Books and Readers in Early Modern England

Books and Readers in Early Modern England

Material Studies

EDITED BY

Jennifer Andersen and Elizabeth Sauer

with an Afterword by Stephen Orgel

PENN

University of Pennsylvania Press

PHILADELPHIA

10 9 8 7 6 5 4 3 2 1

Published by
University of Pennsylvania Press
Philadelphia, Pennsylvania 19104-4011

Library of Congress Cataloging-in-Publication Data
Books and readers in early modern England : material studies / edited by Jennifer Andersen
and Elizabeth Sauer ; with an aferword by Stephen Orgel.
p. cm. — (Material texts)
Includes bibliographical references and index.
ISBN 0-8122-3633-5 (alk. paper) — ISBN 0-8122-1794-2 (pbk. : alk. paper)
1. Books and reading—England—History—16th century. 2. Books and reading—England—
History—17th century. 3. Literature and society—England—History—16th century.
4. Literature and society—England—History—17th century. 5. Book industries and trade—
England—History—16th century. 6. Book industries and trade—England—History—17th
century. 7. England—Intellectual life—16th century. 8. England—Intellectual life—17th century.
I. Andersen, Jennifer. II. Sauer, Elizabeth, 1964– III. Series.
Z1003.5.G7 B69 2001
028'.9'0942—dc21   2001037150

Contents

Current Trends in the History of Reading   1
JENNIFER ANDERSEN AND ELIZABETH SAUER

I. Social Contexts for Writing

Chapter 1: Plays into Print: Shakespeare to His Earliest Readers   23
DAVID SCOTT KASTAN

Chapter 2: Books and Scrolls: Navigating the Bible   42
PETER STALLYBRASS

Chapter 3: *Theatrum Libri:* Burton's *Anatomy of Melancholy* and the Failure of Encyclopedic Form   80
CHRISTOPHER GROSE

Chapter 4: Approaches to Presbyterian Print Culture: Thomas Edwards's *Gangraena* as Source and Text   97
ANN HUGHES

II. Traces of Reading: Margins, Libraries, Prefaces, and Bindings

Chapter 5: What Did Renaissance Readers Write in Their Books?   119
WILLIAM H. SHERMAN

Chapter 6: The Countess of Bridgewater's London Library   138
HEIDI BRAYMAN HACKEL

Chapter 7: *Lego Ego:* Reading Seventeenth-Century Books of Epigrams   160
RANDALL INGRAM

Chapter 8: Devotion Bound: A Social History of *The Temple*   177
KATHLEEN LYNCH

III. Print, Publishing, and Public Opinion

Chapter 9: Preserving the Ephemeral: Reading, Collecting, and the
Pamphlet Culture of Seventeenth-Century England   201
MICHAEL MENDLE

Chapter 10: Licensing Readers, Licensing Authorities in Seventeenth-
Century England   217
SABRINA A. BARON

Chapter 11: Licensing Metaphor: Parker, Marvell, and the Debate over
Conscience   243
LANA CABLE

Chapter 12: John Dryden's Angry Readers   261
ANNA BATTIGELLI

Afterword: Records of Culture   282
STEPHEN ORGEL

List of Contributors   291

Index   295

Current Trends in the History of Reading

JENNIFER ANDERSEN AND ELIZABETH SAUER

To make a false florish here with the borrowed weapons of all the old Maisters of the noble Science of Poesie, and to keepe a tyrannicall coyle, in Anatomizing Genius, from head to foote, (only to shew how nimbly we can carue vp the whole messe of the Poets) were to play the Executioner, and to lay our Cities houshold God on the rack, to make him confesse, how many paire of Latin sheets, we haue shaken & cut into shreds to make him a garment.

> BEN JONSON, Commentary on *The King's Entertainment* (1604)

Truth and understanding are not such wares as to be monopolized and traded in by tickets and statutes and standards. We must not think to make a staple commodity of all the knowledge in the land, to mark and license it like our broadcloth and our woolpacks.

> JOHN MILTON, *Areopagitica* (1644)

These quotations from Ben Jonson and John Milton epitomize the two main ways in which we think of books—as material objects and as systems. Jonson's pun on "sheets" turns on the fact that early modern paper was made of cloth. Paper is the topic of the first chapter in Lucien Febvre and Henri-Jean Martin's *Coming of the Book: The Impact of Printing, 1450–1800* (1990), frequently credited with advancing the concept of "book as object" in the study of book history. Milton, by contrast, regards books as "systems" or parts of a socio-cultural matrix. The latter notion of the contextual and textual nature of books has dominated more recent studies in the history of the book, such as Adrian Johns's *Nature of the Book: Print and Knowledge in the Making* (1997). Despite the dialectical rhetoric that would distinguish a new history of reading from an old book history, physical evidence cannot be so easily separated from its social circumstances and implications; and from its outset early modern book history has treated books not only as bibliographical artifacts, but also as part of social history. In general, early modern books seem to have been more dynamic and fluid, less dogmatic and authoritarian than some modern stereotypes would imply. An overemphasis on concerns with authenticity and authorship may have distracted us from what contemporaries took to be essential features of print culture: its instability, permeability, sociability, and adaptability to particular occasions and readerships.

The twelve original essays in this book contribute to the rich interdisciplinary field of studies on early modern English interpretive practices and reading habits by demonstrating the effects of textual circulation on the larger social, cultural dynamic.[1] This collection limits its scope to the late sixteenth and seventeenth centuries, aiming to present both nuanced case studies and broader pictures of the cultures of reading and writing in this period, which a book by multiple authors can best present. The essays presented here attempt productively to combine the investigation of the "primary" evidence—the hard, bibliographical details of actual books—and the "secondary" historicist implications of an analytical reading of these books in the particular social matrixes of early modern England where they occur. The contributors examine various kinds of evidence to reconstruct interpretive and reading experiences of this period: poems, prefaces, title pages, printer's marks, formats, marginal annotations, pirated editions, bad quartos, the Stationers' Register, library catalogues, newsbooks, tracts, letters, journals, State Papers Domestic, and auction catalogues. Broader contexts of textual provenance, transmission, and consumption are considered as well: the Elizabethan, Jacobean, and Restoration theater; Presbyterian clerical networks; the aristocratic household; humanist circles and university culture; Parliament; and communities of friends, families, and printers. Recovering the bibliographic narratives attached to early modern books helps us extricate them from disciplinary narratives that have dominated their interpretation.

This introductory essay focuses on central themes in the study of early modern books and readers, and on the ways in which essays in this volume analyze them. The history of reading is a large and amorphous field of study with practitioners from various disciplines. Broadly speaking, the field encompasses questions about the production, circulation, and consumption of texts, which are now central for bibliographic, literary, and historical research. Various paths—too numerous and roundabout to investigate individually here—have caused the concerns of subgroups within these disciplines momentarily to intersect. Some bibliographers have turned, for example, from formalist, analytical bibliography toward a sociology of the text; some new historicist literary critics seek a more sophisticated theory of historical context; and some social historians react against an old-style intellectual history.

In all these fields we see a widening of focus in the assessment of textual sources to include not only intrinsic content and structures but also extrinsic patterns of evidence. Indeed, all of these revisionist movements might be characterized as redefining what is considered "outside the text." D. F. McKenzie wants to establish closer links between bibliography and history; he sees the development of analytical bibliography as closely tied to New Criticism, and therefore highly restrictive in nature and narrowly focused on the primary evidence of physical books. Jerome McGann sees the practices of copy-text editors as closely tied to an ideal notion of the purity of authorial intention, which he dissolves into the multivocality of variants and replaces with notions of collective cultural production or social authorship. Adrian Johns repudiates the "technological determinism" of Elizabeth Eisenstein's *Printing Press as an Agent of Change* in order to draw attention to the structures of trust and credibility upon which the functioning of early modern books rested.[2]

At the heart of the junctures of bibliography, literature, and history in early modern England are overlapping definitions of text. For D. F. McKenzie, when bibliography is understood as the sociology of texts, "text" is understood as referring to verbal, visual, oral, or numerical data in the form of maps, prints, music, and so on. His critique of W. K. Wimsatt and M. C. Beardsley's misreading of a line by Congreve in "The Intentional Fallacy" is paradigmatic of the kind of boxes in which he believes readers are hedged by new critical approaches.[3] Indeed, some find McKenzie's Short Title Catalogue, however capacious, too narrowly focused on printed materials to the exclusion of important manuscript sources. Margaret Ezell, Arthur Marotti, and Harold Love, among others, study texts primarily transmitted by manuscript. Ezell argues that scribally authored texts might be even more important than printed ones for examinations of early modern literature. The logical conclusion of McGann's revisionist editorial principles may be seen in Margreta de Grazia's *Oxford Shakespeare*, which employs a "document"-based rather than a "work"-based practice, making no distinction among testimony, eyewitness account, official report, letter, play, and journal entry. Historians such as Alastair Bellany, Peter Lake, and Ann Hughes likewise consider the full gamut of printed sources (formal polemic, sermons, cheap tracts, printed proclamations, parliamentary legislation), as well as circulating manuscripts, rumor, and public performance of a variety of types (sermons, show trials, disputations, executions), in reconstructing events and the manners in which they were retold and interpreted in early modern England.[4] Since Tudor-Stuart historians spend much of their time consulting these kinds of sources, a more informed sense of their provenance and the idiosyncrasies of their production adds a level of sophistication to those readings. For example, in her essay for this volume, Ann Hughes distinguishes between the value of *Gangraena* as a source (of information about radical sects during the civil war) and its value as a text (a polemically situated, rhetorically shaped, collaboratively compiled, serially published, Presbyterian tract).

At the same time as we see a broadening of the kinds of media considered relevant to interpreting historical meaning and the kinds of meaning thought to be found in such texts, we also see a narrowing of the chronological and geographical scope of book history studies. James Raven's coedited volume, *The Practice and Representation of Reading*, amalgamates the world-historical ambitions of older book history in its large chronological reach from the twelfth century to the nineteenth with the microhistorical perspective of newer book history in that it is comprised of narrowly focused case studies. In a review of that book Joad Raymond remarks on the tension in this arrangement which leaves "a puritanical longing for the colossal work of the history of reading which will be both theoretical and empirical, which will squeeze the plethora of evidence into a grand thesis, and effectively capture the reader, frozen in his or her exemplary action."[5] Whereas Elizabeth Eisenstein's research rests on pan-European data, Robert Darnton regularly takes the idiosyncratic but richly documented case as the appropriate unit of study. Darnton offers a prescriptive rationale for his chosen unit of study in his "communications circuit"—a model for the full ambit or life cycle of the text from writing to reading, and through publication, material publication, and distribution. The bibliographical format, the complex alliances their production presupposed, their circulation, and their reception—all this social and bibliographical evidence signifies a text's predicament in its contemporary literary field. Further, each of the variables in the circuit changes in accordance with fluctuating social, political, and economic circumstances. In addition to the synchronic conditions of their production and reception, all of the texts discussed in this volume of course survived the situation in which they originated. They were edited and republished in new forms, and championed and read by new generations of readers who read in innovative ways and found employment for them in other times, places, and canons.

Recent studies on the history of reading are inclined to construct a comprehensive vision through constant exchanges between micro- and macrohistory, and between close-ups and extreme long shots; they thereby regard historical process through apparent exceptions and heterogeneous cases. Carlo Ginzburg invokes the great historical novels of Stendhal and Tolstoy as models for this kind of narration: the private and the public worlds now run along parallel lines, now intersect. A close-up look permits us to grasp what eludes a comprehensive viewing, and vice versa. Essays in this volume likewise aim to present discrete moments in the history of reading in early modern England to illustrate that the intensity and kinds of reading varied greatly over this period, but also to suggest that the sum of such moments is consequential for a broader perspective of historical trends. Like Roger Chartier, we find that as print culture spreads and literacy increases, modes of reading become more various and distinct: "once the book became a more common object and less distinctive by

its merely being possessed, the manners of reading took over the task of showing the variations, of making manifest differences in the social hierarchy."[6]

The general trends and tendencies here adumbrated no doubt overdraw
the differences between the revisionists and their precursors, but they nevertheless indicate evident shifts in focus and method which are reflected in this
volume. The twelve essays are divided into three sections intended to highlight
and exemplify three notions that frequently organize current studies in the
history of reading: social elements that are "outside the author" and that contribute to the construction of texts; the location of readers' intellectual and
affective responses to texts in various kinds of evidence, ranging from front
matter in books to library catalogues; and the relationship of print, publishing,
and public opinion. The following three interrelated subsections discuss each
in turn, while delineating other major issues in the field.

Social Contexts for Writing

Each of the essays in this section suggests that knowledge of particular, extrinsic, historical circumstances and contexts is necessary to understand fully the
intrinsic features of early modern texts. David Scott Kastan suggests that an
earlier school of bibliography overly reliant on internal analysis of Shakespeare's bad quartos constructed a false narrative about the first printers of
Shakespeare's plays. Peter Stallybrass argues that even if bibles were translated
and printed in single volumes in Protestant England, and even though Protestants held that they read the bible through continuously, the Protestant bible in
fact continued to be read discontinuously. According to Christopher Grose,
Robert Burton's abandonment of his original encyclopedic project in the 1621
Anatomy of Melancholy is best understood in the context of religious controversy surrounding Puritan separatists. Ann Hughes reconstructs an elaborate
information network to which Thomas Edwards's *Gangraena* referred and
which supplied him with accounts of sectarian enormities. While each essay
concentrates on an early modern text or series of texts, each draws on a particular expertise to reconstruct the various bibliographical contexts.

The more significant point that the individual essays make about the need
for extrinsic evidence to reconstruct early modern texts' historical significance
is that the primary texts themselves gesture toward it; strategies are built into
them to compensate for the fallibilities and deficiencies of the printed object.
The functioning of early modern books is thus shown to rest on structures of
trust and credibility that lie outside the author. Scholars increasingly realize
that it is incorrect to speak of a sudden transition from aural to visual, from oral
to literate culture. We should not exaggerate the impact of print because there

was a large reading public in the later Middle Ages. Further, hearing and seeing were not mutually exclusive modes of perception, and there were ways of getting around the obstacle of literacy. Most of all, though, early modern writers show signs of anxiety or unease about moving from oral to printed communication, and hence even their printed texts bear a distinctive relation of dependence on the validation of direct speech and the fiction of a speaking presence behind the text.

In "Plays into Print: Shakespeare to His Earliest Readers," David Scott Kastan presents the paradox that Shakespeare, whose name for many moderns is synonymous with professional authorship, himself "had little invested in notions of individuated authorship." By reconstructing early modern conditions for publishing, printing, and selling playbooks, Kastan unravels this apparent paradox. While some of Shakespeare's contemporary playwrights, such as Ben Jonson, Thomas Heywood, and Richard Brome, saw print publication as a means of asserting their proprietary right over dramatic scripts, Shakespeare's lack of interest in print publication in fact made sense considering that publishing play texts was not particularly lucrative for authors. Shakespeare's investment as a shareholder in an acting company guaranteed him an income from performances, and in the context of the theater company, his text was just one element in the economy of the performances that generated income. Consequently, according to Kastan, Shakespeare "worked comfortably within its [the theater's] necessary collaborations."

Many of his plays did of course find their way into print during his lifetime due to the speculations of publishers or printers. Kastan argues that an earlier bibliographical history's stigmatization of these unauthorized publications as "pirated" and "bad quartos" is technically incorrect, for he shares Peter Blayney's views on the prevalence of shared printing in early modern England.[7] Modern pieties about Shakespeare's greatness and fundamental misunderstandings of the usual business practices and collaborations of early modern English printers and publishers, Kastan suggests, contributed to an inaccurate assessment of the stationers responsible for the early unauthorized printings of Shakespeare's plays. As to the charge of illegality, publishers and printers did not need an author's permission to print a text; to obtain legal right to copy they merely had to enter it in the Stationers' Register. Not authorial provenance so much as theatrical success accounted for the excitement surrounding a play and its marketability as a printed text. Printers' use of Shakespeare's name as a marketing strategy in the seventeenth century points to a growing literary reputation and commercial cachet.

Peter Stallybrass's essay dramatically illustrates how the reorganization of meaning in each separate temporal appearance of the medieval and early modern bible reconstitutes the text and reinterprets its meaning. In "Books and Scrolls: Navigating the Bible," Stallybrass identifies the codex, rather than the printed book, as the innovation with the most significant consequences for bible-reading practices. In this he confirms what medievalists like Michael Clanchy have maintained, that the printed book has more continuity with its preprint counterparts than the rhetoric of a print revolution admits.[8] The Renaissance did not invent books, but only printed books; and in many ways the characteristics of those printed books and the fact that there was a market for them at all are properly seen more as the realization of trends that had been developing since the thirteenth century than as a radical departure from them. Thus Stallybrass sees "the invention of printing less as a displacement of manuscript culture than as the culmination of the invention of the navigable book."

Christians in particular embraced the codex form, whose special property was to permit discontinuous reading. In a medieval context the selective reading of the bible was governed primarily by liturgical context. Medieval church services broke up the biblical text to celebrate the liturgical year, and the natural outgrowth of this was the literal dispersal of the bible into multiple service books: missals, graduals, lectionaries, psalters, and sacramentaries. Stallybrass sees the implications of medieval liturgical reading in church artifacts that often brought together scenes from different temporalities in the bible narrative: the Ghent altarpiece, for instance, links disparate bible passages to reinforce central doctrines. While Protestants maintained that they read the whole bible through continuously, elements bound together into Protestant bibles often instruct the reader in discontinuous reading strategies such as liturgical reading or Calvinist reading, as Stallybrass shows through the example of the Newby Bible. This study of bibles thus vividly illustrates how the text is produced in the act of transmission.

Christopher Grose shows Robert Burton's search for a polemically neutral point of view from which to examine the volatile subject of religious melancholy. In "*Theatrum Libri*: Burton's *Anatomy of Melancholy* and the Failure of Encyclopedic Form," Grose chronicles Burton's abandonment of his original encyclopedic project. Grose finds in Burton's revision of the *Anatomy* the end of the European humanist tradition of polymathic chorographies such as those studied by Anthony Grafton and Ann Blair.[9] Because of the newness and topicality of the variety of religious melancholy exhibited by the English Puritans, Burton lacks his "usual supply of prototypes and must abandon his usual reliance on scholarly consensus and rely instead on the dubious authority of eyewitness" to discuss this phenomenon. Burton's section on religious melancholy is relocated from postscript to preface, and Democritus Junior is brought in to address the melancholy of religious separatists in a way that not only pointedly refuses to stigmatize them but also continues to attempt to cure them.

In the device of Democritus Junior, Burton finds a way to treat his controversial subject—the melancholy of Puritan separatists—with a new kind of authority. Interestingly, Burton sets this authority off against books and print culture. In Democritus Junior he takes the theatrical player as the model for his own new kind of authority; specifically, the use of Democritus Junior is the way "his antic energy can incorporate and seem to naturalize the lore of political and religious controversy" because "the volatile materials of religious melancholy have acquired the kind of intractable autonomy" which resists encyclopedic treatment. Inherent in the revision process of Burton's very Jacobean project, as Grose recounts it, is the assumption that textual authority will rely on the assent and engagement of its readers. If the scholarly consensus of encyclopedic knowledge will not consolidate a national readership, the book imagined as theater might do it. Private reading in a world fraught with difference only fragments it further, Burton realizes, so he designs his book to avoid creating division.

Written a few years after Burton's *Anatomy* but moving in a diametrically opposite direction, Thomas Edwards's encyclopedic *Gangraena*, the subject of Ann Hughes's essay, is unapologetically controversial in nature. In "Approaches to Presbyterian Print Culture: Thomas Edwards's *Gangraena* as Source and Text," Hughes analyzes the strategies of the Presbyterian controversialist and his text's impact on religious and political debates of the 1640s. *Gangraena* "was written as part of a campaign for a reformed, comprehensive, and compulsory national Protestant church," but instead of eschewing incendiary invective against separatists as Burton does, Edwards seeks to consolidate Presbyterians through a vehement opposition to separatist movements.

Edwards constructs *Gangraena*'s authority by modeling it on Foxe's *Book of Martyrs* and by reinforcing his written claims with reference to direct oral testimony and letters. Indeed, the production of *Gangraena* depended on elaborate "information networks," including Edwards's London Presbyterian connections, the London lectures, Parliament, the Westminster Assembly, and Presbyterian publishers. Discussion of Edwards's heresiology, in turn, became a means of reinforcing local clerical communities whose networks risked fragmentation and division in the complex debates of the mid-1640s. Edwards was as "anxious for a wide and engaged, active readership as any Leveller or radical sectary. It would be misleading to assume a repressive Presbyterian attitude to print culture, opposed to radical desires for open debate."[10]

Hughes insists that *Gangraena* has a value beyond what it might say about actual events in mid-1640s England; it can tell us how people perceived the threat of sectarianism, how they sought to define orthodoxy, and that the wide dissemination of such notions through print had a real impact on how that world was experienced and understood. Early modern writers were keenly aware of the social nature of their texts, whether that meant that they were given voice in the mouths of players, worshippers, preachers, or polemicists.

Traces of Reading: Margins, Libraries, Prefaces, and Bindings

Evidence about reader responses is essential to demonstrate the part that reception plays in the creation of textual meaning. For directing book historians to study readers, Roger Chartier's contribution cannot be overestimated: he greatly broadened the range of questions that were proper for historians of reading to ask and the types of sources they sought to consult in asking them. Chartier's notion of "appropriation," a reader's prerogative to make creative use of written materials, is the theoretical centerpiece of his approach to the history of reading. This notion emerged out of Chartier's reaction against an old-style Marxist history which claimed the literary world as part of the cultural superstructure "determined" by the economic base, and against sociologists who see social class as the decisive factor in any cultural analysis. In Chartier's words, "retrospective sociology that has long made the unequal distribution of objects the primary criterion of the cultural hierarchy must be replaced by a different approach that focuses attention on differentiated and contrasting uses of the same goods, the same texts, and the same ideas." The *Annales* school of socioeconomic history tried to uncover the general pattern of book production and consumption over long stretches of time and concentrated on the most ordinary sort of books because they wanted to discover the literary experience of ordinary readers. The *Annales* school aspired to make history quantitative and macrohistorical, assuming that if history were analyzed with measurements, graphs, and pie charts we would achieve a truer picture of what was significant or determining for more people. This approach combined scientific method and Marxism and aimed to discover the history of the many, not of the few. It had its heyday from the 1950s to the mid-1970s and favored such evidence as signature counts and library inventories as sources that offered access to written matter.[11]

For early modern England, the equivalent of the French *Annalists*—the counters of books and readers who attempt to uncover a history of the many—have been David Cressy and Margaret Spufford. Margaret Spufford has argued that probably more people could read than could write because many children were removed from school after they could read but before they had completed lessons in writing. Cressy determines that writing skills were limited to 30 percent of the male population and only 10 percent of the female population by 1640, reaching 45 and 25 percent, respectively, by the accession of George I in 1714. Like Chartier, Carlo Ginzburg reacts against this approach to the history of reading: "[to] select as a cognitive object only what is repetitive, and therefore capable of being serialized, signifies paying a very high price in cognitive terms," for "it cancels out many particulars in the existing documentation for the benefit of what is homogeneous and comparable."[12]

Chartier, Darnton, and Ginzburg all felt the loss of the human scale and loss of historical particularity in numerical data. Still interested in the "everyman and -woman," they began looking for sources that could provide more than a statistical view into a generalized class. So they found printing apprentices, millers, and other personalities as the subjects for case studies. They looked for archival sources that could offer not only quantitative, but also particular histories of people's lives and mental habits. Ginzburg's rich and provocative study of the sixteenth-century Friulian miller, Menocchio, challenged the idea that the history of the subordinate classes can only be accomplished through number and anonymity. From such disparate texts as the bible in the vernacular, *The Travels of Sir John Mandeville*, Boccaccio's *Decameron*, and the Koran, Menocchio patched together a cosmology which included a heretical theory of creation ex nihilo. This kind of explosively original reading, Ginzburg suggests, results from the collision between oral culture and the printed page. Ginzburg argues that Menocchio is not passively informed by the texts he reads, but rather that the texts trigger in his memory more deeply rooted oral traditions.[13]

How do we identify and locate early modern English readers? As Keith Thomas reminds us, literacy is not a single, autonomous phenomenon, but takes different forms at different times; its meaning can be studied only in some specific context.[14] In "What Did Renaissance Readers Write in Their Books?" William Sherman examines the traces of reading left in the annotations made on the margins and flyleaves of books, and his conclusions are drawn from a survey of the Huntington Library's holdings of STC books. He finds that in humanist methods for annotating books (published in manuals for Renaissance students) and in heated responses to religious texts we find the marginalia or handwritten annotations that are most easily decipherable and closely tied to texts. Sherman sets out in search of real readers and shows us how to locate them; but he also acknowledges the serendipity involved in finding and identifying significant and substantive marginalia, admits the difficulty of making sense of many marginal markings, and laments the irrelevance of many markings which resulted from the use of blank spaces in books as notepads in an age when paper was expensive. Sherman's survey thus suggests that perhaps one cannot best reconstruct the mentality of Renaissance readers based on scattered evidence from a wide range of readers and contexts.

The results of Sherman's STC survey, as well as his own book-length study of John Dee, point to the more fruitful approaches of focusing on the libraries of well-known scholars or public figures or on a controversy and the texts generated around it.[15] This case study approach is precisely the route taken by Heidi Brayman Hackel in her essay entitled "The Countess of Bridgewater's London Library." Her examination of Frances Egerton's London library offers a rich portrait of an appropriative reader. Brayman Hackel reconstructs the Countess of Bridgewater's library from inscriptions in copies, ownership stamps and signatures, a library catalogue, and her funeral sermon. She discusses the development of her literary tastes with respect to her situation in a powerful, literate family who were patrons of the arts and active in dramatic productions. The Countess energetically acquired books in the 1630s and ordered them with a deliberate and knowledgeable system of organization. Perhaps the most persuasive evidence of such collecting as active appropriation is the discrepancy between the representation of the Countess's learning in her funeral sermon and the actual tastes and interests evidenced in her actual library. The funeral sermon presents Frances Egerton's reading habits as primarily pious and devotional—in the rhetoric of contemporary conduct books, educational treatises, and legal customs which supported the policing of women's reading. While the sermon projects an image of her as a conventional aristocratic matron, Brayman Hackel argues that the intellectual content and range of her library should expand our notion of early modern women as intellectually inquisitive consumers of books. How many other Frances Egertons, unnoticed by their contemporaries, avidly acquired and imbibed a range of texts? Brayman Hackel's Frances Egerton thus joins figures such as Lady Anne Clifford and Lady Anne Southwell as a reader with a richly documented intellectual life.

Margaret Ezell has pointed to the irony that though Chartier has championed studies of reception and real readers such as Frances Egerton, his own research has focused primarily on addresses to the reader in prefatory material in books. In his essay here Randall Ingram offers a critical reading of such evidence in his analysis of addresses to readers in seventeenth-century collections of epigrams. By examining the self-referential poems, remarks, and conventions in collections of epigrams, he shows how conscious authors and publishers were of their books' place in a social and commercial economy. Ingram argues that since print-published epigrammatists and their publishers made a living from their books, they necessarily became keen observers of early modern readers; and their addresses to readers, which attempt delicately to negotiate the transaction between customer and consumable object, are uniquely positioned resources for scholars of reading. Though painfully aware of the status of books as mere fungible objects, the authors of these addresses to readers also recognize and appeal to the book's value as cultural goods which define fashion and taste. In addition, poetic miscellanies had the advantage of continuity with a tradition of scribally circulated verse in manuscript miscellanies; this meant that printed miscellanies fed into an economy of already circulating pre- and para-print practices of commonplacing poems.[16] The exclusivity of scribally circulated poems must have increased the prestige and vendibility of printed miscellanies because of their promise to include readers in a charmed circle of cultural insiders. Ingram thus helpfully complicates the search for real readers in that he shows how reading tastes and publics could also be created and invoked through commercial advertisements.

Texts are implicated in the material processes of textual production. There is in fact no text, Chartier insists, "apart from the physical support that offers it for reading (or hearing), hence there is no comprehension of any written piece that does not at least in part depend upon the forms in which it reaches the reader."[17] The text as a product of scribes or printing presses shapes the process of reception considerably, as shown by David Scott Kastan, for example, and in this section, by Kathleen Lynch. In "Devotion Bound: A Social History of *The Temple*," Lynch examines two case studies in which stationers act as the customers' proxy, making decisions that package and appropriate Herbert's *Temple* for diametrically opposed but also internally incoherent ideological purposes.[18] The two bookbindings Lynch examines in her learned analysis reveal themselves to be statements not only about the devotional identity of their owners but also about scholarly mythologies surrounding the reception of Herbert's poetry. The mistaken attribution of one bookbinding to Nicholas Ferrar's Little Gidding community exhibits the pressure that is exerted by critical orthodoxy and high Anglican genealogy-making on the interpretation of what one might expect to be the most empirical and inexpressive feature of a book—its binding. That *The Temple* lent itself simultaneously to an aesthetic packaging that emphasized a ritualistic, Laudian approach to the word and an austerely puritanical one powerfully indicates the consumer's ability to claim a text. The ideologically incongruous but commercially effective binding together of Herbert's poems with Christopher Harvey's *Synagogue* further complicates the interpretation of the text's religious affiliations. As Lynch's essay indicates, material evidence that reposes in early printed books does not always conform to the neat outlines of intellectual history; rather, it opens up new and imaginative avenues for future investigation. Bookbindings afford opportunities for tracing the history of texts in their circulation, interpretation, and use, not necessarily connected with the circumstances of their production.

In sum, the dialectic overstatements of Chartier and others about the autonomy of readers—meant to compensate for the fact that authors and texts have for so long held the sole focus of our attention—need now to be qualified. For authors, texts, and readers exist in dialectical relationships to one another: texts can win over the sympathies of readerships for commercial, political, or other purposes; but once reading habits and tastes have been developed, readerships can exert their own powers of selection and taste.

Print, Publishing, and Public Opinion

The essays in the final section examine some of the habits and demands that mass reading publics developed and some of the strategies devised by the state and inventive authors to harness those energies. Michael Mendle and Sabrina Baron focus primarily on the 1640s, one of the hot spots in the century in terms of printing activity. Mendle and Baron research aspects of the process whereby the periodical press and polemical pamphlet culture became permanent features of the seventeenth-century English landscape. Once the state realized that it would not be able to muzzle this contentious pamphlet culture, it devised ways of managing and redirecting its energies for its own purposes. Lana Cable, for example, discusses official reactions to publications justified by the principle of "liberty of conscience" and the administrative and polemical modes devised to cope with it. And Anna Battigelli argues that John Dryden, recognizing the effect of a controversial press on readers' tastes, habits, and expectations, adjusts his writing to frustrate, titillate, and satisfy such tastes.

There is a large and burgeoning body of literature about early modern English print culture and public opinion. The pivotal question explored in such studies is whether printed materials reflected or generated public opinion, and to what extent public opinion so generated could matter. A number of scholars have attempted to make the Habermasian notion of the public sphere fit the conditions of seventeenth-century England, but Peter Lake explains why the Habermasian model is a strained and inappropriate description of the circumstances that prevailed in Elizabethan England. He proposes an alternative understanding of the creation and use of public opinion through case studies of four Elizabethan propaganda campaigns: the Anjou Match, the Edmund Campion Affair, the Anti-Theatrical Campaign, and the Marprelate Controversy.[19] To summarize his analysis very briefly here: Lake agrees that printed media were used to appeal to and invoke public opinion; this public opinion was courted not so much for its own sake, however, but as an indirect means or third force to which authorities could appeal in order to legitimate or strengthen their cases. A series of publics could be invoked as providing a reason why the queen either should or should not act. Yet those very publics and the sphere of public appeal and action in and through which they could be deployed eventually became available for opponents or critics of the regime. In this sense public opinion could operate not simply as an instrument called into being and controlled by the powers-that-be for their own ends, but could become an autonomous force in politics.

The process that Lake describes only intensifies throughout the seventeenth century when breaches of the decorum of public speech about matters of church and state become ever more flagrant and frequent. Michael Mendle examines the pamphlet collectors to whom we owe the preservation of so many ephemeral controversial texts from this period. Referring to collectors' marginalia, organizational systems for pamphlets, book auction catalogues, and republications of newsbook separates as collections, Mendle shows the care and expense taken by collectors such as George Thomason, Sir William Clarke, the first Earl of Bridgewater, and William Miller. While such collections may have been exceptional in the early days of pamphlet culture, Mendle suggests that collectors such as Narcissus Luttrell and Anthony Wood indicate that pamphlet collecting was a recognized hobby by the 1670s and 1680s. Mendle contributes to the growing caution, sophistication, and subtlety used by scholars of cheap printed materials to relocate them within the constantly modifying contexts within which they were produced and consumed.[20]

Like Mendle, Sabrina Baron focuses on the reading revolution of the mid-seventeenth century, on the genre of the polemical pamphlet, and on a figure who, like George Thomason, moved easily between scholarly and popular texts. Through a close examination of John Milton's publications of the 1640s, his connections to the book trade (Milton was in fact a patron of Thomason's book shop), and his three-year service as licenser of the press, Baron reconciles Milton's well-known objections to ecclesiastical control of the press from *Areopagitica* (1644) with his career as a state licenser for the press. Baron argues that while Milton objected to the ecclesiastical role in the regulation of printing, "he conceded the necessity for logical, tempered state intervention in printing." Milton's actions as a published author and as a licenser— from the generic format chosen for his title pages, to the absence of the author's name and the authorization of a licenser, to the preference for low-profile, subcontracting printers—no less than his explicit pronouncements in *Areopagitica*, are statements about Milton's advocacy of the freedom to read. Milton's practical contacts and experience with the press in fact suggest a novel interpretation of *Areopagitica*: that it was the freedom to read which Milton was primarily concerned to establish rather than authoritative authorial control.

Moving onto the Restoration period, Lana Cable's essay treats the pamphlet controversy between Samuel Parker and Andrew Marvell, arguing that the earlier radical, republican dominance over pamphlet literature was joined by a more propagandistically savvy cadre of Anglican rhetoricians. At a time when Charles II's tolerationist policies threatened the political authority of the Anglican Church, Parker sought to shore up the Anglican establishment by slaying the dragon of freedom of conscience. Cable suggests that Parker, once a member of a puritan conventicle, republican sympathizer, and friend of John Milton, but later an Anglican licenser of the press, used his insider knowledge to stigmatize nonconformists as enthusiasts and atheists. Parker's Restoration volte-face was likely mirrored by many another career in the London book trade, such as that of John Streater, a republican printer of unauthorized nonconformist literature turned advocate of royal patents. Parker's efforts to stigmatize nonconformist rhetoric involved two main strategies. First, he adopted the prorationalist values of the culturally prestigious Royal Society, as Robert Boyle had, to attack enthusiasts. Like Boyle, Parker found nonconformist reading habits and use of language at the roots of their problem of credibility. By regarding the language of inspired belief as irrational and socially unacceptable, Parker hoped to undermine nonconformist claims to freedom of conscience.[21] Secondly, Parker attempted to impose the values and manners of a cultural elite upon nonconformists by classifying language as a matter of national consensus and style. The focus on language as an issue of aesthetics, capable of being altered without substantial loss, is another attempt to get nonconformists to throw the baby (freedom of conscience) out with the bathwater (unseemly sensory language). Marvell saw through Parker's clericalist agenda which he famously parodied in *The Rehearsal Transprosed*. Aware that censorship would not provide an adequate control of polemical publications, Parker the licenser saw the control of public language through established standards of literary taste as the key to repressing conflict in favor of an elite politics of consensus. Along with the sophisticated audience addicted to pamphlets described by Michael Mendle, the writers of pamphlets became more adept at appropriating and refuting one another's arguments and at manipulating public opinion.

While Samuel Parker as licenser of the press represents one Restoration response to the growing public expectation of a print forum for the exchange of political opinion, Dryden the writer represents another. In "John Dryden's Angry Readers," Anna Battigelli moves between Dryden's texts and the vehement responses they elicited in satires, plays, prefaces, dedications, commentaries, and handwritten annotations. Relating Dryden's strategies of irony, parody, and equivocation to these responses, Battigelli suggests that Dryden deliberately courted controversy to establish a market for his own work and to create a complex reading experience in which the reader must take in alternative opinions without the guidance of authorial judgment. In his willingness to court controversy, Battigelli maintains, Dryden was purveying to a readership for whom reading was closely tied to a public sphere of ephemeral controversy. Dryden frustrated but also intrigued readers who were driven by a partisan climate to search for fixed allusions, identifications, and typologies. Though Dryden's intrusion into traditionally aristocratic spheres of literary and political activity led to considerable abuse and attack, his polemical influence was also feared by noblemen who might fall under the axe of his wit. In Dryden's refined exploitation of controversy for commercial and political purposes, we see the professional writer carving out a permanent place for himself in the economy of print.[22]

*   *   *

This book makes no attempt to provide a synthetic narrative of early modern English reading, but it does suggest some of the basic features that could be deployed at the service of such narratives, which are necessarily comprised of multiple writers, reading publics, and book trade operatives. Such figures jostle together on the pages of this volume, connecting the traditional subjects and approaches of bibliography, literary criticism, and social history. A quick catalogue of some central figures which are discussed in this book indicates how the history of reading brings together topics conventionally studied in separate disciplines: William Shakespeare, John Danter, Robert Burton, Richard Hooker, Francis Bacon, John Brinsley, Anne Askew, Lady Grace Mildmay, Frances Egerton, George Herbert, Philemon Stephens, Christopher Harvey, Thomas Edwards, Thomas Goodwin, Henry Burton, Hugh Peter, Giles Calvert, Henry Overton, John Saltmarsh, John Bachelor, Laurence Clarkson, John Milton, Matthew Simmons, Humphrey Moseley, Georg Weckherlin, Ruth Raworth, Thomas Newcomb, Samuel Hartlib, George Thomason, William Clarke, Anthony Wood, William Miller, Narcissus Luttrell, Andrew Marvell, Samuel Parker, Roger L'Estrange, John Dryden, Mary Evelyn. What was sayable, to whom, and by whom in this period was integrally related to the rising and falling fortunes of institutions and interpretive communities which reproduced themselves in part through their engagement with texts—the stage, the pulpit, the monarchy, the army, the aristocratic family, the gathered congregation, the scholarly society, and so on. In an atmosphere of shifting contexts, highly influential and much-discussed texts could galvanize readers to unite in belief or action; and authors developed rhetorical and commercial strategies for venturing ideas and capital on books. Our efforts to situate early modern writers, texts, respondents, and publishers in terms of these ongoing debates will make us all more sophisticated readers.

Notes

The editors are very grateful to the following people and institutions who made this collaborative project possible: all our contributors for clarifying and enriching the study of the early modern textual matrix; the National Endowment for the Humanities; the Social Sciences and Humanities Research Canada Council; the Folger Library; Steven Zwicker for directing a Folger institute out of which some of these papers grew; Jerome Singerman, editor of the University of Pennsylvania Press, for his support in seeing this book go to press; the Press's anonymous readers who produced exceptionally thoughtful and incisive evaluations of the manuscript; and Anita D'Alfonso, Michelle Orihel, Melissa Smith, and Janice Zehentbauer for their precise and diligent work in helping to prepare the volume for publication.

1. The word *matrix* nicely captures the concrete and abstract poles of book history since it both implies a social network or system as well as being a printing term. A type font is the product of "matrixes" that produced the particular type sorts in a type case. See Lucien Febvre and Henri-Jean Martin, "The Making of Type," *The Coming of the Book*, trans. David Gerard (London: Verso, 1990), 56–60; Cyndia Susan Clegg, "Review Essay: History of the Book: An Undisciplined Discipline?" *Renaissance Quarterly* 54.1 (2001): 221–45.

See attempts to survey the field by Robert Darnton, "What Is the History of Books?" *The Kiss of Lamourette: Reflections in Cultural History* (New York: W. W. Norton, 1990); Anthony Grafton, "Is the History of Reading a Marginal Enterprise? Guillaume Budé and His Books," *Papers of the Bibliographical Society of America* 91 (1997): 139–57; John P. Feather, "The Book in History and the History of the Book," *Journal of Library History* 21 (1986): 12–26. D. C. Greetham discusses at greater length the affinities between *l'histoire du livre* and New Historicism; links between McGann's concept of the disjunctive history of texts, Marxist notions about the creation of social meaning, and Foucault's archaeology of history; resemblances between microhistory, anthropological "thick description" and the new social bibliography in *Theories of the Text* (Oxford: Oxford University Press, 1999).

2. See Adrian Johns, *The Nature of the Book: Print and Knowledge in the Making* (Chicago: University of Chicago Press, 1997). For an account of developments in twentieth-century bibliography see D. F. McKenzie, *What's Past Is Prologue: The Bibliographical Society and the History of the Book* (Munslow, Shropshire: Hearthstone Publications, 1993) and D. F. McKenzie, *Bibliography and the Sociology of Texts* (London: British Library, 1986). For accounts of modern history of the book as a reaction against *Annales* history of the book, see Roger Chartier, *The Cultural Uses of Print in Early Modern France*, trans. Lydia G. Cochrane (Princeton, N.J.: Princeton University Press, 1987), and Carlo Ginzburg, "Microhistory: Two or Three Things That I Know About It," *Critical Inquiry* 20 (1993): 10–35. On book history as offering a more sophisticated theory of context for literary historians, see Peter D. McDonald, "Implicit Structures and Explicit Interactions: Pierre Bourdieu and the History of the Book," *Library*, 6th ser., 19.2 (1997): 105–21. Within literary criticism Jerome McGann perhaps

first articulates a shift towards the study of texts as collaborative creations both in production and consumption: see his *Critique of Modern Textual Criticism* (Charlottesville: University Press of Virginia, 1983). Examples of historical flirtations with literary theory that de-centers the author include Quentin Skinner, "Motives, Intentions and the Interpretation of Texts," *New Literary History* 3 (1972): 393–408; and Martyn P. Thompson, "Reception Theory and the Interpretation of Historical Meaning," *History and Theory* 32 (1993): 248–72.

3. D. F. McKenzie, *Bibliography and the Sociology of Texts* (Cambridge: Cambridge University Press, 1999; rpt. 1986), 10–20.

4. Margaret Ezell, *Social Authorship and the Advent of Print* (Baltimore: Johns Hopkins University Press, 1999); Arthur Marotti, *Manuscript, Print, and the English Renaissance Lyric* (Ithaca: Cornell University Press, 1995); Harold Love, *The Culture and Commerce of Texts: Scribal Publication in Seventeenth-Century England* (Amherst: University of Massachusetts Press, 1993). One needs only think of textual scholarship on the works of Wyatt, Ralegh, Sidney, or Donne to realize the validity of Ezell's point.

Alastair Bellany, "The Poisoning of Legitimacy? Court Scandal, News Culture and Politics in England, 1603–1660," Ph.D. diss., Princeton University, 1995. For the tendency in postrevisionist early modern English history to take discrete events and pursue their causes and ramifications at a number of social, cultural, and institutional levels, see Peter Lake, "Retrospective: Wentworth's Political World in Revisionist and Post-revisionist Perspective" in *The Political World of Thomas Wentworth, Earl of Strafford, 1621–1641*, ed. J. F. Merritt (Cambridge: Cambridge University Press, 1996).

5. Joad Raymond, *The Library* 6th ser., 19.2 (1997): 162–64.

6. Roger Chartier, "Texts, Printing, Readings," *The New Cultural History*, ed. Lynn Hunt (Berkeley: University of California Press, 1989), 174.

7. See Peter Blayney, *The Texts of King Lear and Their Origins* (Cambridge: Cambridge University Press, 1979); for a more general description see Adrian Johns "Press-Pyrats and Pamphlet-Nappers: Knowledge and Authorship in the Realm of the Stationers," *Nature of the Book* (1997): 160–81.

8. M. T. Clanchy, "Looking Back from the Invention of Printing," *Literacy in Historical Perspective*, ed. Daniel P. Resnick (Washington, D.C.: Library of Congress, 1983). Anthony Grafton similarly finds humanist rhetoric to belie itself when he compares practice with propaganda in *Defenders of the Text: The Traditions of Scholarship in an Age of Science, 1450–1800* (Cambridge, Mass.: Harvard University Press, 1991).

9. Anthony Grafton, *Joseph Scaliger: A Study in the History of Classical Scholarship*, 2 vols. (Oxford: Clarendon Press, 1983–93); Ann Blair, *The Theater of Nature: Jean Bodin and Renaissance Science* (Princeton, N.J.: Princeton University Press, 1997).

10. In this Hughes corrects a tendency in collections such as *Pamphlet Wars: Prose in the English Revolution*, ed. James Holstun (London: Frank Cass, 1992) to represent only political radicals as availing themselves of printed polemics. Peter Lake and Michael Questier extend this point also to include English Catholics in "Puritans, Papists, and the 'Public Sphere' in Early Modern England: The Edmund Campion Affair in Context," *Journal of Modern History* 72 (2000): 587–627.

On the divisiveness of printed polemics see Richard Cust, "News and Politics in Seventeenth-Century England," *The English Civil War*, ed. Richard Cust and Ann Hughes (London: Arnold, 1997); R. Malcolm Smuts usefully summarizes recent scholarship in this area in "Print and the Dissemination of Controversy," *Culture and Power in England, 1585–1685* (New York: St. Martin's Press, 1999), 106–22.

11. Chartier, "Texts" (1989), 171. See Traian Stoianovich, *French Historical Method: The* Annales *Paradigm* (Ithaca: Cornell University Press, 1976).

12. David Cressy, *Literacy and the Social Order: Reading and Writing in Tudor and Stuart England* (Cambridge: Cambridge University Press, 1980); Margaret Spufford, "First Steps in Literacy: The Reading and Writing Experiences of the Humblest Seventeenth-Century Spiritual Autobiographers," *Social History* 4 (1979): 407–35. See Cressy's response in "Literacy in Context: Meaning and Measurements in Early Modern England," *Consumption and the World of Goods*, ed. John Brewer and Roy Porter (London: Routledge, 1993). Carlo Ginzburg, "Microhistory," 21.

13. Carlo Ginzburg's seminal study is *The Cheese and the Worms: The Cosmos of a Sixteenth-Century Miller*, trans. John and Anne Tedeschi (Harmondsworth: Penguin Books, 1982). For a recent study of appropriation in an early modern English context see Steven N. Zwicker, "Reading the Margins: Politics and the Habits of Appropriation," *Refiguring Revolutions: Aesthetics and Politics from the English Revolution to the Romantic Revolution*, ed. Kevin Sharpe and Steven N. Zwicker (Berkeley: University of California Press, 1998).

14. Keith Thomas, "The Meaning of Literacy in Early Modern England," *The Written Word: Literacy in Transition*, ed. Gerd Baumann (Oxford: Oxford University Press, 1986), 97–131. This is still the best brief account of kinds of reading competencies and reading matter in the period.

15. Lisa Jardine and Anthony Grafton, " 'Studied for Action': How Gabriel Harvey Read His Livy," *Past and Present* 129 (1990): 30–78. William H. Sherman, *John Dee: The Politics of Reading and Writing in the English Renaissance* (Amherst: University of Massachusetts Press, 1995).

16. For examples of poetic miscellanies see Victoria Burke, "Women and Early Seventeenth-Century Manuscript Culture: Four Miscellanies," *The Seventeenth Century* 12 (1997): 135–50. On the early modern practice of keeping commonplace books and the murky boundary between author, scribe, and reader see Peter Beal, "Notions in Garrison: The Seventeenth-Century Commonplace Book," *New Ways of Looking at Old Texts*, ed. W. Speed Hill (Binghamton, N.Y.: Renaissance English Text Society, 1993), 131–47, and Max W. Thomas, "Reading and Writing in the Renaissance Commonplace Book: A Question of Authorship?" *The Construction of Authorship: Textual Appropriation in Law and Literature*, ed. Martha Woodmansee and Peter Jaszi (Durham, N.C.: Duke University Press, 1994), 401–15.

17. Chartier, *The Order of Books: Readers, Authors, and Libraries in Europe Between the Fourteenth and Eighteenth Centuries*, trans. Lydia G. Cochrane (Stanford: Stanford University Press, 1994), 9.

18. In this sense Lynch's work chimes in with other studies of posthumously printed works by clergymen and poets during the seventeenth century such as Peter McCullough, "Making Dead Men Speak: Laudianism, Print, and the Works of Lancelot Andrewes, 1626–1642," *Historical Journal* 41.2 (1998): 401–24; and Warren Chernaik, "Books as Memorials: The Politics of Consolation," *Yearbook of English Studies* 21 (1991): 207–17.

19. We are grateful to Peter Lake for allowing us to read and cite his essay "Puritans, Papists and Players: Was There a 'Public Sphere' in Elizabethan England?" *The Public Sphere in Early Modern England*, ed. Peter Lake and Steven Pincus (forthcoming). The bibliography on news and public opinion in early modern England is large and burgeoning. The following try to adapt Habermas's public sphere to early

modern English circumstances: David Zaret, "Religion, Science, and Printing in the Public Spheres in Seventeenth-Century England," *Habermas and the Public Sphere*, ed. Craig Calhoun (Cambridge, Mass.: MIT Press, 1997); Sharon Achinstein, *Milton and the Revolutionary Reader* (Princeton, N.J.: Princeton University Press, 1994); David Norbrook, "*Areopagitica*, Censorship, and the Early Modern Public Sphere," *The Administration of Aesthetics: Censorship, Political Criticism, and the Public Sphere*, ed. Richard Burt (Minneapolis: University of Minnesota Press, 1994); Joad Raymond, "The Newspaper, Public Opinion, and the Public Sphere in the Seventeenth Century," *News, Newspaper, and Society in Early Modern Britain*, ed. Joad Raymond (London: Frank Cass, 1999). David Zaret's book, *Origins of Democratic Culture: Printing, Petitions and the Public Sphere in Early Modern England* (Princeton, N.J.: Princeton University Press, 2000), appeared too late for us to review for this introduction, but its subject matter is obviously relevant to the essays in this section.

On news, rumor, and public opinion more generally see Joad Raymond, *The Invention of the Newspaper: English Newsbooks, 1641–1649* (Oxford: Clarendon Press, 1996); Dagmar Freist, *Governed by Opinion: Politics, Religion, and the Dynamics of Communication in Stuart London, 1637–1647* (New York: St. Martin's Press, 1997); Tim Harris, "Propaganda and Public Opinion in Seventeenth-Century England," *Media and Revolution: Comparative Perspectives* (Lexington: University of Kentucky Press, 1995). See the bibliographies of essays in this section for further sources relating to licensing. We are grateful to Sabrina Baron for a preview of her coedited volume (with Brendan Dooley), *The Politics of Information in Early Modern Europe* (London: Routledge, 2001).

20. See Alexandra Walsham, *Providence in Early Modern England* (Oxford: Oxford University Press, 1999); Nigel Smith, *Literature and Revolution in England, 1640–1660* (New Haven: Yale University Press, 1994); and Tessa Watt, *Cheap Print and Popular Pamphlets, 1550–1640* (Cambridge: Cambridge University Press, 1991).

21. See Johns, chpt. 6, "The Physiology of Reading: Print and the Passions," *Nature of the Book*.

22. Battigelli's assessment of the conditions for professional writing that obtained during Dryden's career accords with the account of D. F. McKenzie, *The London Book Trade in the Later Seventeenth Century* (Sandars Lectures, 1976); we are grateful to Peter Blayney for lending us his copy of this work.

I

Social Contexts for Writing

Plays into Print: Shakespeare to His Earliest Readers

DAVID SCOTT KASTAN

—Who's that?
—No one. The author.
Shakespeare in Love

As is well known, Shakespeare, at least in his role as playwright, had no interest in the printed book or in its potential readers. Performance was the only form of publication he sought for his plays. He made no effort to have them published and none to stop the publication or distribution of the often poorly printed versions that did reach the bookstalls. His own commitment to print publication was reserved for his narrative poetry.[1] His *Venus and Adonis* and *Lucrece* were published in carefully printed editions by his fellow townsman, Richard Field, and to each Shakespeare contributed a signed dedication. The published plays, however, show no sign of Shakespeare's involvement. He wrote them for the theater and not for a reading public; for him they were scripts to be acted, not plays to be read.

On such seemingly solid ground, many teachers and scholars have rested their confidence that the proper focus of academic attention is on the plays in performance. Thereby we are assured that Shakespeare's work is returned to the medium in which it lived. There is much to be said for such a focus, and much—too much, I often think—has been said for it. Shakespeare does, of course, "live" in the theater; there he becomes our contemporary, responsive to our needs and interests. And that seems to me to be the problem. Shakespeare in performance yields too easily to our desires. In the theater Shakespeare escapes his historicity, becoming for every age a contemporary playwright, and arguably its most important one. Like the promiscuous Hero of Claudio's tortured imagination, he is not merely our Shakespeare, he is everybody's Shakespeare.

But if age has not withered Shakespeare in the theater, it should not be forgotten that his theatrical vitality is possible only because the plays did reach print. If he does not "live" there quite as animatedly as he does in the theater, at very least in print he is *preserved*. It is not an entirely happy metaphor, I admit. Living beings are preferable to mummies, and print, in any case, does not preserve language as firmly as formaldehyde preserves bodies. Nonetheless, without print there is no Shakespeare for all time. It is in the printing house that his scattered "limbs," as Heminge and Condell say, are collected and cured, re-membered as a body of work.

This re-membering is of course no more exact than any other act of memory. Psychologists know that memory is never a perfect witness to the event remembered; it represses, displaces, and falsifies; nonetheless it is informative, though less as an objective representation of the event than as the overdetermined register of the event's reception and assimilation. Print remembers similarly; it too falsifies even as it recalls and records, incorporating elements separate from that which it would overtly remember. The Shakespeare remembered in the printing house is inevitably something other than Shakespeare—both more and less than his originary presence; his corpus is reconstructed by sets of motivations and practices that leave their marks upon the text, distorting it even as they preserve and set it forth.

This is not to return us to the notion of an ideal text independent of the processes of its materialization; it is to recognize that the text, like the past, is never available in unmediated form. This mediation is precisely what marks it as text, exactly as that which marks the past as past is the impossibility of an unmediated engagement with it. Shakespeare is, of course, available to us only in mediated form. One could say that this means that Shakespeare is never therefore available to us; but to the degree that this is true it is merely an uninteresting literalism. Shakespeare is available precisely because "Shakespeare," in any meaningful sense other than the biographical, is—and has always been—a synecdoche for the involved mediations of the playhouse and printing house through which he is produced.

The printed plays that preserve Shakespeare for us are, however, all in various ways deficient, yet, precisely in their distance from the ideal text of editorial desire, they bear witness to the complex conditions of authorship that shaped his career. Shakespeare has become virtually the iconic name for authorship itself, but he wrote in circumstances in which his individual achievement was inevitably dispersed into—if not compromised by—the collaborative economies of play and book production. Nonetheless, Shakespeare's apparent indifference to the publication of his plays, his manifest lack of interest in reasserting his authority over them, suggests how little he had invested in the notions of individuated authorship that, ironically, his name has come so triumphantly to represent. Literally, his investment was elsewhere: in the lucrative partnership of the acting company. He worked comfortably within its

necessary collaborations, and clearly felt no need to claim his play texts as his own as they began to circulate in print.

In this regard, Shakespeare is perhaps somewhat more anomalous than many have supposed. While plays inevitably were shaped by the demands of performance and the texts legally the property of the acting company (and the genre itself, as we are often reminded, a subliterary form perhaps incapable of sustaining the burden of literary ambition), in fact many playwrights did turn to print to preserve their creation in its intended form. Notoriously, Ben Jonson labored to rescue his plays from the theatrical conditions in which they were produced, seeking to make available in print a play text of which he could be said in some exact sense to be its "author."

The 1600 quarto of *Every Man Out of His Humor* insists on its title page that it presents the play "As It Was First Composed by the Author B. I. Containing more than hath been Publickely Spoken or Acted." Here Jonson asserts the authority of the authorial text over the theatrical script, reversing the tendency to offer the play to a reading audience, in the familiar formula, "as it hath bene sundry times playd," as the 1600 quarto of *Henry V* has it. Even more remarkable is the 1605 quarto of *Sejanus*, to which Jonson contributes a preface in which he again announces that the printed text is "not the same with that which was acted on the publike stage." But in the published quarto, rather than merely restoring theatrical cuts, he has in fact removed and rewritten the work of a collaborator. While admitting that "A second Pen had good share" in what was played, in the printed text Jonson replaces the work of his unnamed coauthor with his own words never acted, disingenuously apologizing for inserting his own "weaker (and no doubt lesse pleasing)" language so as not "to defraud so happy a *Genius* of his right, by my lothed vsurpation" in the published volume (sig. ¶2ʳ).

But if Jonson's aggressive determination to extract his plays from the customary collaborations of the theater is unique, his desire for a printed text that will preserve the dramatist's intended form is not. Other playwrights similarly saw print as the medium in which their intentions could be made visible. Thomas Heywood, for example, insists in his epistle "To the Reader" in the 1608 quarto of his *Rape of Lucrece* that it has not been his "custome . . . to commit [his] plaies to the presse"; nonetheless, on account of the copies that have "accidently come into the Printers handes" in "corrupt and mangled" form, "This therefore I was the willinger to furnish out in his natiue habit" (sig. A2ʳ). In 1640, Richard Brome adds an epistle to *The Antipodes* in which the "Curteous Reader" is told that this playbook too contains "more then was presented upon the *Stage*," where "for superfluous length (as some of the *Players* pretended)," cuts were made. Brome says that for this printed edition

he thought it "good al should be inserted according to the allowed *Original*; and as it was, at first, intended for the *Cock-pit Stage*" (sig. L4ᵛ). For Brome, print restores and preserves the play he wrote, and, incidentally, his remarks reveal that it was the uncut, authorial text that was "allowed" by the Master of the Revels.

Shakespeare, however, never asserted any such proprietary right over his scripts or expressed any anxiety about their printed form. His plays, of course, were subjected to theatrical necessities, revised by various hands to allow them to play successfully within the two hours traffic of his stage, but never did Shakespeare feel obliged to "furnish" the play he wrote in its "natiue habit." Somewhat less than half of his dramatic output ever appeared in print while he lived, and of the plays that were published none is marked by any effort on his part to insure that the printed play accurately reflected what he had written. In their epistle "to the great Variety of Readers" in the 1623 folio, Heminge and Condell tell the would-be purchasers of the volume that the collection contains Shakespeare's plays exactly "as he conceiued the[m]," but that extravagant claim is never one Shakespeare felt inspired to make himself.

Eighteen of his thirty-seven plays were published in his lifetime. With ten reprinted one or more times, all told at least forty-two separate editions reached print before he died. (If one counts *The Taming of a Shrew* as Shakespeare's, there are forty-five surviving editions of nineteen plays.) Clearly Shakespeare was not only a successful theater poet but his plays found a substantial reading audience. The first part of *Henry IV* appeared in six editions before his death, and a seventh before the folio was published in 1623. *Richard II* was published five times, as was *Richard III*. Several other plays were reprinted three times. At the time of his death, the total number of editions of his plays far exceeds that of any other playwright, and indeed no single play to that time had sold as well as *1 Henry IV*. (Even if one extends the time frame to 1640, only three plays—the anonymous *Mucedorus*, Kyd's *Spanish Tragedy*, and Marlowe's *Dr. Faustus*—appear in more editions than *1 Henry IV*'s seven; *Mucedorus*, somewhat improbably to modern taste, topped the list with fourteen printings between 1598 and 1639.)

While he lived, arguably Shakespeare had some competitors for theatrical preeminence, but what has often been overlooked is that as a published dramatist he had none. In our various measures of Shakespeare's greatness, we have usually ignored the fact that in his own age more editions of his plays circulated than of any other contemporary playwright. Eventually the prolific Beaumont and Fletcher would close the gap, but they never actually surpass Shakespeare. Ironically, although he never sought his success in print, he is the period's leading published playwright.

In large part the reason that this has not been observed must be that to us

it seems literally to "go without saying"; it seems to us inevitable that Shakespeare's plays would reach print and thrive in that medium. In his own time, however, that success was hardly assured. We see the drama as the most compelling cultural achievement of the age and Shakespeare as its most extraordinary figure, but Shakespeare wrote in an environment in which plays were the piecework of an emerging entertainment industry. Publishers did not rush to publish new plays because there was not a large or reliable market for them. As Peter Blayney has usefully reminded us, they were at best a risky publishing venture. "No more than one play in five would have returned the publisher's initial investment inside five years," Blayney tells us, and "not one in twenty would have paid for itself during its first year."[2] While Shakespeare provided some publishers with considerable profit, eight of the eighteen plays that appeared in his lifetime did not merit a second edition before he died. And it is worth remembering that *Venus and Adonis* was published in sixteen editions by 1636, seven more than even the most successful of his plays.

In spite of the literary ambitions of some playwrights, plays were generally considered ephemera, among the "riffe-raffes" and "baggage books" that Thomas Bodley would not allow in his library lest some "scandal" attach to it by their presence.[3] Publishers did regularly assume the risk of printing plays (though between 1590 and 1615 on average only about ten were published a year), but they could not have done so imagining either that they were preserving the nation's cultural heritage or about to make their own fortune.

Plays were published in essence because they could be. In a commercial environment where publishing was largely opportunistic, plays were for a publisher a relatively inexpensive investment. If they did not, as Blayney says, offer a reliable "shortcut to wealth" (389), they did allow a publisher the chance to make some money without great financial exposure. Manuscripts became available, probably at a cost to the publisher of no more than two pounds. No record of any payment for a play survives, but evidence like that from the *Second Part of the Return From Parnassus*, where the printer John Danter (of whom more later) is imagined offering an author "40 shillings and an odde pottle of wine" for a manuscript, suggests that this was something like the going rate for a small book.[4] The play text would usually be printed in small pica type on nine sheets of the cheapest available paper. For an edition of eight hundred, all told the costs of copy, registration, and printing probably were about eight pounds. With playbooks retailing at about 6d. and wholesaling at 4d., a publisher, especially one who sold his own books, would break even with the sale of about four hundred copies and would then begin to turn a modest profit, which might average about a pound a year—certainly not a spectacular windfall but a not insubstantial contribution to the financial health of the stationer's business.[5]

The plays that were printed, almost certainly less than a fifth of the number played, arrived at their publishers from a variety of sources, and in the absence of anything like our modern copyright law, the publishers had no obligation to inquire scrupulously into their provenance. All that was legally obligated was that they not violate another stationer's claim to the text. If there was no prior claim, a publisher was free to print his copy with no regard for its author's rights or interests. As George Wither wrote in 1624: "by the lawes and Orders of their Corporation, they can and do setle vpon the particular members thereof p[e]rpetuall interest in such Bookes as are Registred by them at their Hall . . . notwithstanding their first Coppies were purloyned from the true owner, or imprinted without his leaue." Until the first modern copyright law was passed in 1709, this remained the case. Copyright belonged to the publisher not to the author, and the legal situation, as Wither bitterly noted, served the publisher's interest at the expense of that of both the author and the reading public: "If he gett any written Coppy into his powre, likely to be vendible; whether the Author be willing or no, he will publish it; and it shallbe contriued and named alsoe, according to his owne pleasure: which is the reason, so many good Bookes come forth imperfect, and with foolish titles."[6]

In fairness, most stationers did make reasonable attempts to produce an accurate text; still, Wither's main accusation, at least with regard to the drama, is true. Stationers for the most part showed little interest in either the quality of the origin of the dramatic texts they printed; they cared mainly that it be "vendible." Textual scholars, the heirs of Wither's dismay, have often used this fact to motivate their narratives of the transmission of Shakespeare's text. They similarly have stigmatized the stationers, or at least some, as dishonest and incompetent, all too willing to attempt a quick profit by publishing a pirated text of a play. But in truth the pirates, as Blayney and Laurie Maguire have recently reminded us, are largely bogeys of our imagination, functions of an anachronistic understanding of both the playhouse and the printing house.[7] This is not to say that publishers did inevitably purchase their copy from the author or some other apparently legitimate owner; it is, however, to emphasize that stationers knew that the author's permission was not necessary to publish the work, and knew as well that in the case of drama the very notion of authorship is problematic. In any precise sense, the only pirates, and there were some, were those publishers who undertook to print a book that properly belonged to another stationer.

Plays, however, were unquestionably published without their authors' consent or even knowledge, and in forms of which no doubt their playwrights would never have approved; but this should not be taken as anything more than evidence of the usual—and fully legal—procedures of the contemporary book trade. A potential publisher would purchase a manuscript of a play, which

might in some cases be authorial, though it could as well be a scribal copy made for the acting company or for a collector, or a transcript made by one or more actors. For the potential publisher it made no difference; no one of these granted the publisher any clearer authority over the text. All he would have been concerned with was that the manuscript not cost too much, that it be reasonably legible, and that no other stationer have a claim to the play.

There are some examples of writers objecting to the publication of defective versions of their work, although these inevitably reveal how limited was their ability to oppose unauthorized publication. Usually the most they can do is provide authorized copy to replace the unsanctioned printing. Thus, Samuel Daniel explains the publication of the second edition of his *Vision of the Twelve Goddesses* in his dedication to the Countess of Bedford: "*Madame*: In respect of the vnmannerly presumption of an indiscreet Printer, who without warrant hath divulged the late shewe at Court, . . . I thought it not amisse seeing it would otherwise passe abroad to the prejudice both of the Maske and the inuention, to describe the whole forme thereof in all points as it was then performed."[8] Similarly, Stephen Egerton, in a preface to the second edition of one of his sermons that had been taken down by a listener in shorthand, says that had it been his own doing originally he would have "beene more carefull in the manner of handling. . . . And therefore that which I now do, is rather somewhat to qualifie an errour that cannot be recalled, then to publish a worke that may be in any way greatly commodious to other."[9] Both Daniel and Egerton are frustrated by the deficient texts that were published, but neither assumes that the publication of an unauthorized text is a legal issue. In the face of the publication of texts that neither author either delivered to or saw through the press, both realize that they have little recourse except to provide a better text for a new edition.

Plays unquestionably were published in forms that were unauthorized, that is, in editions that differed not only from the author's intended text but also from the text as it had been reshaped in performance, but these were not *illegal* printings; they do not provide evidence of criminal or dishonest business practices. Indeed this is true even for the so-called "bad quartos" of Shakespeare's plays. While these editions differ substantially from the familiar versions in which we know the play, and are arguably inferior if not corrupt, there is nothing to suggest their publishers knew them so. They operated in these cases very much as they did in all others, purchasing a play text on which they thought they might make a small profit.

A published play text, we must remember, was not a priceless literary relic but a cheap pamphlet; it represented not the immortal words of a great writer but the work of professional actors whose skill involved improvisation as much as recall. The play itself had various lives in different theatrical venues, each of which would enforce changes upon the text. Why then would a publisher ever think in terms of the reliability or authority of the text?

Even if, however improbably, he did, how would a publisher recognize textual corruption? We hear a mangled phrase from a bad quarto, and our familiarity with the received text instantly reveals the deficiency. "To be, or not to be, I there's the point." There is no more familiar or compelling evidence of the manifest deficiency of Q1 *Hamlet* (sig. D4ᵛ). But if we did not know the more familiar version would we think the line flawed? And indeed the putative corruption—"I there's the point"—is of course a perfectly uncorrupt Shakespearean line. It appears in *Othello*, after Othello painfully comes to see that his worst fears about Desdemona's betrayal must be true, revealingly in language that shows how fully he has internalized the pernicious racism that Iago exploits: "And yet how Nature erring from it selfe." Iago instantly interrupts, determined that there should be no retreat from the damning knowledge: "I, there's the point" (3.3.231–32, TLN 1855). In *Othello*, the line marks Shakespeare's dramatic genius; in *Hamlet* it marks the corruption of the text.

The example may be too neat, and in fairness when one looks at the whole speech in Q1 *Hamlet* one does find unmistakable signs of logical and syntactic jumble that seems more a function of the troubled transmission of the text than of the troubled mindset of its hero. Nonetheless, the initial question stands. Would a publisher who has come into possession of Q1 have any reason to be suspicious of the text he had purchased? At least at the level of text, the answer, I would insist, is "no," though with *Hamlet* there is another factor that complicates the issue. (I suppose with *Hamlet* there is always another factor that complicates the issue.)

Q1 *Hamlet* was published by Nicholas Ling and John Trundle in 1603; the play, however, had been registered to James Roberts on 26 July 1602. If the quality of the text was not unduly strained, the quality of their right to it seems to be. Roberts's entry establishes his title to the play, a title that is apparently violated by the edition that Ling and Trundle publish. Ling and Trundle are here perhaps truly pirates, not because they print a text in authorized form or one that is come to them via some actor but because they print a text registered to another stationer.

Nonetheless, I wonder if the ease with which we attribute piracy here is still not more a function of our textual expectation than publishing history. The usual account is that Ling and Trundle have indeed published what Fredson Bowers calls "a memorially reconstructed pirate text."[10] A second quarto is, of course, published late in 1604, "Printed by I. R. for N.L.," as its title page has it, that is, printed by James Roberts for Nicholas Ling. This quarto announces itself as "Newly imprinted and inlarged to almost as much againe as it was, according to the true and perfect Coppie." It is consciously designed to supplant the first, offering itself as new and improved, or, actually, new and restored, some 1,600 lines longer than Q1. The deficiencies of the earlier text are here replaced by authorized copy. Trundle's absence from the publishing arrangements of the second quarto have been taken as evidence that he was the supplier of the corrupt copy for Q1, and the cooperation of Roberts and Ling is seen as a pragmatic compromise that acknowledges Roberts's de jure title and Ling's de facto right. In the familiar textual history, Q2 marks the victory of truth and justice. The "memorially reconstructed pirate text" is replaced by a properly authorial version, and the rights of the abused stationer are restored.[11]

It is a good story, but it is not necessarily or even very probably true. Roberts, who was a printer rather than a publisher, had on numerous occasions entered material that was eventually published by another stationer but was printed by Roberts. The entries seem to be for him usually a way of reserving work for himself without risking the capital that publication would involve. Roberts, for example, entered *The Merchant of Venice* in 1598, and two years later printed it for its eventual publisher, Thomas Hayes. Ling, in contrast, was a publisher who, as Gerald Johnson has written, characteristically depended on "other stationers who located copy and brought it to him for help in publishing the editions," often with the printing job reserved for them as their reward.[12] Ling and Roberts also were well known to one another; twenty-three editions published by Ling came from Roberts's press. (Trundle, too, had employed Roberts, indeed in the very year that Q1 *Hamlet* was published.)[13] And title to *Hamlet* seems to have unproblematically settled on Ling, since he transfers it without question to John Smethwick in 1607.

Given these relationships, what seems most likely is that the publication of Q1 *Hamlet* was not piratical but pragmatic, the result of a rather ordinary set of prudent arrangements between stationers. The only thing that fits uncomfortably with this thesis is that Roberts did not in fact get to print Q1 *Hamlet*, though the traffic in his print shop (it was the third busiest year of Roberts's career in terms of the number of books printed and probably the heaviest measured by sheets printed) may well have made it impossible to accept the job when it came due. For us it may seem incredible that a printer would pass up the opportunity to work on *Hamlet*, but job schedules would override any literary considerations; and, in any case, many things for a printer in 1603 might have seemed more compelling than a six-penny pamphlet, perhaps the edition of Drayton's *Baron's Wars* that he printed that year for Ling or Harsnett's *Declaration of Egregious Popish Impostures* or even the two Bills of Mortality that he printed in the autumn of the year. Only an anachronistic sense of *Hamlet*'s value to a printer in 1603 has prevented the more likely version of events from being widely accepted. The putative corruptions of the text, the distortions of Shakespeare's great artistry, demand narratives of motivated villainy. Only a cad would publish a text as "bad" as Q1 *Hamlet*.

But to return to my major point here, it is not obvious to me that Ling and Trundle had any particular reason to think the text they published "bad"—or indeed any to think it particularly good. What they thought was that they had acquired copy that was "vendible," a play text that might be published with some small profit to them. When a new text became available the following year, supplied perhaps by the acting company who might well have been dismayed by what was in print, they were no doubt delighted to produce a second edition that might inspire new sales. This is a less interesting story, I admit, than tales of pirates, but it is almost certainly closer to the truth.

I am not saying that Q1 *Hamlet* is as good a play as the *Hamlet* which we usually read (though I would say that it is a better play than has usually been allowed, and certainly not "*Hamlet* by Dogberry," as Brian Vickers has termed it);[14] I am saying only that such questions of literary judgment should not be allowed to color our understanding of the textual history. When we see that history backward, through the filter of a cultural authority not fully achieved until the mid–eighteenth century, inevitably we get it wrong. Shakespeare, one could say, was not exactly Shakespeare during his own lifetime.

An obvious example: when his plays were first published, his name was not what distinguished them in the bookstalls. As is well known, eight plays were published over four years before a play of Shakespeare's appeared in print with his name on the title page. Cuthbert Burby first included Shakespeare's name on the quarto of *Love's Labor's Lost* in 1598 (and even then hardly as a ringing affirmation of authorship: the title page asserting only that the play was "Newly corrected and augmented, by W. Shakespere," the name set in small italic type) but previously editions of *Titus Andronicus* (1594), *2* and *3 Henry VI* (1594, 1595), *The Taming of the Shrew* (*A Shrew*, 1594), *Romeo and Juliet* (1597), *Richard II* (1597), *Richard III* (1597), and *1 Henry IV* (1598) all had been published with no indication that Shakespeare was the playwright. The plays, with the exception of *2 Henry VI*, all advertise the authority of the text as theatrical rather than authorial, by insisting that it is published "As it was Plaide" by whatever company had performed it.

One should, of course, conclude that what this means is that before 1598 the name "Shakespeare" on the title page was not yet seen as sufficient inducement for a potential customer to purchase a play text at a bookstall. Indeed, most published plays advertised their theatrical auspices, emphasizing for us yet again that the drama was still subliterary, its audience, even for the published play, understood primarily as theatergoers. Play quartos do seem largely

to have depended on playgoers for their sales, the six-penny pamphlets a relatively cheap way of happily recalling a performance or catching up with one that had unhappily been missed. Richard Hawkins reminds the potential buyers of his edition of *Philaster* (1628) that the play "was affectionately taken, and approved by the Seeing Auditors, or Hearing Spectators (of which sort I take, or conceive you to be the greatest part)," though he anticipates also that his edition will be "eagerly sought for, not onely by those that haue heard & seene it, but by others that haue merely heard therof" (sig. A2^v). As excitement about a production waned with time, however, the published play would normally become less marketable: "When they grow stale they must be vented by Termers and Cuntrie chapmen," says Middleton in his preface to *The Family of Love* (1608), distressed that publication of his play had not taken place "when the newnesse of it made it much more desired" (sig. A1^v). Printed plays do seem for the most part to be tied to theatrical success, published with the hope, as Brome says in his epistle to *The Antipodes*, that "the publicke view of the world entertayn it with no lesse welcome, then that private one of the stage already has given it" (sig. A2^v); or, as Heywood writes in his preface to *Greene's Tu quoque* (1614): "since it hath past the Test of the stage with so generall an applause, pitty it were but it should likewise haue the honour of the Presse" (sig. A2^r).

Not surprisingly, then, title pages usually advertise their plays as the records of performance rather than the registers of a literary intention. Whatever the actual status of the underlying manuscript, if the market for playbooks was largely playgoers the strategy makes sense. Within a theatrical economy display of an author's name on a play text offered no particular commercial advantage. It does seem, however, that, at least in Shakespeare's case, this was in the process of changing. In 1598, reprints of both *Richard II* and *Richard III* were published that did include Shakespeare's name on the title page, and in 1599, *1 Henry IV* was reissued with Shakespeare's name added. In the remaining years before Shakespeare died, twenty-nine editions of eighteen separate plays were published, only eight of which appeared without identifying Shakespeare as the playwright.

Unquestionably most remarkable in this regard is the edition of *King Lear* published by Nathaniel Butter in 1608, with a title page not merely identifying Shakespeare as the playwright but trumpeting his authorship at the head of the page and in a larger typeface than had ever before been used for his name: "M. William Shak-speare: / HIS / True Chronicle Historie of the life and / death of King LEAR and his three / Daughters." Here the play is displayed and celebrated as Shakespeare's, but the printed text is no more exclusively "*HIS*" than any of the other published plays that had previously escaped his control. It

is a poorly printed play (indeed the first that its printer, Nicholas Okes, had ever undertaken), and Shakespeare did not oversee its publication or concern himself with the imperfect results.

The play is obviously presented as Shakespeare's, but it literally belongs to Butter, the publisher who owns and controls the text, asserting Shakespeare's authorship as a marketing strategy, both to capitalize on Shakespeare's reputation and to differentiate this play from an anonymous play text of 1605, *The True Chronicle History of King Leir*. Shakespeare's name functions on the 1608 title page perhaps as much to identify the play*book* as the play*wright*. In either role, of course, it serves as a mark of distinction, but Shakespeare is here always the publisher's Shakespeare, not the author himself, a simulacrum invented to protect and promote the publisher's property.[15]

The 1608 *Lear* quarto, then, does at least seem to point to Shakespeare's growing literary reputation. Butter, though he is unconcerned to provide a carefully printed text, is eager to offer what he does publish as Shakespeare's play and not merely as the record of performance by the King's Men. Here is the earliest incontrovertible evidence of what in 1622 Thomas Walkley would claim in his edition of *Othello* (1622): that "The Authors name is sufficient to vent his work." Certainly Butter believed this true, publishing in 1605 an edition of *The London Prodigall* with a title page claiming that is "By William Shakespeare." We cannot know whether or not Butter thought the play was in fact by Shakespeare, but obviously he thought Shakespeare's name would help sell the playbook.

And other publishers apparently thought similarly. The two parts of *The Troublesome Raigne of King John* were published first in 1591 by Sampson Clarke with no authorial attribution but rather with the familiar title page statement that they were set forth "As they were (sundry times) publikely acted by the Queenes Maiesties Players"; but when they were reprinted in 1611 by John Helme, the title page, while announcing that the texts were offered "As they were sundry times lately acted by the Queenes Maiesties Players" ("lately" replacing "publikely," as the Queen's men were now defunct), now included a new (and seemingly inaccurate) assertion that the plays were "Written by W.Sh." And when they were again reprinted in 1622, this time by Thomas Dewe, the name of the acting company had disappeared from the assertion that they were "(sundry times) lately acted" and the title page now proudly claimed they were "Written by W. Shakespeare." For Helme and Dewe it may merely be that they assumed these plays were indeed Shakespeare's *King John*; in any case, it does seem likely that it was the rights to these that were leased by the consortium that published the Shakespeare folio, since the as-yet-unpublished Shakespearean *King John* was not among the sixteen plays "not formerly entred to other men" duly registered by Jaggard and Blount on

8 November 1623. Yet, whatever the publishers' understanding about the plays' authorship, what is absolutely clear is that year by year on the bookstalls the commercial cachet of an old acting company weakened, while the commercial cachet of an old playwright grew.

But if some publishers were indeed convinced that "Shakespeare" on the title page would indeed help sell books, others seemed less certain about the marketability of the name. *Titus Andronicus*, for example, was published in 1594 with no indication of its author, only that it had been "Plaide by the Right Honourable the Earle of *Darbie*, Earle of *Pembrooke*, and Earle of *Sussex* their servaunts." The reticence about authorship here was no doubt because in 1594 the theatrical provenance of the play was more impressive than its still little-known author; but the play was reissued two more times after its first printing (once in 1600 and again in 1611), with title pages that updated its theatrical history but each still with no acknowledgement of Shakespeare's authorship.

Similarly, in 1599, Cuthbert Burby published the second edition of *Romeo and Juliet*, but that title page gives no indication that the play was by Shakespeare; and, lest this be taken only as evidence that even by 1599 the value of Shakespeare's name was still being negotiated, ten years later *Romeo and Juliet*, like *Titus*, was published once again without identifying Shakespeare as the playwright. And indeed about eleven years after that, roughly the time when Thomas Walkley was insisting upon the commercial value of Shakespeare's name, John Smethwick reprinted yet another edition of *Romeo and Juliet*, which again failed to identify is author, though interestingly a variant title page was issued that does claim the play was "Written by W. Shake-speare." This edition was published by John Smethwick, who, on the basis of the titles he controlled, apparently was invited in as a minor partner in the consortium of stationers who combined to publish the first folio. I take it that Smethwick, who had acquired the rights to the play from Nicholas Ling in 1607, had prepared a new edition of *Romeo and Juliet*, a reprint of the 1609 printing, and issued it with a reset version of the earlier title page. The variant title page seems to me likely to have been issued sometime after negotiations for the folio rights revealed to Smethwick the nature of his property. (It is very unlikely that the authorial title page was issued first, as there is no obvious commercial reason to remove Shakespeare's name, but an obvious one to add it.) But until the issue of the variant title page of *Romeo and Juliet*, Smethwick, just like Edward White, the publisher of the later *Titus* quartos, had published two editions of the play he controlled without identifying either as Shakespeare's; and, though it may seem incredible to us, it is at least possible that Smethwick and White did so without knowing that Shakespeare was the author.

How this could be the case is instructive. Both plays were first published by John Danter, *Titus Andronicus* in 1594, the first of Shakespeare's plays to appear in print or at least the earliest surviving publication, and *Romeo and Juliet* in 1597. Danter was an active stationer in London in the 1590s before his death at age thirty-four in October 1599, in his eight-year career printing or publishing 79 editions of 67 separate titles, mainly popular forms, like ballads, pamphlets and plays. Danter's professional behavior, however, has been consistently denigrated as immoral and inept, Chambers, for example, identifying Danter as "a stationer of the worst reputation," and McKerrow, saying of the 1597 *Romeo and Juliet* that "like all his work, it was very badly printed."[16] W. W. Greg agreed, combining the two judgments into general misgiving: "any dramatic quarto with which [Danter] was concerned is necessarily suspect in the first instance."[17] For D. Allen Carroll the whole career is tainted: "Everyone knows of the odor which attaches itself to the name of Danter."[18]

But this may be another case where our anachronistic hopes and expectations for Shakespeare's text have infected our historical judgment; "the odor which attaches itself to the name of Danter" may not be the fetid scent of fraudulence or incompetence but only the homely smell of workmanlike activity. Danter does find himself entangled in various difficulties with the Stationers' Company, but they are for the most part the sorts of disputes that affect almost every one in the company at one time or other. In 1586, Danter was one of six stationers accused of violating Francis Flower's patent to print *Accidence*, a popular Latin grammar, and with the others he was found guilty of illegal printing and "Dyshabled to prynte, otherwyse then as Iourneymen," as the Stationers' Court decreed; nonetheless in 1589 he was admitted a freeman of the company.[19] In 1593 arbitration was ordered for some unnamed conflict that Danter had with Henry Chettle and Cuthbert Burby, a dispute inconsequential enough, however, that three men on and off continued to work together to the end of the decade; and, what was more serious, in 1597, he had his presses and type "defaced and made vnservciable for pryntinge" for printing the *Jesus Psalter*, a work of Catholic devotion, "without aucthoritie."[20]

His court record marks him as at worst a recusant but hardly a wicked or even particularly unruly member of the company. The animus that attaches to him results mainly from his publication of the 1597 "bad quarto" of *Romeo and Juliet*. It is that offense that is "rank" and "smells to heaven"—or at least to the sensitive olfactory organs of the new bibliographers. Danter is guilty of printing an imperfect text of one of Shakespeare's plays. There is no reason, of course, to think he knew it imperfect, and the printing itself is unremarkable, except that halfway through the text the type font changes. Rather typically, the observation of this fact produces more derision: "never was a masterpiece ushered into the world in a worse manner," said Plomer,[21] but in truth the change in font reveals only that the printing was shared, probably with Edward Allde. Such shared printing was not uncommon (Dekker's *The Honest Whore* and the three 1604 quartos of Marsten's *The Malcontent* are examples),[22] and typographically, little marks the composition and presswork as defective. The play, however, was not registered by Danter, and the absence of a license coupled with a text that seems to have been abridged for performance has led to its vilification, most recently by a scholar as normally judicious as David Bevington, who calls it "a pirated edition issued by an unscrupulous publisher."[23]

Danter, however, was no pirate. Printing a play that had been abridged for performance or even one recalled and reassembled by its actors did not violate any law or regulation. No one had a prior claim to the text of *Romeo and Juliet*, and Danter's avoidance of the expected registration procedures may have been motivated by nothing more nefarious than his desire to save the required fees. Danter's usual habits were more conventional. He was involved in the publication of nine plays, three of which he printed for other stationers; of the six he published himself, four were properly registered, including *Titus Andronicus*.

There is no particular reason to see his handling of *Romeo and Juliet* as symptomatic of some character flaw, or indeed as anything worse than somewhat cavalier treatment of what was essentially a pamphlet at a moment when his own career seemed to be in free fall. In 1595 he was involved with nineteen publications; in 1596, with eleven; in 1597, the year *Romeo and Juliet* was published, only three, the following year just one. Late that year or the early the next he died, and in 1600 the Stationers' Company granted his widow and children "twentye Shillinge A yere . . . out of the poores Accompt," the mark of their poverty an addendum that an additional five shillings was to be "gyven vnto her presently in hand."[24] However *Romeo and Juliet* came into his possession it must have seemed a small miracle. We might think better of him if we see his decision to save himself ten pence by denying it both license and entrance less as an effort to put forth a degraded version of one of Shakespeare's plays than as one to put food on the table for his family.

In any case, *Romeo and Juliet* fared better than its publisher. By 1599 Danter was dead, his family destitute; that same year, Cuthbert Burby reissued the play in a new edition, "Newly Corrected, Augmented, and Amended." Printed by Thomas Creede, this second quarto seems to have been printed from Shakespeare's papers, which must have been received directly from the acting company. This seems to be another occasion, like those involving Samuel Daniel or Stephen Egerton, where an effort was made to substitute an authorized text for one that was deemed deficient. But interestingly, the establishment of an authorized text here does not involve the establishment of an author. Q2 may well be, as many bibliographers believe, a "good quarto" deriving from Shakespeare's own papers, but neither the publisher nor the supplier of the good text thought it useful to say so. The play is once again published by Burby as a performance text, printed "as it hath bene sundry time publiquely

acted," though arguably that describes the theatrically abridged text of Q1
more accurately than it does Q2, which, deriving from the playwright's papers,
seemingly deserves what it is denied: the acknowledgment that it is by William
Shakespeare. Such acknowledgment, however, was not forthcoming.

Burby's receipt, in whatever manner, of Shakespeare's papers does not
mark his edition as any more regular than Danter's. Indeed Burby's rights to
the play most likely derive from some negotiation with Danter. They had on
occasion worked together. Danter had printed *The Cobbler's Prophecy* for Burby
in 1594, and, more revealingly, the previous year Danter had entered the play
Orlando Furioso and then transferred his title to Burby with the proviso, as the
Stationers' Register records it, "(Danter to have the printing)." In any case,
though unregistered, Burby's rights to *Romeo and Juliet* are unquestioned, and
in 1607 he transferred his title to Nicholas Ling. Nine months later, Ling
transferred the rights to *Romeo and Juliet*, along with fifteen other titles, to
John Smethwick, who (as we have seen) printed an edition of the play in 1609,
again advertising it as "Newly corrected, augmented, and amended"—though
in fact the title page like the text itself is a simple reprint of Q2—and again
omitting the name of the playwright, as he did once more in 1622, until he
decided to issue the variant title page.

Since its first appearance in 1597, the play had belonged to four men, none
of whom had felt obligated by either bibliographic scruple or commercial
consideration to acknowledge Shakespeare's authorship. As the play became a
less familiar element in the repertory of the King's Men (and indeed no record
survives of any production after 1598), the recurring title page claim that the
play was printed "as it hath beene sundrie times publiquely acted" inevitably
became more gestural than descriptive, and as Shakespeare's name had become
increasingly "vendible" in the marketplace of print, it is hard to imagine that if
he was recognized as the play's author his name would not have been used to
help sell the editions (as indeed it is on the variant 1622 title page).

But play texts, we must again remind ourselves, had not yet fully made the
transition from the ephemera of an emerging entertainment industry to the
artifacts of high culture. They did not yet demand an author, and in some sense
they did not deserve one, the text being so fully a record of the collaborative
activities of a theatrical company. As publishers transferred titles to such works
there is no reason to think the author's name would automatically attach itself
and follow along. Today we hear the title *Romeo and Juliet* and instantly supply
Shakespeare's name. In 1597, in 1599, in 1609, and even in 1622, the Shakespearean canon did not yet exist. The publishers who printed the play were
arguably unaware, and certainly unimpressed, that they were printing a play by
Shakespeare. In this regard it is worth noting that the Stationers' Register

entry that records the transfer of titles from Ling to Smethwick has items like "Master DRAYTONS *Poemes*," "master GREENES *Arcadia*," and "SMYTHS *common Wealth of England*"; the plays, however, are anonymous: "ROMEO and JULETT," "The Taminge of a Shrewe," "Loues Labour Lost," and "a booke called Hamlett."

Authorship is important to us, heirs of a romantic conception of writing as individual and originary, and if it was indeed important to some of Shakespeare's contemporaries, it was not particularly important to Shakespeare himself or to the publishers who first brought his plays to the reading public. They did not see their task as the preservation of the work of the nation's greatest writer as they set forth his plays; they were seeking only some small profit with limited financial vulnerability, as with their six-penny pamphlets they turned Shakespeare into "a man in print" and made his plays available to desiring readers.

Notes

An earlier version of this essay was delivered at University College London as the first of the Lord Northcliffe Lectures that I was privileged to give in March 1999 and which was published (Cambridge University Press, 2001) as *Shakespeare and the Book*. I am extraordinarily grateful to David Trotter and John Sutherland for organizing that occasion and for the comments and questions of colleagues in the audience that helped clarify my interests and argument. I also must thank Zach Lesser, Alan Farmer, and Elizabeth Sauer, who offered much-needed advice, information, and encouragement at various critical stages of this essay's development.

   1. Katherine Duncan-Jones has argued that the 1609 edition of the sonnets was printed from Shakespeare's own revised manuscript and was sold by Shakespeare to Thomas Thorpe; see her "Was the 1609 *Shake-speares Sonnets* Really Unauthorized?" *Review of English Studies* 34 (1983): 151–71. For reasons that are largely irrelevant here, I do not share the view that the volume represents another example of Shakespeare's commitment to print, though, even if it is, it does not affect my argument about Shakespeare's lack of interest in seeing his *plays* in print.

   2. Peter W. M. Blayney, "The Publication of Playbooks," in *A New History of Early English Drama*, ed. John D. Cox and David Scott Kastan (New York: Columbia University Press, 1997), 389. See also Mark Bland, "The London Book-Trade in 1600," *A Companion to Shakespeare*, ed. David Scott Kastan (Oxford: Blackwell, 1999), 450–63.

   3. *Letters of Thomas Bodley to Thomas James, First Keeper of the Bodleian Library*, ed. G. W. Wheeler (Oxford: Oxford University Press, 1926), 219, 222. Two quarto playbooks, however, did in fact find their way into the early collection of the Bodleian; the 1620 library catalogue lists Robert Daborne's *A Christian Turn'd Turke* (1612) and Heywood's *The Four Prentices of London* (1615).

   4. *The Three Parnassus Plays*, ed. J. B. Leishman (London: Nicholson and Watson, 1949), 247–48. John Stephens, in his *Cynthia's Revenge* (London, 1613), speaks of authors who "gape after the drunken harvest of forty shillings, and shame the worthy

benefactors of *Hellicon*" (sig. A2ᵛ); and George Wither, in *The Schollers Purgatory* (London, 1624), similarly notes that stationers "cann hyre for a matter of 40 shillings some needy IGNORAMUS" (sig. 11ᵛ).

5. This analysis is heavily indebted to Peter Blayney's extraordinary reconstruction of the economics of playbook publishing in his "The Publication of Playbooks," esp. 405–13.

6. Wither, *The Schollers Purgatory* (London, 1624), sigs. B6ᵛ–7ʳ, H5ʳ.

7. Blayney observes that "we have been too busy chasing imaginary pirates" to understand how play texts normally found their way into print ("The Publication of Playbooks," 394). Piracy, as Laurie E. Maguire notes, "relates technically to the circumstances of publication, where it means the infringement of one stationer's rights by another." See her *Shakespearean Suspect Texts: The "Bad" Quartos and Their Contexts* (Cambridge: Cambridge University Press, 1996), 16. See also Cyril Bathurst Judge, *Elizabethan Book-Pirates* (Cambridge, Mass.: Harvard University Press, 1934), passim.

8. Daniel, *The Vision of the Twelve Goddesses* (London, 1604), sig. A3ʳ.

9. *A Lecture Preached by Maister Egerton, at the Blacke-friers, 1589* (London, 1603), sig. A4ʳ.

10. Bowers, *On Editing Shakespeare and the Elizabethan Dramatists* (Philadelphia: University of Pennsylvania Press, 1955), 41.

11. For a full and richly suggestive account of the complex "textual situation" of *Hamlet*, see Leah S. Marcus, *Unediting the Renaissance: Shakespeare, Marlowe, Milton* (London: Routledge, 1996), 132–76.

12. See Gerald D. Johnson, "Nicholas Ling, Publisher, 1580–1607," *Studies in Bibliography* 37 (1985): 203–14. On such reservation of printing rights, see, for example, Arber III.92, where Thomas Creede enters *The Cognizance of a True Christian* with a notation: "This copie to be alwaies printed for **Nicholas Linge** by the seid **Thomas Creede** as often as it shalbe printed."

13. STC 16743.2 and 16743.3, *A true bill of the whole number that hath died in the Cittie of London* (London, 1603). See Gerald D. Johnson, "John Trundle and the Book-Trade, 1603–1626," *Studies in Bibliography* 39 (1986), esp. 191–92.

14. *Times Literary Supplement* 24 (December 1993): 5.

15. Some of this material on the *King Lear* title page appears in different form in my *Shakespeare After Theory* (New York: Routledge, 1999), 37, 81.

16. E. K. Chambers, *The Elizabethan Stage* (Oxford: Oxford University Press, 1923), 3, 187; and *A Dictionary of Printers and Booksellers . . . 1557–1640*, gen. ed. R. B. McKerrow (London: Bibliographic Society, 1910), 84.

17. Greg, *Two Elizabethan Stage Abridgements: "The Battle of Alcazar" and "Orlando Furioso": An Essay in Critical Bibliography* (Oxford: Oxford University Press, 1923), 130.

18. Carroll, "Who Wrote *Greenes Groats-worth of Witte* (1592)?" *Renaissance Papers 1992*, ed. George Walton Williams and Barbara J. Baines (Durham, N.C.: Southeastern Renaissance Conference, 1993), 75.

19. *Records of the Court of the Stationers' Company, 1576–1602*, ed. W. W. Greg and E. Boswell (London: Bibliographic Society, 1930), 21 (3 November 1586); and *A Transcript of the Stationers' Register*, ed. Edward Arber (London, 1875), 2, 706 (30 September 1589).

20. Greg and Boswell, *Records of the Court of the Stationers' Company* 46 and 56 (5 March 1593; 10 April 1597).

21. Henry R. Plomer, "The Printers of Shakespeare's Plays and Poems," *Library*, 2nd ser., 7 (1906): 153.

22. See W. Craig Ferguson, *Valentine Simmes* (Charlottesville: University of Virginia Press, 1968), 86–89.

23. *The Complete Works of Shakespeare*, ed. David Bevington (New York: Harper-Collins, 1992), A-14.

24. Greg and Boswell, *Records of the Court of the Stationers' Company* 78 (7 July 1600).

2

Books and Scrolls

Navigating the Bible

PETER STALLYBRASS

Scrolls and Books

Contemporary pronouncements about the death of the book are puzzling, for in many ways, it is the book form—the *combination* of the ability to scroll with the capacity for random access, enabling you to leap from place to place—that has provided the model which these other cultural technologies now seek to emulate. Computers, for instance, with their extraordinary powers of random access, are for most people extremely ungainly and unwieldy in their scroll functions. But computers take to a new level a crucial aspect of the ways in which we often use books—our ability, through bookmarks, to have our fingers in many different places at the same time, and to move rapidly from one to another. We are, I believe, reliving in a different key the moment, analyzed by Roberts and Skeat in *The Birth of the Codex*, when reading practices were radically transformed.[1] If cultural pessimists claim that no one reads anymore, perhaps they mean that it's becoming rarer for people to submit themselves to the scroll function of books. Surfing on TV works against the unwinding of a film scroll and hypertext works against a continuous reading of the *Canterbury Tales*.[2] But that has nothing to do with the death of the book. On the contrary, I would argue that we are living with a new intensity the triumph of the book as a technology. For in a book, as opposed to a scroll, one does not need to read from page 1 to page 2 to page 3 and so on. One can read from page 180 to page 36 to page 297 (as, say, in a collection of poems); or now, with the aid of hypertext, one can thicken a specific moment, reading versions of a single line of verse as it moves from manuscript to manuscript, from manuscript to magazine, from magazine to pamphlet, from pamphlet to "collected works."

The book/codex, as an emergent technology, enabled a reader to mark up places discontinuously. In this sense, the history of the codex is the history of the bookmark. The codex had nearly displaced the scroll for pagan Greek texts by the fourth century. But the adoption of the codex was by no means automatic among pagans, who continued to regard it as a culturally inferior form.[3]

In contrast, the great majority of Christian texts from as early as we have such texts were already in the form of codices, and only 14 of the surviving 172 Christian texts written before the fifth century were written on scrolls.[4] Astonishingly, Christianity immediately adopted the codex as its privileged form. While the codex was more slowly adopted by pagans, it tended to be treated as an inferior, notebook form, even after it became the dominant technology. The most radical contrast, though, is not between Christians and pagans, both of whom converged in the use of the codex by the fifth century. It is between Christians and Jews. Within Jewish culture, while codices may have been used as private notebooks, no Jewish codices have survived from before the tenth century in the Middle East and the eleventh century in Europe. Prior to the tenth or eleventh centuries, Christians and Jews actively differentiated themselves from each other through the adoption of the book or the scroll. The crucial thing for Christians was to make sure that they read *their* Jewish scriptures in a form that was materially as unlike the Jewish scriptures as possible, so as to proclaim the distinctiveness of the Septuagint. For more than six centuries, the distinction of the book from the scroll materially differentiated Christianity from Judaism.[5]

The ideological opposition of the scroll to the codex is powerfully visualized in an engraving of "The Apocalyptic Type" in Joseph Mede's *Key of the Revelation* (Fig. 1).[6] At the top of the engraving, there is a scroll with seven seals. Although the scroll is identified as "Mr HAYDOCK his book sealed," the "book" represents Haydock's conception of a Judaic scroll. The emphasis is upon the scroll as a form that, through its seals, denies easy access. But the seventh seal loops around to the right, first to "THE ENDE" of time (the horizontal axis) and then back to a *codex* at the bottom of the engraving ("Mr HAYDOCK his booke opened") (Fig. 2). The open book shows the suffering of martyrs on the verso with the header "How long o Lord dost thou not aveng" and, on the recto, a quotation from Revelation 5.1: "A booke written within and on the backside sealed with 7 seales." The closed scroll has been transformed into an open codex. But even more striking is what has happened to the seals that keep the scroll closed: they have been transformed into *finding tabs* that will enable the reader to move easily from place to place. The codex is thus marked not only by its openness but by its bookmarks. It is represented as above all *indexical*, a technology that uses bookmarks like prosthetic fingers to take the reader easily from place to place.

As Malcolm Parkes, Mary and Richard Rouse, and Paul Saenger have brilliantly demonstrated, the creation of an easily navigable book was a slow and laborious process, punctuated by moments of rapid development.[7] In the thirteenth century, a moment of such rapid development, all sorts of navigational aids were produced for preachers and university teachers: biblical con-

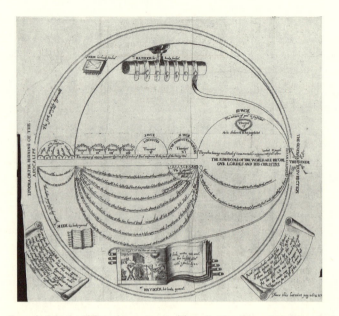

Figure 1. Joseph Mede, "The Apocalyptic Type," *The Key of the Revelation*, trans. Richard More (London: Philip Stephens, 1643), with the book of Revelation as a scroll with seven seals at the top and as an open codex with seven finding tabs at the bottom.

cordances, subject indexes, library catalogues. Reference tools increasingly followed an alphabetical system (like modern indexes), rather than a hierarchical ordering (Rouse and Rouse 221–55). At first, the alphabetic system that we take for granted was actively resisted, because it led to arbitrary relations between words and even to logical inversions, in which the created preceded the creator (*Filia* coming before *Pater*, *Angelus* before *Deus*), and inversions of social hierarchy (*Filia* coming before *Filius*, *Mater* before *Pater*).[8] Manuscripts were given numbered folios or openings, and arabic numerals were increasingly used. The bible and other books were divided into chapters. The fifteenth century was a period of comparable change, and one might want to see the invention of printing less as a displacement of manuscript culture than as the culmination of the invention of the navigable book—the book that allowed you to get your finger into the place you wanted to find in the least possible time. Many of the developments of the thirteenth century were taken up on a much larger and more systematic scale. Tables of contents were added along with lists of chapters, running headlines, more consistent pagination, and a much wider use of indexes (Rouse and Rouse 449–66). Headings and incipits were sometimes written in a formal script which made them stand out from the cursive of the rest of the manuscript. Capitals, often emphasized with a red stroke, were

Figure 2. Detail from Joseph Mede, "The Apocalyptic Type," *The Key of the Revelation*, trans. Richard More (London: Philip Stephens, 1643): the opened codex of Revelation.

used to mark the beginnings of sentences (Saenger 1996: 247, 250–51). Finding tabs were added to books (as in the codex depicted in *The Key of the Revelation*). Elaborate bookmarks are recorded in printing after printing of the fifteenth century, particularly in the Low Countries, as, for instance, in the bookmarks that van Eyck's Virgin uses both in the Ghent altarpiece and in the beautiful *Annunciation* in the National Gallery of Art, Washington.

I have found no images of such book-marking systems before the beginning of the fifteenth century. Do these bookmarks, then, suggest a radical development, not in the art of discontinuous reading as such, but in the *conceptualization* of reading as a practice of discontinuity (a discontinuity already materialized in the fragmentary texts of the most popular late medieval book, the book of hours)? Such random access for specific ends (to learn all that one can about the common loon, for instance) is now enabled by ever more powerful engines for searching the web. Yet my Macintosh computer still uses a little hand to travel around the screen and a pointing finger. And when I find a new website, I add a "bookmark," visualized nostalgically at the top of my screen as a blue ribbon. The navigation of computers is still imagined in the visual language that was elaborated in the fifteenth century for the navigation of books: the language of the index finger and of its prosthetic form, the bookmark.

The manuscript book or codex emerged, I am suggesting, as an alternative to, and sometimes in an antagonistic relation to, the scroll. The scroll as a technology depends upon a literal unwinding, in which the physical proximity of one moment in the narrative to another is both materially and symbolically significant. One cannot move easily back and forth between distant points on a scroll. But it is precisely such movement back and forth that the book permits. It not only allows for discontinuous reading; it encourages it. Indeed, it may even enforce it, as in the case of William Byrd's second book of *Gradualia, ac Cantiones Sacrae*.[9] A chorister using that book will be thrown into panic as he comes to the end of the nineteenth canto, for instance, if he hasn't already made use of the indexical system that the book provides and marked up his copy (with finger or bookmark) ahead of time. Where he would expect to find the "Alleluia," he comes instead to a reference to another canto, *Beata viscera*, and the comment *vt supra* ("as above"). The index at the back of the *Gradualia* refers the chorister to canto eleven and its "Alleluia." In other words, movement back and forth within the codex is necessary simply to sing the piece. In 1592, Hendrik Goltzius depicted Calliope, the muse of epic poetry and eloquence, marking up her oblong music book discontinuously with her fingers, so as to flick back from her present place to two earlier passages. And da capo markings in the seventeenth century would make such flipping back and forth a regular part of music.

Only certain productively perverse uses of the book have transformed it back into a scroll, most notoriously "gripping" novels or "page-turners," where the teleological drive from page to page mitigates against dipping about or turning back (although not, in the case of the unbearable suspense of a mystery, from skipping forward to find out "whodunit"). When cultural critics nostalgically recall an imagined past in which readers unscrolled their books continuously from beginning to end, they are *reversing* the long history of the codex and the printed book as indexical forms. The novel has only been a brilliantly perverse interlude in the long history of discontinuous reading.

Discontinuous Reading

The use of book-marking systems to index discontinuous passages was, and is, central to the Catholic liturgy. A modern missal that I bought secondhand comes with five color-coded ribbons for bookmarks, and to get through a single service in the sixteenth century, one would need to make full use of them.[10] I am far from proficient, but following the High Mass in this missal even today involves something like this sequence (with extra complications for feast days): pages 654, 651, 654–60, 867, 37, 660–62, 867, 37, 868, 37–38, 868, 39, 869, 39–40, 664, 869, 39–40, 666, 869, 666, 869, 40, 666–68, 870, 40, 668–74, 870, 40, 674, 692, 40, 733–35, 698.[11] That's just the bare structure, without the gospel readings and so on. Not surprisingly, it was usually easier, if more expensive, to organize the service via different books, separating out the necessary texts for different functions. Catholic services, particularly in the cathedrals, depended not on the bible as such but on a large number of different books. In the eleventh century, John of Garland listed twelve separate volumes as necessary for a service, including missals, graduals, lectionaries, psalters, and sacramentaries.[12] Separating out the service into separate texts made it less necessary to collate passages from different places—that is, to use your fingers and prosthetic fingers (ribbons, etc.) to mark passages to be read in a single volume from, say, the Pentateuch, the Prophets, the Psalms, the Gospels, the Pauline Epistles, a saint's life, and so on. The discontinuous reading that the codex enabled thus became central to Christianity and led to the cutting up of the bible into specific, usable parts, bound separately.

This is not to say there was no continuity, but the continuity was provided above all by the liturgical year, during the course of which much of the bible would be read (and the Psalms, for instance, would be read repeatedly). How and why, then, did continuous reading become the norm (or at least begin to be perceived as a norm to which one could contrast, say, phone books and technical manuals)?

One answer is that Protestants broke with the Catholic tradition of discontinuous reading. A subtle and complex version of this argument is rehearsed by Patrick Collinson in his groundbreaking article, "The Coherence of the Text."[13] If it is true that Protestants began to read the bible continuously (and, of course, *some* Catholics had done so previously), these readers arguably initiated the practice which novel readers would later naturalize: the perverse habit of reading forward continuously. To imagine continuous reading as the norm in reading a book is radically reactionary: it is to read a codex as if it was a scroll, from beginning to end.

But did Protestants, and specifically English Protestants, read the bible continuously? As Alison Chapman has pointed out, the 1549 Book of Common Prayer specifically addresses problems of discontinuous reading in "The Preface" (reprinted with minor changes until the revised preface of 1662).[14] According to the preface, the "Godly and decent ordre of the auncient fathers, hath been [in the Catholic service] so altered, broken, and neglected, by planting in vncertein stories, Legendes, Respondes, Verses, vaine repeticions, Commemoracions and Synodalles, that commonly when any boke of the Bible was read out, all the rest were vnreade. And in this sorte, the boke of Esaie was begon in Aduent, and the booke of Genesis in Septuagesima: but they were onely begon, and neuer read thorow." Moreover, the preface claims, the indexical system (or "Pie") for reading the scriptures, has such "numbre and hardnesse of the rules" that "to tourne the boke onely, was so hard and intricate a matter, that manye tymes there was more busynesse to fynde out what shoulde be read, then to reade it when it was founde out." This readerly objection is combined with an economic justification for the transformation of the service. In the new Protestant dispensation, "the curates shal nede none other bookes for their publique service, but this book [the Book of Common Prayer] & the Bible: by the meanes whereof, the people shall not be at so great charge for bookes, as in tyme past they haue been."

There are additional changes which also emphasize continuous reading. The simplified calendar is, the preface claims, "plaine and easy to be vnderstanded, wherein (so much as maie be) the readyng of holy scripture is to be set furthe, that all thynges shall bee doen in ordre, without breakyng one piece therof from another. For this cause be cut out Anthemes, Respondes, Inuitatories, and suche like thynges, as did break the continuall course of the readyng of the scripture." Moreover, the abolition of most of the Catholic saints' days meant that it was far easier to follow a linear progression through the church year, even if Sundays and feast days continued to complicate this progression.[15] Ideally, one would start reading Genesis chapter 1, verse 1, Matthew chapter 1, verse 1, and Romans chapter 1, verse 1 on 1 January and then scroll through the "significant" parts of the bible. In fact, that wasn't possible. Large chunks of the Apocrypha were inserted, and the conclusion of the year was dominated by

Isaiah, because of his supposedly central role in the prophecy of Christ; he was thus the appropriate reading for Advent. And the end of the year was disrupted by a series of feast days which had been preserved and which each had its own special readings: Christmas on 25 December (Isaiah 9 and Matthew 1 for "Matins" in the 1549 prayer book; Isaiah 9 and Luke 2 for the renamed "Morning Prayer" in the 1552 prayer book); Saint Stephen on 26 December (Isaiah 56 and Acts 6 and 7 in both prayer books, although Isaiah is replaced with Proverbs 28 in, for instance, the King James Bible of 1611); Saint John the Evangelist on 27 December (Isaiah 58 and Revelation 1 in both prayer books, although Isaiah is replaced by Ecclesiastes 5 in 1611); Innocents' Day on 28 December (Jeremiah 31 and Acts 25 in both prayer books).[16]

Perhaps the most strikingly disruptive feast is the one which pushes Genesis chapter 1, verse 1, Matthew chapter 1, verse 1, and Romans chapter 1, verse 1 back to January the *second*, when one would expect them to be read on 1 January. But 1 January was already reserved for remembering that Christ was a *Jewish* boy. It was the Feast of the Circumcision, with readings from, in the morning, Genesis 17 ("every man-child among you shall be circumcised") and Romans 2 (Paul trying to finesse Christ's Judaism by emphasizing the circumcision of the heart and the spirit as opposed to the circumcision of the flesh and the letter), and, in the evening, Deuteronomy 10 and Colossians 2. In fact, the church year did not officially begin on 1 January anyway. It was traditionally dated from Advent Sunday (a movable feast, usually four, but sometimes five, Sundays before Christmas). But Advent itself was never used, as far as I know, for the actual dating of the year, which normally began on 25 March (Lady's Day). Thus George Herbert begins his poem "The British Church":

> I joy, deare Mother, when I view
> Thy perfect lineaments, and hue
>   Both sweet and bright.
>
> Beautie in thee takes up her place,
> And dates her letters from thy face,
>   When she doth write.[17]

Herbert conflates the church with the Virgin/Mother, who "dates" the beginning of the year from the feast of the Annunciation, just as Herbert himself in his correspondence dated the year from 25 March. But this latter official calendar was clearly contradicted by the order of readings from the bible. One would begin at the beginning of Genesis and the beginning of Matthew on 1 January, were it not for the inconvenient fact (for gentile Christians) that Christ was a Jew.

In examining the Church of England's attempt to produce an "orderly" (i.e., sequential) reading of the bible, the crucial point remains that there were innumerable exceptions (including Sundays and feast days, the very days when the congregations were largest). And, of course, the service still depended on flicking back and forth between the Jewish scriptures, the Gospels, and the Epistles (i.e., on the technology that Christianity had used and refined from the second century C.E.).

But doesn't the Christian bible, whether read by Catholics or Protestants, seem to be organized for a continuous method of reading? After all, it begins with the beginning and ends with, or even after, the end: Genesis to Revelation, with, George Herbert claimed, everything in between. The story of the Jews, he wrote, "pennes and sets us down." It is, like God's works, "wide" and "let[s] in future times."[18] It is such a scroll reading of the bible that Lady Grace Mildmay seems to advocate at the opening of her autobiography: "I have found by experience [and] I commend unto my children as approved, this to be the best course to set ourselves in from the beginning unto the end of all our lives. That is to say: first to begin with the scriptures to read them with all diligence and humility, as a disciple, continually every day in some measure until we have gone through the whole book of God from the first of Genesis to the last of the Revelation and then begin again and so over and over without weariness" (Pollock 23). This would appear at first sight to be a recommendation to read the bible we would read a novel. Only here, Mildmay ends the book only to begin reading it all over again. She appears at first sight to be reading the bible as a single continuous loop. Novel readers may well envy Mildmay her ability to read the same book "over and over without weariness." But what I want to emphasize here is that *if* she read the bible like a novel (an "if" to which I'll return), there were material obstacles in her way.

One of the obstacles to scroll reading is made clear by John Locke, in a book that Don McKenzie has drawn attention to. In *A Paraphrase and Notes on the Epistles of St. Paul*, John Locke attacks "the dividing of [the Epistles] into Chapters and Verses, as we have done; whereby they are so chopp'd and minc'd, and as they are now printed, stand so broken and divided, that not only the common People take the Verses usually for distinct Aphorisms; but even Men of more advanced Knowledge, in reading them, lose very much of the Strength and Force of the Coherence."[19] Locke goes on to attack sectarians who depend on "the Benefit of loose Sentences, and Scripture crumbled into Verses, which quickly turn into independent Aphorisms" (vii).

The bible has become for Locke a bad kind of food: it has been chopped and minced, broken into scraps. And while Locke thinks of this kind of piecemeal reading as a boon for sectarians, the mincing of the bible, as he is clearly aware, is right at the heart of institutionalized Christianity in England. The division of reading, day by day, breaking off in the middle of a chapter is, as we've just noted, the way lessons were and still are read in the church service. And Locke is surely right in refusing to distinguish too easily between the different reading practices of different denominations. Technologically, what most denominations share in common is an emphasis upon techniques of discontinuous reading. Patrick Collinson is particularly acute on this point, and he notes the following passage from Herbert's "The H. Scriptures. II.":

> This verse marks that, and both do make a motion
> Unto a third, that ten leaves off doth lie:
> Then as dispersed herbs do watch a potion,
> These three make up some Christians destinie.[20]

If, as John Donne writes, "The world is a great Volume, and man the Index of that Booke," men and women are crucially the indexers of *actual* volumes.[21] Different techniques of indexing could certainly have different theological functions, but it's still important to emphasize the centrality of indexical reading to nearly all Christians in early modern England.

The Newby Bible

As I've been looking at Renaissance bibles off and on over the past few years, I've become increasingly aware of how often actual copies are compilations. That is, if we talk about the Geneva Bible, the Bishops' Bible, the Authorized Bible as separate translations, there are in fact elements that migrate from one translation to another or that are in some editions of a specific translation but not in another. Moreover, readers could add, and less often subtract, all kinds of materials beside what we might like to think of as "the bible proper" when they had their composite bibles bound and rebound. Bibles were, indeed, *usually* composites.[22] That is, they incorporated a wide range of navigational aids—aids that showed one how to read the bible other than as continuous narrative.

I want to turn now to a specific bible to see what it can tell us about Protestant reading habits over a period of two centuries. The Newby Bible is a quarto in the Folger Library, STC 2129 Copy 1. The scriptures themselves are the 1580 edition of the Geneva Bible, with its elaborated Protestant marginalia. But that tells us little or nothing about the owners' beliefs, since the Geneva Bible was relatively cheap and it was the most popular bible at least for the first

half of the seventeenth century. Even Archbishop Laud, antipathetic as he was
to its radical Protestant interpretations, probably grew up on it, since he quotes
it, as well as the King James Bible, even in his sermons.

The Newby Bible has stamped on its covers in Roman capitals: "FRANCES
NEWBY HIS BOOKE GIVEN HIM BY / HIS FATHER SAMVEL NEWBY 1645"
(Figs. 3 and 4). On a blank page at the back, there's the following inscription:
"My: ffather Samuell: Newby: gaue: mee this: booke ye: 7th of october 1644
with a chargh to keep it as: long as I liue: F: N:" (Fig. 5). The Newby Bible, then,
was rebound over sixty years after it was printed. But the book was previously
in the Newby family, as appears from an inscription on the opposite page:
"ffrancis: Sonne of: Samuell Newby & Elizabeth his wife: was babtised the 2d
of aprill: 1624 at St. Donstons: Church: In fleete streete. Londone—Iohn:
Benson is Clarke etc" (Fig. 6). An ancient pressed violet, preserved at Psalm 107
when I last looked at the Folger volume, has stained the pages brown, and there
are two thin green ribbon bookmarks of indeterminate date.

I have not yet discovered who the Newbys were. But Francis Newby was
baptized in St. Dunstan's only two weeks after John Donne had been installed
as vicar there (18 March 1623/4).[23] The parish was a highly fashionable one, just
within Temple Bar and so within the City, but surrounded by the law courts.
Judges and lawyers frequented the church, as did members of the book trade,
including, at one time or another, William and John Jaggard, John Smethwick,
John and Richard Marriot, Matthew Lownes, Thomas Dewe, Anne Helme,
Richard More, William Washington, and George Winder.

The Newby Bible is a compilation that gathers together an extraordinary
range of navigational aids into a single book. It includes, for instance, the Book
of Common Prayer, together with its calendar and tables of lessons and psalms.
These tables encourage a liturgical reading—that is, a reading that follows the
order of the church service through the year. "The summe of the whole Scripture" and "Certaine questions & answers touching the doctrine of predestina-
tion," in contrast, suggest reading the bible in an explicitly Calvinist way (a
theological reading that has no relation to the liturgical year). Among the
navigational aids are Robert Herrey's *Two Right Profitable and Fruitfull Concordances, or Large and Ample Tables Alphabeticall* (Fig. 7). Geneva Bibles
printed in quarto between 1580 and 1615 often have the concordances (with the
exception of those with Laurence Tomson's revision of the New Testament).
The titles of such bibles (including the Newby Bible) draw attention to the
presence of Herrey's work, advertising both the scriptures "And also a most
profitable Concordance, for the readie finding out of any thing in the same
conteyned" (Fig. 8). Patrick Collinson made use of Herrey's concordance,
bound with his Geneva Bible, until 1991, when his wife gave him Cruden's
concordance for Christmas.

The first of Herrey's concordances, "The first Alphabet of directions to Common places, containing all the Hebrewe, Chaldean, Greek, Latine, or other strange names," draws attention to a peculiar aspect of translation.[24] Why have the Hebrew proper names *not* been translated, when they are shown to *have meaning*? Of course, we do not generally translate proper names (my own means "Rock Barley-Field Steel-Arm" [Peter Bigland Stallybrass]), but the effect in reading the bible, if one does not know Hebrew, is to give an experience of "lumpy" reading, where unfamiliar words like *Lámech, Adáh, Hábel* (the accents are those of the Geneva Bible) are combined with tongue twisters like the Egyptian word *Zaphnáth-paanéah.* The latter is the name that Joseph is given, along with an Egyptian wife, after Pharaoh "toke of[f] his ring from his hand, and put it vpon Iosephs hand, and araied him in garments of fine linen and put a golden cheine about his necke" (Genesis 40.45, 42). The marginal gloss tells us that Joseph's new name means "the expounder of secrets."

Herrey's "First Alphabet" is a wonderful key to reading the bible as a form of deep play with proper names. The first entry is: "AARON or Aharon: *A teacher,* or *teaching,* or *conceiuing,* or *a hill or mountaine,* or *a man of the mountaine,* or *the mountaine of fortitude,* or *a stronge hill.* The sonne of Amram. Exo. 6.20." A dazzling array of possible meanings is opened up by this concordance. Imagine a reading of the bible that used the concordance to follow the progress of *Zion,* when it means, according to the "First Alphabet," "a heape, a tombe, looking glasses or drought." "*Looking glasses*" *or* "a tombe"? "A heape" *or* "a drought"? I am equally enchanted with *Zuph,* meaning "a watch, or couering, or a hony combe, or a swimming, or looking for." Even the most imaginative of Derrideans would be hard put to come up with such a wild proliferation of meanings from a single word.

The "Second Alphabet," on the other hand, attempts to control against such proliferating meanings, guiding the reader "to common places . . . containing all the Englishe wordes conducing vnto most of the necessariest and profitablest doctrines, sentences and instructions." In fact, the "necessariest and profitablest doctrines" have a heavily anti-Catholic slant. This concordance begins:

Abominable. Abominations. Idolatry to be counted most Abominable. Deut. 7.26.
The punishment of the Abominable. Reue. 21.8, 27
What things are Abominable to the Lord. Deut. 7.25 and 27.15. Isa. 41.24.

The concordance moves on to entries like the following:

The cup and mother of Abominations. Reuel. 17.4, 5.

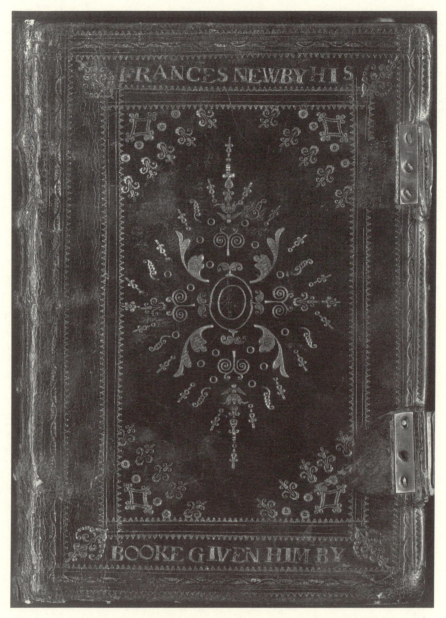

Figure 3. Front cover of the *Newby Bible. The Geneva translation* (London, 1580);
Folger STC 2129. By permission of the Folger Shakespeare Library.

Figure 4. Back cover of the *Newby Bible. The Geneva translation* (London, 1580); Folger STC 2129. By permission of the Folger Shakespeare Library.

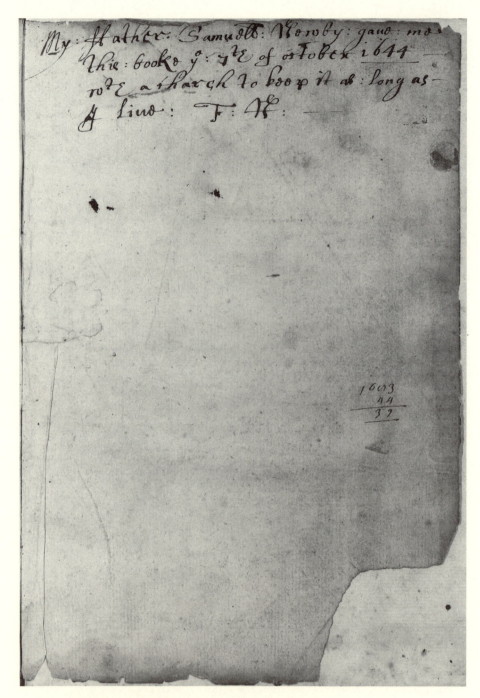

Figure 5. Frances Newby's record of the bible as his father's gift in 1644 at the back of the *Newby Bible*. *The Geneva translation* (London, 1580); Folger STC 2129. By permission of the Folger Shakespeare Library.

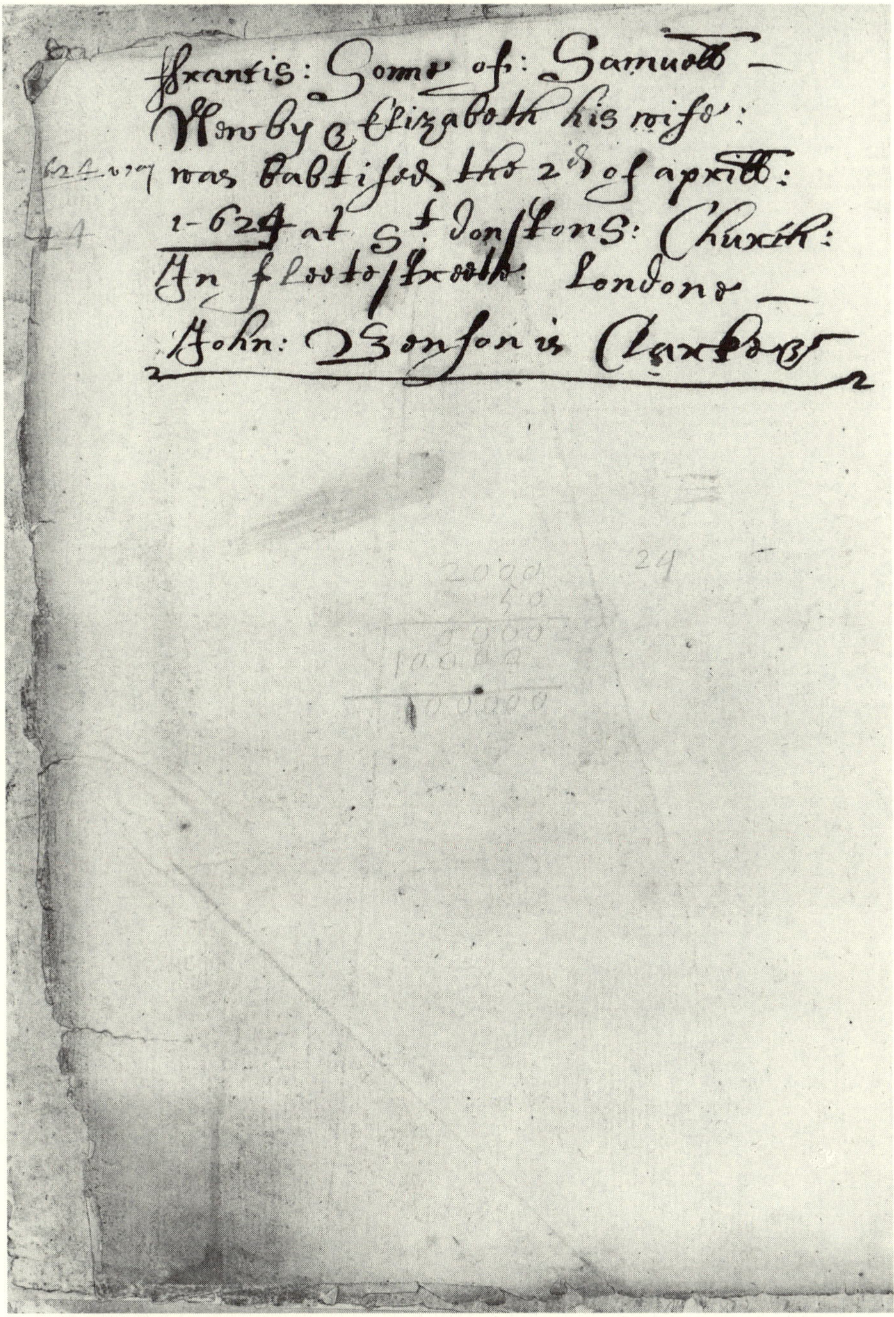
ffrantis: Sonne of: Samuell
Newby & Elizabeth his wife:
was baptised the 2d of aprill:
1-624 at St Donstons: Church:
In fleetestreete London
John: Benson is Clarke

Figure 6. Record of the birth of Frances Newby in 1624 at the back of the *Newby Bible. The Geneva translation* (London, 1580); Folger STC 2129. By permission of the Folger Shakespeare Library.

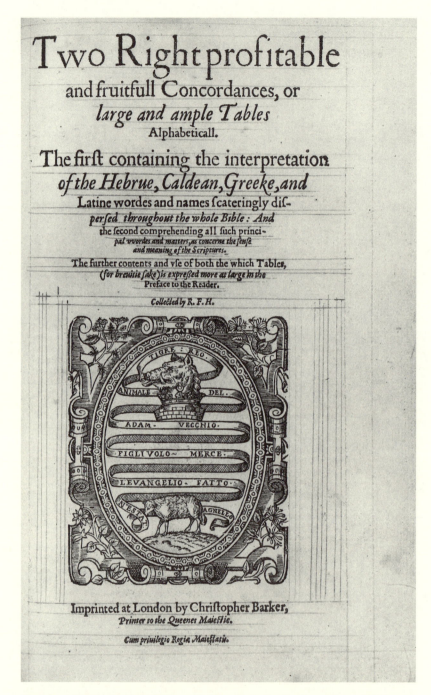

Two Right profitable

and fruitfull Concordances, or

large and ample Tables

Alphabeticall.

· The first containing the interpretation

of the Hebrue, Caldean, Greeke, and

Latine wordes and names scateringly dis-

persed throughout the whole Bible : And

the second comprehending all such princi-

pal wordes and matters, as concerne the sense

and meaning of the Scriptures.

The further contents and use of both the which Tables,

(for breuitie sake)is expressed more at large in the

Preface to the Reader.

Collected by R. F. H.

TIGRE · REO ·

ANIMALE ————— DEL ·

ADAM · ———— VECCHIO ·

FIGLIVOLO~ ——— MERCE ·

L·EVANGELIO · ——— FATTO ·

NESIA ————— AGNELLO ·

Imprinted at London by Christopher Barker,

Printer to the Queenes Maiestie.

Cum priuilegio Regiæ Maiestatis.

Figure 7. Title page, Robert Herrey's *Two Right Profitable and Fruitfull Concordances, or Large and Ample Tables Alphabeticall* in the *Newby Bible. The Geneva translation* (London, 1580); Folger STC 2129. By permission of the Folger Shakespeare Library.

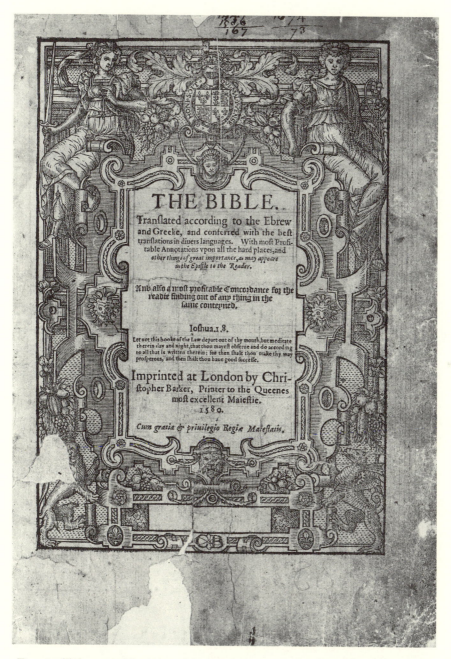

THE BIBLE.

Translated according to the Ebrew
and Greeke, and conferred with the best
translations in diuers languages.   With most Profitable Annotations vpon all the hard places, and
other things of great importance, as may appeare
in the Epistle to the Reader.

And also a most profitable Concordance for the
readie finding out of any thing in the
same conteyned.

Ioshua.1.8.

Let not this booke of the Law depart out of thy mouth, but meditate
therein day and night, that thou mayest obserue and do according
to all that is written therein; for then shalt thou make thy way
prosperous, and then shalt thou haue good successe.

Imprinted at London by Christopher Barker, Printer to the Queenes
most excellent Maiestie.
1580.

Cum gratia & priuilegio Regiæ Maiestatis.

Figure 8. Title page of the *Newby Bible. The Geneva translation* (London, 1580); Folger STC 2129, drawing attention in the middle of the page to the presence of Herrey's concordances: "And also a most profitable Concordance, for the readie finding out of any thing in the same conteyned." By permission of the Folger Shakespeare Library.

If the reader follows this reference, he or she finds the following at 17.3–6 in the Geneva translation:

3 So he caried me away into the wildernes in the Spirit, and I sawe a woman sit vpon a skarlat coloured ᵈ beast, full of names of ᵉ blasphemie, which had seuen heads, & ten hornes.
4 And the ᶠ woman was araied in purple & skarlat, & guilded with golde, & precious stones, and pearles, and had a cup of golde in her hand, ful of ᵍ abominations, and filthines of her fornication.
5 And in her forehead *was* a name written, ʰ A Mysterie, great Babylon, the mother of whoredomes, and abominations of the earth.
6 And I sawe the woman drunken with the blood of Saintes, & with the blood of the Martyrs of Iesus: and when I sawe her, I wondered with great marueile.

The marginal notes read:

d The beast signfieth yᵉ ancient Rome: yᵉ woman that sitteth thereon, the newe Rome which is the Papistrie, whose crueltie and blood shedding is declared by skarlat.
e Ful of idolatrie, superstition and contempt of the true God.
f This woman is the Antichrist, that is, the Pope with yᵉ whole bodie of his filthie creatures, as it was expounded, vers. 18, whose beautie only standeth in outwarde pompe & impudencie and craft like a strumpet.

In other words, while the first concordance emphasizes readerly possibilities, the second attempts to secure an interpretation of the bible in which the main threat is Catholic idolatry. There are, indeed, no less than forty-seven entries under "idole," "idolatry" etc. The only thing that the two concordances have in common is that, as is the way with concordances, they suggest nonlinear readings of the text, in which one can detach a word from its narrative context and/or reattach a word to other seemingly disconnected passages in which the same word occurs.

The Newby Bible thus suggests a wide range of ways to read the scriptures, *none* of them continuous. And to the reading strategies I have mentioned could be added, on the one hand, the random opening of the bible to find out one's fate, and, on the other, mathematical calculations to discover scriptural secrets. My favorite example of the latter strategy can be found in a 1631 "Wicked" Bible (the King James Bible in which it is commanded that "thou *shalt* commit adultery") at Indiana University. At the front of the bible are manuscript notes made by Edmund Burn, dated 10 August 1798. Burn notes that there are 39 books in the OT and 27 books in the NT; 926 chapters in the OT and 260 chapters in the NT; 23,214 verses in the OT and 7,959 verses in the NT; 592,493 words in the OT and 181,253 words in the NT; 2,728,100 letters in the OT and 838,380 letters in the NT. The table "shows" that the "navel" of his bible is the eighth verse of Psalm 118—"It is better to trust in the Lord, than have confidence in man." But what appears at first to be the personal idiosyncrasy of Burn's was in fact a cultural practice.

One finds the same figures written at the front of a 1611 Geneva bible at the University of Pennsylvania (Forrest BS 170), including the fact that "Jehova" occurs 6,855 times and the word "And" occurs 35,543 times in the Old Testament. Such tables work against consecutive reading. The most interesting evidence about actual reading practices in the Newby Bible comes from considerably later than the Renaissance. In the 1790s, a family of dissenters owned the Newby Bible and systematically recorded by date, preacher, and place the texts of the sermons they heard (Fig. 9). For instance, in Genesis one finds the following marginalia: "3rd August 1794 Mr Groves text at tabernacle 7th chapter latter part of the 16th verse—And the Lord shut him in. On account of the sufferers at the fire at Hadcliffe Cross a collection." Or in Proverbs, we get this: "27 Feb 1793 my dear Joey went to hear Mr Thomas his text the 14 Chap 26 verse"; in Luke: "9 December 1792 Emly heard Mr Thomas his text 7 chap 50 verce." The following annotations are on a single page of St. John's gospel: "27 Sep 1795 Mr Parsons at Tabernacle Ch 5 vers 3" (top of page); "3rd February 1793 at Tabernacle Mr Wilks 5 Chapter 35 verse A funeral sermon for the Rev Mr Berredge who died on the 22 of January at 1/2 past 3 in the afternoon hope his soul is gone to glory who Laboured in the cause of Christ 36 years" (bottom of page). In a different hand, four pages back, we find the following confusing annotation: "3 Feb 1793 Mr Joss text at Totenham Cort chappel Chap 1 verse 47 for that Man of God Mr Beridge who Did 31 of ⟨Feb⟩ 1793 Jan" (bottom of page). When *did* Mr. Beridge/Berredge die? On 31 January or 22 January? And who were the two people who, on 3 February, attended two different funeral sermons for him and marked up the bible accordingly?

John Berridge (1716–93) was an evangelical clergyman, born in Nottinghamshire on 1 March 1716. He became "head of a sect called Berridges in the neighbourhood of Cambridge." Although his sermons at St. Mary's gave offense to the orthodox, he developed a large following in the countryside. In 1758, he became friends with Wesley and Whitefield, and preached in their chapels in London, while they preached in the church of Everton, Bedfordshire, where he had been inducted in 1755. He gave his first sermon out of doors on 14 May 1759, after which he went on several preaching tours. Wesley called him "one of the most simple as well as sensible of men." He died in Everton on 22 January 1793 and was buried on the twenty-seventh. So the later entry in the Newby Bible gets the date of his death right.

The dissenting family has noted sermons that they heard throughout the bible. Not surprisingly, given radical Protestant emphases, they heard more sermons on the Pauline Epistles than on the Gospels. A single page of Colos-

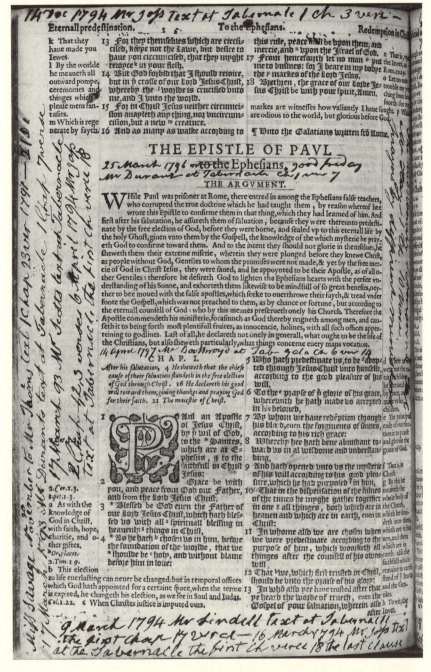

Figure 9. Marginalia by the dissenting family who owned the *Newby Bible* (London, 1580); Folger STC 2129, and recorded the sermons they attended in the 1790s. By permission of the Folger Shakespeare Library.

sians, for instance, has four different hands from the family noting sermons. But in noting the passage that the preacher took as his text, the dissenters of the 1790s are conforming to a practice *explicitly advocated* in the Geneva Bible of 1580 that they owned. Their bible, as we have seen, included the Ramist diagram, "Howe to take profite in reading of the holy Scriptures" (Fig. 10). The final point on the diagram is that one should "Take opportunitie" to "Heare preaching and to proue by the Scriptures that which is taught. Acts 17.11" (Fig. 11). The scriptural text referred to is: "These were also more noble men then they which were at Thessalonica, which receiued the worde with all readines, and searched the Scriptures daily, whether those things were so." The Geneva Bible mentions the verse in the chapter heading: "11 To search the Scriptures." In the longer chapter heading of the King James translation, though, this instruction goes missing. And it is probable that by 1611 the practice of taking bibles to church to check what the preacher was saying against the scriptures seemed contentious to the translators. But such use of the bible was central to the reformed faith as it was articulated by the Geneva Bible, which adds two marginal glosses to the one verse. The second gloss reads, "This was not onely to trie if these things which thei had heard were true, but also to confirme them selues in the same, and to increase their faith."

That the King James Bible reduces the significance of searching the scriptures is the more striking in that the title page of the first edition of its official predecessor, the Bishops' Bible, has a woodcut of Elizabeth I, her throne supported by Fortitude and Prudence, while she is crowned by Justice and Mercy (Fig. 12). Beneath Elizabeth, in a strapwork cartouche, is the scriptural quotation: "Search the Scriptures, for in them ye thynke ye haue eternal lyfe, and they are they which testifie of me. Iohn. v." (Fig. 13).[25] Beneath the cartouche, a minister in a pulpit (his head bare, an hourglass beside him) preaches. Women and men sit or stand below him, and one of the women holds open her bible, while others hold theirs closed (Fig. 14).[26] In other words, the congregation is encouraged to bring their bibles to church and to check the preacher's interpretation against their own reading of the text.

The polemical intention of this "searching the scriptures" is clarified by the title page of Foxe's *Actes and Monuments*. As Margaret Aston and Elizabeth Ingram note, the format is that of a medieval doom, but it is here appropriated for distinctly polemical purposes. In the 1570 edition, the left hand images (i.e., the column to God's right) are labeled at the bottom of the page "The Image of the Persecuted Church." The right hand images are labeled "The Image of the Persecuting Church." The Catholic scene at the bottom right shows a "shaveling" priest, wearing the four-cornered hat that was anathema to reforming Protestants, preaching to men and women, four of whom have prayer beads (Fig. 15).[27] These "inappropriate" materializations of prayer will be denounced

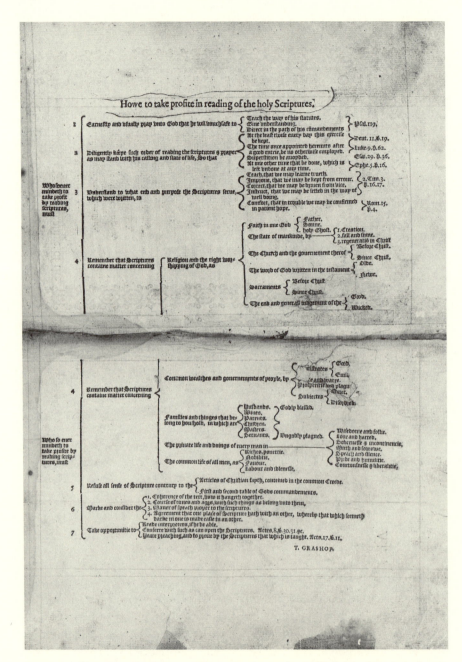

Figure 10. The Ramist diagram, "Howe to take profite in reading of the holy Scriptures," in the *Newby Bible. The Geneva translation* (London, 1580); Folger STC 2129. By permission of the Folger Shakespeare Library.

Refuse all sense of Scripture contrary to the { Articles of Christian fayth, conteined in the common Creede.

Marke and consider the {
1. Coherence of the text, how it hangeth together.
2. Course of times and ages, with such things as belong vnto them.
3. Maner of speach proper to the scriptures.
4. Agreement that one place of Scripture hath with an other, whereby that which seemeth darke in one is made easie in an other.

Take opportunitie to {
Reade interpreters, if he be able.
Conferre with such as can open the Scriptures. Actes. 8. 30, 31 &c.
Heare preaching, and to proue by the Scriptures that which is taught. Actes. 17. 8. 11.

T. GRASHOP.

5

6

7

Figure 11. Detail from "Howe to take profite in reading of the holy Scriptures," in the *Newby Bible. The Geneva translation* (London, 1580); Folger STC 2129: the final point in the diagram is "Heare preaching, and to proue by the Scriptures that which is taught. Acts 17.11." By permission of the Folger Shakespeare Library.

Figure 12. Title page, Bishops' Bible (London, 1573), Folger STC 2108. By permission of the Folger Shakespeare Library.

Figure 13. Detail from title page, Bishops' Bible (London, 1573); Folger STC 2108: "Searche the Scriptures, for in them ye thynke ye haue eternal lyfe, and they are they whiche testifie of me. Iohn.v." Either side of "Iohn.v.," Ann Russell has added her initials. By permission of the Folger Shakespeare Library.

by Foxe and many other reformers as "trinkets" if not "idols" (see Kearney 2001). To the right of the image, a Corpus Christi procession carries the host under a canopy, with tonsured monks singing before it. Led by a man carrying a cross and a boy with a candle, they process toward a statue on a wooden pedestal. On the left, a simply capped preacher, wearing a beard that proclaims him marriageable and no "eunuch before God" (in antithesis to the "shavelings"), exhorts his congregation (Fig. 16). To the left, two men are following the text of his sermon in a bible. Just below him, a woman sits with an open bible and points to a passage. Above her, a youth also follows the sermon in his bible (Collinson 1995: 106–7). Godly Protestants, in other words, read the word of God while godless Catholics use rosaries for rote learning and worship false idols. On the right of the "godly" scene, even those who look up to heaven are reading. Where God might be in Catholic iconography, they read the Hebrew tetragrammaton.

The title page of Foxe's *Actes and Monuments*, like the title page of the Bishops' Bible and the Ramist diagram that the Newby Bible contains, encourages those who possess bibles to bring them to church and to follow the text of the sermon. Patrick Collinson directs our attention to John Earle's depiction of "A She Precise Hypocrite": "Her deuotion at the Church is much in the turning of her ey, and turning downe the leaf in her book, when she heares named, Chapter and Verse."[28] But while Collinson finely notes the relation of this passage to the Foxe title page, he perhaps misses its novelty. The

Figure 14. Detail from title page, Bishops' Bible (London, 1573); Folger STC 2108: a preacher giving a sermon, some of the congregation with closed bibles and one woman with an open bible. By permission of the Folger Shakespeare Library.

Figure 15. Detail from title page, John Foxe, *Actes and Monuments* (London, 1596). The bottom right panel, depicting a Catholic "shaveling" wearing a four-cornered hat, preaching to men and women, some of whom have prayer beads. By permission of the Folger Shakespeare Library.

passage is in fact quoted by the *OED* as the first example of the phrase "chapter and verse." The *OED* is not, of course, infallible in its dating of first occurrences. But the lateness of the emergence of this phrase (the *OED* gives the date as 1628) is still striking. How are we to explain it?

One of the most powerful of Foxe's stories of Protestant martyrs is that of Anne Askew. Askew appears constantly to be citing "chapter and verse" to her tormentors. Indeed, they claim that she "was much to blame for vttering the scriptures. For S. Paule . . . forbode women to speake, or to talke of the word of God."[29] Christopher Dare, one of her inquisitors, tells her that

there was a woman, which did testifie that I should read, how God was not in Temples made with hands. Then I shewed him the 7. and 17. chapters of the Actes of the Apostles, what Stephen and Paule had said therein. Whereupon he asked me how I tooke those sentences: I answered, I would not throwe pearles among Swine, for Acornes were good inough.

[H]e asked me wherefore I said that I had rather to reade fiue lines in the Bible, then to heare fiue Masses in the Temple: I confessed that I said no lesse: neither for the dispraise of the Epistle or the Gospell, but because the one did greatly edifie me, and

Figure 16. Detail from title page, John Foxe, *Actes and Monuments* (London, 1596). The bottom left panel, depicting a bearded Protestant preacher wearing a plain cap, with some of the congregation following his text in their bibles. By permission of the Folger Shakespeare Library.

the other nothing at all. As S. Paule doth witnes in the 14. chapter of his first Epistle to the Corinthians [marginal note: "*I.Cor.14.*"], where as he saith, If the trumpet giueth an vncertaine sound, who will prepare himselfe to the battell? (Foxe 1125)

Dare is concerned with Askew's ability to detach "sentences" from the interpretative place that they have been given within Catholic tradition. Against that tradition, Askew arranges her "sentences" in a countertradition, here weaving together the seventh and the seventeenth chapters of the Acts of the Apostles with the fourteenth chapter of 1 Corinthians.

Like Dare, Bishop Bonner attacks Askew's use of the bible, claiming that "I had alledged a certaine text of ye scripture. I answered that I alledged none other but S. Paules owne saying to the Athenians, in the xviii. chap. in the Acts of the Apostles, that God dwelleth not in Temples made with hands. Then asked he me what my faith and beliefe was in that matter? I answered him, I beleeue as the Scripture doth teach me. . . . Then he asked me why I had so few words: And I answered, God hath giuen me the gift of knowledge, but not of vtterance. And Salomon saith: *That a woman of few words is a gift of God. Prou. xix*" (Foxe 1126).

Askew legitimates both her speech and her silence by an appeal to the "chapter and verse" of the scriptures. Her dependence upon her own reading of the bible against the authority of the Church is made explicit in her final confession of faith: "I beleeue all those scriptures to be true, which [Christ] hath confirmed with his most pretious bloud. Yea, and as S. Paule saith, those scriptures are sufficient for our learning and saluation, that Christ hath left here with vs: so that I beleeue we need no vnwritten verities to rule his church with. [Marginal note: 'Scripture sufficient to our saluation. *Psal. 28.*'] Therefore looke what he hath saide vnto me with his owne mouth in his holie gospell, that haue I with Gods grace closed vp in my heart, and my full trust is (as David saieth) that it shall be a lantern to my footsteps, Psal.28" (Foxe 1129). But in fact, at the most literal of levels, Askew does *not* cite "chapter and verse." Nor could she if she wanted to, for the simple reason that the bible she used had no verse numbers. None of the early English bibles (Coverdale's, the "Matthew," the Great Bible, etc.) had verse numbers, although they did have chapter numbers and letters ("A," "B," "C," etc.) as navigational aids for the reader. The first English bible with verse numbers was the Geneva translation, printed in 1560, fourteen years after Anne Askew had been burned at the stake.

This makes all the more remarkable Askew's feat of remembrance in finding and putting together the passages she needs.[30] Such an interlacing of quotations is radically emphasized in Foxe's *Actes and Monuments*, where Askew's citation of book and chapter (but not verse) of the bible are doubled by the marginal notes that re-cite her scriptural quotations in the second and later editions. The most readily available modern copy of Foxe, W. Grinton Berry's cheap paperback Foxe's *Book of Martyrs*, not only abridges the *Actes and Monuments* (God knows, a necessary feat given its encyclopedic prolixity), but also deletes the marginal notes and some of the citations within the body of the text. In *Actes and Monuments*, Askew tells Bishop Fisher "that in the mouth of two or three witnesses, euery matter should stand, after Christes & Paules doctrine, Matthew xviii. ii.Cor. xiii." (Marginal notes: "*Matth. 18.*"; "*2.Cor.13.*") In Berry's edition, this becomes Askew saying (as if in her own words) "in the mouth of two or three witnesses every matter should stand."[31] Berry thus partially constructs Askew's "own" voice by erasing the extent to which her voice is haunted by the scriptures that she collates, even as she is interrogated. It is Askew's acts of collation, as much as of courage, that are materialized on the pages of *Actes and Monuments*.

Nowhere is Askew's feat of collation more apparent than in "The confession of me Anne Askew, for the time I was in Newgate, concerning my beliefe":

I finde in the Scriptures (said she) that Christ tooke the bread and gaue it to his disciples, saying: *Take, eate, this is my body which shall be broken for you,* meaning in substance, his owne very body, the bread being thereof an only sign or sacrament. For after like manner of speaking, he said, he would breake downe the temple, and in three daies build it vp againe, signifying his own bodie by the temple, as S. Iohn declareth it, Iohn 2. and not the stony temple it selfe. So that the bread is but a remembrance of his death, or a sacrament of thanks giuing for it, whereby we are knit vnto him by a communion of christian loue. Although there be many that cannot perceiue the true meaning thereof, for the veile that Moises put ouer his face before the children of Israel, that they should not see the clerenes thereof, Exod.24. and 2.Cor.3. [Marginal notes: "*Exod.24.*"; "*2 Cor.3.*"]³² I perceiue the same veile remaineth to this day. But when God shall take it away, then shall these blinde men see. For it is plainly expressed in the history of Bell in the Bible, that God dwelleth in no thing materiall. *O King* (saith Daniel) *be not deceiued, for God will be in nothing that is made with hands of men,* Daniel. 14. [Marginal notes: "*Dan.14.*"; "*Actes.7.*"] And what stiffnecked people are these, that will alwaies resist the Holy Ghost? But as their fathers haue done, so do they, because they have stonie harts.

> *Written by me Anne Askew, that neither wisheth*
> *death, nor yet feareth his might, and as*
> *merie as one that is bound towards heauen.*

Truth is layd in prison, Luke.21. The law is turned to Wormewood, Amos.6. And there can be no right iudgement go forth, Esay. 59. [Marginal notes: "*Luke.21.*"; "*Amos.6.*"; "*Esay.59.*"] (Foxe 1128)

In a single paragraph, Askew collates John 2, Exodus 34, II Corinthians 3, the history of Bell, Daniel 14, Acts 7, Luke 21, Amos 9, Isaiah 59 (one reference to the Pentateuch, three references to the Prophets, one reference to the Apocrypha ["The idole Bel and the dragon," as the Geneva Bible calls it, one of the apocryphal books dear to many radicals in the sixteenth century], two references to the Gospels, and two references to the Epistles).

Such collation would become considerably simpler with the Geneva Bible of 1560 which, following the lead of Pagnini's Latin translation of 1528 and Estienne's French translation of 1553, systematically divided the chapters into verses for the first time in English.³³ With such a tool (and subsequent verse-numbered translations like the Bishops' and the King James), Earle's "She Precise Hypocrites" (i.e., later radical Protestants, following in the footsteps of Anne Askew) could indeed cite chapter *and verse*. It became simpler, as a result, to move between "sentences" in different places in the bible, and the navigational aids added to the Geneva Bible (including the concordances) made full use of this new reference system. In other words, the desire of the Book of Common Prayer that "the readyng of holy scripture" should be "doen in ordre, without breakyng one piece therof from another" must be set against the navigational aids that made it increasingly easy to do what Locke so feared: to "crumble" the scriptures into "loose sentences" and "independent aphorisms." But in attacking these new techniques of disassembling and reassembling "sentences" (witness Anne Askew), Locke turned his back upon the codex and the printed book as machines that enable discontinuous reading.

In conclusion, let me return to Lady Grace Mildmay. She began her autobiography, we may recall, by apparently extolling a reading of the bible as continuous narrative: "I have found by experience [and] I commend unto my children as approved, this to be the best course to set ourselves in from the beginning unto the end of all our lives. That is to say: first to begin with the scriptures to read them with all diligence and humility, as a disciple, continually every day in some measure until we have gone through the whole book of God from the first of Genesis to the last of the Revelation and then begin again and so over and over without weariness" (Pollock 23). In fact, it's only the projection backward of our own reading habits (developed through reading Jane Austen or Ian Fleming) that makes us imagine Lady Grace "unscrolling" her book as a single continuous narrative. That is not how she read the bible, as she makes clear later in her autobiography: "First, in divinity every day as my leisure would give me leave and the grace of God permit and draw me, I did read a chapter in the books of Moses, another in one of the Prophets, one chapter in the Gospels and another in the Epistles to the end of the Revelation and the whole Psalms appointed for the day, ending and beginning again and so proceeded in that course. Wherein I found that as the water pierceth the hard stone by often dropping thereupon, so the continual exercise in the word of God made a deep impression in my stony heart . . ." (Pollock 3435). In other words, Lady Grace Mildmay read through the bible *liturgically*, following the readings of the church service, which would cover much of the bible every year, but only through discontinuous daily readings. It was the collation of widely separated passages in a single book that worked the magic of making "a deep impression" (like the work of a seal on wax or a printing press on paper) upon Lady Grace's "stony heart"; it was such widely collated passages that Anne Askew "closed vp in [her] heart" (Foxe 1129). But such collation depended upon the long history of Christianity in the creation of systematic methods of discontinuous reading. The codex as a technology of discontinuity made at first possible and finally easy the collation of the Pentateuch, the Prophets, the Gospels, the Epistles, and the Psalms on a daily basis.

Lady Grace's liturgical reading was, of course, a very different practice of discontinuous reading from Anne Askew's. Askew's method, at least at her examinations, was forensic not liturgical. And the dissenters who owned the Newby Bible in the 1790s used yet a different discontinuous technique when they followed whatever text the preacher had chosen. We need to explore in greater detail the extraordinary diversity of such uses that the codex made possible and encouraged. But we should equally remember that all these strategies depended upon the bible as a *book* as opposed to a scroll. The codex and the printed book were the indexical computers that Christianity adopted as its privileged technologies.

Notes

I have incurred an unusual range of intellectual debts in the long gestation of this piece: to Juliet Fleming, Margreta de Grazia, David Kastan, and Matthew Rowlinson, with whom I've discussed concepts of materiality over many years; to Deborah Linderman and Dan Warner, who started me on this project; to Lisa Jardine, Ann Matter, Bill Sherman, William Slight, Evelyn Tribble, and Steve Zwicker, who first got me thinking about marginalia and the reading practices embedded in books; to Joe Farrell, Don Fowler, Bridget Murnaghan, and Ralph Rosen, who have generously shared their knowledge of scrolls and codices in classical antiquity; to Malachi Beit-Arié, Ora Limor, David Stern, David Ruderman, and the Center for Advanced Judaic Studies, University of Pennsylvania, who have taught me all I know about Judaic texts; to Roger Chartier and Stephen Orgel for suggestions and criticisms; to John Pollack, Michael Ryan, and Dan Traister, and the Rare Book Room staff, University of Pennsylvania; to Mandi Pratt and Rita Copeland for pointing out at least some of my errors; to Laetitia Yeandle and the Folger Library; to Jim Green and the Library Company of Philadelphia; to Elizabeth Fuller and the Rosenbach Museum and Library; to Martin Antonetti and the Smith College Library; to Peter Lindenbaum and Indiana University; to Mark Dimination, Cornell University Library, and the Library of Congress; and above all, to Patrick Collinson, Jim Kearney, and Jessie Ann Owens, whose influence is everywhere in this paper, if never fully acknowledged.

1. Colin H. Roberts and T. C. Skeat, *The Birth of the Codex* (London: Oxford University Press, 1983).

2. In fact, it would have been materially impossible to read the *Canterbury Tales* in the late Middle Ages as the continuous narrative that the modern Riverside edition, for instance, constructs.

3. So, for that matter, did Christians trained in the classical tradition. "Such was the force of convention that even when the codex was in common use for books Augustine felt obliged to apologize for writing a letter in codex form, and Jerome, who remembers that he is a gentleman as well as a scholar, writes his letters correctly on rolls, even though he keeps his books in codices" (Roberts and Skeat, *The Birth of the Codex*, 24).

4. For a different account of why Christians adopted the codex, see Harry Y. Gamble, *Books and Readers in the Early Church: A History of Early Christian Texts* (New Haven: Yale University Press, 1995), 63–81.

5. See Malachi Beit-Arié, *Hebrew Manuscripts of East and West: Towards a Comparative Codicology*, the Panizzi Lectures 1992 (London: British Library, 1993), 11–12. There are, however references to Jewish codices from the end of the eighth or the beginning of the ninth centuries (see Beit-Arié, 11). For the whole of this paragraph, I

draw upon Irven M. Resnick's important article, "The Codex in Early Jewish and Christian Communities," *Journal of Religious History* 17.1 (1992): 1–17. My thanks to David Stern for drawing my attention to Resnick's work. See also Gamble, *Books and Readers*, 210–11. It is important to note that the Torah scroll never necessitated treating the bible as a continuous narrative. While the Torah was unscrolled continuously in the synagogue, the Rabbinic tradition placed extraordinary emphasis upon oral ways of moving discontinuously from one place in the scriptures to another, according to the sound or the meaning of a word or phrase. Christianity *textualized* these discontinuous practices, and later tended to mistake the opposition between the scroll and the book as a simple opposition between Judaic and Christian cultural practices of reading and learning. The ideological opposition between the Judaic scroll and the Christian book remained operative in Christian thought long after Jewish codices (above all, the Talmud) had become common. In 1481, for instance, Vittore Crivelli painted five panels for an altarpiece. The central panel depicts the Virgin and Child, with (from left to right) Saints Bonaventura, John the Baptist, Louis of Toulouse, and Francis of Assisi. John has a scroll, because he comes before Christ. St. Louis of Toulouse wears an orphrey, depicting Old Testament prophets, all of whom carry scrolls. St. Bonaventura, on the other hand, wears an orphrey with images of Franciscan saints and three apostles, all of whom are carrying codices. But, disappearing behind St. Bonaventura's neck, one can just make out John the Baptist, again carrying a scroll. Crivelli thus marks the distinction between Old Testament and New Testament, between Judaism and Christianity, as the difference between scroll and codex. St. John the Baptist, because he comes before Christ, still carries a scroll. Those who come after carry codices. (I am deeply indebted to David Ruderman and David Stern for correcting at least some of my earlier misconceptions about the implications of Jewish scrolls.) It was equally or more important for Jews to distinguish their scriptures from the "corrupted" version that Christians had stolen from them.

6. Joseph Mede, "The Apocalyptic Type," *The Key of the Revelation*, trans. Richard More (London: Philip Stephens, 1643). It is worth noting that the distinction between codex and scroll has little *textual* support in Mede's book.

7. See Malcolm Parkes, *Scribes, Scripts and Readers: Studies in the Communication, Presentation and Dissemination of Medieval Texts* (London: Hambledon Press, 1991), particularly chpt. 3, "The Influence of the Concepts of *Ordinatio* and *Compilatio* on the Development of the Book"; Mary A. Rouse and Richard H. Rouse, *Authentic Witnesses: Approaches to Medieval Texts and Manuscripts* (Notre Dame, Ind.: University of Notre Dame Press, 1991); Saenger, "The Impact of the Early Printed Page on the History of Reading," *Bulletin du Bibliophile* 2 (1996): 237–301. See also Saenger's *Space Between Words: The Origins of Silent Reading* (Stanford: Stanford University Press, 1997), which is a marvellous analysis of word separation and the construction of navigable texts (see, for instance, 257–61). I remain deeply skeptical, however, about Saenger's argument for the origin of silent reading in word separation. On silent reading (and other aspects of reading) in classical antiquity, we await the posthumous publication of Don Fowler's important work.

8. See Lloyd W. Daly, *Contributions to a History of Alphabetization in Antiquity and the Middle Ages*, Collection Latomus, vol. 90 (Brussels: Latomus, 1967), particularly 69–84.

9. William Byrd, *Gradualia, ac Cantiones Sacrae* (London: Richard Redmer, 1610), STC 4244.

10. Such elaborate bookmarks are depicted in Jan and Hubert van Eyck's Ghent altarpiece. Lotte Brand Philip, *The Ghent Altarpiece and the Art of Jan van Eyck* (Princeton, N.J.: Princeton University Press, 1971), Otto Pächt, *Van Eyck and the Founders of Early Netherlandish Painting*, trans. David Britt (London: Harvey Miller, 1994), and Elisabeth Dhanens, *Hubert and Jan van Eyck* (New York: Alpine Fine Arts, n.d.). Both John the Baptist and the Virgin, sitting on either side of the enthroned Christ, use pippes with decorated pearl heads. A pippe is a metal rod inserted into a book to which multiple ribbons were attached as bookmarks. The only reference I have to the naming of these bookmarks as "pippes" is from John Harthan's *Books of Hours and Their Owners* (London: Book Club Associates, 1982). Harthan writes: "inside the metal rod known as a pippe [could be] inserted to which the signaux or book-marks were attached. When completed the book was either provided with a box for safe keeping or sewn into a covering known as a chemisette (or chemise), usually made of a fine kid-leather called chevrotin or of cendal, a silk fabric. When picked up by the corners the chemisette formed a bag in which the book could be conveniently carried. When laid open on a priedieu or held in the hands for reading, the chemisette was unwrapped to serve like a napkin to keep the pages clean" (37).

Other examples of pippes can be seen in Jan van Eyck, *Virgin and Child with the Chancellor Rolin* (the Louvre) and *Annunciation* (National Gallery of Art, Washington, D.C.); Hugo van der Goes, *Maria Portinari with Daughter and Saints* (Uffizi); the Edinburgh altarpiece (National Gallery of Scotland); Bruges Master of 1499, *Diptych of Virgin and Child and Christian de Hondt* (Koninklijk Museum voor Schone Kunsten, Antwerp); Geertgen tot Sint Jans, *Holy Kinship* (Rijksmuseum, Amsterdam); Master of the Retable of the Reyes Católicos, *Christ Among the Doctors* (National Gallery of Art, Washington, D.C.); Master of Frankfurt, *St. Anne with the Virgin and Child* (National Gallery of Art, Washington, D.C.).

11. *The Missal in Latin and English* (London: Burns, Oates and Washbourne, 1958).

12. See David M. Robb, *The Art of the Illuminated Manuscript* (New York: A. S. Barnes, 1973), 331, and, more generally, Andrew Hughes, *Medieval Manuscripts for Mass and Office: A Guide to Their Organization and Terminology* (Toronto: University of Toronto Press, 1982).

13. Patrick Collinson, "The Coherence of the Text: How It Hangeth Together: The Bible in Reformation England," *The Bible, the Reformation, and the Church*, ed. W. P. Stephens (Sheffield: Sheffield Academic Press, 1995), 84–108.

14. *The First and Second Prayer Books of Edward VI* (London: J. M. Dent, 1949), 2–5. I am deeply indebted to Alison Chapman, who first drew "The Preface" to the Book of Common Prayer to my attention, and who generously shared with me her research on the topic. On the frequency with which prayer books were bound together with bibles (and implicitly provided navigational aids to the reading of scripture), see Judith Maltby, *Prayer Book and People in Elizabethan and Early Stuart England* (Cambridge: Cambridge University Press, 1998), 26. Maltby's book is invaluable on the importance of the Book of Common Prayer in the period.

15. See the calendars in *The First and Second Prayer Books of Edward VI*, 9–20 and 335–46.

16. *The First and Second Prayer Books of Edward VI*, 20 and 346.

17. George Herbert, *The Temple* (Cambridge: Thomas Buck, 1633), STC 13183, 102.

18. Herbert, "The Bunch of Grapes," *The Temple*, 120–21.

19. John Locke, *A Paraphrase and Notes on the Epistles of St. Paul* (London: A. Betterworth and C Hitch, 1733 [1707]), vi–vii. Like the first two editions, the third edition, which I follow here, is in complex tension with Locke's declared approach, since it looks remarkably like a glossed bible. The inner columns of the page have the biblical text *with verse numbers* in small type. The outer columns, in larger type, give Locke's paraphrase, linked by verse number to the text, and there are often lengthy footnotes at the bottom of the page, also keyed to the traditional verse numbers. On the other hand, Locke's prominent section headings work against the conventional divisions by chapter and verse. Thus, Locke's first section of Galatians is Galatians 1.1–5, his second section 1.6 to 2.21, his third section 3.1–5, his fourth section 3.6–17, and so on.

20. Herbert, "The H. Scriptures II.," *The Temple*, 50; Collinson, "The Coherence of the Text," 105.

21. John Donne, "A Sermon Preached at the funeral of Sir William Cokayne Knight, Alderman of London, December 12. 1626," *Selected Prose*, ed. Evelyn Simpson, Helen Gardner, and Timothy Healy (Oxford: Clarendon Press, 1967), 281.

22. Important accounts of the "customizing" of English books in the Renaissance include Lisa Jardine and Anthony Grafton, " 'Studied for Action': How Gabriel Harvey Read his Livy," *Past and Present* 129 (1990): 30–78; Lisa Jardine and William Sherman, "Pragmatic Readers: Knowledge Transactions and Scholarly Services in Late Elizabethan England," *Religion, Culture, and Society in Early Modern Britain*, ed. Anthony Fletcher and Peter Roberts (Cambridge: Cambridge University Press, 1994), 102–24; and John Kerrigan, "The Editor as Reader: Constructing Renaissance Texts," *The Practice and Representation of Reading in England*, ed. James Raven, Helen Small, and Naomi Tadmor (Cambridge: Cambridge University Press, 1996), 102–24.

23. All the information for this paragraph is drawn from R. C. Bald, *John Donne: A Life* (Oxford: Clarendon Press, 1970), 457–64.

24. My thinking on printed and manuscript marginalia is deeply indebted to William W. E. Slights, "The Edifying Margins of Renaissance English Books," *Renaissance Quarterly* 42.4 (1989): 682–716, and his " 'Marginall Notes that spoile the Text': Scriptural Annotation in the English Renaissance," *Huntington Library Quarterly* 55 (1992): 254–78; Evelyn B. Tribble, *Margins and Marginality: The Printed Page in Early Modern England* (Charlottesville: University Press of Virginia, 1993), especially chpt. 1; James J. Kearney, "Glossing the English Reformation: Scriptural Annotation and *The Shepheardes Calender*" (M. Phil. thesis, Cambridge University, 1995); Monique Hulvey, "Not So Marginal: Manuscript Annotations in the Folger Incunabula," *Publications of the Bibliographical Society of America* 92.2 (1998): 159–76; William H. Sherman, " 'The Book Thus Put in Every Vulgar Hand': Impressions of Readers in Early English Printed Bibles," *The Bible as Book: The First Printed Editions*, ed. Paul Saenger and Kimberly van Kampen (London: the British Library, 1999), 125–33, and his "What Did Renaissance Readers Write in Their Books?" (in this volume) and "Life in the Margins" (unpublished ms.); Steven Zwicker, "Reading the Margins: Politics and the Habit of Appropriation," *Refiguring the Revolution: Aesthetics and Politics from the English Revolution to the Romantic Revolution*, ed. Kevin Sharpe and Steven N. Zwicker (Berkeley: University of California Press, 1998), 101–15, and "Consuming Passions: Habits of Reading and the Creation of Early Modern Literary Culture" (unpublished ms.); Stephen Orgel, "Marginal Materiality: Reading Lady Anne Clifford's *Mirror for Magistrates*" (unpublished ms.). I am deeply indebted to Jim Kearney for drawing my

attention to the significance of Herrey's concordances. See his "Matters of the Book: The Incarnate Text in the English Renaissance" (Ph.D. diss., University of Pennsylvania, 2001).

25. *The holie Bible* (Bishops') (London: R. Jugge, 1568), STC 2108. The title page was reused for the 1572 edition (STC 2107).

26. In the Folger copy of the 1573 edition of the Bishops' Bible (STC 2108), the reference to St. John 5 ("Searche the Scriptures") is framed by the initials "A" and "R," referring to the owner of the book, who, a year after the bible was printed, wrote her name at the top of the page: "An. Mushart. Russell. / her book. 1574."

27. The Image reproduced here is taken from the 1596 edition, but the title page was a constant in the early editions. I have deliberately chosen to use a later edition of Foxe to conform to a widespread Renaissance view that later editions were normally preferable to earlier editions, since they usually contained "more" of everything. This is particularly the case with Foxe, where the later editions, as the title pages claim, have been "newly recognized and inlarged by the Author IOHN FOXE." Not only were there additional texts and corrections (as well as additional misprints), but the 53 cuts of the first edition were increased to 105 in the second edition. The second edition also adds a wide range of navigational aids: an extraordinary increase in typefaces to distinguish, e.g., letters from the narrative, in paragraph divisions, and in marginal notes. And the running headers of 1563 have been replaced with the relevant monarch's name and headers related to the specific contents of each page. The 1597 edition also adds line numbers (10, 20, 30, etc.) between the two columns of text.

28. John Earle, *The Autograph Manuscript of Microcosmographie* (Leeds: Scolar Press, 1966), 117; Earle, *Micro-Cosmographie* (Cambridge: Cambridge University Press, 1903), 87; cited in Collinson, "The Coherence of the Text," 107 n. 55.

29. John Foxe, *Actes and Monuments* (London: R. Day, 1596), STC 11226, p. 1125. Foxe's account is largely drawn from John Bale's *The firste examinacyon of A. Askew* (Wesel, 1546) and *The lattre examinacyon* (Wesel, 1547). For an excellent modern edition of all the early texts of Anne Askew, see Elaine Beilin, *The Examinations of Anne Askew* (New York: Oxford University Press, 1996). I am also indebted to her "Anne Askew's Dialogue with Authority" in ed. Marie-Rose Logan and Peter L. Rudnytsky, *Contending Kingdoms* (Detroit: Wayne State University Press, 1991), 313–22 and her "Anne Askew's Self-Portrait in the Examinations," in ed. Margaret P. Hannay, *Silent but for the Word* (Kent: Kent University Press, 1985), 77–91.

30. Remarkable to us, that is. Askew's feats of remembrance are frequently replicated by Catholics and Protestants alike in early modern England, although their techniques of interlacing quotations are significantly different.

31. Ed. W. Grinton Berry, *Foxe's Book of Martyrs* (Grand Rapids: Spire, 1998), 331.

32. As Mandi Pratt has kindly pointed out to me, the Exodus 24 reference is a mistake. It should be Exodus 34. The mistake originates in the first edition and is simply repeated.

33. M. H. Black, "The Printed Bible," *The Cambridge History of the Bible: The West from the Reformation to the Present Day*, ed. S. L. Greenslade (Cambridge: Cambridge University Press, 1963), 408–75, 436, 442. See also Gerald Hammond, *The Making of the English Bible* (Manchester: Manchester University Press, 1982), 116ff; and, on the relation of the English to the French Geneva Bible, Basil Hall, "The Genevan Version of the English Bible: Its Aims and Achievements," *The Bible, the*

Reformation, and the Church, ed. W. P. Stephens (Sheffield: Sheffield Academic Press, 1995), 124–49; and Elizabeth Ingram, "Dressed in Borrowed Robes: Religious Discipline and the Making and Marketing of Catholic Bibles in France, 1550–1600" (unpublished ms.). I am grateful to Elizabeth Ingram for showing me her essay prior to publication and for her insights into the Geneva Bible generally.

3

Theatrum Libri

Burton's Anatomy of Melancholy *and the Failure of* Encyclopedic Form

CHRISTOPHER GROSE

[There is] a total body of vision that poets as a whole class are entrusted with, a total body tending to incorporate itself in a single encyclopaedic form, which can be attempted by one poet if he is sufficiently learned or inspired, or by a poetic school or tradition if the culture is sufficiently homogeneous.
—Northrop Frye

The beguiling manners of Burton's Democritus Junior make it easy to suppose that the *Anatomy of Melancholy* performs more or less what it promises in its dauntingly preemptive Ramistic chart, supplemented by an index or "Table" beginning in the second edition of 1624. Readers have persisted in this understandable acquiescence despite their likely resistance to Burton's résumé for the historical Democritus, featuring, at the outset, a virtually Orphic link with the natural order (I.2–3), proceeding with travels mapped so as to suggest a scheme of complementary sojourns in Egypt and Athens (including hints of the Alexandrian conquests envisioned by Prince Henry), and culminating with the unlikely spectacle of sages "breathing libraries" in the manner of Ficino's friend Pierleonus (I.28).[1]

Such appreciation is not entirely unprovoked, historically: the same agreeably academic terms were occasionally applied to James I, making him a kind of prototypal Dr. Johnson. In 1609, William Barlow sees something like "Constantine's Court, *Ecclesiae instar*, a little *Universitie*, compassed with Learned men in all professions; and his Majesty in the middest of them . . . a living Library, furnished at all hands, to reply, answer, obiect, resolve, discourse, explane."[2] And even in the "satyrical" preface to the first edition of the *Anatomy*, we encounter Burton's own extravagant adulation of James I as "a wise, [learned, religious, 1624, ed.] king, another Numa, a second Augustus, a true Josiah" (I.75), together with the usual tactics of critique, targeting the Scottish favorites, those "bad weedes, and enormities, which much disturb the peace of this body politick, [eclipse, 1628, ed.] the honour and glory of it, fit to bee rooted out, and with all speede to be reformed."[3]

What makes Burton such a fascinating figure in Stuart studies, among other things, is the timing of his book and the unusual span involved in the *Anatomy*'s gestation and extensive revisions, from its first edition in 1621 to (and seemingly beyond) his death in 1640. But even in the first edition of 1621, we find other notes, as in the call for "some generall visiter in our age," in effect a better James to address a situation apparently grown tragic: "Another Attila, *Tamberlane*, Hercules, to strive with Achelous, Augeae stabulum purgare, to subdue tyrants, as he did *Diomedes* and *Busiris*: to expell thieves, as he did *Cacus* and *Lacinius*: to vindicate poor captives, as he did *Hesione*: to pass the Torrid and the deserts of *Lybia*, and purge the World of monsters and *Centaures*: or another *Theban Crates* to reforme our manners, to compose quarrels, end controversies, as in his time he did, and was therefore adored for a God in *Athens*" (I.84).[4] Given the clear disparity between such conditions and the prerequisites for Frye's encyclopedism, it may be worthwhile to reconsider our suspicions of the Democritan résumé, and to look more closely at the *Anatomy*'s early contrasting juxtaposition of its delightfully garrulous presenter and Burton's narrative of the historical Democritus.

* * *

In the best Jacobean manner, Burton's Democritan model is certainly Frye's kind of encyclopedic author: a physician, politician, and mathematician all in one, "*omnifariam doctus*" also engaged in pursuit of the book's conspicuous desideratum of middle ways (I.2). But although panoptic ambitions seem involved in the ideal book as Burton conceives it, the *Anatomy* also shows how the encyclopedic is often imagined as an imperiled item, endangered by threats similar to the "hoarse or mute" impediments to Milton's project in heroic verse, similarly panoptic, and in its way equally deferred. Even Frye's account acknowledges the multiple contingencies which are likely to destabilize such a recuperative form. In particular, the cultural homogeneity and the social integration of that whole class of poets (or Frye's deceptively innocuous surrogate, a "tradition") show how readily an encyclopedic work falls apart into an admittedly failed "anatomy," its informing system devolving into an itinerary or list of keywords, signs of the particularism which, as Richard Helgerson has observed, seem almost inherent in such chorographic projects.[5]

Contemporary discussions were no less skeptical. In Hooker's preface to *The Laws of Ecclesiastical Polity*, Frye's "total body of vision" has become the reward of a committed and patient reading of an author whose "travels" have removed him, at least temporarily, from the community (Frye's "class") of poets. Thinking to contain the day's controversy with the ground plan of a discursive mansion or garden, Hooker's preface succeeds much better in highlighting a process of historification. As the mere epitome or "brief of these my travels" and not the full register, the *Laws* can at best prompt a deferred restoral of the lost proportions: "it shall be no troublesome thing for any man to find each particular controversy's resting place, and the coherence it hath with those things, either on which it dependeth, or which depend on it." Hooker likens his kind of work to "the stateliness of houses, [and] the goodliness of trees," even as he addresses the difficult gestation of the *Laws*, and the way in which, book by book, his discourse grew increasingly reactive, in this way less "artificial."[6] The preface thus intimates a systematic or organic wholeness at the very moment when changing circumstances virtually compel Hooker to rely upon the concealment of his polity's essential mysteries, sounding almost wistful in projecting an ideal reception that would make "innocents" of his readers (*Laws* 1:6; 1:218).

If Francis Bacon shares with Hooker in supposing chorographic powers to be somehow inherent in the authorial office, his discussion of the bible also illuminates the contingencies betrayed in Hooker's preface. Bacon redisposes Hooker's secrets to the context of an authorial intent deferred in time, in the manner of human gestation.[7] Addressing the matter of controversy and the general problem of disconnection between a text and its readings, Bacon in effect relocates the very occasion of Hooker's preface to an antecedent position: his emphasis on the oblique discursive transactions of Christ and the Pharisees enables him to situate the Scriptures themselves between a primeval conflict (or the evasion of one) and a progressive revelation of divine intent. The "infinite springs and streams of doctrine to water the church in every part" are the definitive and necessarily encyclopedic expression of an original intent to address the thoughts and not the mere words of men. Hence the uniquely unprofane status of Bacon's ideal book, "written to the thoughts of men, and to the succession of all ages, with a foresight of all heresies, contradictions, different estates of the church, yea and particularly of the elect." It is such doubts about the likely fate of encyclopedic intents that are reflected in Burton's emphatic distinction between an historical Democritus, *omnifariam doctus*, and the indefinitely deferred work which the present author sets about to "complete and finish in this treatise."[8]

*   *   *

Readers less susceptible than Hooker's "innocents" have grown accustomed to regarding the apparatus as a kind of prolegomenal afterthought. But in the fashion of Bacon's Bible—and unlike the anthropological projects studied by James Clifford—Burton's book requires us to deal with the co-originality of the book proper and seeming prolegomenal apparatus, as in the proemia of *Paradise Lost*.[9] Such as it is, the evidence suggests that the divagations inevitable in ordinary travel were built into the encyclopedic venture itself; the prefatory top-heaviness of the *Anatomy* was integral to the first edition (1621) of this heavily revised and much reprinted book. Indeed, Burton's preface narrates a fundamental deflection for his project, in terms recalling Hooker's trope for his own encyclopedic travels: "At this time I was fatally driven upon this rock of melancholy, and carried away by this by-stream, which, as a rillet, is deducted from the main channel of my studies, in which I have pleased and busied myself at idle hours, as a subject most necessary and commodious" (I.20). Despite its confusions, this sentence seems more specifically focused than the autobiographical evocation with which it is commonly identified. In its ambiguity of situation (just where has he "pleased and busied" himself for work on that "most necessary and commodious" subject?), it conjoins authorial vocation and literary form to the point of identifying a new locus for "divinity" (I.23). For all his complaints elsewhere about the current "precipitate" age, Burton seems to feel at home in Montaigne's world of geological process. We seem to encounter a field of study in itself dynamic, and encountered at a moment of historical transition—a likely point at which Frye's imagined cultural matrix for encyclopedic form is no longer "sufficiently homogeneous."

Whatever we may attribute to Burton in the way of the talents and plenary intentions enjoyed by the inspired Pierleonus, the narrative of Baconian shipwreck serves to originate a more particular and volatile authority for the *Anatomy*'s actual presenter. With Milton and others, Democritus Junior shares a conspicuously belated condition situated somewhere between academic study and that most generic of professions, "divinity"—a prolonged moratorium that does not augur well for fully realized encyclopedic works. There is a decidedly transgressive aspect to this discussion of a vocational destiny complicated by an instinctive attraction to medicine, by no means a legitimate sister art at the time, whether in the view of James's *Daemonologie* (1597) or of those readers ironically promised atonement in the form of "some Treatise in Divinitie" should they find the present approach too medicinal or "humane" (I.23). Unlike his well-traveled "historical" namesake, he remains enclosed, "still a collegiat student," an oddly immobile "rover" who has toured only "in Mappe and Card" (I.4)—a writer, indeed, whose subject *came to him*. In the hands of Democritus Junior, the seemingly recuperative itinerary of the historical Democritus acquires the nomadic tinge of a "wandering life."

In the pages that follow, I will argue that even the first edition of the *Anatomy* (1621) marks the site of another, earlier project. In the claim that the historical Democritus practiced "according to the divinity of those times" (I.2), Burton looks back upon his own erstwhile recuperative or encyclopedic intentions, in order to distinguish them from the frankly nonpanoptic, fragmentary mode actually suggested by the title of his book. The virtually final version which I will call the "Eventual" *Anatomy* originates in the incompletely understood links between its intended final phase as an "Encyclopedic" project—the predetermined destination called "religious melancholy," as indicated on the Ramistic chart for Burton's "travels"—and the eventually pervasive effects of its prefatory frame, which was advertised from 1621 on as "a satyricall preface, conducing to the following discourse."

The story of the partition between the shape and mode of Burton's Eventual book and the Intended *Anatomy*, considered as a project, begins with the postscript and virtual signature of the 1621 edition, parts of which Burton relocated from its concluding position to the preface, itself already in place, as we have just seen. And the evolution of the book—it is just the wrong term if we measure the result against the Intended project—continues with further additions to "Religious melancholy" and the extravagant expansion of the preface well into the long publishing history of the *Anatomy*. Relatively early in the book (1.1.3.3), there is a section on the "matter" of melancholy, as though the entire category could be addressed encyclopedically, all at once. The preface's claim of the many "honourable Presidents for this which I have done" (I.6), including anatomies similarly organized, is central to the project in this early phase. Behind Burton's sense of "the scholarship" is the encyclopedist's presumption of the timeless network linking the world's categories, following nature's method "with the aliment of our bodies": "We can say nothing but what hath beene said, the composition and method is ours onely, and shewes a Schollar" (I.11). Even in speaking of himself, Burton has "only this of Macrobius to say" (ibid.).

As represented on the panoptic table and in the early encyclopedic phase of Burton's project, religious melancholy was just another pigeonhole in the classic file, a branch of melancholy's perpetual, familiar tree, to be treated in the familiar chorographic procedures of scholarly collation. A presumed subspecies of love melancholy, an object of Burton's continuing investigation well into the book's publishing history, religious melancholy ought to have been subject to the assumptions still intact as Burton changed course at the beginning of Part 3: "There is nothing here to be excepted at; Love is a species of melancholy, and a necessary part of this my treatise, which I may not omit" (3.1.1.1; III.2). When we arrive at "Religious melancholy" in mid-Part 3, however, we encounter a fundamental alteration in the conceptual basis of melancholy, innocuously couched in the complaint that "No Physician hath as yet distinctly written of [religious melancholy]" (3.4.1.1; III.873). The passage testifies to the sense of a material "distinction" to match the scholarly deficiency—the need for a specialized literature for a subspecies somehow uncovered by the previous discussions of an indivisible, encyclopedically conceived "matter" for melancholy. Although the remark itself is characteristically masked in quotation, the insistent point that for this juncture there is "no pattern to followe, as in some of the rest, no man to imitate" hints at the need for a new kind of author to fill the gap left by authorities like Zanchio (3.4.1.1; III.330). Lacking his usual supply of well-documented prototypes and analogies in ethnic experience either among the ancients or at either of the overseas "Indies," Burton must abandon his usual reliance on scholarly consensus at this point in his progress through the schematic itinerary, and rely instead on the dubious authority of the eyewitness (3.3.4.2; III.866)—a necessity unaltered by his low opinion of such testimony.

Along with the continuing expansion of religious melancholy, Burton's relocation of materials from the 1621 postscript to the preface suggests that religious melancholy became an epitome for his journey, an unanticipated "*rem substratum*" rather than its intended concluding port of call.[10] The phase of his project which carried Burton beyond the constitutive literature of melancholy eventually functioned in his book as a transmigrated version of the *Anatomy*'s erstwhile, recuperative master category. It is at this point that Burton's book became a more reflexive and explicitly theatrical "playing labour" and his Democritus Junior the kind of inspired invention which Conrad found in Marlowe: not so much the encyclopedic traveler or visiting anthropologist as a product of the culture Burton came to study in such sharp and sympathetic detail.

For my purposes, the potential convergence between Democritus Junior and the subjects of Burton's intended report on religious melancholy may originate in the moment Burton steps backstage to unmask in the 1621 postscript, addressing a gentle complaint to a reader he styles a "rigid censurer": "If ought be amisse, I require a friendly admonition, no bitter invective" (Ddd2^{vo})—not an appropriate response, he supposes, in exchanges among antagonists presumably linked by a common "scholarly" identity itself conventionally susceptible to melancholy. Seemingly addressed to readers studiously engaged with the book's issues and perhaps also to fellow sufferers of melancholy, the postscript's brief afterthought shows a tone of wounded surprise altogether missing in its new location in the Eventual preface (I.19).

The concluding section of the Eventual *Anatomy* shows some interesting marks of the shift in Burton's project. This is partly owing to the incompletely realized presence of Democritus Junior in the definitive, fully edited *Anatomy* that some readers might prefer to what I am calling the "Eventual" one. Burton's presentation of the book's final, as yet undocumented subspecies of melancholy remains unleavened by a more fully ironized presenter. The category which seems to have provoked Burton's famous sympathy requires the inves-

tigative work of a first-person speaker who addresses "us" at times confiden-
tially, and occasionally turns to (and sometimes on) a rhetorically estranged
third party, "them." Here, the investigator loses his bearings, in something like
dramatic imbrication: "Many of them are so close, you can hardly discerne it,
or take any just exceptions at them, they are not factious, oppressours as most
are, no bribers, no simoniacall contractors, no such ambitious, lascivious persons as some others are, no drunkards, . . . they rise sober and goe sober to bed,
plain dealing, upright honest men, they do wrong to no man, and are so
reputed in the worlds esteeme at least, very zealous in religion, very charitable,
meeke, humble, peacemakers, keepe all duties, very devout, honest, well spoken of, beloved of all men" (3.4.2.1; III.406). "Discernment" is just what Burton
seems unable to manage here. The diagnostician has so entered into the formulae of self-justification that we may be surprised by the verdict of hypocrisy
offered by "he that knowes better how to judge, he that examines the heart"
(3.4.2.1; 3.406). Whoever might be capable of the conclusion's pronouncement
(Hawthorne's Chillingworth comes to mind here), it is presumably neither us
("you") nor, as yet, the prefatory Democritus Junior.[11] Depending on our approach, the moment seems either forgetful of Burton's sympathy or as yet
uninformed by it. It is not the only place in the Eventual *Anatomy*'s conclusion
where Burton's enactment of sympathy does not altogether fill the space separating the investigator from his subjects: "The last maine torture and trouble of
a distressed minde, is not so much this doubt of Election, and that the promises
of grace are smothered and extinct in them, nay quite blotted out as they
suppose, but withall Gods heavy wrath, a most intollerable paine and griefe of
heart seaseth on them" (3:4:2:6; III.439). Hard on the heels of that proto-
Miltonic "nay quite blotted out," the qualifying "as they suppose" and the
ensuing turn, "To such persons I oppose Gods mercy and his justice" (3:4:2:6;
III.439), seem arbitrary and forced. Just a moment ago, after all, we fell among
"such persons" ourselves: "A blacke cloud of sinne as yet obnubilates thy soule,
terrifies thy conscience, but this cloude may conceave a rainbowe at the last,
and be quite dissipated by repentance" (III.430). At such close quarters with
the very consideration that produced Democritus Junior, we may be jarred by
the more isolated and somehow official "I" who informs us of what "these men
must know," to the point of tendering amnesty for those who have separated
from the national body.[12]

    Our sense of isolation from Democritus Junior's company, and the mate-
rials now helping to establish his presence elsewhere in the book, seems even
more pronounced in the conclusion to Burton's Eventual book as a whole.
Here, in the space originally occupied by the 1621 postscript, we are told that
despite a divine permission to "possess us inwardly to molest us," there are
nonetheless limitations to Satan's power: "[Satan] is Prince of the Ayre, and

can transforme himselfe into severall shapes, delude all our senses for a time, but his power is determined, hee may terrifie us but not hurt; God hath given *his Angell charge over us, hee is a wall round about his people*" (III.443). As though he has forgotten the virtual ubiquity of "spirits" urged in the impressive "Digression," Burton speaks of Satan as a minor annoyance seemingly bounded by physical realities. Without quite erasing the operative contingency of that lingering, "obnubilating" cloud or the *Anatomy*'s pervasive imagery of deluge, the divine "wall" of Burton's quotation retrieves something like John of Gaunt's geography for a safely moated British citadel. Having testified virtually throughout the *Anatomy* to a latter-day devolution—something like a reversion to the original Satanic hegemony prior to the messianic silencing of the heathen oracles—Burton concludes his book, in effect, by cancelling the point.[13] Even the program of repentance offered in the final pages of the Eventual *Anatomy* undoes itself by promising to "effect prodigious cures, make a stupend metamorphosis" (III.429), employing the very epithet, disturbing in the hyperbole of its reassurance, with which he had earlier spoken of the British penchant for idolatry "in all ages."

The effect seems quite different from the palpably rhetorical encirclement practiced by the Eventual preface, expressly designed to convince us that all are melancholy, none of us "excepted." Even the moralizing so abundant in the body of the book includes us within Burton's discursive "commonwealth" when he assures us, with a schoolmasterly geniality, that "Sicknesse is the mother of modesty, putteth us in minde of our mortality, and when wee are in the full careere of worldly pompe and jollity, she pulleth us by the eare, and maketh us knowe ourselves" (II.135). Lacking the manifestly ironized garrulity of Democritus Junior in the Eventual book's conclusion, we may well feel isolated from his more communal folly, and unlikely to escape the predicament from which he seems almost anxious to secure us.

*   *   *

In Burton's Eventual *Anatomy*, we deal with a postencyclopedic book constructed in antithetic reaction to the "close" and suffering Protestant victims presented in such sympathetic (and un-Democritan) fashion in the book's concluding pages. The 1621 postscript makes it clear that the significant shift in Burton's project was couched in theatrical terms, in keeping with Burton's telling citation of John of Salisbury's dictum *totus mundus agit histrionem*. But here, the men and women who are "merely players" in the eyes of Shakespeare's melancholics have become Burton's "fools." The *Anatomy*'s striking translation of John's *histrione[s]* (I.37) bridges the gap between the humane, "medicinal" encyclopedia and the theatrical realm also famously reliant on Salisbury's words in the motto of the Globe Theater. Indeed, the textual evidence suggests that Burton began with a conventional antitheatricalism—the complaint that, in Ralegh's words, "we are all become comedians in religion"—and went on to employ the lore of "saintly" culture to feed a comic estrangement fundamentally different from the discursively separated "them" (or "these men") of "Religious melancholy."[14] Having urged his reader "by all means [to] open himself (III.45), Burton models the process begun so paradoxically with the decision, in the postscript of 1621, "to cut the strings of Democritus' visor, to unmaske and shew him as he is" (1621, Ddd; 783). In the eventual relocation of the 1621 postscript and other materials of the ever-expanding file on religious melancholy, Burton's reporter fully merges with "Democritus Junior." In doing so, the would-be encyclopedic "scholar" becomes inextricably involved with his subject, thereby participating in the reversionary metamorphosis for which the contemporary theater, in the eyes of its Puritan antagonists, provided the obvious type.

The qualification is operative. In the Eventual *Anatomy*'s preface as in "Religious melancholy," Burton's empirically inclined presenter is the disgusted viewer of all things theatrical, as in "To see a man turn himselfe into all shapes like a Camelion, or as *Proteus, Omnia transformans sese in miracula rerum*, to act twenty parts and persons at once" (I.52). But while the reformist mentality remains prominent in "Religious melancholy" in all editions of the *Anatomy*, inviting us to consider the looks and gestures of the day as something like "theater" in the devalued sense of masks or costumes easily detached (III.142), the Eventual preface shows a new attitude toward Burton's own "playing labour." Even as he moves toward the remarkable claim that those who would "freely speak and write, must be forever no subject, under no prince or law," the jaded spectator dissolves into loquacious babble: "But I must take heede, . . . that I doe not overshoot my selfe, *Sus Minervam*, I am forth of my element, as you peradventure suppose, and sometimes veritas odium parit, as he said, *verjuce and oatmeale is good for a Parret*" (1.84). Having affiliated the subjects of his book with the common sites of what we may call "virtual ethnicity"—heathen, woman, child, madman, and now mimic beast—Burton adds the epitome of all Protean spirits, the theatrical player as the outrageous model for his own new kind of authority.[15]

It is significant in this context that Burton's caustic remarks about books and the various aspects of early modern print culture do not extend to many of the sources for his own work, recently discussed by Vicari. "News" and travel narratives do not seem to count, for this avid reader of the current and earlier expeditions, as "books." Indeed, what makes for learning—the constitutive literature which alone can "show a scholar"—is tactically set off, not (as we might expect) against "neoterics" like the admired Gesner, but vernacular sources like essays and the drama. Burton seems to have imagined "plaies," in particular, as somehow unbookish, belonging to a category altogether different from the commodified items which prompt his frequent attacks on "our mercenary stationers." And to Burton's mind, plays differ most significantly from printed sermons and "treatises of divinity"; in the *Anatomy*, the latter become virtual paradigms of the overly digested discursive performances which Burton eventually decided to avoid.[16]

Burton explicitly registers the nature of his countertextual alteration in the second edition of 1624, even as he persists in his long-standing reconsideration of the presumed encyclopedic affiliation between "Love melancholy" and the adjacent category of religious melancholy. Advertising material "which was not in the former editions," his introduction sheds the conventional antitheatricalism inherent in complaints like Ralegh's; he declares the intent "boldly to shew my selfe in this common Stage, and in this Trage-comedy of love, to Act severall parts, some Satyrically, some Comically, some in a mixt Tone, as the subject I have in hand gives occasion, and present sceane shall require or offer it selfe" (3.1.1.1; III.8). The brash announcement of a mixed tone appropriate to his materials and occasion both grounds and enhances the perspective offered in the *Anatomy*'s opening allusion to "This antic or personate actor" who "so insolently intrudes upon this common theatre, to the world's view." Thus situated, the announcement confirms the leavening and subversive presence of Democritus Junior within Burton's discussion. Considered as a phase in his encyclopedic project, it marks the decision to abandon it as such, by extending the "playing" personality of Democritus Junior deep into the now virtually canonical or Eventual *Anatomy*.[17]

The result, audible here and there in the body of the Eventual *Anatomy*, is the vocal assimilation of Burton's multifarious materials in which Dr. Johnson thought he heard Burton's own voice. In a fashion similar to metaphysical "conceits," Democritus Junior's heavily advertised juvenility/madness informs a bit of zoology present in the 1621 edition, impressively transforming it into a biologically grounded Stuart politics of union, and envisioning the dark consequences in store for those lacking in such zeal for commonwealth: "Wee see them here some in Somer, some in winter, *Their coming and going is sure in the night: in the plaines of Asia (saith he) the storkes meet on such a set day, he that comes last is torn in peeces, and so they get them gone*" (II.37).[18] An emblem of James's arch-Protestant "humor," the belated stork becomes an instance of "heroicall passion," in which the victims, recalling and updating Isaiah's contending nations, "furiously rage, are tormented, and torne in peeces by their predominate affections" (3.2.5.5; III.257).

Despite the attributive emphasis and the citations hinting at a scholarly consensus, the passage is a nice instance of the vocal authority Dr. Johnson appreciated. All the more important, then, that this densely allusive writing comes from the "Digression of Air," present in 1621 but, on the face of it, an anomalous space within the book's original encyclopedic scheme, and a momentary interruption which inevitably calls attention to the book's own "aerial progress" (II.48). Well into the encyclopedic voyage, the "Digression" hints at the fine line separating the original *Anatomy* from its "Eventual" successor; the regularly scheduled interval ("Member 3") within Part 2, Section 2 reminds us of how early in the project Burton might have discovered the potential use of Democritus Junior and the way his antic energy can incorporate and seem to naturalize the lore of political and religious controversy.

Among the various readings which enabled Burton to pursue the imbricative act to which his materials and human sympathy had subjected him, the "plaies" most significantly affected his demarcation between the procedures of his presenter and the victims of religious melancholy. Rooted as it is in the rapidly evolving Protestant culture of his day, Democritus Junior's folly becomes a pointed illustration of the view Dr. Johnson attributed only to Shakespeare's *audience*, that "the stage is only a stage, and the players are only players."[19] The authorial hilarity of Burton's own book seems to emulate the primitive martyrs whose "cheerful and merry" behavior "in the midst of their persecutions" differs so sharply from the modern "saints," inwardly "tossed in a Sea, and that continually without rest or intermission" (III.421).

The distinction, so sharply formulated in relation to religious melancholy, is writ large in the Eventual preface and often echoed in the later additions to the body of the Eventual book. Among other things, Burton's "play" applies to the preface's concluding boast of "independence"—"I care not. I owe thee nothing, (Reader) I looke for no favour at thy hands, I am independent, I feare not" (I.112). Addressed as they are to the very "captious" or "rigid" readers who serve as the subject of "Religious melancholy['s]" report, moments like this perform the work of a writer who is "no subject, under no prince or law" (I.84). Almost necessarily, they are also of a piece with the various reminders of an author absconded, one who "dwells not in this study" or who is even "gone."[20]

Burton's most striking play on the commonplace that "the tongues of dying men / Enforce attention like deep harmony" recalls St. Laurence's kind of perfected alienation, in the wit of "I have layd my selfe open (I know it) in this Treatise, turned mine inside outward" (I.13), where we encounter an antique instance of Michel Foucault's notion of madness as "the déjà là of death."[21] The kind of double consciousness displayed by Richard II (and Gaunt before him) informs Burton's revisionist analogy of Zisca's drum, Montaigne's illustration of imagination carrying us "beyond ourselves" in the unacknowledged source of Burton's conceit. Johan Vischa ("Zisca") "would have a drumme made of his skinne when he was dead, because he thought the very noise of it would put his enimies to flight." By this token, Democritus Junior professes no doubt that "these following lines, when they shall be recited, or hereafter read, will drive away Melancholy (though I be gone) as much as Zisca's drumme could terrify his foes" (I.24). Burton's "great captain" has been tactically reduced from the more complicated status he enjoys in Montaigne, as one who "brought insurrection to Bohemia in defence of the errors of Wyclif." Indeed, Montaigne proceeds to link the device to the Indians' "defences" against the Spanish conquerors, to be warded off by the thought of their own potential fate—as drumsticks.[22] For all the signs of the Anatomist's preoccupation with the continuing predations of the "Hungry Spaniard," Burton's prolonged meditation on Christian rage and other symptoms (I.13) serves to displace the erstwhile common enemy of England and Indians alike in favor of his undocumented, newly activated field of investigation. Nor has Burton forgotten Montaigne's appreciation of the ideologically pointed "Indian" ripostes which were a common feature of early colonial narratives.

Whether overtly critical or officially sanctioned, such defiances in "a shaft of wit that by no means savours of barbarism" made for intellectually licentious theater and literature in England long before Ralegh cited Bartolomé de Las Casas in 1596.[23] The abundant travel literature works together with Foxe and the "plaies" in enabling Democritus Junior's folly to rediscover the oppositional status (and alleged insanity) of the authentic saints, already well-sanctioned and affiliated in Burton's "playing labour" with court jesters and, quite likely, with the folly of Shakespeare's most enduring royal martyr, Richard II. The Anatomy's references to the crucial Jacobean predecessor are all the more intriguing for the conspicuous overlap between the book's gestation and publication history—from relatively early in James I's reign, say, to the closing of the theaters in 1642. As an occasion to comment on the Scottish favorites of James, Richard's presence eventually made the Anatomy another of the period's prophetic works, in conjunction with allusions to "our Pharsalian fields" past and perhaps future. But it is also rewarding to put Democritus Junior on good terms with the Shakespearean matrix of the Anatomy's own "mixed passion," and in particular with Richard's belated recognition of the "many people" represented by the royal "player," and the reality—mastered by the mythic Hal and notoriously neglected by James himself—of something like Donne's "universal monarchy of wit."[24]

Under the circumstances, it seems clear that when a project like Burton's turns out "neither as I will nor as thou wilt," the authorial "captain" has been deposed. The Anatomy's prefatory "lightening" recognizes that the volatile materials of religious melancholy have acquired the kind of intractable autonomy which seems alien to Frye's view of the encyclopedic venture. Might it also suggest an independence shared between presenter and reader, in the fashion of that "utopian parity" which Democritus Junior realistically concedes is "To be wished for, rather than effected" (I.89)? Such a convergence between presenter and reader might even underlie the bold claim of the preface that "Thou thyself art the subject of my discourse," in which Burton's authorial hegemony reaches its apogee. Much will depend on whose voice we hear in this remarkable declaration, where Burton may be thought to recognize and seal the encyclopedic intent which we have seen to be incompletely realized in the more analytic final pages of the Eventual *Anatomy*'s conclusion. Once we put King Richard's mirror into Democritus Junior's hand for this brief "recitation," have we not met once again, as fellow performers, with the occasionally "excepted" presenter? Such an encounter is certainly a prime effect in Burton's citation of "Epichthonius Cosmopolites" and the now familiar fool's-cap-framed world map that so aptly updates the mentality of Hooker's "innocent" readers.[25] Recalling and topically applying Hugh's memorable formulation describing the entire world as "a foreign land" for the man who is perfect in *contemptus mundi*, the juxtaposition of cartographic prospect and folly's badge nicely captures Burton's contrast between an authentic saintly "perfection" and those contemporary "deified spirits" whose un-Democritan symptoms provoked some of his most impressive writing (I.60).[26]

Thus constructed and partly deployed, the lens through which we follow Burton's encyclopedic itinerary also functions as the means of its radical qualification or erasure. But though the project as such cannot survive this brilliant and only partly editorial stroke, it seems clear that the older encyclopedic fit between book and reader has not entirely been abandoned in the alterations that eventually produced Burton's "playing labour." The idea of a "ventilating" function for the antic mask, and in general the decision to "open up" his book from a scholarly Latin compactness in order to address an English audience itself perhaps shipwrecked by "actual" melancholy (I.24), carry his project well beyond the 1621 postscript's "unmasking" of an author now presumably off-stage. An integral part of the somatic focus which makes his book dangerously medicinal, the prevalent expressive emphasis of this theatrical model provides an inward situation for the *Anatomy*'s discourse. And the illusion of immedicacy promoted by Democritus Junior's claim that his prose "flows remissly as it was first conceived" further serves to obliterate any textual gap between author and auditory, like the well-advertised "aerial progress" of the book as a seeming whole. Imagined as theater, such a book might yet consolidate a national readership, by recreating the old fit between recuperative speaker and auditory.

In different ways, the multifarious reception history of the *Anatomy* testifies to the central place Burton gives to his saints' behavior, both in his conclusion and in the prefatory folly of Democritus Junior. Lilburne's frequent insistence (in *A Work of the Beast*, 1638) on his own "cheerfulness" ("as cheerful and merry in the Lord . . . as if I were to receive my present liberty") may serve to illustrate the *Anatomy*'s impact on readers made uncomfortable by Burton's inventive adaptation of James's arch-Protestant "humors."[27]

More broadly revealing is Humphrey Moseley's shrewd attempt to capitalize on the *Anatomy*'s commercial success. Like Burton, Edmund Gregory's *Historical Anatomy of Christian Melancholy* (1646) hints at the imminent death of its author, pictured (at thirty) in the frontispiece. And no less than Burton, Gregory's book seeks to address the age's loss of an inward and silent "conscience" which has been displaced by the controversies and printed discourses of those who have failed in the tacit argumentation of *imitatio Christi*.[28] As committed as Burton to the proposition that the "natural disposition and temper of man [is] much addicted to Melancholy" (1; B1), Gregory's little book would nonetheless serve only as an aid to devotion. Explicitly foregoing anything like authorial hegemony, Gregory highlights the contrast between private reading in a world fraught with difference and the vestigial aims of Burton's quasi-dramatic "recitation": "what I have written is not the Experience of all men . . . Let it not, I pray, by any means offend you, if you chance to meet with that thing which concurs not with the Experience and Motion of your own soul; for I intend nothing herein as a positive Doctrine or an absolute Rule" (A3^{vo}–A4).

Notes

Note to epigraph: Northrop Frye, *Anatomy of Criticism* (Princeton, N.J.: Princeton University Press, 1957), 55.

1. Against Ficino's claims for Pierleonus's originality, that he understood the secrets of nature by "a divine kind of infusion" before he read the works of "Grecian and barbarian philosophers," Burton finds a symptom of "evil spirits," which are especially adept with "humours decayed" (I.427–28). Except where noted, Burton is quoted from the edition of Faulkner, Keissling, and Blair (Oxford: Clarendon Press, 1989).

2. William Barlow, *An answer to a catholike Englishman* (1609), quoted in Patrick Collinson, *The Religion of Protestants: The Church in English Society, 1559–1625* (Oxford: Oxford University Press, 1982), 28.

3. Ibid., with dated additions to *1621* in brackets.

4. Here I follow the text and punctuation of UCLA's copy of 1621, departing from the familiar "quarrels and controversies," which first appeared in 1632. The Oxford edition reports no pointing for 1621–28 (I.486).

5. Richard Helgerson, *Forms of Nationhood: The Elizabethan Writing of England* (Chicago: University of Chicago Press, 1994).

6. *Laws* 1:1; *The Works of . . . Richard Hooker*, 3 vols. (Oxford: Clarendon Press, 1907), 1:171, 197.

7. In the second book of the *Advancement of Learning*, Bacon contends: "For it is an excellent observation which hath been made upon the answers of our Saviour Christ to many of the questions which were propounded to him, how that they are impertinent to the state of the question demanded; the reason whereof is, because not being like man, which knows man's thoughts by his words, but knowing man's thoughts immediately, he never answered their words, but their thoughts: much in the like manner it is with the Scriptures, which being written to the thoughts of men, and to the succession of all ages, with a foresight of all heresies, contradictions, differing estates of the church, yea, and particularly of the elect, are not to be interpreted only according to the latitude of the proper sense of the place, and respectively towards that present occasion, whereupon the words were uttered, or in precise congruity or contexture with the words before or after, or in contemplation of the principle scope of the place; but have in themselves, not only totally or collectively, but distributively in clauses and words, infinite springs and streams of doctrine to water the church in every part" (*The Works of Francis Bacon*, ed. Basil Montague [Philadelphia: Hart, 1852], 1:242–43).

8. Fox's encyclopedist reading, *The Tangled Chain: The Structure of Disorder in the Anatomy of Melancholy* (Berkeley: University of California Press, 1976) seeks to correct Stanley Fish's reading of Burton's preface in *Self-Consuming Artifacts: the Experience of Seventeenth-Century Literature* (Berkeley: University of California Press, 1972). For essentially similar approaches, see also William Osler, "Burton's Anatomy of Melancholy," *Yale Review* 3 (1914): 251–71; and David Renaker, "Robert Burton and Ramist Method," *Renaissance Quarterly* 24 (1971): 210–20.

9. James Clifford, *The Predicament of Culture* (Cambridge, Mass.: Harvard University Press, 1988).

10. For the expatiation of religious melancholy, see (in addition to the textual notes of the Oxford edition) Dennis Donovan, "Burton's *Anatomy of Melancholy*: 'Religious Melancholy,' a Critical Edition" (Ph.D. diss., University of Illinois, 1965). Genetically focussed studies also include Reinhard Friederich, "Training His Melancholy Spaniel: Persona and Structure in Robert Burton's 'Democritus Jr. to the Reader,'" *Philological Quarterly* 55 (1976): 195–210; Devon Hodges, *Renaissance Fictions of Anatomy* (Amherst: University of Massachusetts Press, 1985), 107–23; James Roy King, "The Genesis of Burton's *Anatomy of Melancholy*," in *Studies in Six Seventeenth-Century Writers* (Athens: Ohio University Press, 1966); and William Mueller, *The Anatomy of Robert Burton's England* (Berkeley: University of California Press, 1952).

11. Compare the effect to a similar moment in the Eventual preface where Democritus Junior more clearly mediates the attack on a similar target by the Holy Ghost, who "calls them Fooles" (1.27).

12. E. Patricia Vicari's homiletic model for the *Anatomy* as a whole (*The View from Minerva's Tower: Learning and Imagination in "The Anatomy of Melancholy"* [Toronto: University of Toronto Press, 1989]) seems most appropriate to the Eventual book's conclusion, isolated from the preface's protracted hostility towards sermons, regarded by Democritus Junior as among the most vendible of the books sold by "our mercenary stationers" (I.16).

13. "*All the world over before Christ's time he* [that is, Satan and friends] *freely domineered, and held the souls of men in most slavish subjection (saith Eusebius) in diverse forms, ceremonies, and sacrifices, till Christ's coming, as if those devils of the air had shared the earth amongst them, which the Platonists held for gods . . . , and were our governors and keepers*" (3:4:1:2; III.344). The implications of Burton's counterstatements, available in

the "Digression on Spirits" as in the preface and other sections of "religious melancholy," are in keeping with the dehistoricizing corrections of James's own *Daemonologie* (1597). In *1621*, the digression's title lacks the mechanical import of Robert Burton's somatized "spirits": "A Digression of Divels, and how they cause Melancholy" (D5; p. 57).

14. *Sir Walter Ralegh: Selected Works*, ed. G. Hammond (Harmondsworth: Penguin, 1984), 140.

15. Discussed by Jonas Barish in *The Antitheatrical Prejudice* (Berkeley: University of California Press, 1981), chapter 4. In this case, though, Puritan and Protean have converged.

16. It should be added, in light of the preface's ironic promise of some treatise in divinity to atone for the book's medicinal and "human" emphasis, that Burton's exploitation of a renovated kind of theater also addresses the contemporary Reformers' antipathy to the academic remedies advanced by Bacon: "not so much as degrees some of them will tolerate, or universities, all human learning ('tis *cloaca diaboli*), hoods, habits, cap and surplice, such as are things indifferent in themselves, and wholly for ornament, decency, or distinction'-sake" (III.387).

17. For a strikingly similar itinerary, see M. Certeau, "Melancholique et/ou Mystique: J. J. Surin," *Analytique* 2 (1978): 35–48.

18. The passage, initially similar to Holden Caulfield's curiosity about the winter whereabouts of the ducks in Central Park, ends as a parabolic epitome of the healthy body politic: the birds are often found "in the bottom of lakes and rivers, spiritum continentes . . . two together, mouth, wing to wing; and when the spring comes they revive again, or if they be brought into a stove [~body?], or to the fire-side." The Democritan conceit converts them to emblems of alchemical rarefaction in species. If not a spirit in itself, a bird becomes a vessel of spirit, requiring another such body (or the stove, a characteristic Burtonian replacement) for its very survival. Even off the ground, they fly "familiarly," and Egypt is the favored resort—a healthy geographical body on its own account, with its well-"ventilated" uplands and the "serene" air that makes its human inhabitants a "conceited and merry nation" (2.58).

19. Similarly, Bacon's *New Organon* adopts a reforming stance in its discussion of the Idols of the Theater, which "have immigrated into men's minds from the various dogmas of philosophies." Bacon regards the "received systems" of the day as "but so many stage plays, representing worlds of their own creation after an unreal and scenic fashion" (Aphorism 44, *Francis Bacon: A Selection of His Works*, ed. S. Wahrhaft [Indianapolis: Bobbs-Merrill, 1965], 337). Bacon further ties such "playbooks" to the way in which a contemporary preoccupation "with religion and theology" has in effect displaced the philosophical sects which would otherwise have arisen (347). Johnson's preface is quoted from *Johnson on Shakespeare*, ed. Walter Raleigh (Oxford: Oxford University Press, 1908; rpt. 1957), 27.

20. Such recollections continue even in Burton's own inscription for the monument in the Cathedral of Christ Church, commemorating "*Democritus junior / Cui vitam dedit et mortem / Melancholia*."

21. *Madness and Civilization: A History of Insanity in the Age of Reason*, trans. Richard Howard (New York: Vintage, 1965), 16.

22. *Essays* 1:3, Screech, 14, citing Francisco Lopez de Gomara's *History of the Indies*.

23. Such critiques can be found in Lopez de Gomara, the source (via Fumee's translation of 1578) of Montaigne's Indian materials in 1:3. Lopez is frequently attacked

by Bartolomé de Las Casas for his standing as an official historian. Burton presents Las Casas himself as "their owne bishop" (1.44) Bartolomé's *Narratio Regionum Indicarum* (Frankfurt, 1598) was among the books presented to the Bodleian Library under the terms of Burton's will. See S. Gibson and F. Needham, eds., "Two Lists of Burton's Books in the Bodleian Library, in Christ Church Library," *Oxford Bibliographical Society: Papers and Proceedings* 1 (1927): 222–46.

24. *Richard II*, 2:1:5–6. Hayward's life of Henry IV (London, 1599) is among the books bequeathed to Christ Church in Burton's will. In light of James's penchant for citing the printed record of his own writings, it is ironic that he was widely criticized specifically for his lack of Hal's extemporal talents: a "king-in-law" only, "not a Prince of any natural Affections to the People of this Nation." Francis Osborne, *Memoires of Q. Elizabeth and K. James* in *Works of Francis Osborne Esq . . . in Four Several Tracts* (London, 1689), 426.

25. Hooker's passage (*Laws* 1:6, 1:218) is hedged with qualifications and anticipates the charge of "over hyperbolical" speech.

26. Montaigne, *Essays*, 1:19, citing Lucretius's *eripitur persona, manet res*; Screech, 87. Attributed to Jean de Gourmont, the map now serves as virtual logo for the Norton edition of Shakespeare. It is reproduced and discussed by William Engell in his *Mapping Mortality: The Persistence of Memory and Melancholy in Early Modern England* (Amherst: University of Massachusetts Press, 1995), 153–54. Hugh is quoted from the translation of Jerome Taylor (*The Didascalicon of Hugh of St. Victor: A Medieval Guide to the Arts* [New York: Columbia University Press, 1961], 101). Petronius's *numina* is applied to men who "think too well of themselves" (I.60), a circumstance distinguished from the legitimate category of "holy madnesse, even a spirituall drunkennesse in the Saints of God" (I.65).

27. *Tracts on Liberty in the Puritan Revolution*, ed. William Haller (New York: Columbia University Press, 1934), 2:7.

28. Burton's most forthright answer to the rhetorical question "whom shall I except" is "such as are silent . . . no better way to avoid folly and madness, then by taciturnity" (I.107).

4

Approaches to Presbyterian Print Culture

Thomas Edwards's Gangraena *as Source and Text*

ANN HUGHES

The phenomenon of cat baptism, associated with sectaries in the London of mid-1640s, can be illustrated from two very different sources. Surviving Middlesex quarter sessions records reveal that in August 1644 John Platt, a Golding Lane heel maker, and his wife Susan were bound over to appear in court, "for depraveing the two sacraments of Baptisme and the Lords Supper . . . (saying) that a Catt or a dogg may be as well baptised as any Child or Children in their Infancie." This case dragged on for some months, prompting "tumult" in the streets with insults exchanged and physical assaults on Susan. By October it was being alleged that Susan Platt as "a matter of fact" had christened a cat. The Platts' opponents denounced the partiality of Robert Dawlman, one of the justices involved: two men were bound to "answere for saying in my [Dawlman's] presence I would heare none but Theefes, whores and Annabaptists" as well as for defaming Susan. One of the Platts' sureties was the radical printer, Thomas Paine, later to be associated with the Levellers, while Dawlman was a stationer, specializing in the publication of books by Congregationalist or "Independent" ministers such as Thomas Goodwin, and a close associate of the ageing radical Independent Henry Burton.[1] Burton, in turn, was a main target in all the polemical writings of Thomas Edwards, whose most notorious work, *Gangraena*, is the focus of this chapter (Fig. 1). Edwards's *Gangraena* is the second source for cat baptism. Error 104 in Part One was, "That Paedobaptisme is unlawfull and antichristian, and that tis as lawfull to baptize a Cat or a Dog or a Chicken, as to baptize the Infants of beleevers." One of Edwards's most characteristic techniques was a bludgeoning repetition and he presented a similar account in the narrative part of his book: the sectaries "have done and practised many strange things in reference to baptisme of children, dressing up a Cat like a child for to be baptized . . . ," inviting the neighbors round in a mockery of infant baptism.[2]

Edwards echoed the move in the court proceedings from a form of words to an actual profane reenactment of the sacrament, and it may be that the court

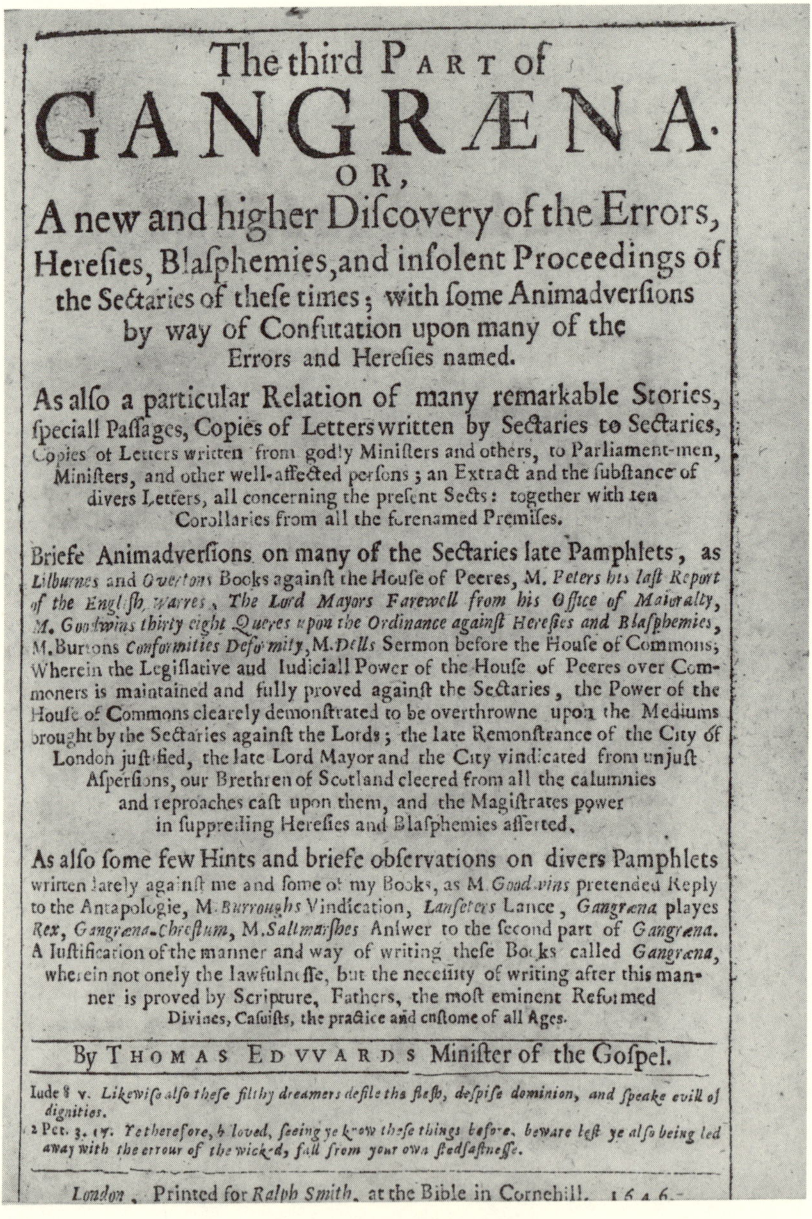

The third PART of

GANGRÆNA.

OR,

A new and higher Discovery of the Errors,
Heresies, Blasphemies, and insolent Proceedings of
the Sectaries of these times; with some Animadversions
by way of Confutation upon many of the
Errors and Heresies named.

As also a particular Relation of many remarkable Stories,
speciall Passages, Copies of Letters written by Sectaries to Sectaries,
Copies of Letters written from godly Ministers and others, to Parliament-men,
Ministers, and other well-affected persons; an Extract and the substance of
divers Letters, all concerning the present Sects: together with ten
Corollaries from all the forenamed Premises.

Briefe Animadversions on many of the Sectaries late Pamphlets, as
Lilburnes and Overtons Books against the House of Peeres, M. Peters his last Report
of the English warres, The Lord Mayors Farewell from his Office of Maioralty,
M. Goodwins thirty eight Queres upon the Ordinance against Heresies and Blasphemies,
M. Burtons Conformities Deformity, M. Dells Sermon before the House of Commons;
Wherein the Legislative and Iudiciall Power of the House of Peeres over Com-
moners is maintained and fully proved against the Sectaries, the Power of the
House of Commons clearely demonstrated to be overthrowne upon the Mediums
brought by the Sectaries against the Lords; the late Remonstrance of the City of
London justified, the late Lord Mayor and the City vindicated from unjust
Aspersions, our Brethren of Scotland cleered from all the calumnies
and reproaches cast upon them, and the Magistrates power
in suppressing Heresies and Blasphemies asserted.

As also some few Hints and briefe observations on divers Pamphlets
written lately against me and some of my Books, as M. Goodwins pretended Reply
to the Antapologie, M. Burroughs Vindication, Lanseters Lance, Gangræna playes
Rex, Gangræna-christum, M. Saltmarshes Answer to the second part of Gangræna.
A Iustification of the manner and way of writing these Books called Gangræna,
wherein not onely the lawfulnesse, but the necessity of writing after this manner is proved by Scripture, Fathers, the most eminent Reformed
Divines, Casuists, the practice and custome of all Ages.

By THOMAS EDVVARDS Minister of the Gospel.

Iude 8 v. Likewise also these filthy dreamers defile the flesh, despise dominion, and speake evill of
dignities.
2 Pet. 3. 17. Ye therefore, b loved, seeing ye know these things before, beware lest ye also being led
away with the errour of the wicked, fall from your own stedfastnesse.

London, Printed for Ralph Smith, at the Bible in Cornehill. 1646.

Figure 1. Title page of Thomas Edwards, *The Third Part of Gangraena* (London, 1646); E237 Bd. w. E228. By permission of the Folger Shakespeare Library.

proceedings, continued into 1645, were at some remove the source for his accounts. We do not know. Many historians, sceptical about Edwards's accounts of radical religion, feel more comfortable about court proceedings in suitably grubby archives, although of course the significance and meaning of legal cases may be equally problematic.[3] The truth of what "actually" occurred is unrecoverable, as is its representativeness. We cannot be sure of the full significance of the Platts' prosecution: is it the tip of a much larger iceberg of transgressive activity, is it evidence of local outrage at an exceptional travesty, or perhaps an end product of local malice provoked by a variety of personal concerns?

This analysis of *Gangraena* is founded on the refusal of a clear contrast between printed and manuscript sources, or a preference for either one. It argues for the value of studying print culture in its own right—undeterred by squeamishness about its value as a source—as evidence for something beyond itself. *Gangraena: or a Catalogue and Discovery of many of the Errours, Heresies, Blasphemies and Pernicious Practices of the Sectaries of this time, vented and acted in England in these four last years*, (as Part One was titled), the work of the London Presbyterian controversialist and lecturer Thomas Edwards, was published in three parts in February, May, and December 1646. In over eight hundred pages it offered readers obsessive lists of errors, outraged stories about the political machinations, religious disorders, and immoral behavior of sectaries and independents, and pages of alarmed commentary. *Gangraena* was "an ephemeral best seller";[4] "the last book *Gangraena* being now in the Presse the third time within lesse then two months," wrote Edwards as he finished Part Two. A second printing of Part One had apparently been necessary within a fortnight (2.42, 48). Part Two, *A fresh and further Discovery of the Errors, Heresies, Blasphemies, and dangerous Proceedings of the Sectaries of this time*, had at least one further edition, but for the Third Part, *A new and higher Discovery of the Errors, Heresies, Blasphemies, and insolent Proceedings of the Sectaries of these times . . .*, one printing seems to have sufficed (Fig. 1), and there were no reissues of any part until a facsimile edition was produced in 1977. It was very much a product of debates and anxieties centred in London in the mid-1640s.

Gangraena aroused wide debate in print and elsewhere; some twenty pamphlets in 1646–47 directly addressed it, while countless other tracts commented on Edwards and his work. It was discussed in London streets, in Essex parsonages, and in Parliament's army, becoming indeed an army grievance in the spring of 1647, when the soldiers denounced the "many scandalous Books, such as Mr Edwards Gangraena," whose "false calumnies" made them "odious to the kingdom."[5] Book and author ultimately acquired a single notorious personification so that Hugh Peter could defend the army's conduct in London in August 1647 by insisting, "I doe professe I conceive even *Gangraena* himselfe might have marcht through the Army unmolested."[6]

This was a profoundly controversial notoriety. *Gangraena*, like all of Edwards's published works, was written as part of a campaign for a reformed, comprehensive, and compulsory national Protestant Church; he has become one of the archetypal high Presbyterians of the mid–seventeenth century, one of the minority of English figures willing to accept a Scottish-style church-government.[7] We will search his writings in vain, however, for any extended positive justification of the Presbyterian way. His polemical instincts were most often negative, driven by a long-standing opposition to separation from a national church. Much of his adult life was spent in combating moves toward any form of religious liberty, even for relatively respectable Congregationalists, denouncing "toleration" as the doorway to a horrifying eruption of blasphemy, separatism, and heresy. It is not surprising that he aroused widely contrasting contemporary judgments. Edwards located himself in a tradition of defenders of orthodoxy from Paul, through Augustine, Epiphanius, and Theodoret to Luther, Calvin, and Beza, and sought consolation in the knowledge that his predecessors too had "suffered many reproaches, and yet rejoyced, counting their sufferings a signe of their greater glory." He appropriated also the authority (through criticism) of the most potent product of orthodox, zealous Protestant print culture, Foxe's *Book of Martyrs*: "as the Jesuits and Papists did by Mr Foxes Book of Martyrs, give out it was a Book of lyes . . . and yet all the Protestants know it was full of truths and is of pretious esteem in the Church of God. Just so do the Sectaries now by my Book" (1, sig. B2ᵛ; 2.45).

For Edwards's friends and supporters, he was the "faithful friend of truth," valiantly unmasking the evil doctrines and foul behavior of radical sectaries. For those attacked in *Gangraena*, and for others sympathetic to liberty of conscience, however, his book was, in the words of John Goodwin, one of Edwards's prime targets, a work of "shameless untruths." Another reader, Cheney Culpeper, considered it so intemperate and destructive it was best used for lavatory paper: "I . . . doe . . . repine at the price, of which I can fine noe returne but to spend by peecemeale in a house of office." To the Baptist Edward Drapes, Edwards was "the father of lyes"; to another, anonymous, radical, "the famous forger of these latter dayes." Most famously, Edwards attracted the opprobrium of John Milton, a minor target of *Gangraena*: "Men whose life, learning, faith and pure intent / Would have been held in high esteem with Paul / Must now be named and printed heretics / By shallow Edwards and Scotch What-d'ye-call."[8]

Modern judgments have been equally polarized, with twentieth-century historical debate focusing on the value of *Gangraena* as a source for radical beliefs and behavior.[9] Christopher Hill and J. Colin Davis represent contrasting stances. Hill has of course used *Gangraena* frequently and straightfor-wardly as a source for religious radicalism—for general comments on the atmo-sphere of the 1640s, and for specific radical opinions and activities. In one essay, he concludes: "We need not accept the alarmist accounts of professional heresy-hunters like Edwards, Baillie, Rutherford, Pagitt, Ross, and several more—though Edwards's *Gangraena* at least is well documented and seems to stand up quite well to examination: we need a critical edition."[10]

Colin Davis, on the other hand, regards Edwards and other "heresiogra-phers" as forerunners of the "yellow press" journalists who, in his view, created the "Ranter Sensation" in 1650–51: "Before the Ranters worshipped pewter pots and practised all indency, Independents and Baptists were apparently busy doing so." In passing, he stresses the need for work on *Gangraena*, taking up Hill's remarks: "What does 'well documented' mean in this context? Where has been the sustained examination of Edwards' documentation and its qual-ity? Isn't the need for a critical edition an admission that these things have not been done?"[11]

Until recently, there has been no sustained examination of Edwards's methods and sources, perhaps because of profound—and contradictory—pre-suppositions about his plausibility. Put simply, Hill believes *Gangraena* to be broadly true, because Edwards's account of the range and importance of radi-calism accords with his own (although their attitudes toward the phenomenon are obviously entirely different) and so there is little need to check his material. Davis, on the other hand, has offered some salutary warnings about using polemically or generically structured printed works as sources for the beliefs and actions of their radical targets. His book focuses on the distortions of the pamphlet polemic, rather than alternative sources, perhaps because he assumes there are few sectaries to be found: "The heresiographers are suspect, if not worse, as sources of what, *if anything*, was *actually* happening on the margins of religious orthodoxy" (Davis 127). It is not clear how we could discover, defini-tively, what actually happened or what purer, presumably manuscript, source would be decisive. Indeed it is almost as if religious radicalism did not exist precisely because alarmed orthodox writers exaggerated or misrepresented it.

* * *

Connected to the cleavage between Hill and Davis about the nature and im-portance of radical ideas and movements, there are contrasting attitudes to printed sources, one perhaps too credulous, the other too sceptical. It is in this context that any judgement about the value of *Gangraena* as a source must be made. This is not the place for an extensive study of the accuracy—I would prefer to say the plausibility—of *Gangraena*. Detailed historical research can check alternative sources and contrasting interpretative frameworks for many of Edwards's stories and errors.[12] There is little sign that Edwards invented his material, and many of his details of name, time, and place can be confirmed from other sources. But these bare facts take us only so far; more often we discern profoundly divergent interpretations of what are recognizably the same books or the same incidents. Contextualizing *Gangraena* most often serves to confirm the provisional and contested nature of any "true" account; no easy and definitive conclusions can be reached. Suffice it to say that much of Edwards's material is worth taking seriously as one account of what was going on; but that *Gangraena* should not be regarded as some comprehensive, systematic catalogue, notwithstanding its self-presentation as such. It was a Londoner's book, concentrating on radical excesses in the city and the pernicious impact of Londoners (and soldiers) on the provinces rather than presenting a local perspective. It was a book that focused on political activists and open troublemakers rather than on intellectual heresies per se. And it was, as Colin Davis has insisted, a book that sought to smear respectable Independents by stealth, through associating them with the outrageous exploits of more radical sectaries. Besides these structural "biases" it is clear that *Gangraena* presented often a random picture of what came to the hands of an author, working under great pressure, through his particular contacts and networks. Edwards's versions of radical books, for example, were as often careless as deliberately distorted.

As we have seen, Edwards appealed to Foxe as a model of embattled truth telling. In an important study, Patrick Collinson has suggested, "the question of Foxe's strict veracity, though by no means unimportant, is perhaps the smallest of the problems facing historians."[13] This chapter likewise argues that we will have an impoverished understanding of the importance of *Gangraena* if we explore it only as a source, and not also as a text, as a phenomenon in its own right, rather as historians are beginning to do for crucial sixteenth-century works such as the *Book of Martyrs* or John Knox's *History of the Reformation*.[14] On the whole, until recently, in England as in France, the importance of print culture in revolutionary upheavals has been undervalued or misconceived: "Historians generally treat the printed word as a record of what happened, instead of as an ingredient in the happening."[15]

My crucial presupposition is that books matter, they are an "ingredient in the happening," created out of a mysterious engagement of an individual author with the concerns of the day, and the materials and methods available to him. Books have an impact on how people understand their experiences and on how they act. A book like *Gangraena* is thus an event in itself, as much as a record of events, part of the "context" for religious conflict in 1646–48, both highlighting the dangers of error and separatism and stimulating an orthodox fight back. Insofar as print culture has been explored for the revolution, the stress has been on the radical pamphleteers, and I hope there may be particular value in discussing the (superficially) less attractive orthodox or Presbyterian parliamentarian approaches to print culture.[16] A full study would address a variety of issues: generic parallels and models for Edwards, the methods by which *Gangraena* was made to look true, its readership, and its connections with political and religious mobilization in the mid-1640s.[17] This chapter concentrates on what Edwards's *Gangraena* reveals about the nature of print culture itself.

Edwards wrote in a world where many people were becoming confidently literate for the first time, and where civil war and parliamentarian factionalism brought into being an effervescent, relatively cheap, extremely responsive print culture, producing a multitude of small printed texts—newsbooks and other pamphlets—which were a very rapid response to open-ended dilemmas and unresolved crises.[18] Print was a crucial aspect of political and religious conflict and debate but one not yet to be taken for granted. There is a notable self-consciousness about the processes of writing, print, and publication within *Gangraena*. Edwards did not present his work as a smooth, seamless, finished product, but as a rough and unfinished reflection of the ever emerging, ever more frightening burgeoning of religious dissent. This indeed is one of the many techniques (if technique does not imply too deliberate a policy) by which *Gangraena* acquired a "look of truth."

The very construction of his books, Edwards insisted, was the result of a continuous struggle between his own decisions and purposes on the one hand, and unpredictable outside pressures on the other. He explained why he could not include as much material as he wished: "because I have already exceeded that number of sheets I intended," a refrain which occurs over and over again to justify the omission of a reply to the "Erastian" Thomas Coleman, an extended account of the subversive preaching of Hugh Peter or the "insolent loose ungodly practices" of John Lilburne (although these two last targets are allocated many pages each) (1.115; 3.146, 153).

A particularly good example of the foregrounding of printing processes for readers is found in Edwards's discussion at the end of Part Three of the death of the respectable Independent Jeremiah Burroughs, with whom Edwards had conducted an extended and complex dispute about the accuracy of *Gangraena*, through printed works, manuscript exchange, and bookshop debate: "it hath pleased God (before my Third Part of *Gangraena* could be printed) to take Master *Burroughs* out of this life (for which I am heartily sorry, and the more, besides that I should have bin glad he might have read my book, because I do conceive the putting it forth after his death may be liable to . . . mis-constructions." Edwards also regretted, that two or three places might be said to be "a speaking evill of the dead, I desire to let the Reader know, they were both written and printed off long before Master *Burroughs* sicknesse and death . . . no understanding man will once imagine a Booke of above Forty sheets could be made, written out, and printed in a month . . . the Book-seller and Printer can testifie this Third Part hath been above this quarter of a yeare in the Presse a printing" (3.286–87, 290).

Printing practices were open and transparent in revolutionary London, as Edwards's polemical career revealed at many points. His earlier work, the *Antapologia* (written against the Assembly Independents' *Apologeticall Narra-tion*) was responded to (by Sidrach Simpson) before it was published; while Edwards's most bitter antagonist, John Goodwin, enraged him by entering another reply in the Stationers' Company Hall book, and then not publishing it for over a year.[19] Edwards himself took advantage of a preview of a reply to Part One of *Gangraena*: "I hear that one *Web* hath an Answer in the Presse to what I relate of him in *pag.* 106, 107. which Answer, before it went to the Presse, by a providence came to my hand without ever seeking it, or indeed imagining that ever *Web* (such an Heretick and Blasphemer) durst have appeared in print" (2.110, 137).

Publishing was for Edwards an entirely partisan affair. He denounced the radical publishers, "One [Giles] Calvert a Sectary and a Book-seller on Lud-gate hill," and Henry Overton, "an Independent Book-seller and a member of Master *John Goodwin*'s Church" (adding a marginal note, "All kind of un-licensed Books that *make* any ways for the Sects and against the Presbyterians are sold at his shop"). But his most virulent attacks were reserved for the Independent licenser of religious books, John Bachelor, who gave a spurious respectability to sectarian books. Edwards subjected Bachelor's licensing to an analysis as meticulous as ever Prynne did Laudian press censorship, noting his glosses on a second edition of an Anabaptist argument for toleration, Leonard Busher's *Religious Peace*, first published in 1614, as well as his revisions to Webb's text (3.9; 3.103–5; 2.137–39).

A polemicist like Edwards could respond very rapidly to events. Part One of *Gangraena* was registered with the Stationers' Company on 8 January 1646, but not received by Thomason until 26 February (although it was described by the Scots minister Robert Baillie as among "some late books" on 20 Febru-ary).[20] The first seventy-six pages of Part One were printed separately from the rest, and the complicated, extended production process meant that Edwards could report on recent correspondence and events and note recent tracts. He quoted several items which were not licensed, completed, or received by Thomason until after 8 January, including the second edition of the Con-fession of Faith of the London Baptist churches, "which came not to my hand till Feb. 13." The postscript to Part One also reported on the London Common

Council meeting of 16 January where complaints were heard of the preaching of Hugh Peter and William Hawkins (1.183–84).[21]

* * *

Furthermore, in the political culture of the 1640s, there was an intimate inter-action between fundamental religious and political crisis where basic assump-tions and basic truths were called in question, and there was profound ques-tioning over the validity of different types of communication and the status of various categories of "evidence."[22] This is seen clearly both within *Gangraena* itself and in the ensuing, wide-ranging contemporary debate it provoked. In his initial narratives, and even more when his accounts were challenged, Ed-wards was always insistent—over insistent—on validating his stories in an overt and elaborate fashion. Much of his discussion focused on the mutually rein-forcing claims of direct oral testimony and written material. A well-known account of a *"Disputation held at the Spitle* about *the Immortality of the Soul,"* featuring the first appearance in *Gangraena* of the future Leveller, Richard Overton, was justified at length: "This Relation was given me under the hand of a godly honest Citizen, who was an eare and eye witnesse of all the said passages, who also named to me other persons that were present, and he delivered me this Relation in writing before two sufficient witnesses, and de-clared himself ready to make proof of this before Authority when ever he should be called" (2.17–18).

As this shows, Edwards himself was sharply aware both of the specifici-ties of print, and of the competing claims of other, oral and manuscript forms. Modern discussions to some extent represent or re-present a range of seventeenth-century positions.[23] The authorizing "presence" of an individual speaker could give direct speech a validity lacking in mutable printed forms, whose meaning could not be controlled. Publication of written material in printed form, as opposed to "scribal publication," remained controversial and required specific justification as a strategy for achieving influence, throughout our period. Yet print, which "fixed" a message and subjected it to wide public scrutiny, had in other contexts an authority which speech lacked. *Gangraena's* controversial authority was based on a variety of communication strategies— printed, written, and spoken. It was their juxtapositions, their mutual rein-forcement, that carried conviction: direct ear and eyewitness reports communi-cated orally and backed up by written testimony; oral endorsement of printed works. No claim was made for the inherent superiority of particular types of evidence.

Gangraena, a part work and a composite production, was an interactive text par excellence. It presupposed an existing print culture, drawing on earlier accounts of error, notably Prynne's *A Fresh Discovery of Some Prodigious New Wandering Blasing-Stars & Firebrands, Stiling themselves New-Lights* (London: for Michael Sparke, 1645) and Thomas Gataker's attack on "Antinomians" in *Gods Eye on his Israel* (London: for Fulke Clifton, 1645); as well as on the radical or wicked books themselves. Edwards's only direct sighting of the veteran radical Clement Writer was "On April the 9. 1645. being that day commonly called Easter Wednesday in Peter Cole's book-shop in Cornhill, I going to him to help me to an unlicensed Book" (1.82–83).

The production of *Gangraena* depended on elaborate information networks, many characteristic of 1640s London, through which stories and lists of errors were given to Edwards by word of mouth or in writing. Edwards could take advantage of a wide personal acquaintance through London Presbyterian connections, forged at Sion College and elsewhere. But much other material came from people who did not know him personally, but had come to hear of him as an author and lecturer, dedicated to opposing error and separatism. A London lecture was "a brave center for all kindes of correspondencey." Edwards, "the controversie Lecturer" performed regularly at Christ Church, Newgate, "the heart of the city"—the epithets come from John Tombes and Robert Baillie.[24] This church was the venue for many of the great set-piece occasions where city and parliamentary authorities met for fast and thanksgiving sermons. It was convenient for news of Common Council and other meetings at the Guildhall, as Edwards's knowledge of the investigation of Hugh Peter reveals; for the bookshops and other news-gathering venues of Cornhill, the Exchange, and Pauls. *Gangraena* offers many vivid insights into city gossip networks: Edwards explained how he had come across startling blasphemies uttered by Robert Cosens in Rochester, through a chance meeting with a member of the Westminster Assembly, a "reverend, learned, godly, humble, retired man . . . who . . . did not make it his businesse or work to tell mee this story . . . but I, going in London upon my occasions, this Minister accidentally being in a shop with a friend of his, a Citizen whom I know also, I spake to them as I was going by . . . the last sheet of my Book being either printing off, or quite printed off, I put it in a Postscript, as the Reader sees" (2.127).

We should note again Edwards's presentation of his work as an ever developing process, but this passage, chosen from many possibilities, also suggests the particular advantages a Londoner compiling something like *Gangraena* had in the 1640s. A permanently sitting Parliament gave provincial people the opportunity to correspond regularly with their MPs; two ministers from each English county sat in the Westminster Assembly, preaching in city churches while they kept in touch with friends at home. Both Assembly and Parliament received formal complaints about dangerous books and religious radicals from 1643; many of the same targets, John Archer's *Comfort for Be-*

lievers, or the opinions of Paul Best and Thomas Webb, feature in *Gangraena*, as do very many individual letters sent to MPs or members of the Assembly and passed on to Edwards.[25] Finally, Edwards drew on contacts within Presbyterian publishing networks. Edwards's usual publisher, Ralph Smith of Cornhill, specialized in official declarations of the Westminster Assembly and other decidedly Presbyterian works. John Brinsley of Yarmouth, another of Smith's authors, contributed material to *Gangraena* (2.161–62), while stories about Independents in Manchester and West Yorkshire were sent in by Thomas Smith, a Manchester bookseller.[26] Edwards's fame as the controversial author of *Antapologia* and then of Parts One and Two of *Gangraena*, in which he urged those alarmed by sectarian activity to send him further evidence, produced many letters of denunciation.

Gangraena thus drew on other books, other texts, on angry and alarmed conversations. Once published it stimulated a range of other controversial encounters as it became embroiled in fierce competition for meaning with other texts. It was not simply challenged in print, but provoked manuscript denials and denunciations as well as direct confrontations. In the preface to Part Three (see Fig. 1), Edwards described how some of those "mentioned in Letters written up to friends, and printed by me, have come to my house, denying peremptorily those things spoken of them in the Letters" (sig. *4^r–^{v}). Robert Cosens, John Mascall of Dover, John Saltmarsh, John Lanseter, Thomas Collier, and Henry Pinnell of Poole were amongst Edwards's opponents who came to challenge him in person. There was a particularly vivid encounter with Hugh Peter. On 3 June 1646, Edwards was "walking in *Westminster* Hall, Master *Peters* meeting me, spake to me, that I had abused him in Print, and that I had broken a Gospel rule, which was, *If thy Brother offend thee, go and tell him his fault between him and thee alone*" (3.127). Edwards was unrepentant, and when Peter complained, "coming twice up from the Army; each time he found himself in a Book of mine: I told him . . . he was like to be in a third Book; whereupon he call'd me Knave, and stincking fellow" (3.126).

Debates over the validity of *Gangraena* stimulated further manuscript material; letters of support and elaboration are one obvious phenomenon, as is the solicitation of written denials or corroboration of Edwards's stories. One brief but crucial story, taking up less than a page in Part One, provoked much further discussion, manuscript rebuttals, and extended discussion in at least four printed works besides the later parts of *Gangraena*.[27] This was Edwards's assertion that the relatively respectable Independents Jeremiah Burroughs and William Greenhill were so alarmed by the "wicked opinions" of one "Nichols who lives about Moor-Fields, that comes into Stepney parish sometimes to draw away people" that they held a special meeting to see what could be done to curb him (thus compromising their commitment to liberty of conscience).

John Goodwin printed a denial solicited from Burroughs, that it was "all false . . . I never heard there was such a man in this world, till I read it in Mr Edwards his book."

Edwards had to respond to criticism from such respected men, including a twelve-page justification of the original story in *Gangraena*, Part Two. An eyewitness Mr. Allen [in fact Mr Alle], "of Stepney parish . . . related it to divers in Master Bellamy's shop, in my hearing," after which Edwards wrote a full account in his diary. But Burroughs got Alle to sign a note confirming his rival version, and printed this further manuscript in own rebuttal of Edwards. Then Alle largely reiterated Edwards's account in print, providentially he claimed: "Seeing the hand of providence, for so it is that hath ordered it, and doth order all things, for I had no thought nor knowledge of my being brought upon the Stage in Print, untill I saw my name in Master Edwards His Book called Gangraena." However, this accidental turn to print is rendered suspicious by the fact that Alle's work is produced by Edwards's printers and publisher. Burroughs's tract then appeared where he had some fun with the fact that Edwards got his supposed ally's name wrong, and Edwards was left fuming because of Burroughs's premature death, as we have seen.[28]

* * *

Colin Davis has suggested that one problem with *Gangraena* as a source is its "indiscriminate jostling of different groups, sources and types of information" (*Fear*, 127). I have tried to suggest that this becomes an advantage in explorations of *Gangraena* as a text within the religious culture of the period. It was a text that both depended on and helped to foster lively and bitter pamphlet confrontations, which were themselves inextricably connected with the circulation of letters and other manuscripts and were both the product and the subject of oral controversy. This is not to suggest that print was interchangeable with other forms of communication or debate—a point amply demonstrated in the careful distinctions drawn by Edwards himself.

One specific importance of print is its capacity to forge abstract communities. Eisenstein's classic account holds that "Printed materials encouraged silent adherence to causes whose advocates could not be found in any one parish and who addressed an invisible public from afar." Local loyalties were overlaid by larger collectivities.[29] Yet *Gangraena* can be seen to harness a variety of local communities to its own production and the ensuing debate over its validity. Edwards's text built on, relied on, but also constructed and reconstituted opposed abstract communities of (in his judgement) the godly and orthodox versus heretics and sectaries. The creation of his books depended, as we have seen, on information from a range of supporters, some personally already familiar to him but others who knew him only from reading his books:

"I would bee glad to know of Mr Edwards the Antagonist of Hereticks what to do in this matter; To whom though unknown, I present my love in the Lord," wrote one Oxfordshire minister in June 1646, sending in an alarmed account of the disorderly preaching of army chaplains (*Gangraena* 3.62).

Discussing Edwards's books or the errors and sectaries described in them was a means, in itself, of reinforcing local communities of the clergy whose networks risked fragmentation and division in the complex debates of the mid-1640s.[30] One letter from a group of ministers included in *Gangraena* acknowledged the great service Edwards had done for the defense of the church against schism and heresy. He was "well known to us all," through his books which had been discussed at their weekly meeting (2.48–49). "A worthy and godly Minister in Suffolk" wrote "in the name, and by the consent and agreement of other Ministers of the County at a meeting of theirs." "God make you as *Augustine, Malleum Haereticorum*," they prayed, informing Edwards of "late prancks of some Sectaries . . . One is of *Oates* the Anabaptist (whom your Gangraena takes notice of)." Another was "one *Lanchester of Bury*"; this latter brief account stimulated an extended pamphlet defense by John Lanseter and another awkward personal encounter (2.20–21).[31]

In such a fashion, *Gangraena* surely contributed to Presbyterian petitioning campaigns and collective condemnations of error in 1646–48. Furthermore, the mutual printed citations and defenses of each others' work among London polemicists like Edwards, Josiah Ricraft, John Jones, and John Vicars, as well as in the more extended polemics of Prynne, Bastwick, and Robert Baillie, attempted to suggest a community united against error. Affectionate citation evaded the real differences between Prynne, say, and Edwards, particularly over the extent of clerical power, in the cause of unity.[32]

As far as the sects were concerned, Edwards himself insisted he was dealing with abstract communities, partly in response to accusations of personal animosity (1.178): "I can say it truly of all those men whom I principally lay open, and give the people warning of, that I have had nothing to do with them, and they have not wronged me at all, but as they have wronged the truth, and the glory of God; and among all these notorious sectaries, excepting *Wrighter*, and one or two more, I know them not so much as by face, having never so much as to my knowledge as seen them: I never saw *Den, Hich, Clarkson, Paul Hobson, Web, Lamb, Marshal*, with many others named in this Book."

His opponents too constituted themselves as a community in print, in some cases reacting in ways which seemed to justify Edwards's blurring of distinctions between Independents and more radical sectaries. John Goodwin, for example, replied to *Gangraena* on his own account, but also defended many other radicals with whom he was acquainted (but not necessarily in agreement), amongst them William Kiffin, William Walwyn, Jeremiah Burroughs,

Hugh Peter, and Samuel Eaton. He wrote on behalf of others whom he had
met only to discuss their mutual featuring in *Gangraena*, such as Cosens of
Rochester and still others, such as John Ellis of Colchester with whom he had
merely corresponded about Edwards's attacks.[33]

One of Edwards's main polemical purposes was to implicate "respectable
Independents" in the encouragement of pernicious error and sectarianism, as
seen in his comments on John Bachelor's help for Webb: "so that wee may see,
the Independents will not lose any of the most blasphemous, Atheisticall he-
reticall men, but further them, and joyn with them against the Presbyterians"
(2.138). Repeatedly in *Gangraena*'s general sections on the practices of sectaries
or in the deductions or corollaries he drew from the contemporary religious
ferment, Edwards coupled together "sectaries and Independents" interchange-
ably. The response of Burroughs, along with the generous scope of Goodwin's
writings against *Gangraena*, helped to make plausible Edwards's notion of a
continuum between the relatively respectable and the completely horrifying.

The attempt to construct such a continuum in all three parts of *Gangraena*
was intended to have an immediate, practical impact: as Edwards declared at
the end of Part Three in December 1646: "Oh if so few [sectaries] have done so
much, and that in a bad cause, what might not we doe in a good cause, if
courageous, zealous and intent upon it? . . . we might in a short time break the
hearts and the neck of that faction" (281). The city of London in particular was
urged to lead the assault against sectarianism. Edwards repeatedly bemoaned
Presbyterian backsliding: "*such a time have we fallen into of Lukewarmnesse*" (3,
sig. [ ]r).

In order to encourage Presbyterian determination, Edwards was as anxious for a wide and engaged, active readership as any Leveller or radical sectary.
It would be misleading to assume a repressive Presbyterian attitude to print
culture, opposed to radical desires for open debate. *Gangraena* was to be "a
manuall that might be for every ones reading," as Edwards "(. . . took a reso-
lution in the entrance of this worke, not to be too large) that so the more might
both buy and read it" (1.8, 41–42). He wanted also an active, judicious readership, urging all readers to weigh up the evidence presented, to compare his own
account "with what *Cretensis* has written anent his businesse." His targets
included sectaries themselves: hoping that many "who have been deceived . . .
many in the way who are not of the way . . . that all such upon the discovering
to them, the dangerous Errors, Heresies, pernicious practices" will "forsake
them . . . and return to the publike Assemblies" (2.120, 203).

Edwards's accounts of rival communities were not, initially at least, accurate descriptions of political/religious divisions in 1645–46, but attempts to
conjure up such a rigid polarization. As such *Gangraena* worked on fluid politi-

cal identities during a period of massive disruption and shifting possibilities, where disparate groups could be united, for a time at least, against a perceived common enemy. *Gangraena* contributed to a fatally simplified polarization of beleaguered orthodox Puritan Presbyterians on the one hand, and threatened radical sectaries, soldiers, and Independents on the other; the writing and reading of this book made a difference.

Apparently more trivial or particular matters, however, can as effectively highlight some of the less tangible effects of print in the religious culture of the 1640s. *Gangraena* contributed to the notoriety of its targets (as well as its author). Samuel Oates and Laurence Clarkson are among several examples of sectaries whose very appearance in *Gangraena* was a crucial part of their notoriety. Edwards's correspondents looked out for the radicals he denounced and then sent further alarmist accounts for inclusion in later volumes: "The last Sabbath day we had one *Clarkson* a Seeker that Preached at *Butolph* Church, the same man I beleeve that Mr. *Edwards* mentions in his Book: His sermon tended to the vilifying of the Scriptures, all Ordinances, Duties, Ministers, Churchstate" (2.165).

The pernicious books they write are crucial to the fame of the sectaries: "one Lawrence Clarkson, a Seeker, spoken of in my *Gangraena*, *pag.* 104, and 105. who put forth a pamphlet called *The Pilgrimage of Saints*" (2.7). This is not to argue that such men were merely "media stars" and had no "real" influence; as Edwards's whole project reveals, Presbyterians feared intensely the real power they believed radical writings had.

Ironically, of course, Edwards massively added to the publicity accorded men like Clarkson and their books. In his later spiritual autobiography, *The Lost Sheep Found*, Clarkson described a journey to Gravesend, where he sought the "strange opinionated people."[34] In the alehouse they frequented "a few words uttered" by Clarkson ensured a warm welcome. The victualler "brought me some bread and cheese, with which I was refreshed, and bid me take no care, for I should want for nothing, you being the man that writ *The Pilgrimage of Saints*." This was a very rare book with no surviving copies, in contrast to the many copies of *Gangraena*. It is not fanciful to suggest that the strange opinionated people of Gravesend knew Edwards's Clarkson rather than the original book.

We do not need to accept *Gangraena* as an accurate description of "reality" to assess its value in discussions of the role of print in the upheavals of the 1640s. The labels, categories, or stereotypes through which people seek to define what is true or orthodox, to demonize opponents as outsiders, as "other," have a real impact in a real world because they influence (to put it no stronger) how that world is experienced and understood. Furthermore, labels have to have some plausibility—some recognizable connection to how individuals behave—if they are to have any polemical effect. Hence in both drawing on existing stereotypes and divisions and seeking to reinforce them, Edwards's *Gangraena* had a major impact on contemporary perceptions and contemporary action.

Gangraena did not convince readers primarily through intellectual arguments about heresy, but through tapping into a range of profound cultural themes or scripts—some concerned with gender or family dramas, others with narratives of danger and deceit, still others with transgressive behavior involving animals, as we began this chapter. The cultural resources, resonance, and impact of *Gangraena* can finally be demonstrated by returning to the baptism of cats. A legal case does not prove Edwards's story was true, but it does suggest how in the crowded, intimate milieu of the city of London, many people would have discussed the sectarian outrage and the acquiescence of an Independent magistrate, and thus found Edwards's account familiar and plausible.

But the legal case itself should be related to preexisting assumptions. There is a prehistory of plausibility for such incidents. Stories that sectaries baptized animals were long-established.[35] We should be cautious in concluding that animal baptism was widespread, but it is possible that such traditions provided a script to follow for would-be Anabaptists, and more likely that the orthodox expected and believed sectaries would do such things. Of course, *Gangraena* extended the currency of such stories, both directly and through the recycling of Edwards's material in a range of antisectarian print. In the Dr. Williams's library copy of one such work, Samuel Clarke's *Golden Apples . . . sundry Questions and Cases of Conscience*,[36] a later seventeenth-century reader included a comment dated 19 May 1692, "The Anabaptists are very angry with Mr Slater for saying thay baptize dogs & Cats in degradation of infant Baptizme. see the 149 page of this Book words to the same Efect." Again we see books in juxtaposition with previous assumptions and conversations. Turning to page 149, Clarke's "error 28" reads, "That it's as lawfull to Baptize Dogs, and Cats, and Horses, as Infants of Believer." It is Edwards's error 104 again, probably conflated with the story of Eastern Association soldiers baptizing a horse in Huntingdonshire, also spread by *Gangraena* (3.17–18). To be effective, Edwards's stories about religious radicals had to have some relation to readers' other experiences and frameworks for interpreting those experiences, they had to chime in with other contemporary versions of reality. In turn, whether he was writing of the dangerously radical ambitions of the New Model Army, or the propensity of Anabaptists to baptize naked women and animals, Edwards's stories and lists of errors had a most significant impact on contemporary understandings of religious divisions. His book was clearly "an ingredient in the happening."

Notes

My work on *Gangraena* has been supported by generous grants from the British Academy, the Leverhulme Trust, and the Humanities Research Board, and has benefited enormously from the skilled research assistance of Kate Peters.

1. The cases involving the Platts are discussed in Keith Lindley, "London and Popular Freedom in the 1640s," *Freedom and the English Revolution*, ed. R. C. Richardson and R. M. Ridden (Manchester: Manchester University Press, 1986) and idem, *Popular Politics and Religion in Civil War London* (Aldershot: Scholar Press, 1997), 291, 301–2. For Dawlman see Henry R. Plomer, *A Dictionary of the Booksellers and Printers who were at work in England . . . 1641–1667* (London: Bibliographical Society, 1907), 63. For his support for Burton see Henry Burton, *Truth still Truth Though shut out of Doores* (London: for Giles Calvert, 1645), 25. The sessions' records are in London Metropolitan Archives, MJ/SR 952/56–57, 956/32–37, 215, 958/125, 959/22, 25.

2. *Gangraena* I.28, 67. For convenience all quotations are from the facsimile edition of *Gangraena* published by the Rota at the University of Exeter in 1977, although this is something of a hybrid. All editions of all three parts were originally published by Ralph Smith in London in 1646.

3. Diane Purkiss, *The Witch in History: Early Modern and Twentieth-Century Representations* (London: Routledge, 1996), 70–71.

4. Murray Tolmie, *The Triumph of the Saints: The Separate Churches of London, 1626–1649* (Cambridge: Cambridge University Press, 1977), 134.

5. *Divers Papers from the Army* (London: May, 1647), quoted in Austin Woolrych, *Soldiers and Statesmen: The General Council of the Army and Its Debates, 1647–1648* (Oxford: Clarendon Press, 1987), 83, 92.

6. Hugh Peter, *A Word for the Armie and two Words to the Kingdome* (London: for Giles Calvert, 1647), 7–8.

7. Valerie Pearl, "London Puritans and Scotch Fifth Columnists: A Mid–Seventeenth Century Phenomenon," *Studies in London History*, ed. A. E. J. Hollaender and W. Kellaway (London: Hodder and Stoughton, 1969): 317–51.

8. [John Jones,] *Plain English or the Sectaries Anatomized* (London: for Ralph Smith, 1646), B.L. E 350 (11), with Thomason's note that it was by "Captaine Jones," a well-known Presbyterian activist. "The Letters of Sir Cheney Culpeper, 1645–1657," *Seventeenth Century Political and Financial Papers*, ed. M. J. Braddick and Mark Greengrass (Camden Miscellany, 33, Camden Fifth Series, vol. 7 [1996]): 266 (24 February 1646); Edward Drapes, *A Plain and Faithfull Discovery of A Beame in Master Edwards his Eye* (London: for William Larner, 1646), 21; *A Letter to Mr Thomas Edwards* (London: for Thomas Veere, 1647), 10; John Goodwin, *Cretensis or A Briefe Answer to an Ulcerous Treatise . . . Intituled Gangraena* (London: for Henry Overton, 1646, pp. 49, 50. Milton's book, *The Doctrine and discipline of Divorce*, was cited in Part I, p. 34; for his sonnet, "On the New Forces of Conscience under the Long parliament," which ends, "New Presbyter is but old Priest writ large," see *John Milton*, ed. Stephen Orgel and Jonathon Goldberg (Oxford: Oxford Authors, 1990), 83–84.

9. A recent stimulating treatment by a literary scholar is Kristen Poole, "Dissecting Sectarianism: Liberty of Conscience, the Swarm and Thomas Edwards' *Gangraena*," *Form and Reform in Renaissance England: Essays in Honor of Barbara Kiefer Lewalski*, ed. Amy Boesky and Mary Thomas Crane (Newark, Del.: Associated University Presses, 2000), 45–69.

10. Christopher Hill, *The World Turned Upside Down* (Harmondsworth: Penguin, 1972; rpt. 1975); see, for example, 191, 166, 148, 187–89; Hill, *Milton and the English Revolution* (London: Faber, 1977; rpt. 1979), 293, 308 on antitrinitarianism and mortalism where Edwards is quoted as an introduction to Milton's views; Hill, "Irreligion in the "Puritan Revolution," *Radical Religion in the English Revolution*, ed. J. F. McGregor and B. Reay (Oxford: Clarendon Press, 1984), 198, 200, 203, 206.

11. Colin Davis, *Fear, Myth and History: the Ranters and the Historians* (Cambridge: Cambridge University Press, 1986), 129.

12. Alternative accounts of religious radicalism in London and provincial England occupy Part 3 of my forthcoming book on *Gangraena*.

13. Patrick Collinson, "Truth and Legend: the Veracity of John Foxe's *Book of Martyrs*," *Elizabethan Essays* (London: Hambledon Press, 1994), 177.

14. A British Academy project is exploring all aspects of Foxe's text, see *John Foxe and the English Reformation*, ed. David Loades (Aldershot: Scolar Press, 1992); Roger A. Mason, "Usable Pasts: History and Identity in Reformation Scotland," *Scottish Historical Review*, 76 (1997).

15. "Introduction," *Revolution in Print: The Press in France 1775–1800*, ed. Robert Darnton and Daniel Roche (Berkeley: University of California Press, 1989), xiii.

16. Sharon Achinstein, *Milton and the Revolutionary Reader* (Princeton, N.J.: Princeton University Press, 1994); Neil Keeble, *The Literary Culture of Nonconformity in later Seventeenth-Century England* (Leicester: Leicester University Press, 1987) are pioneering studies in this field.

17. Again I must refer readers to my forthcoming book.

18. For general treatments of these developments see Dagmar Freist, *Governed by Opinion. Politics, Religion and the Dynamics of Communication in Stuart London, 1637–1645* (London: Tauris Academic Studies, 1997); Nigel Smith, *Literature and Revolution in England, 1640–1660* (New Haven: Yale University Press, 1994); Joad Raymond, *The Invention of the Newspaper: English Newsbooks, 1641–1649* (Oxford: Oxford University Press, 1996).

19. Sidrach Simpson, *The Anatomist Anatomis'd: or a short Answer to An Anatomy of Independencie* (London: for Peter Cole, 1644), mainly intended as a reply to Alexander Forbes, discussed *Antapologia* in a preface. Goodwin's work was entered in July 1645 but did not appear until August 1646: *A transcript of the registers of the Worshipful Company of Stationers from 1640–1708* (London: Privately printed, 1913–14), 179; *Anapologesiates Antapologias* (London: for Henry Overton, 1646). The city clergy seem to be an exception to Adrian Johns's account of the Stationers' jealous guarding of the mysteries of their trade: *The Nature of the Book. Print and Knowledge in the Making* (Chicago: University of Chicago Press, 1998), 102–3, 128, 137, 196–97.

20. *Stationers' Register*, p. 210; B.L. E 323 (2) for Thomason's copy of Part One; *The Letters and Journals of Robert Baillie*, ed. David Laing, 3 vols. (Edinburgh: A. Lawrie, 1841), 2: 352.

21. City of London Record Office, Journal of the Common Council 40, f. 166r. Dates have been taken from Thomason, Prefaces and *Stationers' Register*. Part Two was similarly up to date.

22. See Smith, *Literature and Revolution*, chpt. 1.

23. There is a burgeoning literature on such matters. Among much else I have found the following particularly useful: Roger Chartier, *The Order of Books* (Oxford: Polity, 1994); Harold Love, *Scribal Publication in Seventeenth-Century England* (Ox-

ford: Clarendon Press, 1993); D. F. McKenzie, "Speech—Manuscript—Print," *New Directions in Textual Studies*, ed. Dave Oliphant and Robin Bradford (Austin, Tex.: Humanities Research Center, 1990); Jonathan Barry, "Literacy and Literature in Popular Culture: Reading and Writing in Historical Perspective," *Popular Culture in England, c. 1500–1850*, ed. Tim Harris (Basingstoke: Macmillan, 1995); Walter Ong, *Orality and Literacy: The Technologizing of the Word* (London: Routledge, 1984), 118; Adam Fox, "Custom, Memory and the Authority of Writing," *The Experience of Authority in Early Modern England*, ed. Paul Griffiths, et al. (Basingstoke: Macmillan, 1996). Cf. Ann Hughes, "The Meanings of Religious Polemic," *Puritanism: Transatlantic Perspectives on a Seventeenth-Century Anglo-American Phenomenon*, ed. Francis Bremer (Boston: Massachusetts Historical Society, 1993), for a discussion of the principles of oral debate.

24. "The Letters of Sir Cheney Culpeper," 266; John Tombes, *An Apology or Plea for the Two Treatises Concerning Infant Baptism* (London: for Giles Calvert, 1646), 8–9; Baillie, *Letters*, 2: 215–16.

25. For Edwards's treatment of Archer, Best, and Webb see *Gangraena*, 1.20–22, 37–39, 54–57 (second sequence), 3.100; for proceedings in Parliament and Assembly see *Lords Journals*, 7: 71, 80, 494; Baillie, *Letters*, 2:306; *Minutes of the Sessions of the Westminster Assembly of Divines*, ed. A. F. Mitchell and J. Struthers (Edinburgh: Blackwood, 1874), 105, 111–12.

26. For Smith see the brief account in Plomer, *Dictionary*, 167. Amongst Brinsley's works published by Smith were *A Looking-Glasse for Good Women* (London, 1645), and *The Arraignment of the Present Schism of New Separation in Old England* (London, 1646). For Thomas Smith see Richard Hollingworth, *An Examination of Sundry Scriptures* (London: for Thomas Smith, 1645); Plomer, *Dictionary*, 167–68.

27. These were Goodwin, *Cretensis*, 41–42; John Vicars, *The Schismatick Sifted, or the Picture of Independents Freshly and Fairly Washt-over again* (London: for Nathaniel Webb and William Grantham, 1646), 11, 35; Jeremiah Burroughs, *A Vindication of Mr Burroughs Against Mr Edwards* (London: for Henry Overton, 1646); Thomas Alle, *A Brief Narration of the Truth of Some Particulars in Mr Thomas Edwards his Book called Gangraena* (London: for Ralph Smith, 1646).

28. For Edwards's accounts see *Gangraena*, 1.78–79; 2.85–97; cf. Burroughs, *A Vindication*, 4–8; Alle, *A Brief Narration*, 3–5.

29. Elizabeth L. Eisenstein, *The Printing Revolution in Early Modern Europe* (Cambridge: Cambridge University Press, 1993), 95–96.

30. For the importance of print to nonconformist identity see Neil Keeble, *The Literary Culture of Nonconformity* (Leicester: Leicester University Press, 1987). In contrast Love, *Scribal Publication*, shows how manuscript circulation worked to "define communities of the like-minded," more intimate, and more restricted, than the communities of print (33).

31. *Lanseter's Lance for Edwardses Gangrene* (London, n.p., 1646).

32. Thirteen counties printed manifestos of support for *A Testimony to the Truth of Jesus Christ, And to Our Solemn League and Covenant, As Also Against the Errours, Heresies and Blasphemies of these times and the Toleration of them*, signed by fifty-two London ministers in 14 December 1647 (London: for Thomas Underhill, 1648). Jones, *Plain English*; Vicars, *Schismatick Sifted*; Bastwick, *The Utter Routing of the Whole Army of all the Independents and Sectaries* (London: for Michael Sparke, 1646); Josiah Ricraft, *A Nosegay of Rank-smelling Flowers* (London: for Nathaniel Webb and Wil-

liam Grantham, 1646); Robert Baillie, *Anabaptism. The True Fountaine of Independency* (London: for Samuel Gellibrand, 1647); William Prynne, *The Sword of Christian Magistracie Supported* (London: for John Bellamy, 1647).

33. Goodwin, *Cretensis*, and John Goodwin, *Hagiomastix or the Scourge of the Saints Displayed in his Colours of Ignorance and Blood* (London: for Henry Overton, 1647).

34. Lawrence Clarkson, *The Lost Sheep Found* (London: for the author, 1660), 21.

35. David Cressy, *Travesties* (Oxford: Oxford University Press, 2000), has a full account of such reenactments. I am very grateful to David Cressy for allowing me to see a proof copy of the relevant chapter.

36. Clarke, *Golden Apples, . . . sundry Questions and Cases of Conscience about Divisions, Schismes, Heresies, and the Tolleration of them . . .* (London: for Thomas Underhill, 1659).

II

Traces of Reading: Margins, Libraries, Prefaces, and Bindings

5

What Did Renaissance Readers
Write in Their Books?

WILLIAM H. SHERMAN

Roger Stoddard has recently reminded us that "When we handle books sensitively, observing them closely so as to learn as much as we can from them, we discover a thousand little mysteries. . . . In and around, beneath and across them we may find traces . . . that could teach us a lot if we could make them out."[1] During the past two decades, scholars have been increasingly concerned with making out, and making sense of, the mysterious traces that readers leave behind in their books. Both historical and literary studies have seen a renewed interest in the interaction of past texts and readers, especially at moments when that relationship was unusually charged, as it was during the religious and political upheavals of the sixteenth, seventeenth, and eighteenth centuries. And a renewed appreciation of the extent to which textual scholars must also be anthropologists and archaeologists—asking what (as Stoddard put it) "traces of wear can tell us [about] how artifacts were used by human beings" (32)—has prompted us to look in new ways at the books that have come down to us from the past. As a growing number of researchers are noticing, when observed closely these volumes turn out to be startlingly full of marks left by the hands through which they have passed.

In my own work on two of Elizabethan England's most prolific annotators, John Dee and Gabriel Harvey,[2] and in the more general survey that informs this essay, I have focused on one particular category of readers' marks: manuscript marginalia, or notes written in the margins and other blank spaces of texts. Marginalia are not, of course, the only sources of evidence for the encounters of readers and writers, either inside or outside the covers of individual volumes. They are part of a circuit of production and consumption involving a wide range of agents and techniques, and they need to be set alongside prefaces, printed marginalia, and other guides to the reader; commonplace books, diaries, and library inventories; and contemporary portraits—both verbal and visual—of readers in action. But contemporary annotations represent an extensive and still largely untapped archive of information about the lives of books and their place in the intellectual, spiritual, and social lives of their readers.

Most important, marginalia have begun to play a key role in bringing together theories and histories of reader response, and in returning our attention to the "actual reader." Long placed in subordination to actual authors (to the extent that readers were important, as makers of meaning, only if they were authors in their own right),[3] and more recently displaced by an exhaustive array of theoretical stand-ins (so that scholars could talk about "implied," "inscribed," "model," or "ideal" readers without any reference to real ones),[4] individual readers and communities of readers are now playing a central role in research across the humanities and social sciences.[5] As the history of reading has come into its own, scholars have been combing the margins of books for evidence provided by the actual readers of the past.

As anyone who has looked for overviews of the subject will know, however, generalizations about Renaissance marginalia are hard to come by. As I will suggest in the final section of this essay, the nature of marginalia itself makes them hard to produce; and the most valuable work to date has focused on the practices of individual readers (including Dee, Harvey, Ben Jonson, Robert Cotton, Inigo Jones, and William Drake). But there is a pressing need for information that will generate some larger patterns across a wider range of books and readers. In pursuit of a more general sense of Renaissance readers and their marks, I carried out a reasonably comprehensive survey of one of the major repositories of English Renaissance books—the STC collection[6] at the Huntington Library in San Marino, California. I searched for traces left behind by early readers and, while I tried to take note of the presence of owners' signatures and of nonverbal markings, I was primarily concerned with more substantial annotations. I recorded the presence of marginalia in books according to their date of publication, format, and subject matter, and then took a closer look at individual items of particular interest.[7] This essay will offer a brief introduction to what I found and will indicate, I hope, some of the promises and problems involved in working with the marginalia of Renaissance readers.[8]

Marking Readers, Circa 1600

It is important to note, at the outset, the changing place of marginalia in the training of readers since the early modern period. While many readers still write notes in the books they read, only rarely do marginalia play a part in the education of students. They are generally seen as antithetical to the respect toward books that teachers try to inculcate, and university libraries regularly display books that have been "defaced" by the pens and pencils of readers.[9] For their part, students tend to be reluctant to write in the books they buy because it affects their value when they want to sell them at the end of their courses (to other students or, more commonly in the United States, back to university bookstores, which pay higher prices for unmarked books). But at times readers have been encouraged and even taught to mark their books as a way of making them more useful for their present and future needs, and in the early modern period marginal annotations played a central role in pedagogical theory and practice. In 1612, the schoolmaster John Brinsley published his *Ludus Lite-rarius: Or, the Grammar Schoole*, an influential handbook for training students to translate, interpret, and apply the texts they encountered in their educational and professional careers. Records of professors and students at the universities of Renaissance England and France testify to their use of marginalia for parsing Latin sentences and storing useful phrases, but from the *Ludus Literarius* it is clear that the same practices were introduced at a much earlier age.[10] In several places Brinsley touches on marginalia and offers some remarkably detailed instructions for "marking" books: "difficult words, or matters of speciall obseruation, [which] they doe reade in any Author, [should] be marked out. . . . For the marking of them, to doe it with little lines vnder them, or aboue them, or against such partes of the word wherein the difficulty lieth, or by some prickes, or whatsoeuer letter or marke may best helpe to cal the knowledge of the thing to remembrance."[11] When working with Latin texts, Brinsley suggests that beginning readers should take the time to "note the Declension with a *d*, ouer the head, and a figure signifying which Declension," "The Coniugation with a *c*, and a figure," and so on. "As they proceede to higher fourmes," Brinsley continues, they should "marke onely those which haue most difficulty, as Notations, Deriuations, figuratiue Constructions, Tropes, Figures, and the like." The reason for all this marking—what a printed marginal note signals as "The ends of marking their bookes"—was that the students "shall keepe their Authours, which they haue learned" (140–41). Such annotations are, first and foremost, an aid to the memory, which is "the reason that you shall [find] the choysest bookes of most great learned men, & the most notablest students, all marked through thus." But for Brinsley and his contemporaries, the knowledge stored up was not just to be kept in mind but put into use: "To read and not to vnderstand what wee read, or not to know how to make vse of it, is nothing else but a neglect of all good learning, and a meere abuse of the means & helps to attaine the same."[12]

As Paul Saenger and Michael Heinlen have concluded, the readers of early printed books simply did not share our "modern book etiquette, which views the printed page as sacrosanct and consequently all handwritten additions to the printed page as . . . detrimental."[13] Some Renaissance readers did have concerns about writing in their books, however, and Brinsley offered reluctant teachers and students several ways to avoid "marring" them. First, they could write in "a fine small hand [which] will not hurt their bookes" (124). They could also choose to use pencil rather than pen for some of their notes, since—even before the invention of the rubber eraser—they could later be removed: "For the manner of noting, it is best to note all schoole books with inke; & also all others . . . whereof we would haue daily or long practice, because inke will indure: neither wil such books be the worse for their noting, but the better, if they be noted with iudgement. But for all other bookes, which you would haue faire againe at your pleasure, note them with a pensil of black lead: for that you may rub out againe when you will, with the crums of new wheate bread" (46–47). And finally, if they wanted to keep their books completely clean, they could take their notes elsewhere, by constructing "a little paper booke" (124).[14]

Surveying the Margins

Within what might be described as "Renaissance book etiquette," then, elaborate systems for marking books coexisted with a desire (either economic or aesthetic) for keeping them "faire." Not surprisingly, the majority of the Renaissance books that we take off the shelf today will show no sign of marginalia. But just over 20 percent of the books in the Huntington's STC collection contain early manuscript notes, and there are several reasons why the practice must have been much more widespread than that figure suggests. First, the copies of Renaissance texts that have survived represent only a fraction of those that were produced. It would seem that the more heavily a book was used, the more vulnerable it was to decay; "wear," as Stoddard explains, "is the eradicator of vital signs. The squeeze and rub of fingers stain and wear away ink and color, fraying paper thin, breaking fibers, and loosening leaves from bindings. Rough hands sunder books, and over time even gentle hands will pull books apart" (32). Second, the desire that some Renaissance readers had to keep their books clean has been more than matched by later readers, binders, and booksellers, many of whom (especially during the nineteenth and early twentieth centuries) felt no compunction about effacing the marks of earlier readers. Monique Hulvey has pointed out that "The destruction of manuscript annotations reached its peak in the nineteenth century, when printed leaves were washed and bleached in a concerted effort to 'clean' the margins of the books, and the edges were cropped as much as possible in rebinding, in order to get rid of all the 'mutilating' marks" (161).[15] Many STC items were (fortunately) not considered valuable enough to warrant this special treatment, but no less than 40 percent of the Huntington's incunables bear evidence of one or both of these methods. And third, while Henry Huntington did not himself express an antipathy to marginalia, the copies in the libraries that he bought tended to be unusually clean, and other (more randomly assembled) collections are likely to have a higher proportion of annotated books.[16]

Even discovering marginalia in just one book in five, I began to find the actual readers of the past obtrusively present in the visual field of the Renaissance page, and their traces struck me not as desecrations but as potential sources of evidence. My experience was comparable to that of the medievalist John Dagenais who, turning to manuscripts after years of working with pristine modern books, found texts that "had rough edges, not the clean, carefully pruned lines of critical editions; . . . edges . . . filled with dialogue about the text—glosses, marginal notes, pointing hands, illuminations . . . activities by which medieval people transformed one manuscript into another."[17]

Dagenais's terms, I would suggest, could be extended to the texts of early print culture: Renaissance readers regularly transformed one printed book into another and, indeed, they occasionally turned one back into a medieval manuscript.[18] There are significant continuities not only in the visual forms of books but in the transformative techniques employed by their readers. Some of them have passed from scribal culture into electronic culture, such as the pointing hand (☞) which few of us still use in our marginal notes but which was revived as a typographic symbol that can now be produced by most word-processing programs. Another scribal tradition which enjoyed a surprisingly rich afterlife was the "anathema" (or book curse) which owners inscribed on their books to prevent them from being lost or stolen.[19] Even well into the seventeenth century, owners of books were adding such curses to their signatures: on the last page of a 1639 psalter at the Huntington we find, "To Stephen Dance this book belong / and he that steale it dowth him rong / lev it alone and pase there by / in euery place where it doth lye,"[20] while the owner of Thomas Blundeville's 1613 *Exercises* was more aggressive, warning "hee that douth this bouke stayll hee shall be hanged" (HEH RB 46130).

Looking at Renaissance marginalia from the other end of the period, we find that these transformative manuscript marks do not die away as quickly as traditional narratives would have us believe. As printed books gradually freed themselves from the visual and organizational models of the manuscript tradition, there is no question that the use of the margins for authorial or editorial annotations increased steadily. Since many of these notes provided the kinds of apparatus which readers were used to writing in for themselves, scholars have assumed that manuscript marginalia decreased proportionally. In their important essay on fifteenth-century reading habits, Saenger and Heinlen argued that in the first few decades of printing, books still contain enough in the way of illuminations, rubrications, and annotations that they deserve to be catalogued as if they were manuscripts. But, they claim, by the second decade of the sixteenth century this was no longer the case: "The printer's provision of all the aids that previously had been added [by hand] . . . effected the final step in the transformation of reading. In antiquity reading had implied an active role in the reception of the text. . . . Throughout the Middle Ages readers, even long after a book had been confected, felt free to clarify its meaning through the addition of . . . marginalia. Under the influence of printing, reading became increasingly an activity of the passive reception of a text that was inherently clear and unambiguous" (253–54). Adrian Johns has recently cast doubt on whether the texts that printers produced were ever "inherently clear and unambiguous" (at least during the handpress period): in his account, the "credit" of printed books and the knowledge they conveyed remained in question throughout the seventeenth century.[21] The marks of readers in surviving books cast further doubt on whether reading became "an activity of passive reception" at any point in the sixteenth century. While the average proportion of annotated books from the incunable period is very high (between 60 and 70 percent), it is not much lower a full century later: among the books printed as late as the 1590s, 52 percent still contain contemporary marginalia. While the numbers do decline after that date (before rising again in the 1640s and 1650s), the proportion for some subjects—such as religious polemics and practical guides to law, medicine, and estate management—remains well over 50 percent for the entire STC period. The evidence left in English Renaissance books suggests that readers continued to add to texts—centuries rather than decades after the invention of printing—and that printers did not provide everything that every reader needed to make sense of the text (and with the text, by domesticating, digesting, or applying it). Insofar as individual books (like all artifacts) pick up pieces of history as they pass through time, for many purposes, including cataloguing, it may be more useful to approach them as if they were manuscripts.[22]

A typical scene can be found on the last page of the Huntington's copy of *The treasurie of Amadis of Fraunce*, a popular collection of speeches and letters (Fig. 1).[23] At least two early readers have filled the page with scribbles, penmanship exercises, and a set of surprisingly complex notes of ownership. The long note at the top reads, "Thomas Shardelowe ow[n]eth this book God geue him grace on it to look[.] if I it lose and you it find I pray you be not so vnkind but geue to me my booke againe and I will please you for yor payne[.] the rose is red the leafe is grene God preserue our noble king and queene but as for the Pope God send him a rope and a figge for the King of spayne." Lower down the page, another reader has drafted a series of phrases from which an ownership formula finally emerges: "Be it knowne Dale Heaver," "Dale Havers oweth me

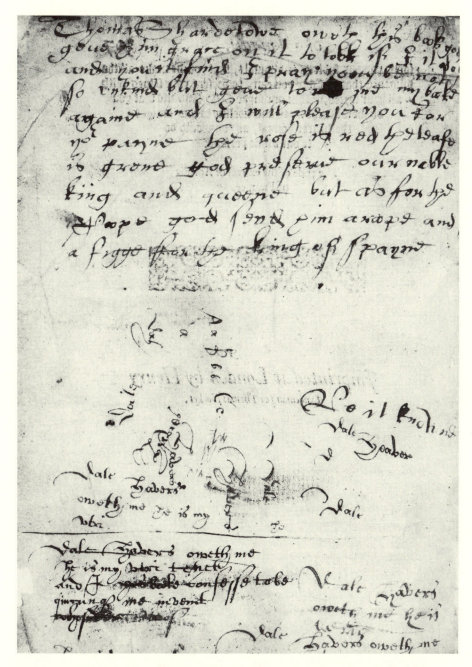

Figure 1. Amadis de Gaula, *The most excellent and pleasaunt booke, entituled: The treasurie of Amadis of Fraunce* (London: Henry Bynneman, 1572?); HEH RB 12924: verso of final page. Reproduced by permission of The Huntington Library, San Marino, California.

he is my veri," "Dale Havers oweth me he is . . . Dale Havers oweth me," and, finally, "Dale Havers oweth me / he is my veri tenet [owner] / and I this booke confesse to be / quicunque me invenit [whoever finds me]." These notes may not say much about Shardelowe or Havers, and they offer next to nothing about their interpretation of this particular text, but they do preserve a human presence that makes this copy unique.[24] More importantly, they capture a set of textual formulae—which must have circulated, formally or informally[25]—for displaying one's property, handwriting, and political beliefs.

As this relatively simple illustration suggests, marginalia provide some wonderfully literal examples of the way in which a printed book must be understood (in Natalie Zemon Davis's words) "not merely as a source for ideas and images, but as a carrier of relationships."[26] It is not unusual, for instance, to find the phrase "et amicorum [and friends]" accompanying a signature on a Renaissance title page or binding. The familiar practice of inscribing bibles (and other texts) with generations of family history was already well established in the sixteenth century (Sherman, "The Book" 128). And complex relationships of friendship and patronage were captured by the inscriptions on books given as gifts.

Renaissance marginalia usually offer clues not just about the contexts in which books were circulated and read, but about how they were used; indications of the kinds of training that readers brought to bear on their encounters with texts, and the kinds of needs they could be made to serve. They sometimes record a general judgment, such as that offered by Frances Wolfreston in the Huntington's copy of Shakerley Marmion's play, *A Fine Companion* (1633). Beneath the list of dramatis personae she wrote, "A resnabell prity bouk of a usurer and his 2 daughters and their loves with other pithy pasiges."[27] At times such judgments could be more politically pointed (as in a compilation containing Edmund Spenser's *View of the Present State of Ireland*, where a reader has remarked that "the Rebellion of Oct[ober] 23. 1641 justified Spencers wisedome and deep insight into that barbarous nation")[28] or more consequential (as in a collection of medical recipes, where a reader has deleted many passages, noting that "All theas receiptes ar verye falsly written. but being corrected heer they ar trew").[29] Underlinings can indicate which passages an individual reader picked out, making them easier to locate for future readings and readers. It is surely significant that in a 1574 Bishops' Bible a reader (perhaps the Thomas Taylor who signed the first page of Matthew in 1619) saved his heaviest underlining for the Book of Esdras, and has systematically picked out verses on angels, omens, and prophecies (HEH RB 292510).

Marginalia can identify other texts a reader associated with or even read alongside a particular book. Cross-references and passages copied verbatim from other books are frequent enough to attest to the widespread practice of what has been called "extensive" rather than "intensive" reading, and to suggest that (for some groups of readers at least) this mode started in England well before what Robert DeMaria has called the "reading revolution" of the eighteenth century.[30] While we might expect readers from the legal profession to have knowledge of and access to a wide range of statutes and precedents, it is striking how often readers of sermons, herbals, or husbandry manuals were able to reference other books and authors in their reading.

Another indication that printing did not automatically, or immediately, render readers passive was the kind of active and appropriative reading uncovered by recent studies of sixteenth- and seventeenth-century readers. The "actual" reader was, after all, originally understood as "act-ual," linked by Brinsley's advice and by etymology itself to action.[31] Ironically, what the actual (or act-ual) reader insists on most immediately is the potential that any particular text represents. On the one hand, as Lisa Jardine and Anthony Grafton have shown with their study "How Gabriel Harvey Read His Livy," the same reader can read in different ways, acting different roles as circumstances allow or require.[32] On the other, students of reading from Stanley Fish to Roger Chartier have wrestled with the fact that the same text can be interpreted or used in radically different ways.[33] Perhaps the most potent example at the Huntington is a copy of *A Christian Directory*, published in 1585 by the English Jesuit Robert Parsons (HEH RB 433864). This text generated both pro- and anti-Catholic responses, but the Huntington's copy records voices from both camps within the covers of a single book [Figs. 2 and 3]. One sympathetic reader has written such sober endorsements as, "Reade over thes two portions over [*sic*] manye Tymes: diligentlye." A different hand records the outrage of an obviously Protestant reader with such comments as "A most lewd & grosse lie, & Popish slaunder." It is no coincidence that this example concerns religion: few texts have divided opinion as much as those that grew out of the Protestant Reformation, and as they moved through those years, many were modified in accordance with new beliefs. In England, many prayer books were destroyed outright but some remained in circulation after the break with Rome: in these, readers often censored their copies by scratching out newly offensive terms like "Pope" and "Virgin Mary" or by deleting sections that were no longer endorsed. This did not only apply to bibles and prayer books: in her study of surviving copies of Caxton's *Royal Book* (printed in 1485 and 1507), Elaine E. Whitaker found that approximately half of them were later censored, removing (in various copies) the phrase "of rome" after the word "church," an entire section on purgatory, and even a woodcut illustration of a liturgical procession.[34]

In what might be described as radically customized copies—copies, that is, where the text is not just annotated but physically altered, sometimes even

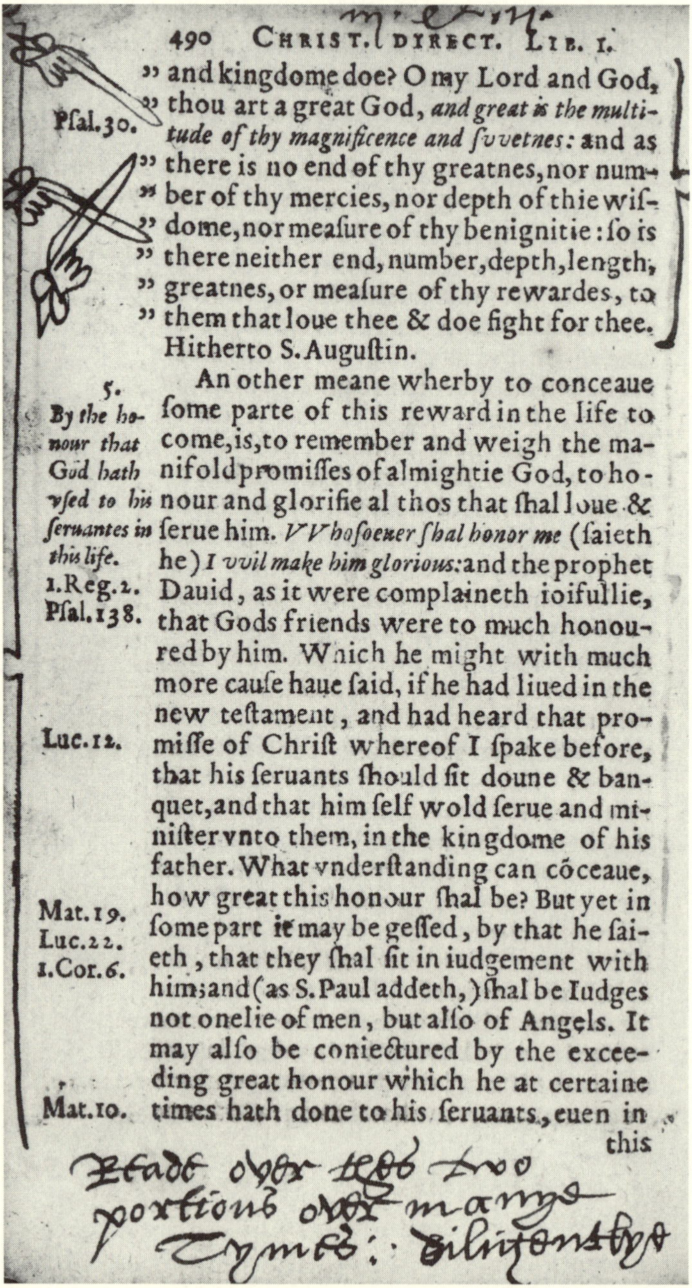

490　CHRIST. DIRECT. LIB. I.

" and kingdome doe? O my Lord and God,

Pſal. 30. " thou art a great God, *and great is the multi-*
tude of thy magnificence and ſwetnes: and as
" there is no end of thy greatnes, nor num-
" ber of thy mercies, nor depth of thie wiſ-
" dome, nor meaſure of thy benignitie: ſo is
" there neither end, number, depth, length,
" greatnes, or meaſure of thy rewardes, to
" them that loue thee & doe fight for thee.
Hitherto S. Auguſtin.

5.　　　An other meane wherby to conceaue
By the ho-　ſome parte of this reward in the life to
nour that　come, is, to remember and weigh the ma-
God hath　nifold promiſſes of almightie God, to ho-
vſed to his　nour and glorifie al thos that ſhal loue &
ſeruantes in　ſerue him. *VVhoſoeuer ſhal honor me* (ſaieth
this life.　he) *I vvil make him glorious:* and the prophet
1. Reg. 2.　Dauid, as it were complaineth ioifullie,
Pſal. 138.　that Gods friends were to much honou-
red by him. Which he might with much
more cauſe haue ſaid, if he had liued in the
new teſtament, and had heard that pro-
Luc. 12.　miſſe of Chriſt whereof I ſpake before,
that his ſeruants ſhould ſit doune & banquet, and that him ſelf wold ſerue and mi-
niſter vnto them, in the kingdome of his
father. What vnderſtanding can cōceaue,
how great this honour ſhal be? But yet in
Mat. 19.　ſome part it may be geſſed, by that he ſai-
Luc. 22.　eth, that they ſhal ſit in iudgement with
1. Cor. 6.　him; and (as S. Paul addeth,) ſhal be Iudges
not onelie of men, but alſo of Angels. It
may alſo be coniectured by the exceeding great honour which he at certaine
Mat. 10.　times hath done to his ſeruants, euen in
this

Figure 2. Robert Parsons, *A Christian Directory* (1585), 22, 490; HEH
RB 433864. By permission of The Huntington Library, San Marino,
California.

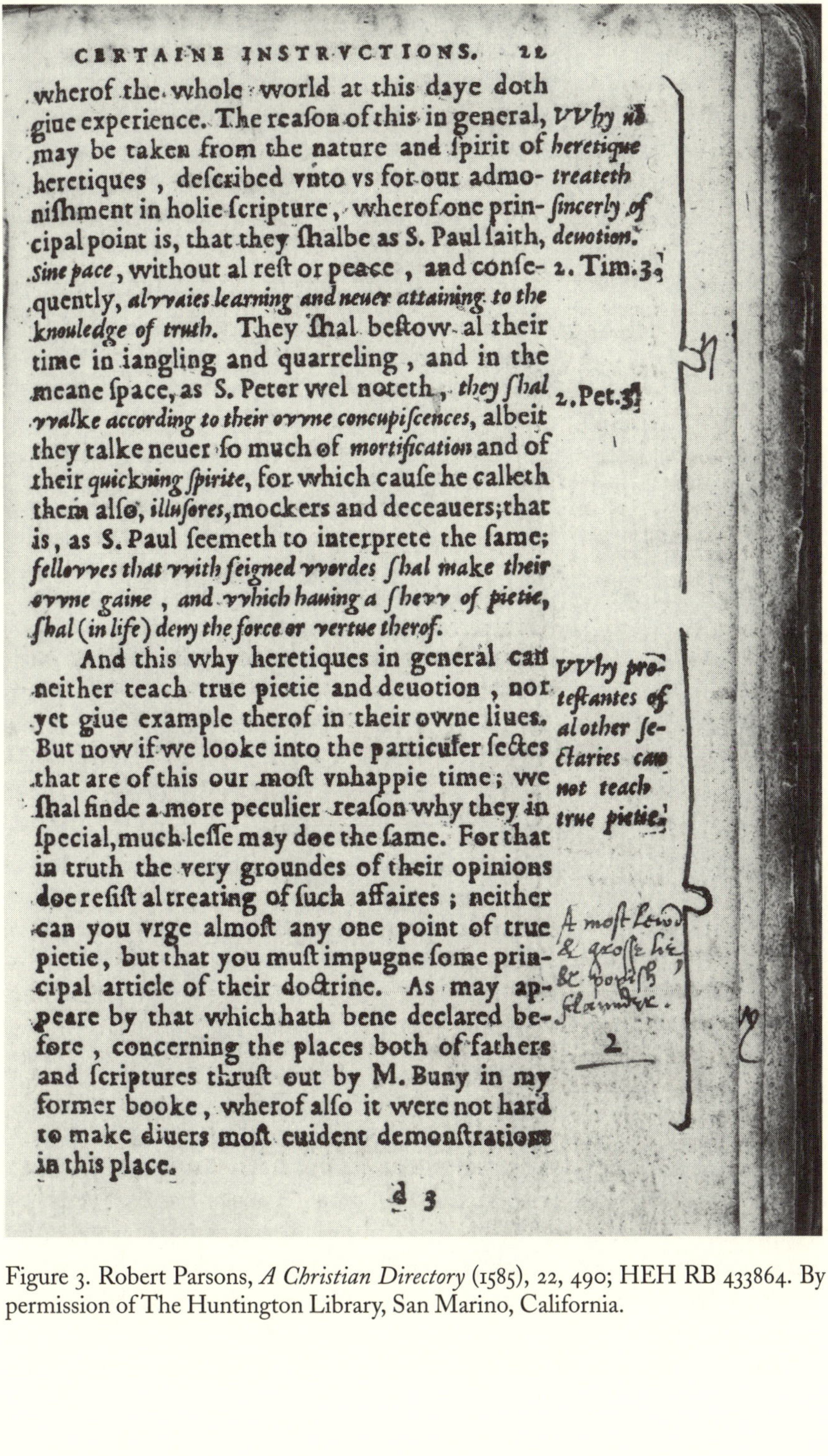

CERTAINE INSTRVCTIONS.   22

wherof the whole world at this daye doth
giue experience. The reason of this in general, *VVhy a̅*
may be taken from the nature and spirit of *heretique*
heretiques , described vnto vs for our admo- *treateth*
nishment in holie scripture , wherof one prin- *sincerly of*
cipal point is, that they shalbe as S. Paul saith, *deuotion.*
sine pace, without al rest or peace , and conse-   2. Tim. 3.
quently, *alvvaies learning and neuer attaining to the*
knouledge of truth. They shal bestow al their
time in iangling and quarreling , and in the
meane space, as S. Peter wel noteth , *they shal*   2. Pet. 3.
vvalke according to their ovvne concupiscences, albeit
they talke neuer so much of *mortification* and of
their *quickning spirite*, for which cause he calleth
them also, *illusores*, mockers and deceauers; that
is , as S. Paul seemeth to interprete the same;
fellovves that vvith feigned vvordes shal make their
ovvne gaine , and vvhich hauing a shevv of pietie,
shal (in life) deny the force or vertue therof.

And this why heretiques in general can   *VVhy pro-*
neither teach true pietie and deuotion , nor   *testantes of*
yet giue example therof in their owne liues.   *al other se-*
But now if we looke into the particuler sectes   *ctaries can*
that are of this our most vnhappie time ; we   *not teach*
shal finde a more peculier reason why they in   *true pietie.*
special, much lesse may doe the same. For that
in truth the very groundes of their opinions
doe resist al treating of such affaires ; neither
can you vrge almost any one point of true   *A most lewd*
pietie , but that you must impugne some prin-   *& grosse lie*
cipal article of their doctrine. As may ap-   *& popish*
peare by that which hath bene declared be-   *slaunder.*
fore , concerning the places both of fathers
and scriptures thrust out by M. Buny in my   *2*
former booke , wherof also it were not hard
to make diuers most euident demonstrations
in this place.

d 3

Figure 3. Robert Parsons, *A Christian Directory* (1585), 22, 490; HEH RB 433864. By
permission of The Huntington Library, San Marino, California.

cut up and combined with other texts—there is evidence of reading so active
and appropriative that it challenged the integrity not just of the word or page
but of the entire printed book. Readers could actively alter their books (when
they were bound or re-bound) by inserting blank leaves for extensive marginalia, by rearranging the sections, or even by combining sections from different
texts.[35] In 1673, for instance, a reader signing himself only "GF" filled the
margins of a 1638 textbook on mathematics with a running summary of the
principles of geometry, and inserted several diagrams cut out of other books.[36]
In more extreme cases, the results make it difficult to identify which is the
primary text that is being added to: in the Huntington volume which is catalogued as John Bate's *Mysteryes of nature, and art*, all that remains of Bate's text
is the third of its four books (HEH RB 60330). In the place of Books 1 and 2 are
large sections of Books 1 and 2 of Henry Peacham's *Gentleman's Exercise*, while
Book 4 is replaced by nine pages of manuscript notes—turning Bate's encyclopedic text into a narrowly focused anthology on drawing and painting.

What Are Marginalia Evidence Of?

One of the most pervasive—and problematic—features of Renaissance marginalia is that by no means all of the notes left behind by readers engage directly
with the text they accompany, and more have to do with the life of the reader
than the life of the text. The blank spaces of Renaissance books were used not
just to record comments on the text but penmanship exercises, prayers, recipes,
popular poetry, drafts of letters, mathematical calculations, shopping lists, and
other glimpses of the world in which they circulated. This is not only true of
almanacs, which were the most conventional repositories for this sort of information. The Huntington's copy of Boccaccio's *Amorous Fiammetta* contains
only one manuscript note: on the verso of the title page an early owner has
inscribed a recipe for a leek and herb sauce.[37] And in a copy of Erasmus's
De Copia, the only note written by its owner, William Anderson, records that
"On the 18th of May anno Domini 1585 there was heard a great terrible
thundering."[38]

    Clearly, the project of reading marginalia comes up against a range of
methodological and practical challenges. There has been a growing awareness
among those who have gone in search of actual readers that the "actual" is
neither as accessible nor as self-evident as it sounds.[39] Reading often leaves no
trace, and that evidence which survives is often difficult to find and to read
(both to decipher and to interpret). Moreover, once this evidence has been
recorded and (when possible) connected with a person, place, or time, there
remains the challenge of relating individual readers and their marks to the

larger patterns that most literary and historical scholars have as their goal.[40] As cases like the Boccaccio and Erasmus above suggest, marginalia are often too fragmentary or decontextualized to contribute much to that kind of project. This information may take us beyond (or fail to achieve) what we understand by "reading"; and as anyone who has travelled to a library to consult an "annotated" volume only to find a shopping list or even some anonymous underlinings will agree, the practices which made books useful to Renaissance readers are not always interesting to us.[41] Finally, while the leek and herb sauce recipe would no doubt be of interest to a culinary historian, the chances of one coming across it, given the finding aids that are currently available, are very slim indeed.

While most of these notes remain hidden from those who might be most interested in them, they do suggest that marginalia played a crucial—and still largely undefined—role in what we might call the "archival economy" of Renaissance readers.[42] An important factor was, of course, the price of paper: it was relatively expensive in the STC period and accounted for much of the cost of a book—which meant that, unlike today, the scraps of paper most readily available for miscellaneous notes were those which surrounded printed texts. It is also possible that the white space around texts would have been an important place to store memoranda: certain books were likely to occupy special places in the households—and memories—of Renaissance readers.[43]

One final example can be taken as exemplary of the paradoxical way in which Renaissance marginalia tended to follow rules in unpredictable ways. It is one of the Huntington's four copies of the 1605 edition of Francis Bacon's *Advancement of Learning*[44] (Fig. 4). These annotations were the work of the Genevan scholar Isaac Casaubon, perhaps the finest philologist of his day.[45] Here, then, is an encounter between two of Europe's most learned men, in the margins of a work that is itself concerned with the management and application of information.[46] Casaubon marked up the book in his usual scholarly fashion. At the bottom of the page reproduced here he has transcribed a lengthy passage from another work (by the Greek orator Themistius) which praised the ruler in terms similar to those contained in Bacon's address to King James. We can also find him translating some of Bacon's English phrases into Latin and Greek (across from "wisest," for example, he has written "Sapientiss."), and labelling rhetorical devices (next to Bacon's "And as the Scripture sayth of the wisest King: *That his heart was as the sands of the Sea*," Casaubon has written "Cor Regis Simile"). But alongside these standard philological techniques there is a more original and enigmatic practice: Casaubon has marked (or had someone mark for him) the accented syllable of every word with more than one syllable, suggesting that he read it aloud and used the text, at least in part, to practice his pronunciation of English.[47]

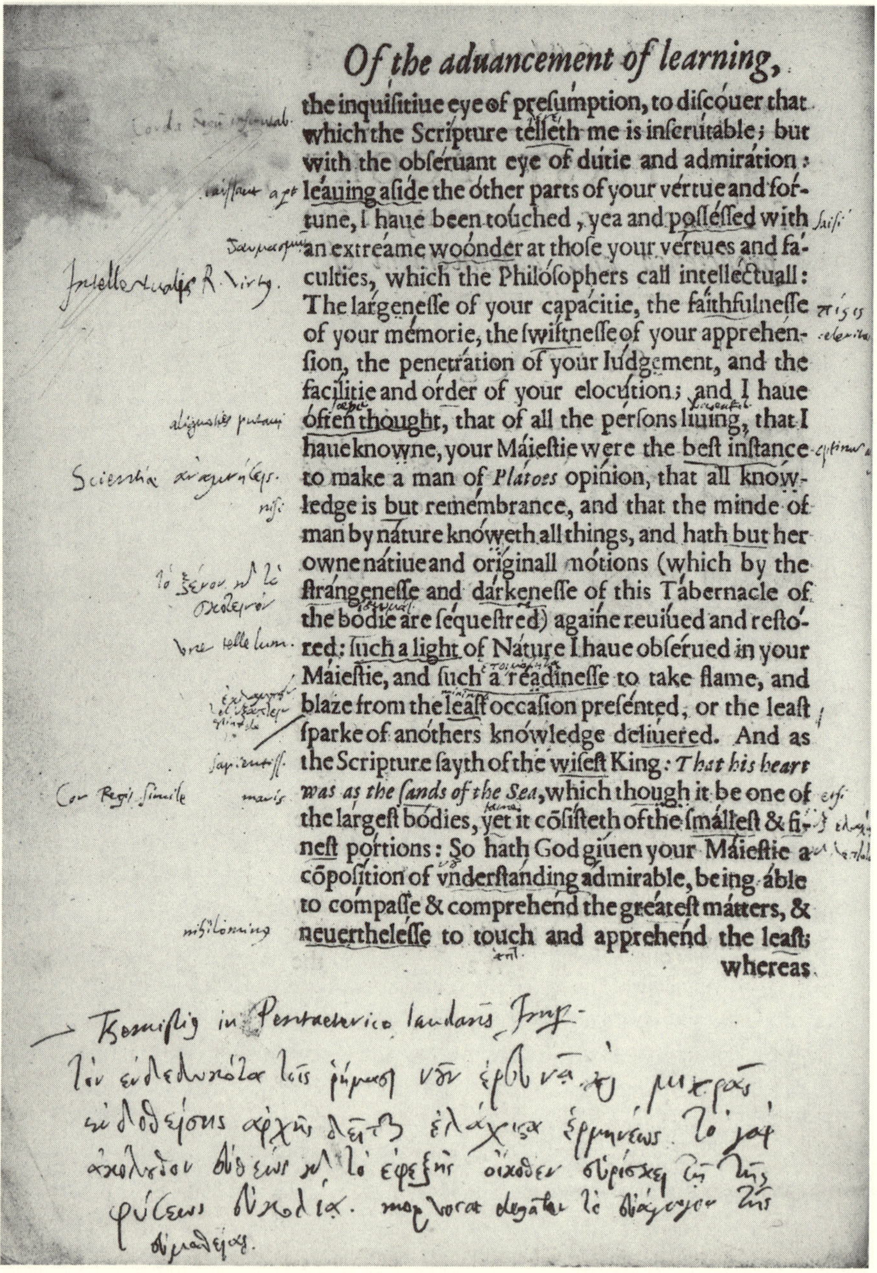

Of the aduancement of learning,

the inquiſitiue eye of preſumption, to diſcouer that which the Scripture telleth me is inſcrutable; but with the obſeruant eye of dutie and admiration: leauing aſide the other parts of your vertue and fortune, I haue been touched, yea and poſſeſſed with an extreame woonder at thoſe your vertues and faculties, which the Philoſophers call intellectuall: The largeneſſe of your capacitie, the faithfulneſſe of your memorie, the ſwiftneſſe of your apprehenſion, the penetration of your Iudgement, and the facilitie and order of your elocution; and I haue often thought, that of all the perſons liuing, that I haue knowne, your Maieſtie were the beſt inſtance to make a man of *Platoes* opinion, that all knowledge is but remembrance, and that the minde of man by nature knoweth all things, and hath but her owne natiue and originall motions (which by the ſtrangeneſſe and darkeneſſe of this Tabernacle of the bodie are ſequeſtred) againe reuiued and reſtored: ſuch a light of Nature I haue obſerued in your Maieſtie, and ſuch a readineſſe to take flame, and blaze from the leaſt occaſion preſented, or the leaſt ſparke of anothers knowledge deliuered. And as the Scripture ſayth of the wiſeſt King: *That his heart was as the ſands of the Sea*, which though it be one of the largeſt bodies, yet it cōſiſteth of the ſmalleſt & fineſt portions: So hath God giuen your Maieſtie a cōpoſition of vnderſtanding admirable, being able to compaſſe & comprehend the greateſt matters, & neuertheleſſe to touch and apprehend the leaſt; whereas

Figure 4. Francis Bacon, *The tvvoo bookes of Francis Bacon. Of the proficiencie and aduancement of learning, diuine and humane* (1605); HEH RB 56251. By permission of The Huntington Library, San Marino, California.

It should be clear, even from this brief survey, that the margins of Renaissance books contain, in Nicolas Barker's words, "a wealth of evidence" that is "temptingly available[;] so much larger, so delightfully accessible, when compared with census returns, state papers, [and] parish registers."[48] But Barker was referring to Renaissance books in general, and when applied to manuscript marginalia the phrase "delightfully accessible" no longer seems so appropriate. They require privileged access and specialized skills, and they have a tendency to frustrate disciplinary expectations and personal hopes—usually telling us something different from what we expected and often less than we need to do much with them. Many of the traces of Renaissance reading will remain invisible, indecipherable, or (worst of all) boring. But when we are patient, and lucky, they can allow us to catch glimpses of individual and collective habits of thought; to trace the reception of particularly important books and the perception of large-scale shifts in education, religion, and politics; and to challenge some of our most deep-seated assumptions about the readers and libraries of other times and places.[49]

Notes

This essay is part of a long-term project on Renaissance readers and their marks. For their encouragement and advice along the way, I am grateful to Julie Biggs, Anthony Grafton, Heidi Brayman Hackel, Heather Jackson, Lisa Jardine, Roy Ritchie, Kevin Sharpe, Peter Stallybrass, Steve Zwicker, and the members of seminars at the University of Pennsylvania and the Folger Shakespeare Library. My research was supported by several short-term fellowships from the Huntington, a grant from the Bibliographical Society (UK), and funding from the University of Maryland General Research Board. I would like to thank the staff at the Huntington, and especially its rare books librarian, Alan Jutzi, for allowing me to access large numbers of rare books and for showing an interest in what I found in them.

1. "Looking at Marks in Books," *The Gazette of the Grolier Club*, New Series 51 (2000): 27–47; 27. This passage first appeared in Stoddard's *Marks in Books, Illustrated and Explained* (Cambridge, Mass.: Houghton Library, Harvard University, 1985).

2. William H. Sherman, *John Dee: The Politics of Reading and Writing in the English Renaissance* (Amherst: University of Massachusetts Press, 1995); Lisa Jardine and William H. Sherman, "Pragmatic Readers: Knowledge Transactions and Scholarly Services in Late Elizabethan England," *Religion, Culture and Society in Early Modern Britain: Essays in Honour of Patrick Collinson*, ed. Anthony Fletcher and Peter Roberts (Cambridge: Cambridge University Press, 1994), 102–24, which forms part of a book-length study with Lisa Jardine and Anthony Grafton, currently entitled *Professional Reading in Renaissance England: Gabriel Harvey's Marginal Career*.

3. It is no coincidence that the resurgence of interest in the actual reader has followed the "death of the author" (as pronounced by the theorists of the late 1960s), nor that traditional narratives of the history of reading locate the emergence of private and passive reading at the same moment as the "birth of the author" (i.e., with the

advent in the seventeenth and eighteenth centuries of a print-driven literary marketplace, accompanied by new professional roles and protocols).

4. *Readers and Reading*, ed. Andrew Bennett (London: Longman, 1995), 3.

5. For recent overviews of this work see *A History of Reading in the West*, ed.
Guglielmo Cavallo and Roger Chartier (Amherst: University of Massachusetts Press,
1999); *The Practice and Representation of Reading in England*, ed. James Raven, Helen
Small, and Naomi Tadmor (Cambridge: Cambridge University Press, 1996); *The Eth-
nography of Reading*, ed. Jonathan Boyarin (Berkeley: University of California Press,
1993); and *Pratiques de la lecture*, ed. Roger Chartier (Marseille: Rivages, 1985).

6. That is, the books catalogued in A. W. Pollard, G. R. Redgrave, and K. F.
Pantzer, *A Short-Title Catalogue of Books Printed in England, Scotland, and Ireland and
of English Books Printed Abroad, 1475–1640*, 2nd ed., 3 vols. (London, 1976–91). In the
Huntington's rare book stacks, the STC books are stored as a group, in the order of
their STC numbers. Other STC titles are scattered throughout the more specialized
collections (e.g., the fine bindings), and in the vaults that house the especially rare
volumes.

7. I created a database that has been deposited with the librarians at the Huntington and incorporated, to some extent, in their on-line catalogues. While some
libraries have traditionally kept index card files of former owners, better catalogues of
marginalia are badly needed to help future scholars locate the past readers and readings
that interest them; and researchers will need to communicate and even collaborate with
cataloguers. Robin C. Alston's *Books with Manuscript: A Short Title Catalogue of Books
with Manuscript Notes in the British Library* (1994) is a useful start, but since it is based
entirely on the incomplete listings in the British Library's old printed catalogues it will
need to be updated and added to the fuller records that electronic catalogues allow. In
this respect, the ESTC is already a vast improvement on the printed STC and Wing
catalogues since, for some libraries at least, it gives details of copy-specific features
(including marginalia).

8. Others have been carrying out similar surveys with other materials: Steven
Zwicker has been examining the Wing books at the Huntington and the Folger Shake-
speare Library; see his "Reading the Margins: Politics and the Habits of Appropriation," *Refiguring Revolutions: Aesthetics and Politics from the English Revolution to the
Romantic Revolution*, ed. Kevin Sharpe and Steven Zwicker (Berkeley: University of
California Press, 1998). And Monique Hulvey has worked through the Folger's incunables—see "Not So Marginal: Manuscript Annotations in the Folger Incunabula,"
PBSA 92.2 (June 1998): 159–76. See also Stephen Orgel's essay on Renaissance marginalia, "Margins of Truth," *The Renaissance Text: Theory, Editing, Textuality*, ed. Andrew Murphy (Manchester: University of Manchester Press, 2000), which appeared
too late for me to use here.

9. Cf. H. J. Jackson, "Writing in Books and Other Marginal Activities," *University of Toronto Quarterly* 62 (1992–93): 217–31.

10. See the references in Sherman, *John Dee*, 66–70, and Eugene R. Kintgen,
Reading in Tudor England (Pittsburgh: University of Pittsburgh Press, 1996), chpt. 2.

11. John Brinsley, *Ludus Literarius: Or, the Grammar Schoole* (London: Thomas
Mann, 1612), 46. Appropriately enough, the Huntington's copy of this text (shelfmark
29028) has been very heavily annotated. I am grateful to Ben Deneault for reminding
me of these passages in Brinsley's text.

12. Brinsley, 46, 42. Brinsley is here citing what he calls "that olde rule," "Legere

& non intellegere negligere est," and it is significant that he interprets *intellegere* as not only understanding but application.

13. "Incunable Description and its Implications for the Analysis of Fifteenth-Century Reading Habits," *Printing the Written Word: The Social History of Books, circa 1450–1520*, ed. Sandra L. Hindman (Ithaca: Cornell University Press, 1991), 225–58; 254.

14. Brinsley devotes several long sections to the praise, and use, of commonplace books.

15. Stoddard's comments on this process—while perhaps unfair to today's more sensitive conservators—are nonetheless chilling for the student of readers' marks: "Rare is the binder who has deliberately preserved historical evidence. Old covers and end-papers are jettisoned along with their library marks, ownership marks, booksellers' marks, index notes, annotations, documents, or verses. . . . Then stains, both finger marks and marginalia, are bathed away in bleach before the results are squeezed flat in a standing press, obliterating from paper the bite of type and ornament and the dents and scratches scribed or pressed blind without pigment" ("Looking at Marks in Books," 32).

16. For instance, the Bridgewater library, which forms the core of the Huntington's STC collection, displays a clear preference for clean copies: its proportion of annotated books is considerably lower than the average for the whole collection (though this may be partly accounted for by the high proportion of literary texts, since that is the subject with the fewest annotations—across the board). For an account of Huntington's strategies as a collector, see Donald C. Dickson, *Henry E. Huntington's Library of Libraries* (San Marino, Calif.: Huntington Library, 1995).

17. John Dagenais, *The Ethics of Reading in Manuscript Culture: Glossing the "Libro de Buen Amor"* (Princeton: Princeton University Press, 1993), xvi. Cf. Stephen G. Nichols, "On the Sociology of Medieval Manuscript Annotation," *Annotation and Its Texts*, ed. Stephen A. Barney (Oxford: Oxford University Press, 1991), and Michael Camille, *Image on the Edge: The Margins of Medieval Art* (London: Reaktion Books, 1992).

18. There is a manuscript copy of the Book of Common Prayer in the James R. Page collection at the Huntington which copies the text and, to some extent the layout, of the 1561 printed edition, but by pasting in illuminated initials cut out from earlier manuscripts captures something of the look of a medieval book of hours. For a discussion and illustration see William H. Sherman, " 'The Book thus put in every vulgar hand': Impressions of Readers in Early English Printed Bibles," *The Bible as Book: The Earliest Printed Editions*, ed. Paul Saenger and Kimberly van Kampen (London: British Library, 1999), an essay which offers a parallel, but more narrowly focused, report on the Huntington's STC marginalia.

19. Marc Drogin, *Anathema! Medieval Scribes and the History of Book Curses* (Totowa, N.J.: Allanheld, Osmun, 1983).

20. Henry E. Huntington Library [henceforth HEH] Rare Book [henceforth RB] 30108.

21. Adrian Johns, *The Nature of the Book: Print and Knowledge in the Making* (Chicago: University of Chicago Press, 1998), chpt. 1 passim.

22. When Saenger revisited his and Heinlen's earlier essay (in Paul Saenger, "The Implications of Incunable Description for the History of Reading Revisited," *PBSA* 91:4 [December 1997]: 495–504), he proposed some valuable modifications to their

paradigm for cataloguing incunables, but did nothing to extend their argument to later printed books.

23. HEH RB 12924: Amadis de Gaula, *The most excellent and pleasaunt booke, entituled: The treasurie of Amadis of Fraunce* (London: Henry Bynneman, 1572?).

24. This is not, however, to endorse James Nielson's suggestion that manuscript materials embody or give access to authentic personalities, or that the "chirographic chaos" of Gabriel Harvey's manuscript writings and notes "allow or even force us, as practical readers . . . to feel that we can get at the 'real Harvey' through his handwritten text" ("Reading Between the Lines: Manuscript Personality and Gabriel Harvey's Drafts," *Studies in English Literature, 1500–1900* 33.1 [winter 1993]: 43–82; 44–45).

25. More work needs to be done on how and where Renaissance readers picked up these rhyming texts.

26. Natalie Zemon Davis, "Printing and the People," *Society and Culture in Early Modern France* (Stanford: Stanford University Press, 1975), 192.

27. HEH RB 62472. Paul Morgan lists many of Wolfreston's books—though not this one—in "Frances Wolfreston and 'Hor Bouks': A Seventeenth-Century Woman Book-Collector," *Library*, 6th ser., 11 (1989): 197–219; and Heidi Brayman Hackel discusses Wolfreston's collection of playbooks in her contribution to *A New History of Early English Drama*, ed. John D. Cox and David Scott Kastan (New York: Columbia University Press, 1997), 126.

28. HEH RB 28118: James Ware, preface, *The History of Ireland* (1633).

29. HEH RB 432871: Alexis Piedmont, *The Secretes . . . containyng excellente remedies against diuerse diseases* (1580), Book 3, fol. 65ʳ.

30. "Samuel Johnson and the Reading Revolution," *Eighteenth-Century Life* 16 (November 1992): 86–102. For a critical overview of this argument (which derives from the theories of Rolf Engelsing) see Reinhard Wittmann, "Was there a Reading Revolution at the End of the Eighteenth Century?" *A History of Reading in the West*, ed. Cavallo and Chartier.

31. According to the *Oxford English Dictionary*, *actual* derives from the Latin *actual-is*, meaning "of or pertaining to action."

32. Lisa Jardine and Anthony Grafton, "'Studied for Action': How Gabriel Harvey Read his Livy," *Past and Present* 129 (November 1990): 30–78; passim. Reader-response criticism and speech-act theory have acknowledged this fact, but it may be that performance studies—which is mapping the interface between rhetoric and role-playing and is most attuned to the problematics of acting—has more to offer students of the actual reader. For example, Stanton B. Garner Jr., *Bodied Spaces: Phenomenology and Performance in Contemporary Drama* (Ithaca: Cornell University Press, 1994), 7, has referred to "the play of possible *actuality* already posited by the dramatic text"—or, I would suggest, any text.

33. Stanley Fish, "Interpreting the *Variorum*," *Is There a Text in This Class?* (Cambridge: Harvard University Press, 1980); Roger Chartier, "Communities of Readers," *The Order of Books: Readers, Authors, and Libraries in Europe Between the Fourteenth and Eighteenth Centuries*, trans. Lydia G. Cochrane (Stanford: Stanford University Press, 1994).

34. Elaine E. Whitaker, "A Collaboration of Readers: Categorization of the Annotations in Copies of Caxton's *Royal Book*," *Text* 7 (1994): 233–42; 236.

35. In academic communities these composite texts are still common in the form of photocopy packets, or "readers," compiled by instructors. Some publishers of text-

books have started to offer customized texts of their own: in cooperation with the Ohio State University History Department, Simon and Schuster recently made available *Retrieving the American Past*, which they call "A Customized U.S. History Reader." A sticker on the front cover of sample copies invites instructors to "Choose from over 60 modules to create a custom book!"

36. HEH RB 271828: John Wells, *Sciographia, or the Art of Shadowes* (1635).

37. HEH RB 99544: Giovanni Boccaccio, *Amorous Fiammetta* (London, 1587).

38. HEH RB 376333: Desiderius Erasmus, *De duplici copia verborum, et rerum* (1569).

39. That the "actual" is neither readily accessible nor self-evident is an observation made by Randall Ingram in his contribution to this volume.

40. This last challenge has been most clearly articulated by Roger Chartier in "Texts, Printing, Readings," *The New Cultural History*, ed. Lynn Hunt (Berkeley: University of California Press, 1989).

41. For instance, if we look for personal or creative intensity in marginalia, we will most likely be disappointed. Heather Jackson's lively article on modern marginalia provides a useful contrast with the typical features of early modern marginalia: she defines them as "responsive," "personal," "critical," "self-indulgent," and "spontaneous," and proposes that we "dismiss . . . what we can call the *professional* marking of books, the more or less systematic underlining of passes, noting-down of topics or keywords, and similar means by which readers since the birth of print . . . have tried to improve their grasp or recall of the works they read" ("Writing in Books," 217–20). Needless to say, what Jackson would dismiss is precisely what we are most likely to find in Renaissance marginalia.

42. Jacques Derrida's discussion of the *"eco-nomic* archive" is very suggestive: see his *Archive Fever: A Freudian Impression* (Chicago: University of Chicago Press, 1996), 7.

43. I owe this suggestion to Peter Blayney.

44. HEH RB 56251: Francis Bacon, *The tvvoo bookes of Francis Bacon. Of the proficiencie and aduancement of learning, diuine and humane* (1605).

45. Casaubon's reading habits are in need of detailed study, but see Mark Pattison, *Isaac Casaubon, 1559–1614* (London: Longmans, Green, 1875).

46. It seems to have been one of the most regularly annotated books in the period: four of the six copies at the Folger Shakespeare Library contain manuscript notes. And in another remarkable instance of a customized book, Sir William Drake cut out pages from his already annotated copies of *The Advancement of Learning* and pasted them into two of his commonplace books (Kevin Sharpe, *Reading Revolutions: The Politics of Reading in Early Modern England* [New Haven: Yale University Press, 2000], 76–77, 87–88).

47. Casaubon was in exile in England from 1610 to his death in 1614 and may have been making a late, enforced attempt to work on his English at this time.

48. *A Potencie of Life: Books in Society*, The Clark Lectures, 1986–87, ed. Nicolas Barker (London: British Library, 1993).

49. Cf. Anthony Grafton, "Is the History of Reading a Marginal Enterprise? Guillaume Budé and His Books," *PBSA* 91.2 (June 1997): 139–57.

6

The Countess of Bridgewater's London Library

HEIDI BRAYMAN HACKEL

A recent survey of early modern women's reading follows earlier scholarship in assuming that "few women developed libraries of their own."[1] As a challenge to this widely held belief, this essay presents a case study of the London library of Frances (Stanley) Egerton, Countess of Bridgewater (1585–1636),[2] a collection, I argue, that was not extraordinary in its day. Many other women, particularly among the aristocracy, also amassed collections that left traces in the historical record. As I situate Lady Bridgewater's case in the broader context of gendered reading and book ownership, I will explore the circulation of books in households, the integration of reading into domestic life, and women's responses to the well-documented policing of their reading.

Reconstructions of early modern book ownership are nearly always laborious and partial, and these methodological difficulties become compounded when the book owner is a woman. Common law restricted a married woman from making a will and allowed a widower to claim all of his late wife's property; accordingly, wills and probate inventories do not survive in the same numbers for women as for men.[3] While some wives did leave wills—a gesture Mary Prior considers "an extraordinary event"—their husbands' consent was generally required and could be revoked at any point before probate.[4] Not surprisingly, therefore, wives' wills make up less than one percent of the wills recorded between 1558 and 1700 (Prior 208). Further, a woman did not have to die in order for her husband to subsume her property, and women's libraries seem often to have been incorporated into their husbands' holdings during their lifetimes. The history of a book given to Lady Jane Lumley typifies the ways in which women's libraries disappear from view.[5] Nicholas Bacon sent a book to Lady Lumley "at her desire" in the mid 1570s. At some point "Lumley"—that is, *her husband*'s ownership mark—was written in the book by his secretary. Only the record of Bacon's inscription to Lady Lumley marks this book as once distinct from Lord Lumley's vast holdings. One seventeenth-century woman, clearly aware of the danger of her book being mistaken for someone else's property, inscribed her copy of *Culpeper's Directory for Midwives* with her name three times on different pages of the book, one with the further clarification "Elizabeth Hunt her Book not his."[6] Occasionally, the physical separation of "her books" from "his" in large households leaves a trace in the historical record. When a woman's books were kept in a discrete and gendered space like "my ladies book closett," a record of her collection may survive in household inventories. Listed among "An Inventorye of all such goods as I william More Esquiere had the 20th day of August Aº Domini 1556" are books "In my wyfes closet." The books and trifles in this closet belong to More's household estate, yet their location in a separate chamber is enough to preserve their identity as a woman's collection.[7]

Despite the practices and assumptions—both contemporary and modern—that obscure women's book ownership, detailed records attest to the existence of women's private libraries in early modern England. This evidence survives in many different forms: ownership stamps and signatures in extant copies of books, references in journals and letters, passages in commonplace books, representations in portraits, bequests in wills, and lists in probate and household inventories. Often, such records offer partial views of a woman's holdings. In a commissioned portrait, for example, Lady Anne Clifford is shown flanked by forty-eight books identified on their spines by title, but her diaries and funeral sermon mention another ten books, and a binding and annotations mark still another two books as hers.[8] Some records indicate substantial holdings without providing details about individual books. Catherine, Duchess of Suffolk, owned a "chestful of books" in 1580, Lady Anne Southwell moved three "truncks of bookes" to her new household in 1631, and Anne, Viscountess of Dorchester, left at her death in 1639 books worth nearly seventy-seven pounds, a sum that would have bought nearly one hundred fairly elaborate folio volumes or four hundred more modest books.[9] Other records, however, provide more precise information about women's book holdings. "An Inventory of Lady [Elizabeth] Sleighs bookes May 12 1647" documents the titles and formats in her library of fifty-three volumes. Lady Mohun took out a newspaper advertisement in 1679, offering a forty-shilling reward for the return of books stolen from her closet: "A Cambridge Bible in Folio, Mrs. Philips's Poems in Folio, a French Dictionary in Folio, Heylen's Geography in Folio, Two Volumes of Playes, one Mr. Drydens, in a large Quarto, A French Grammar in Quarto, Two English Dictionaries in Quarto, one Blunts, The New Testament in French, in two Parts, in Quarto; and several other Books."[10] Printed marks of ownership survive for thirty women between 1590 and 1700.[11] While an extant book label alone is not evidence of a large private library, it does point to a book owner who valued her books. And then there are the surviving books themselves. Remnants of what must have been a substantial collection, at least ninety-six extant books bear ownership marks of Frances

Wolfreston (1607–77). Countless other women recorded their ownership by hand in individual copies of books: "Anne Pay her Booke 1641," "mary crewe her Book," "This book perteins to me wryttin with my awn hand in march iii anno 1622 Elizabeythe forbes." These scattered ownership marks, particularly in books unlikely to be someone's sole volume, hint at the breadth of female book ownership in the period.[12]

On a much grander scale, some early modern women, primarily Continental royalty, made their mark in the world of books by building great libraries. Dianne de Poitiers built a library at Anet, a place so associated with her as to bear the nickname "Dianet," and Christina of Sweden hired a librarian and sent buyers all over Europe for books for the great European library she was assembling around the core library started by her father. After having abdicated the throne to her cousin in 1654, Christina traveled to Rome leading a procession of coaches bearing over two thousand books and manuscripts, a collection that in her time in Rome would more than double in size.[13] Lady Bridgewater's library of 241 separate volumes was then, I expect, not extraordinary among the aristocracy. Perhaps it was even modest. It is unusual only in that a clear, detailed catalog survives along with the larger family library with which many of its books were later merged.[14]

Frances Stanley was born into a family with great social ambitions and literary ties; with her mother's second marriage and her own marriage, she became doubly aligned with the powerful Egerton line as both stepdaughter and daughter-in-law to Lord Chancellor Ellesmere.[15] Steven May has identified her father, Ferdinando Stanley, Lord Strange, as a "courtier poet" active at court and author of several extant poems. With interests in verse, military shows, and tilting, Lord Strange performed in the Accession Day Tilts of 1590, and Edmund Spenser mourned him as "Amyntas" in *Colin Clout Comes Home Again.*[16] The Stanley family had, since the reign of Henry VIII, patronized troupes of players and tumblers known as "Derby's men" and "Strange's men."[17] The Countess's collection of drama and particularly of play quartos, therefore, continues this family interest in the theater and popular literature.

Alice (Spencer) Stanley, the Countess's mother, has been described as "a great lady, who had more close associations with more great literary figures [of the Renaissance] than any other single person that I am aware of" (Fogle 25). Lady Stanley at least briefly continued her late husband's patronage of an acting company in the 1590s, and later, as the wife of Lord Chancellor Ellesmere and a favorite of Queen Anne, she acted in court masques by Daniel and Jonson (Fogle 11–14, 22). She commissioned works by Davies and Marston, and Milton's *Arcades* was performed in her honor. The family's connection to literature and performance did not end with this generation: Frances Egerton's sister performed in Ben Jonson's *Masque of Beautie* and *Masque of Queenes,*[18] and her own children performed in Milton's *Comus*. The Countess had a model in her parents for her literary interests; her father's and husband's families similarly provided precedents for a rich private library. While only a few manuscripts survive, her paternal grandmother must have had an impressive collection (Fogle 14), and Lord Chancellor Ellesmere amassed one of the great early modern libraries, which included a traveling collection of miniature books housed in a special case shaped like a folio.[19]

Born into this powerful, literate, even bookish family, Frances Stanley Egerton leaves only one record of her learning and intellectual interests: her library. All the other surviving documents that I have examined reveal nothing of her education or love of books. She is portrayed as an early modern woman exemplary for her piety and obedience. "A Meditation on the Countess" is typical in its praise: "I neuer knew (nor any body els, I belieue) a more Obedient Daughter, a more Affectionate Sister, a more Carefull Mother, nor a Better Wife in all respects."[20] Her sister Elizabeth Hastings, Countess of Huntingdon, in contrast, is praised in her funeral sermon for a "mind of most excellent composure, of a noble & generous height" and an "understanding . . . of great perspicacity," so impressive that her husband professed "how much he hath in the estate of the minde beene bettered by her."[21] Certainly, the intelligence that the elegist celebrates is one "attempered" with sweetness and humility, and Lady Huntingdon's knowledge and literacy are inextricably bound up with her piety. Nevertheless, we learn that she was "an unwearied reader" of Scripture and that she habitually wrote down her observations and meditations after perusing the bible.[22] Two of Lady Bridgewater's daughters are similarly extolled in their funeral sermons as readers and collectors of devotional books.[23] But it is only from Lady Bridgewater's library that we learn that this mother of fifteen probably read French and was interested in history, theology, epistolary style, French music, foreign travel, and English drama. An examination of the Countess's private library reveals a woman who emerges as altogether more vigorous and educated than she seems in her contemporaries' portrayals.

"A Catalogue of my Ladies Bookes at London" contains three dated lists and several additions. The bulk of the catalogue was "Taken October. 27th. 1627," and books are identified by short title, format, and publication date, thus making exact identification possible for most entries. English printed books are grouped by format—"Bookes in Folio," "Bookes in Quarto," and "Bookes in Octauo and Lesse"—and manuscripts and French books are listed under separate headings.[24] Additions were made in 1631 and 1632, and a few titles were later added to each of these dated lists. The addition of some sixty-seven books between late 1627 and 1633 represents an increase of more than 38 percent of the 1627 holdings: the Countess was clearly actively acquiring a range of books into the 1630s. Because the catalogue was compiled in at least three distinct stages, we can learn both about the Countess's collection as it stood in 1627 and about her habits of acquisition between 1627 and 1633.

The Countess's library does not seem to have been made up of gifts, and it was not an inherited library. Especially in a family with other substantial private holdings, it is important to establish the Countess's agency in the acquisition of this collection. Two books are described as gifts: an English bible "giuen by Mrs Bagner" and *The New Covenant* "giuen mee by my Sister Huntington." Since these entries are explicitly distinguished as gifts, it seems unlikely that the rest of the books were gifts as well. The library was certainly not inherited from the Countess's father: only ten of the books in the catalogue were printed before his death. As for other potential bequests, the Countess was outlived by her mother—otherwise the most likely candidate—and by her husband. At the time of the catalogue, her two sisters were alive as well.

With Elizabeth Hunt's proprietary claim as a caution—that is, this book is "hers not his"—I want to argue that Lady Bridgewater's collection was distinct from her husband's library. She and Lord Bridgewater certainly owned "his and hers" copies of at least one book. The marks of their individual ownership in two extant copies point toward the existence of two discrete book collections during their lifetimes, a suspicion that the presence of many duplicates within the later family library strengthens.[25] The catalogue seems to be a shelf list since the entries are arranged by size, which was considered the most efficient way to store books. This probable arrangement suggests that the Countess's library was stored separately, perhaps in a book closet, an early modern version of a "room of one's own."[26] The fact that other English gentlewomen had their own book closets as early as the 1550s suggests that the Countess may have had such a room in the 1620s. Her sister, her daughters, and her daughter-in-law all had such rooms.[27] Her eldest daughter, Lady Frances Hobart (1603–64), stocked her closet with "most valuable English books," devotional texts that she consulted daily (Collinges 26–29). The closet of her daughter-in-law, Elizabeth (Cavendish) Egerton, the second Countess of Bridgewater, is described in an inventory taken after her death: "The Clossett for ye vpperpart is hung with white imbroderd satten naild to ye Cubbords. The lower part of ye clossett is hung with 4 Curtens of rich taffaty wrought with flowers of needleworke 2 window Curtens a Carpett, & a window cloth of Stained taffaty 1 little square table, & 2 stooles of Irishstitche 1 old Japan Cabbonett with drawers."[28] A pretty room with two stools and a table: perhaps the Countess too had such a retreat in which to read her books.

"My Ladies Bookes at London" seem to have constituted an active, ordered library. Within the divisions by size, the books are arranged by subject and author. Each section of the library opens with the bibles and psalters of that size, and other books follow by genre and topic. Among the folios, for instance, classical histories are grouped together, followed by French histories, then English histories. Of the twenty-six authors who are represented more than once in the collection, all but four are shelved side-by-side wherever their formats permit. This attention to a system of organization—to the placing of books—suggests the presence of a book owner who was both deliberate and knowledgeable. The publication dates of the books in Lady Bridgewater's library indicate a steady pattern of acquisition throughout her adulthood. Of the 241 books in the library, only 15 were published before she reached adulthood and married. The Countess appears to have acquired her books quickly: the April 1633 book list, for example, includes George Herbert's *The Temple*, hot off the press. The folios, typically the most expensive books at the time, seem to have been acquired steadily from 1600 to 1632, at a rate of roughly one folio per year. Further, fully two-thirds of the folios and quartos are first editions.

The currency of the Countess's library is matched by its breadth. As might be expected in a woman's library—or any early modern library for that matter—half of the Countess's books were religious texts. She owned thirteen bibles, seven prayer books, and three psalters, and indeed these were some of the oldest books in her library. Nevertheless, the Countess's library was not a narrow collection of devotional works of comfort and guidance. Many of her religious books were treatises, sermons, and books of doctrine. Further, many of these books represent opposing religious and political positions. Her funeral eulogist's praise of her "firme and vnshaken" allegiance "to the Truth of Religion" is reflected in her possession of a large number of Protestant tracts, many of them virulently anti-Papist, like John Rawlinson's *The Romish Judas* and Thomas Morton's *The Grand Imposture of the (Now) Church of Rome*. But, as befits the "dangerous times" to which the funeral sermon alludes, the Countess also owned several books with Marian or recusant connections: *A Right Godly Rule* (a prayer book based on a Marian edition), a *Iesus Psalter* (a popular Catholic book of devotion), and several works by the recusant poet Robert Southwell. The shelving of *A Right Godly Rule* next to an edition of Southwell printed by the Catholic secret press confirms that the Countess was, in fact, aware of the Marian and recusant influences in her library.

After religious books, the next largest category of books in the Countess's library is literature and history, which comprise nearly 100 of the 241 books in the catalogue. Along with a rich collection of classical, Continental, and English histories, the Countess owned literary works by Spenser, Shakespeare, Jonson, Donne, Drayton, Herbert, Wroth, and Bacon. Her collection of drama included masques, closet dramas, and plays from the public theaters, and she counted among her books Ben Jonson's 1616 *Workes*, *The New Inne*, and a manuscript of *The Gypsies Metamorphosed*, Fulke Greville's *Tragedy of Mustapha*, Mary Sidney's *Antonius*,[29] "Diuers Playes by Shakespeare," and seven other volumes of "Diuerse Playes." In addition to quarto playbooks, several other volumes of cheap, recreational literature survive among the octavos in the book catalog: Thomas Overbury's *Characters*, John Scoggin's *Jests* (listed as his "Merry Tayles"), and *Greenes Ghost Haunting Conie-Catchers*.

The breadth of the Countess's library suggests a resistance to the expectations of publishers and authors for women's reading. Frances Dolan and Jacqueline Pearson have documented the "policing" of women's reading during the period, pointing to conduct books, educational treatises, and legal customs that circumscribed women's reading.[30] At once catering to and trying to contain a growing female readership, authors and publishers produced books with prefatory letters addressed to "ladies" or "gentlewomen" and volumes whose subject matters—like cooking or midwifery—were destined for a largely female audience. Suzanne Hull has described and analyzed these books, compiling a list of these "Books for Women." Of the Countess's 241 volumes, only six books appear in Hull's list of 163 "Books for Women." In fact, the Countess shared more titles with one of her male relatives, the Earl of Huntingdon, than she does with this list of women's books.[31] Based largely on prefatory definitions of audience, Hull's finding list usefully records what authors and publishers hoped women would read; lists of women's holdings show the extent to which early modern women contested these constraints. Lady Bridgewater, for example, owned books addressed to "the vulgar sort" and to "young gentlemen."

The absence of herbals and medicinals and other "books for women" may partly be a consequence of the location of this collection in London, where one had access to pharmacists and doctors in the seventeenth century. These books may have been valued primarily in less urban areas like the family seat in Ashridge, where the Countess may have had another library. It seems quite possible that she assembled or had access to two distinct collections—a London library and a country library—each appropriate to her local needs and activities. And indeed an extant Donne manuscript stamped with her initials is not recorded among the "Paper Bookes" in her London library; perhaps this manuscript was part of a collection housed elsewhere.[32] One of her contemporaries, Lady Anne Merricke, refers in a letter to a country collection, which must suffice while she is away from London: "I must content my selfe here with the studie of Shackspeare, and the historie of woemen, all my countrie librarie."[33] While Merricke's two "countrie librarie" books can both be found in Lady Bridgewater's London library, Merricke's letter nevertheless supports the possibility of a gentlewoman's multiple, distinct collections housed at her various residences.

Though the Countess's library is not a prescriptively feminine collection, it is unlike the libraries amassed by her most bookish male peers in its preponderance of English books. The assumed language in the organization of John Dee's catalog, for example, is Latin; in Lord Lumley's library, less than 7 percent of the books were in English, and a full 88 percent were in classical languages.[34] Lady Bridgewater, in contrast, owned nothing in Latin or Greek: except for eighteen French books, everything in her collection is in English. Roughly 15 percent of the Countess's books were translations into English from Latin, Greek, Italian, Spanish, and French. This proportion of translations is unsurprising given that a fifth of all books printed in Elizabethan England were translations, and women were one of the targeted audiences for vernacular texts.[35] The translations in the collection made available to her texts she otherwise could not have read:[36] Plutarch's *Lives*, Tacitus's *Annales*, Boethius's *Books of Philosophicall Comfort*, Tasso's *Godfrey of Bulloigne*, Cervantes's *Don Quixote*, and Boccaccio's *Decameron*, among others. Along with these literary texts, she owned Tycho Brahe's *Astronomicall Conjectur* and several descriptions of foreign lands, particularly Turkey and the Indies.

Lady Bridgewater owned quite an interesting set of books to pluck off the shelf, but did she read these books? And, if so, what did she make of them? Much as the library catalogue reveals something of the breadth of the Countess's collecting and possible reading, extant copies of her books, to which the catalogue directs us, also hold clues in their bindings, flyleaves, and margins.[37] Most frequent in the surviving copies from the Countess's library are ownership marks: her holograph initials and the signature of her son, to whom she gave at least three of her books and probably several, perhaps her entire library. In her *Booke of Homilyes*, the Countess wrote the initials of each of her daughters—"EE:CE:ME:PE:KE:ME:AE:AliceE:"—the sort of inscription that often appears in families' treasured books.[38] Other marks of ownership similarly indicate that the Countess took great care with her library: her stamped initials, often in gilt and often on elaborate and beautiful bindings, suggest the importance of the collection to her. Further, the very fact that she had her library cataloged implies a certain literary self-consciousness, for a private library, unlike a public institution, does not need a catalogue. And unlike a probate inventory, a private library catalogue is not motivated by economic or legal concerns. The compilation of such a catalogue, therefore, may very well have been a gesture to announce her relation to the world of books and her position as a book owner.

Yet no marks of active readership survive in any of the Countess's books that I have located. What are we to make of this absence? Did Lady Bridgewater merely possess her books as objects of status? Were they read aloud to her? Did she read them without marking in them? If so, another series of questions arises about why she did not mark her books as an active reader: did she not consider herself a serious reader? Did she not re-read her books? Or did she, like her daughter-in-law, read them and make notes elsewhere?[39]

The Countess's library catalogue stands in many ways as a ghost pointing provocatively at what can now only be guessed. It is not just Lady Bridgewater's seeming silence that puzzles me: in general, early modern women seem to have left very little marginalia—just one of the signs of active, engaged reading in the period. Some women, however, certainly did annotate their books. As a dowager in her eighties, Lady Anne Clifford produced an elaborate record of the reading of *A Mirror for Magistrates* in her household. Sometimes in her own shaky hand, more often in the hand of her secretary, marginal annotations record the place, date, and circumstances of the reading of various sections, and they provide assessments and summaries of passages: "A remarkable side of a Leffe," "A most brave ver[s]e," "A fine description of the tempest of the Sese."[40] Other women may have annotated the sorts of books that do not survive in great numbers: almanacs, herbals, recipe books. So, too, these women may have made notes in books as they prepared to teach their children the rudiments of reading. Eliza Bradburn leaves a nineteenth-century account of such a scene of instruction:

EMILY.—Mamma, I often see you reading Dr. Clarke's Commentary on the Bible: Is any thing said in it about the woman's obeying the man before God passed sentence upon them?

MAMMA.—I will read a few lines to you, which I marked last evening; expecting this subject would interest you.[41]

Like Eliza Bradburn, Lady Bridgewater emerges from her books and book list as both an attentive book owner and as a mother.

Additions to the catalogue and marks in the books themselves provide a glimpse of the circulation of books within a network of family members and associates. Along with the two books initially registered as gifts in the catalogue, several other volumes are marked as being given or lent later: a duodecimo book of prayers, *The Enemy to Atheisme*, was "giuen to my Lady Penelopie," the Countess's daughter, while a 1612 quarto Bible "of the new trans" (presumably the King James version) was "sent to my lady Ma[?]e beinge the 16 of No: 1628." The *Book of Homilyes* inscribed with her daughters' names found its way later to her daughter-in-law Elizabeth, who passed it to her son in 1663. The social life of these books offers an instructive contrast to the list as a whole. For while the catalogue documents a library of striking breadth of subjects and a resistance to the narrow devotional libraries sometimes urged upon early mod-

ern women, the recorded circulation of books supports the contemporary notion that the most appropriate gifts for women were devotional works and
bibles. Her son John Brackley, on the other hand, was the recipient of a far more
various set of books: Boethius's *Five Bookes of Philosophicall Comfort*, Jonson's
The Gypsies Metamorphosed in manuscript, and the *Tableau historique des ruses et
subtilitez des femmes*. The Countess also owned Heywood's defense of women,
the *History of Women*, but it was this antifeminist French work, the *Tableau
historique*, that her son later counted among his own books.

Celebrated after her death for her exemplarity as daughter, sister, mother,
and wife, Lady Bridgewater emerges from her library catalogue not as a para-
gon of learning but as a woman connected to familial networks and responsive
to cultural expectations. She is an "Affectionate Sister" noting the gift of a book
of sermons and a "Carefull Mother" recording her daughters' initials in a book
of homilies, passing bibles and devotional works on to her daughters and a book
for "Young Gentlemen Readers" to her son. Unlike Lady Anne Clifford, who
seems remarkable at every turn in her own self-presentation and in her contemporaries' portrayals of her, Lady Bridgewater does not ripple the historical
record with signs of curiosity, resistance, or exceptional intelligence.[42] It is her
very conventionality, I would argue, that makes her library collection so striking, for its existence does not seem to have been considered worthy of remark.
And if a woman's library of 241 volumes did not warrant attention in 1633, then
we must expand our notions of early modern women as consumers of books.

* * *

Note: In the following transcription I have silently expanded abbreviations and
dropped periods following many of the entries and dates.[43]

A Catalogue of my Ladies Bookes at London;
Taken October. 27th. 1627.

Bookes in Folio   Printed. Anno.

Speeds Chronicle in 3 volumes	
His mappes	} 1611
The Turkish History	1610
The Treasury of aunceint and moderne times	1613
The Catalogue of Honour. by Milles	1610
The Booke of Homilyes	1623
Dr Halls Workes	1621
Hookers Ecclesiastical Policy	1604

Plutarch's Liues	1579
The Roman History Engl. by Holland	1609
Tacitus with Sir Henr. Savills Notes	1612
The French History by Commines	1601
Lewes the 11th Engl. by Grimston	1614
Martin's Chronologie	1615
Henry the 7th by the Lord Verulam	1622
His Natural History	1627
A World of Wonders	1607
Sandys his Trauells	1615
The Diall of Princes	1619
The History of Women	1624
The Countesse of Montgomery's Vrania	[n.d.]
Barcklay's Argenis	1625
Johnsons Workes	1616
Drayton's Workes: part 2d	1627
The Fayery Queene	1609
Godfrey of Bulloigne	1600
A Discouery of erours in the firste Edition of the Cottalogue of Honnor Raphe Brooke}	1621
Annalls of England. per B: Hereford	1630
Evsebius his Eclesiasticall History	1619

Bookes in Quarto

Three Bibles 1	1611
2	1612
3	1609
The Bible in two volumes.	1619
Three Common. prayer bookes 1	1596
2	1607
3	1614
A Booke of Christian prayers	1590
Our English Liturgie in French	1616
A forme of prayer for the dangerous times	1626
The History of the Church by Simson	1624
Pseudomartyr	1610
Mount Caluary by Guevara	1595
Cases of Conscience by Perkins	1611
The Buckler of Faith, by Moulin	1620

The Liues of the three Norm. Kings by Hayward		1613
The Natural and moral History of both Indyes		1604
The Court of King Iames		1619
King Iames his Apology for the Oathe of Allegeance		1609
False Complaints by Paschalius English		1615
Of true Happines by Boulton		1611
Christ's Crosse by Andrewes		1614
A Thankefull Remembrance of Gd's mercy by Bishop Carleton		1627
Dr Kinges Lectures on Ionas		1611
Dr Benfeild on Amos		1613
Smiths Sermons		1597
Quadriga Salutis or The Chariot of Saluation 4 Sermons by Dr Rawlinson		1625
His Viuat Rex }	1	1619
His Romish Iudas } Three Sermons	2	1611
His Fishermen }	3	1609
The Holy Roode by Io. Dauies		1609
St Peteres Complaint		1602
A Sermon by Dr Donne		1626
Another		1622
A Sermon by Dr Balcanquall		1623
More Worke for a Masse-Priest		1621
History of Trebizond		1616
Don Quixot by Shelton		[n.d.]
The English Secretary		1607
Sir Edward Hobby's Letter		1609
Du Bartas Engl. verse by Sylvester Edit. 4		[n.d.]
Posthumus Bartas		1607
Diuers Playes by Shakespeare		1602
Diuerse Playes in 5 thicke Volumes in Velum		[n.d.]
A Booke of Diuerse Playes in Leather		1609
The Tragaedy of Mustapha		1609
A Booke of diuerse Playes in Velum		1601
A Quip for an vpstart Courtier		1620
The grand Imposture of the church of Roome		[n.d.]
Davids teares		[n.d.]
The Rule of Faith or an Exposicion of thappostles creed		1626
The life of Queene Eliz:		[n.d.]
[??] booke of beastes fishes fluers gardin[?] [??]		[n.d.]
The English Bible with a Ruffe Couer		[⟨1588⟩?]

Bookes in Octavo and Lesse

Two English Bibles 1	1619
2	1620
Two new Testaments 1. with singing Psal	1600
2. with ye paper green'd	1603
Two Bookes of Common prayer 1	1573
2	1610
Two Psalme Bookes in meter with 1	1623
the Reading Psalmes in the marg. 2	[n.d.]
Grounds of Religion by Virell Impress. 8°	1609
Directions to know the true Church by Dr Carleton	1615
A Briefe Catechisme for Housholders with	
godly Prayers, by Dering	1602
The sixt and 1.	1622
seauennth volumes of Dr Halls Contemplacions 2.	1623
His meditacions and Vowes; Two of them 1	1616
2	1621
An Exposition of the 15th Psal. by Epinas with	
other Treatises annext	1548
An Exposition on the Reuelacion by Dent	1611
Three small Treatises of Diuinity in one Vol	[n.d.]
Hyggons his motiue to suspecte his Religion	1609
The Imitacion of Christ by Rogers	1589
The Practice of Christianity by Rous. Edit. 2ᵃ.	[n.d.]
The Practice of Piety	1615
Dr Donnes Devotions	1624
Featlyes Handmaide to Devotion	[n.d.]
A Helpe to Devotion by Hieron	1608
The Sanctuary of a Troubled Soul by Hayward	1602
The euer burning Lamp of Piety and Devotion	1619
The Art of true Happines by Rous	1619
Oyle of Scorpions by Rous	1623
Times Curtaine drawne, Or the Anatomy of	
Vanity by Brathwayte	1621
A Strappada for the Diuell by Brathwayte	1615
The Romish Chaine by Gurney	1624
A pretious Pearle Engl. by Couerdale	1560 [1605]
Crummes of Comfort, Engl. by Couerdale	1627
Dauid's sling by Hutchins	1606
The Card and Compasse of life by midleton	1613

A staffe of Comfort by Bernard	1616
A Dyet for the Christian Soule	1607
The dayly watch of the soule by Gerhard	1611
The Enemy to Atheisme	[n.d.]
The Enemy of Security Engl. by Rogers	1591
A right godly Rule	1602
Shorte Rules of a good life	1602
Mary Magda: Funerall Teares with other Treatises annext	[n.d.]
Heraclitus his Teares or Humane Misery by Darcie [?]	1624
Meditacions on the Sacrament by Sutton	1622
Meditations of Instruction Exhortacion and Reproofe	1616
Prayers and Meditacions 14 by Lewis de Granada	1602
An Exhortatory Instruction to Repentance by Lennard	1609
A Garden of Spirituall Flowers	1612
The Posy of Godly Prayers, by Themilthorpe	1613
Supplications of Saintes. Two of them.	1[n.d.]2[n.d.]
The Poore mans Reste	[n.d.]
A Pensiue Mans Practice by Norden	1610
The Princes Prayers	1607
Godly Prayers	[n.d.]
An Eye to see God	1624
The Diseases of the Time, by Rous	1622
A Patterne for a Kings Inauguracion by King Iames	1620
A briefe Remembraunce of Engl. Monarchs by Taylour	1618
Boetius English	1609
Quintus Curtius English	1602
Florus English	[n.d.]
The wellspring of Sciences, by Barker	1612
The Parlament of Virtues Royall, by Syluester	[n.d.]
Scotts Philomythie	1616
The Shepheards Hunting, by Withres	1615
Two funeral Elegyes in black velum	1624
A Funerall Sermon, for the Lady Mary	1607
Iesus Psalter	[n.d.]
Sir Thomas Overbury's Characters	[n.d.]
King Iames his Aphorismes	[n.d.]
The Heauenly Banquet by Denison	1619
An English bible with siluer claspes	1628
An English Testament with greene couer	1598
A ladyes present to a princes	1627
A sermone by the B: of Exeter supr[?]	1628

A sermon by the B: of Lincolne	1628
Sco[gg]ons Merry tayles	1626
Greenes ghoste	162[?]
History of lazarello de Tormes	1624
Esops Fables	162[?]
The Greate Assyze or day of Iubile sermon S.S.	1628
Vade Mecum a Manualle of Essayes	1629
The Marrow of the orackles of god	[n.d.]
Stepes of Assention into god	[n.d.]
The light of Faith per Richard Bifeild	1630
A Collection of private devotions B: London	1627
The Isle of Man	1629
The Imitation of Dauids Resolution	162[?]
Horae subrasiuae, or spare howers of Meditation	1630
The English Mans Doctor	1624

French Bookes of diverse Volumes

D'Ossats Letters	1627
Le Secretaire des Secretaires	1610
L'Astree, Seconde Partie	1614
Another the same	1615
Les Amours de Clidamant et Marilinde	1603
Le Decameron de Bocace	1579
Les Pensees de l'Eternite	1626
A French Musick booke	[n.d.]
A French Testament	[n.d.]
A litle Prayer Booke	[n.d.]
la Golatee	1626
les oeuures de Mounsieur de Balzac	1627
Tableau historique des Ruses	1623
La Pratique de piete	1628[?]
A French Bible	[n.d.]
An other French bible	[n.d.]
Saintes prieres recuielles	[n.d.]

26 Aprill 1631

Buttleres Bees with the orchard	[n.d.]
A Catechisticall docktrine	[n.d.]

Eclesiasticall History	[n.d.]
Practice of piety	[n.d.]
Granadoes meditations	[n.d.]
Gerrards Praiers	[n.d.]
The Heavenly Banquett	[n.d.]
A Chaine of pearle	[n.d.]
A Threefold resolution by Denyson	[n.d.]
A Discourse of life & death by Morney	[n.d.]
The Counter scufle	[n.d.]
Clavells recantation	[n.d.]
Felthams Resolues	[n.d.]
Brittaines remembrance	[n.d.]
Devout Communicant	[n.d.]
English psalmes by King Iames translated	[n.d.]
A misticall Marriadge	[n.d.]

Paper Bookes of diverse volumes

A Sermon-Booke, in 4to
A Sermon of Mr Mores, at Ashridg. 1622
The Lamentacions of Ieremy in verse by Dr Donne, 8°
A Prayer Booke: 32°
Three Bookes of French Songes
The Gypsies masque. 4to
A litle cleane Paper-booke, 12°
Two Accompt Bookes, in 4to
a booke of the psalmes translated
      after a new manner written, Master Rauenscroft

17° Aprill 1632

The masse of Christe & bookes per B Coventrey	1631
Two bookes of seuerall sermons per B Andrewes	1632
Dr donnes sermons	1622
Dod on the Lords Supper 2	1628
The new covenante per Mr Attersole	1614
Ticho Brahe's conclucion	1632
Two bookes of Sir Franc Bacon	1632
Three bookes of wisedome per Pet. Charron	[n.d.]
An english bible giuen by Mrs Bagner	[n.d.]

Theatre of gods iudgments per Dr Bearde   1631
The New Couenant or the Sayntes porcion
    giuen mee by my Sister Huntington   1632
Randall vppon the Sacrament in 23 sermons   1633
A Testament in Dec°: octauo in turkish Leather guilte   [n.d.]
The New Inn   [n.d.]
The Church Porch   [n.d.]

Notes

The Huntington Library in San Marino, California, funded my initial work on the
Countess of Bridgewater, and its curatorial staff (especially Mary Robertson and Alan
Jutzi) taught me much about the Bridgewater collection. Two fellow Huntington
readers contributed especially to this project: James Knowles first alerted me to the
Countess's catalog, and Victoria Burke, who had worked independently on the manu-
script, generously read this essay in draft and offered many useful suggestions. The
Duke of Sutherland has kindly permitted me to publish a transcription of the manu-
script here, based upon the Huntington's facsimile.

    1. Jacqueline Pearson, "Women Reading, Reading Women," *Women and Liter-
ature in Britain, 1500–1700*, ed. Helen Wilcox (Cambridge: Cambridge University
Press, 1996), 82. In his still influential *Library Catalogues of the English Renaissance*
(Godalming, Surrey: St. Paul's, 1983), Sears Jayne reports, "Records of the ownership
of books by women are unfortunately very sparse; there are only three lists of books
owned by women included in this survey, and two of these are clearly collections left by
deceased husbands" (46). Curiously, even Jayne's own volume includes five records of
women's libraries that he does not count in this tally. Suzanne W. Hull and Caroline
Lucas cite Jayne when they note the absence of early modern records of female book
ownership (Hull, *Chaste, Silent, and Obedient: English Books for Women, 1475–1640* [San
Marino, Calif.: Huntington Library, 1988], xi; Lucas, *Writing for Women: The Example
of Woman as Reader in Elizabethan Romance* [Philadelphia: Open University Press,
1989], 14). Peter Clark challenges Jayne by broadening the basis of his study, but he does
not much improve upon Jayne's dismissal of female book collectors ("The Ownership
of Books in England, 1560–1640: The Example of Some Kentish Townsfolk," *Schooling
and Society: Studies in the History of Education*, ed. Lawrence Stone [Baltimore: Johns
Hopkins University Press, 1976], 99, 102–3). In an essay published while this book was
in press, David McKitterick surveys the field and describes the collection of about one
hundred books owned by Elizabeth Puckering (c. 1621–89) ("Women and Their Books
in Seventeenth-Century England: The Case of Elizabeth Puckering," *The Library*, 7th
ser., 1 [2000]: 359–80).
    2. A family manuscript from 1636 records the year of her birth as 1585, calculat-
ing the span of her life in years, months, and days (Huntington Library EL 6846).
Citing a monumental inscription, Cokayne dates her birth as 1583, *The Complete
Peerage of England, Scotland, Ireland, Great Britain, and the United Kingdom: Extant,
Extinct, or Dormant*, new edition by Vicary Gibbs (London: St. Catherine's Press,
1912), 2:312.
    3. Amy Louise Erickson, *Women and Property in Early Modern England* (Lon-

don: Routledge, 1993), 25, 139–43. For the methodological challenges associated with probate inventories, see Clark, 98; and Margaret Spufford, "The Limitations of Probate Inventory," *English Rural Society, 1500–1800: Essays in Honour of Joan Thirsk*, ed. John Chartres and David Hey (Cambridge: Cambridge University Press, 1990), 139–74. Examples of wills and probate inventories documenting men's book ownership are readily available in E. S. Leedham-Green, *Books in Cambridge Inventories: Book-Lists from Vice-Chancellor's Court Probate Inventories in the Tudor and Stuart Periods*, vol. 1, *The Inventories* (Cambridge: Cambridge University Press, 1986); and *Playhouse Wills, 1558–1642: An Edition of Wills by Shakespeare and His Contemporaries in the London Theatre*, ed. E. A. J. Honigmann and Susan Brock (Manchester: Manchester University Press, 1993).

4. Mary Prior, "Wives and Wills, 1558–1700," *English Rural Society, 1500–1800: Essays in Honour of Joan Thirsk*, ed. John Chartres and David Hey (Cambridge: Cambridge University Press, 1990), 214, 202–3.

5. For a discussion of this manuscript volume, see Elizabeth McCutcheon, "Sir Nicholas Bacon's Great House Sententiae," *English Literary Renaissance Supplements* 3 (1977): 5–12. The volume is listed in Lumley's library catalog as item 2208: "Sentences painted in Sir Nicolas Bacons lorde Keepers gallerie at Goramburie, and by him sent to the la: Lumley" (*The Library of John, Lord Lumley: The Catalogue of 1609*, ed. Sears Jayne and Francis R. Johnson [London: British Museum, 1956], 249). While this edition reports seven items that bear Jane Lumley's signature, this volume bears only Lord Lumley's ownership mark.

6. I am grateful to Suzanne Hull for showing me this inscription in her personal copy.

7. Sir William More's Account Book, 1556 (Folger Shakespeare Library L.b.550, ff. 2–7). Among the bottles and brushes and spices are "a boke de parte muliers," "the pomeander of prayers," and three "other bokes of prayers" (ff. 6–7).

8. For a seventeenth-century transcription of the titles in the portrait see George C. Williamson, *Lady Anne Clifford, Countess of Dorset, Pembroke & Montgomery, 1590–1676* (1922; rpt., East Ardsley, Wakefield: S. R., 1967), 498–500; Richard T. Spence adds two titles and provides fuller bibliographic identifications, *Lady Anne Clifford, Countess of Pembroke, Dorset and Montgomery (1590–1676)* (Phoenix Mill, England: Sutton, 1997), 190–91. Mary Ellen Lamb documents nine other books mentioned in Clifford's diary, "The Agency of the Split Subject: Lady Anne Clifford and the Uses of Reading," *English Literary Renaissance* 22 (1992): 349, n. 8; Edward Rainbowe recalls her praise of *"William Barklay's Dispute* with *Bellarmine"* in *A sermon preached at the funeral of the Right Honorable Anne Countess of Pembroke, Dorset, and Montgomery . . . with some remarks on the life of that eminent lady* (London, 1677), 39. Stephen Orgel has identified a book in his library as once belonging to Clifford (see n. 40 below); Maggs Bros., Ltd., recently offered for sale Clifford's copy of *The Generall Historie of Spaine* (1612), which bears her crest and initials. Much like Clifford, Margaret Hoby also recorded her reading in her diary, from which Lamb culls the books, authors, and titles that Hoby mentions by name, "Margaret Hoby's Diary: Women's Reading Practices and the Gendering of the Reformation Subject," *Pilgrimage for Love: Essays in Early Modern Literature in Honor of Josephine A. Roberts*, ed. Sigrid King (Tempe, Áriz.: Arizona Center for Medieval and Renaissance Studies, 1999), 87–91.

9. Lawrence Stone lists the collection of the Duchess of Suffolk, *The Crisis of the Aristocracy, 1558–1641* (Oxford: Clarendon Press, 1965), appendix 37, 794. Francis Steer

has transcribed the Viscountess of Dorchester's inventory in "The Inventory of Anne, Viscountess Dorchester," *Notes and Queries* 198 (1953): 94–96, 155–58, 379–81, 414–17, 469–73, 515–19; the appraiser's valuation of "1 great chronicle booke" at 16s. provides one key to the number of the Viscountess's "Bookes in the lowe gallery" together valued at £76 18s. 10d. For a list of contemporary book prices, see Francis R. Johnson, "Notes on English Retail Book-prices, 1550–1640," *The Library*, 5th ser., 5 (1950): 94–112. Southwell's trunks are listed in "An Inventorye of the Lady Anne Southwells goods," which appears in the Southwell-Sibthorpe commonplace book, as does her husband's "List of my Bookes," which seems to incorporate his late wife's books (Folger MS V.b.198 59ʳ, 60ᵛ, 64ᵛ–66ʳ; edited by Jean Klene, *The Southwell-Sibthorpe Commonplace Book: Folger MS. V.b. 198* [Tempe, Ariz.: Medieval & Renaissance Texts & Studies, 1997], 93–96, 98–101). For a discussion of this list of 110 books, many of which probably filled Southwell's three "truncks," see Klene, xix; and Jean Carmel Cavanaugh, "The Library of Lady Southwell and Captain Sibthorpe," *Studies in Bibliography* 20 (1967): 244–46.

10. The inventory of Sleigh's books appears in MS 751 at the Wellcome Institute for the History of Medicine; I am grateful to Jennifer Stine for sharing her transcription of this list with me. Mohun advertised in the *Domestick Intelligencer* 28 (10 October 1679); I am indebted to William Burns for this reference.

11. This tally includes book labels, bookplates, book stamps, and gift labels listed under STC 3368.5 and in Brian North Lee, *Early Printed Book Labels: A Catalogue of Dated Personal Labels and Gift Labels Printed in Britain to the Year 1760* (Pinner, Middlesex: Private Libraries Association and Bookplate Society, 1976), #39, 68, 69, 93, 129, 135, 139, 141a, 151, 154, 185, 187, 196, 202, 204, 210, 214, 215, 219, 221, 222, 229, 233; and Lee, *British Bookplates: A Pictorial History* (Newton Abbot, England: David & Charles, 1979), #211 and 218.

12. These three signatures appear in Huntington Library Rare Books 19826, 15856, and 42618. Ninety-five of Wolfreston's books are identified by Paul Morgan, "Frances Wolfreston and 'Hor Bouks': A Seventeenth-Century Woman Book-Collector," *The Library*, 6th ser., 11 (1989): 197–219. William Sherman alerted me to another extant copy bearing her signature. Ownership marks of little-known readers are not routinely catalogued in modern libraries' provenance files, but two computer-based projects promise at least a glimpse beyond the chance findings in individual books. Alan Nelson has begun to record contemporary signatures in STC books in the UMI microfilm collection, making a preliminary listing available at his website (http://socrates.berkeley.edu/~ahnelson/). And the Reading Experience Database solicits scholars' findings of individual accounts of reading and book ownership, which it will compile into a growing database: http://www.open.ac.uk/Arts/RED/index.htm.

13. On Dianne de Poitiers, see Sandra Sider, "The Woman Behind the Legend: Dianne de Poitiers," *Women Writers of the Renaissance and Reformation*, ed. Katharina M. Wilson (Athens: University of Georgia Press, 1987). For an account of Christina's bibliophilia, see Charles I. Elton, "Christina of Sweden and Her Books," *Bibliographica* 1 (1895): 5–30. Although it is dated and includes only noblewomen, Ernest Quentin Bauchart's work provides an overview of women's book ownership in France, *Les femmes bibliophiles de France (XVIe, XVIIe, et XVIIIe siècles)*, vol. 1 (Paris, 1886).

14. The Huntington Library holds a facsimile (EL 6495) of the manuscript now owned by the Duke of Sutherland. With his kind permission, a transcription of the library catalog follows this essay. For earlier mentions of the catalog, see Cedric C.

Brown, *John Milton's Aristocratic Entertainments* (Cambridge: Cambridge University Press, 1985), 33; and Margaret J. M. Ezell, *The Patriarch's Wife: Literary Evidence and the History of the Family* (Chapel Hill: University of North Carolina Press, 1987), 15–16.

15. For biographical information about members of her family, I have relied on the *Dictionary of National Biography*; Brown, *John Milton's Aristocratic Entertainments*; French R. Fogle, "'Such a Rural Queen': The Countess Dowager of Derby as Patron," and Louis A. Knafla, "The 'Country' Chancellor: The Patronage of Sir Thomas Egerton, Baron Ellesmere," *Patronage in Late Renaissance England, Papers Read at a Clark Library Seminar, 1977* (Los Angeles: Clark Library, 1983); and several manuscripts owned by the Duke of Sutherland and available at the Huntington Library in facsimile (EL 6841, EL 6846, EL 6847, EL 22/F/39).

16. Steven W. May, *The Elizabethan Courtier Poets: The Poems and their Contexts* (Columbia: University of Missouri Press, 1991), 369–76; Fogle, 15–16. For information on surviving poems attributed to Lord Strange, see May, "Spenser's 'Amyntas': Three Poems by Ferdinando Stanley, Lord Strange, Fifth Earl of Derby," *Modern Philology* 70 (1972): 49–52.

17. For their patronage of minstrels, see Tessa Watt, "Publisher, Pedlar, Pot-Poet: The Changing Character of the Broadside Trade, 1550–1640," *Spreading the Word: The Distribution Networks of Print, 1550–1850*, ed. Robin Myers and Michael Harris (Winchester: St. Paul's Bibliographies, 1990), 68.

18. *The Progresses, Processions, and Magnificent Festivities, of King James the First*, ed. John Nichols (London, 1828), 2: 174, 245.

19. One of only four such extant English collections, the Ellesmere traveling library survives at the Huntington Library (RB 88313).

20. Huntington Library EL 6888 (facsimile). She is similarly eulogized in John Carter's funeral sermon (EL 6883, facsimile); Aurelian Townshend's "A Funerall Elegie" (*The Poems and Masques of Aurelian Townshend with Music by Henry Lawes and William Webb*, ed. Cedric C. Brown [Reading: Whiteknights, 1983], 54–55); Thomas Maye's elegy (EL 6843, facsimile); Robert Codrington's volume of verses (EL 6850, facsimile); and a Latin inscription for her funeral monument (EL 6845, facsimile). Jennifer Andersen kindly helped me untangle the linguistic and paleographic difficulties of EL 6845. Originals of these manuscripts are held by the Duke of Sutherland.

21. I. F., *A sermon preached at Ashby De-la-zouch . . . At the funerall of . . . lady Elizabeth Stanley [Hastings]* (London, 1635), 33–36.

22. Some of these meditations may be included among the prayers and notes gathered as "Certaine Collections of the right honourable Elizabeth late Countesse of Huntingdon for her owne private vse. 1633" and bound as memorial copies (Huntington Library HM 15369, EL 6871, HA Literature 1 [6], HA Religious 2 [8]).

23. J[ohn] C[ollinges], *Par Nobile. Two Treatises* (London, 1669), 22, 25–27, 29–30, 268, 272.

24. Although originally separated from these other categories by a good deal of blank space, which was then filled in on 26 April 1631, the list of "Paper bookes of diverse volumes" seems to have been made in 1627: the hand and system of arrangement are the same, and unlike any of the later lists, this section provides formats for most of the volumes.

25. The Huntington Library owns the copy of Augustine Vincent's *A Discoverie of Errours* (1622) that was Lord Bridgewater's (RB 69784); David Scott Kastan owns the copy that was Lady Bridgewater's. I am grateful to him for alerting me to this volume's

provenance. Several sales of duplicates from the Bridgewater family library can be documented, most notably in the early nineteenth century and by the Huntington Library after acquiring the collection: (Stephen Tabor, "The Bridgewater Library," *Dictionary of Literary Biography* 213: 47, 49–50).

26. For discussions of book closets, particularly as they may have been gendered spaces, see Lena Cowen Orlin, "Gertrude's Closet," *Shakespeare Jahrbuch* 134 (1998): 44–67; Alan Stewart, *Close Readers: Humanism and Sodomy in Early Modern England* (Princeton: Princeton University Press, 1997), 163–70; James Knowles, "'Infinite Riches in a Little Room': Marlowe and the Aesthetics of the Closet," and Sasha Roberts, "Shakespeare 'Creepes into the Womens Closets about Bedtime': Women Reading in a Room of their Own," *Renaissance Configurations: Voices/Bodies/Spaces, 1580–1690*, ed. Gordon McMullan (New York: St. Martin's, 1998).

27. In an early example, Lady More kept books in her book closet, which her husband inventoried in 1556 (Folger L.b.550). Lady Bridgewater's sister, the Countess of Huntingdon, had a book closet (Huntington Library Hastings Inventories Box 1 [13], f. 2^v), as did two of her daughters (Collinges 25, 29, 272). In examples from contemporary drama, Lavinia, Lady Macbeth, Ophelia, and Gertrude all spend time in their own closets (*Titus Andronicus* III.ii.81–85; *Macbeth* V.i.7; *Hamlet* II.i.77–84, III.iv).

28. Huntington Library EL 8094, 21 December 1663.

29. Published with *A Discourse of Life and Death* by Phillippe de Mornay, which the Countess of Pembroke also translated.

30. Dolan, "Reading, Writing, and Other Crimes," *Feminist Readings of Early Modern Culture*, ed. Valerie Traub, M. Lindsay Kaplan, and Dympna Callaghan (Cambridge: Cambridge University Press, 1996).

31. Huntington Library Hastings Inventories 1 (13), ff. 18^r–24^r. I am grateful to James Knowles for alerting me to this manuscript and sharing his transcription with me.

32. Titled "Dr Donne" and bearing the Countess's stamped initials on its covers, Huntington Library EL 6893 is not the Donne manuscript listed in the catalog as "The Lamentacions of Ieremy in verse."

33. Merricke to Mrs. Lydall, 21 January 1638, *Calendar of State Papers*, Conway Papers 142. In the early eighteenth century, Lady Anne Coventry catalogued her impressive collection, setting apart from the main collection "Books in my closett at Crombe," "Books and Papers brought from the Vicarage House," and "Books from Edston" (Ruth Perry, *The Celebrated Mary Astell: An Early English Feminist* [Chicago: University of Chicago Press, 1986], appendix B).

34. The section of Latin books is not titled in Dee's catalog, whereas English, French, Spanish, Hebrew, and Italian books are given separate headings (*John Dee's Library Catalogue*, ed. Julian Roberts and Andrew G. Watson [London: Bibliographical Society, 1990]). For Lumley, see Jayne and Johnson 11.

35. Eve Rachele Sanders, *Gender and Literacy on Stage in Early Modern England* (Cambridge: Cambridge University Press, 1998), 104.

36. For other evidence that Lady Bridgewater could not read Latin, see Huntington Library EL 6514, a 1634 letter that includes an English copy of a Latin document for her to read.

37. Of the 241 entries in the catalog, I have located fifty-nine copies from the Bridgewater family library, some of which may not have been the Countess's; eighteen

of these bear further marks identifying them conclusively as hers. James Knowles has generously helped me trace several Bridgewater books.

38. Huntington Library 473000 Page Collection 328. A modern cataloger's note describes this volume as her daughter Alice's copy, but by the time Alice Egerton (b. 1619) would have been old enough to write this accomplished hand, several of her sisters had married, and so she probably would not have referred to them by the initials of their maiden name. Alice's name may be written out to distinguish her from her sister "A[rbella]E."

39. Elizabeth (Cavendish) Egerton recorded her reading of the Bible in a manuscript book of meditations (Huntington Library EL 8374, facsimile, of which RB 297343 is a fair copy).

40. Stephen Orgel kindly allowed me to examine his copy of the 1609/10 *Mirror*, which he has identified as Clifford's. These representative annotations appear on pp. 817, 830, and 836 in Haywood's *England's Eliza* at the end of the volume. Orgel's forthcoming essay "Marginal Maternity: Reading Lady Anne Clifford's *Mirror for Magistrates*" provides an excellent analysis of Clifford's reading and annotating of this volume.

41. Quoted in Joseph Wittreich, *Feminist Milton* (Ithaca: Cornell University Press, 1987), 78.

42. See Lamb, "Agency," for one discussion of Clifford's resistance to patriarchal conventions.

43. For a fully annotated transcription of Huntington Library EL 6495 in which I identify nearly all the books, see the appendix to my dissertation, "Impressions from a 'Scribbling Age'" (Columbia University, 1995).

7

Lego Ego

Reading Seventeenth-Century Books of Epigrams

RANDALL INGRAM

If each reading by each reader is actually a secret, singular creation, is it still possible to organize this indistinguishable plurality of individual acts according to shared regularities? Is it even possible to envision knowing anything certain about it?
ROGER CHARTIER, 1989

Of all companions Books be the secretest, there a man may solace himselfe, and yet heares nothing but the Echo of his own words.
HENRY HARFLETE, 1653

Epigrammatists routinely refer to their own labor as writers, including the work of revising their poems, and for reasons that will soon become clearer, I start by invoking and participating in that tradition.

As I researched Robert Herrick's *Hesperides* (1648) a few years ago, I became interested in how frequently and urgently Herrick addresses his readers, particularly how he attempts to accommodate readers of disparate tastes in a single, flexible, but still monumental book.[1] After having published that research, however, I became concerned that I had been studying Herrick's book primarily in terms of implied rather than actual readers, and reviewing Roger Chartier's influential prescriptions for "a history of reading" deepened that concern. Instructions to readers cannot be considered to have determined reading, Chartier observes, because "experience shows that reading is not simply submission to textual machinery. Whatever it may be, reading is a creative practice, which invents singular meanings and significations that are not reducible to the intentions of authors of texts or producers of books."[2] Chartier therefore recommends researching traces of actual reading—what a recent session at the convention of the Modern Language Association calls "Real Readers Reading"[3]—because those traces may record individual readers departing from the prefixed instructions of authors and publishers and instantiating their autonomy from the protocols dictated by books. For this essay, then, I initially proposed to follow Chartier's two-part model: I would both analyze addresses to readers in seventeenth-century collections of epigrams (since concern with reading is more characteristic of epigrammatists generally than of Herrick specifically), and, having seen scattered marks in copies of *Hesperides*, I would gather and examine handwritten marginalia from these collections. In short, I would compare how authors and stationers wanted their books read to how contemporary readers actually read them. The new emphasis on actual readers suited the empiricism of this collection.

But other than reaffirming and enriching my fascination with epigrams, this essay has not turned out as first planned, partly for reasons that historians of reading might have predicted: I found very few handwritten traces of reading in books of epigrams, and the traces I found in a necessarily partial search answer dubiously and darkly to the twenty-first-century scholar. These traces raise familiar questions of sequence and consequence. When, for instance, a seventeenth-century reader of *Hesperides* corrects faults ascribed to the printer, precisely as a poem addressed to readers instructs, has the reader followed the poem or the reader's own habits? Has the poem effectively prescribed or described reading? As William Sherman's contribution to this collection demonstrates, traces of early modern reading can multiply rather than resolve questions about readers and their habits.

Perhaps in an attempt to make a slender virtue of a pressing necessity, I have omitted from this essay any consideration of the sparse marginalia in seventeenth-century books of epigrams, and I argue instead for the value of studying authors' and stationers' addresses to their readers, regardless of whether evidence from readers themselves can be found. I do not question the enormous value of studying evidence of past reading—I realize that the grapes I have not reached are not sour—but I do hope to reconsider the vexed category of "implied readers," a reconsideration inspired by seventeenth-century epigrams but applicable more broadly. Scholars of reading have frequently and justifiably dismissed implied readers, because such "readers" have seemed to be figments of authors' and stationers' hopes and fears. But seventeenth-century books of epigrams often attempt to address actual readers whose pleasure or displeasure, when expressed with actual currency, meant actual success or failure for stationers and authors competing in a literary market. Because stationers and authors so situated were materially invested in closing the gap between "implied" and "actual" readers, and because the process of realizing tastes while reading blurs the neat opposition of "implied" and "actual," I have returned to the implied readers I once discarded, but with a renewed appreciation for the complexity of such an approach. This essay accordingly explores some of the possibilities for a cultural study of readers implied by literary texts, a study not limited to explication of epigrams and their figurations of readers, but sensitive to the social, commercial, and bibliographic circumstances of those figurations.

Even more troubling than the (perhaps predictable) paucity and opacity of marginalia in books of epigrams have been the methodological challenges that these books pose. Seventeenth-century books of epigrams often insist that would-be anatomists of reading acknowledge one group of readers that anatomists strategically overlook: the anatomists themselves. Many books of epigrams require scholars to recognize their own activity as mediation rather than as revelation, as further reading rather than as lifting the veil. If past reading was "a creative practice," these books suggest that so too is current reading; if scholarly papers claim to show "real readers reading," they also inevitably show real readers being read. Consequently, as I consider the intersections among epigrams and their readers, such as Henry Harflete's compelling reading of an epigram by John Owen in *A Banquet of Essayes* (1653), I also reflect on the implications of these intersections for studies of reading, particularly this essay. As the title of this essay indicates, I am interested in the intertwined meanings of the Latin verb *legere* (gather, select, read), a verb that appears in countless titles for vernacular epigrams. Books comprising hundreds, even thousands, of small poems implicitly and explicitly invite reading that is unavoidably partial—in multiple senses. This tight conjunction of reading and selecting assumes a subject-centered process of reading that complicates the impartial, object-centered activities of anatomists. Reading seventeenth-century books of epigrams, I will argue, can enrich our understanding of how readers' tastes exerted pressure on authors and stationers, how, in turn, the books produced by authors and stationers helped realize readers' tastes, and finally, how current reading informs accounts of past reading.[4]

Ad Lectorem, ad Infinitum

Collections of epigrams generally and seventeenth-century collections specifically are almost obsessively preoccupied with their own reception. They routinely address readers directly, not only at the thresholds of books, but throughout, so that engaging readers is a central rather than an ancillary concern. The topics of seventeenth-century epigrams vary drastically—indeed, often vary drastically within the same book—but many share this preoccupation with readers and their habits. As a result, some contemporaries seem to have recognized these discussions of reading as significant features of books of epigrams: when, in 1653, Henry Harflete wanted to explain the right way of reading, he chose as his text not a passage of scripture, but a seemingly secular epigram written by John Owen.

Early modern epigrammatists may have inherited a preoccupation with readers from their Greek and Roman predecessors, but the persistent recurrence of these addresses demonstrates that, in addition to connecting early modern epigrammatists to a classical tradition, they also provided a relatively stable and familiar space for confronting changing conditions of publication and reading. Epigrams flourished in England during the long, unsteady transition from (in Dustin Griffin's words) "a patronage economy" to "a literary marketplace"[5] partly because books of epigrams were suited to negotiating this transitional market. As Thomas Churchyard's prefatory poem of 1594 shows, visitors to bookstalls might flip through books and read brief excerpts, deciding whether to buy:

> Some steps in hast, and leanes on Stationers stall,
> To aske what stuffe, hath passed Printers Presse,
> Some reades awhile, but nothing buyes at all
> For in two lines, they give a pretty gesse,
> What doth the booke, contayne such schollers thinke,
> To spend no pence, for paper, pen, and inke.[6]

Although Churchyard is exasperated by this browsing, epigrammatists and their stationers hoped that readers would linger in the stalls and eventually make the purchase; in the stark language of a prefatory poem to William Slatyer's *History of Great Britanie* (1621): "Reader, abide, marke, buy."[7] Poets and stationers scattered brief appeals to readers throughout their collections, both to entice potential buyers who might glance beyond the opening pages and to confirm the good taste of customers who had purchased the book.

For scholars attuned to the submerged vocabulary of patronage in, say, Elizabethan sonnet sequences, the frank commercial appeals of these epigrams can come as a shock. At times, epigrammatists appeal to booksellers as their most immediate sources of income. John Heath's epigram "To the Bookseller" from *The House of Correction* (1619) jokes nervously about the uncertainty of his book's commercial success:

> Nay, feare not Bookeseller, this Booke will sell:
> For be it good, as thou know'st very well,
> All will goe buy it; but say it be ill,
> All will goe by it too: thus thou sel'st still.[8]

Heath and other epigrammatists bring to the center of the page the transactions of reading that preceded and made possible the publication of their books, but addresses to stationers as a special class of readers also convey an important message to potential customers. The inclusion of Heath's "To the

Bookseller" in his published book reminds these customers that he has successfully sold the book to at least one influential reader, the bookseller, who,
within the poem, functions as an exemplary book buyer.

More often, epigrammatists sell their books directly to booksellers' customers. Paul Voss has recently surveyed advertisements for books in late Elizabethan England as a "reaction to the changing literary landscape" that "helped
mitigate the effects of decreased patronage as the sixteenth century came to a
close" (Voss 733). Christine Ferdinand has similarly shown the important role
of newspapers in selling books during the seventeenth and eighteenth centuries, but as Voss demonstrates, advertising for books was often part of the
books themselves. Some bibliographic features—title pages, prefatory material, lists of recent publications included at the ends of some books—operated
as rudimentary advertisements.[9] Indeed, some epigrams addressed to readers
give the book a voice to sell itself. An epigram entitled *"Liber ad Lectorem"*
from *Wits A.B.C.* (1610) keeps the unmentioned author aloof from the process
of selling and has the book beg for mercy and money:

> I hardly did escape the Printers Presse,
> It did so rudely crush my tendernesse:
> And now I feare more harme will me befall,
> If I long lye vpon the Stationers stall.
> Some-time I shall be nayld vnto a post,
> And som-time rashly torne, pincht, scratcht, & crost:
> Reader therefore, in kindnesse let me wooe thee:
> To free me hence, sixe-pence will not vndoe thee.[10]

The vestigal associations of epigrams with writing on walls and carving on
stone allowed early modern poets to meditate on the materiality of their poetry,
including the alarming possibility that their poems might be used to line
pastries, to wrap fish, or even, in one of Herrick's epigrams, to "wipe (at need) /
The place, where swelling *Piles* do breed."[11] In *Wits A.B.C.*, the book's material
vulnerability grounds its appeal to readers; for six pence, kind readers can
preserve from further suffering a book that has been oppressed. Six pence
seems to have been the advertised price for some books of epigrams in the first
decades of the seventeenth century, for the second poem entitled "The Booke
to the Reader" in John Davies's *Wits Bedlam* (1617) also quotes this price.
Rather than complain about its own injuries, Davies's book warns readers to
beware of its corrective power:

> Art good; and bad thy wit? then, touch me not:
> For, I doe often ierke the honest *Sot*.

Art bad, and they wit good? Forbeare, much more,
To touch mee: for, I lash such till they roare.
Or, art thou good, and great thy Wits extent?
Th'wilt loue me, tho thou loathe mine Excrement.
But be thou good or bad: for Six-pence, I
Will glad and grieue thee, make thee laugh & cry[.]
   O! take my money
   For this Sowre-Honey.[12]

Like the author of *Wits A.B.C.*, Davies discreetly keeps himself out of the commercial transaction between the book and its potential buyer, and once again, a book advertises itself. Unlike the earlier poem, however, Davies's epigram begins by refusing some readers ("touch me not" and "Forbeare") and engaging others ("Th'wilt loue me"). But by the seventh line, the poem gives up on these distinctions; "good" and "bad" alike are invited to spend their six pence. The remarkable final couplet closes the poem and the pitch: once the initial pretense of selecting a readership has been abandoned, the reader given voice here may be of good or bad morals, good or bad wit, as long as the reader will enthusiastically ("O!") hand over the money. That the poem so quickly abandons its attempt to select fit readers indicates that the attempt is itself a ploy to attract a broad readership, a readership defined not by wit or morals but by a willingness to buy.

  When epigrammatists and stationers attempt to sell books to as many of these unknown book buyers as possible, their addresses to readers become as much solicitous attempts to meet potential customers' perceived desires as authoritarian attempts to direct reading through restrictive "textual machinery." Poets and stationers seem to have found books of epigrams well suited to the emerging market of book buyers because collections of many short poems allow numerous opportunities to please anonymous, diverse readers. Authors of epigrams often repeat that, in Francis Quarles's words from "To the Readers" (plural) of *Divine Fancies* (1632), "All cannot affect all";[13] that is, different readers will appreciate different poems, so the larger and more varied a book of epigrams, the better the chance that at least some of its poems will please at least some of its readers. According to an epigram in *Wits Recreations* (1640), attempting to satisfy these perceived desires can be exasperating:

Mirth pleaseth some, to others 'tis offence,
Some co[m]mend plain conceits, some profound sence,
Some with a witty jest, some dislike that,
And most would have themselves they know not what.

Then he that would please all, and himselfe too,
Takes more in hand than he is like to doe.[14]

Trying as the work of accommodation seems to have been for this epigram-matist, epigrammatic collections' capacity for accommodation made them par-ticularly attractive to authors and stationers facing a slowly changing literary economy. Griffin observes that "there was no rapid or complete changeover . . . from an aristocratic culture to a commercial culture, no sudden change from a patronage economy to a literary marketplace" (Griffin 10). Books of epigrams may have been published so steadily throughout the seventeenth century be-cause they allowed stationers and authors not only to appeal either to specific patrons or anonymous customers of bookstalls, but to appeal to both at once. Within a book of short poems, an author like Herrick could have it both ways: he could address a number of potential patrons by name in some poems, and in others, he could address the nameless readers/customers who had begun to influence the publication and distribution of literary works. Collections of epigrams thus allowed authors and stationers to straddle divergent economies by appealing simultaneously to specific patrons and to a wide variety of un-known book buyers.

As attempts at engagement and accommodation, these projected re-sponses can at least provide contemporary accounts of the tastes, habits, and abilities of readers whose readings usually left no trace. If Chartier's questions in the epigraph nag at scholars of reading as they consider readers retro-spectively, similar questions also troubled seventeenth-century authors and stationers as they surveyed their market prospectively: where retrospective "shared regularities" allow scholars to organize disparate reading practices, these prospective "shared regularities" could help protect entrepreneurs against the speculative risks of publication. Like scholars of early modern reading, seventeenth-century authors and stationers often seemed acutely aware of the great variety of readers—differences in literacy, local and national politics, religion, gender, class—and this variety presented obvious difficulties for those who might hope to sell many copies of a single book. Beside the many general addresses entitled "To the Reader" or "*Ad Lectorem*," epigrammatists iden-tify readers as soure, generous, unfruitfull, neate, gentle, equall, captious, iudicious, enuious, foolish, vertuous-minded, indifferent, plaine-dealing, un-gentilized, vulgar, intelligent, kinde, displeased, and perhaps most accurately, various.[15] This elaborate taxonomy, barely sketched here, responds to and per-petuates a perceived fragmentation of the market for epigrams, a fragmenta-tion that corresponds to the diversity of authors and compilers who published epigrams. To recast Chartier's questions, could any book of poetry unite this fragmented population into a consensus of appreciative, paying customers? Or could a book hope at least to find an understanding audience within the apparently vast and varied field of books and readers? Faced with this "indistinguishable plurality," epigrammatists and their publishers necessarily became early modern observers of early modern readers, and as such, their addresses to readers are uniquely positioned resources for scholars of reading. In the case of some seventeenth-century collections of epigrams, then, implied readers may not be simply fanciful abstractions or representations of authorial hopes and fears; they may be market forecasts, projected by seventeenth-century agents who based their livelihoods on the accuracy of their projections.

Se/lectio

So far, I have argued that epigrammatic addresses to readers can serve as on-the-scene interpretations of readers' habits and desires. By itself, such an argument could imply that taste exists, fully formed, before the market and before reading, that readers choose books according to their stable, established tastes, and that poets and stationers must therefore scramble to find a subpopulation of fit readers. But seventeenth-century epigrammatists and stationers often seem to understand that consumers' tastes could be realized in the ongoing process of reading/selecting, and they worked within the extreme hypotheses described by Pierre Bourdieu, "the hypothesis of a sovereign taste compelling the adjustment of production to needs" and "the opposite hypothesis, in which taste is itself a product of production."[16] In the market of cultural goods, Bourdieu writes, neither of these hypotheses holds true; producers neither simply dictate nor simply conform to existing tastes but, whether deliberately or not, offer goods that activate consumers' latent desires.[17] The realization of those desires allows for expressions of taste that distinguish one producer from another and one consumer from another. As he looks over the many goods that allow twentieth-century consumers to differentiate and distinguish themselves—"drinks (mineral waters, wines and apertifs) or automobiles, newspapers or holiday resorts, design or finishing of house or garden"—Bourdieu argues that cultural goods (art, music, literature) are particularly effective instruments of distinction:

If, among all these fields of possibles, none is more obviously predisposed to express social differences than the world of luxury goods, and, more particularly, cultural goods, this is because the relationship of distinction is objectively inscribed within it, and is reactivated, intentionally or not, in each act of consumption, through the instruments of economic and cultural appropriation which it requires. It is not only a matter of the affirmations of difference which writers and artists profess ever more insistently as the autonomy of the field of cultural production becomes more pronounced, but also of the intention immanent in cultural objects. (226)

Unlike some of the twentieth-century cultural goods that Bourdieu studies, seventeenth-century books of epigrams can be quite explicit about the distinguishing functions "objectively inscribed" within the books themselves and about the reactivation of those functions "in each act of consumption." Seventeenth-century producers and consumers of books of epigrams found those books rich fields for realizing, confirming, and legitimizing multiple tastes. If addresses to readers can show some seventeenth-century responses to perceived tastes, they can also illuminate the formation of those tastes and the corollary formation of individual readings and readers.

Many seventeenth-century epigrams addressed to readers promise pleasures of reading indistinguishable from pleasures of selecting, first selecting a book from among others for sale and then selecting poems within a book. These addresses to readers further imply that, because readers' tastes and habits differ so drastically, no single book is a single book. Following Martial, epigrammatists frequently observe that the quality of their collections wavers, so readers should expect to appreciate some poems and overlook others, their choices shaping the books. This epigram from Henry Parrot's *Cures for the Itch* (1626) is representative:

> *Ralph* reads a line or two, and then cries mew,
> Deeming all else according to those few:
> Thou mightst haue thought, (& prov'd a wiser lad)
> (As *Ioan* her puddings boght) some good, some bad.[18]

Like many other epigrammatists, Parrot concedes that his book contains "some good, some bad" and literalizes this matter of taste by likening the consumption of books to the consumption of puddings. Of the many epigrams on this theme, none specifies which poems are good or which bad; the boundaries among these floating categories are not determined by authors but by readers, by each *lectio*, each reading/selecting. Even a carefully designed monument such as Herrick's *Hesperides* resembles less famous books of epigrams in its requests that readers shape the book:

> See, and not see; and if thou chance t'espie
> Some Aberrations in my Poetry;
> Wink at small faults, the greater, ne'rthelesse

Hide, and with them, their Fathers nakedness.
Let's doe our best, our Watch and Ward to keep:
Homer himself, in a long work, may sleep. (32)

Herrick, too, refuses to indict his book by specifying where "Aberrations" or "faults" might appear, imagining a process of reading indistinguishable from a process of selection. Reading so figured enables rather than threatens Herrick's model of authorship, for the collaborative work of doing "our best" compensates for the author's inevitable lapses. As Gordon Braden has observed, Herrick's invitation to "spot reading" is consistent with Martial's instructions to his readers:

Si nimius uideor seraque coronide longus
esse liber, legito pauca: libellus ero.
terque quaterque mihi finitur carmine paruo
pagina: fac tibi me quam cupis ipse breuem.

[If I seem too big, a long book with a delayed conclusion, just read selections, and I'll turn into a booklet. Quite a few pages end with a short poem—make me as small as you like.][19]

In the bookstall, epigrams to readers can offer customers membership in a sympathetic community, working together to do "our best," and after the purchase, these epigrams can consolidate that community. But as defined by Martial and by some seventeenth-century epigrammatists, books of epigrams can also become sites of divergence rather than convergence, instruments for expanding rather than contracting the range of possible readings.

Because of this expanded range of possible readings, many seventeenth-century epigrams to readers can offer a process of reading that individuates readers.[20] By alleging a nearly infinite variety of tastes, these poems predict that each person will respond differently to the same mechanically reproduced object and that differing responses mark defining differences among potential customers. Consequently, and consistent with Bourdieu's analysis, collections of many brief poems simultaneously satisfy and perpetuate a wide variety of tastes. A small book of one hundred epigrams, such as *Wits A.B.C. Or A Centurie of Epigrams*, allows readers many chances to explore and assert their own tastes by approving or disapproving, and a larger book permits even more possibilities. If the 1,130 poems of *Hesperides* were ranked from "good" to "bad," the possible arrangements, and hence the possible expressions of individual taste, would exceed 1.4175 followed by nearly three thousand zeros. In the face of such nearly infinite possibility, each *lectio* seems to be a *selectio*—a selection, but also a reflexive reading, *se legere*. Addresses to readers imply that reading amid so many possibilities requires a constant process of selection and that the constant choosing defines and affirms individual taste. In a literary market increasingly influenced by anonymous, undistinguished book buyers, books of epigrams could offer opportunities for individuation.

These books of epigrams thus seem to reinforce Cecile M. Jagodzinski's recent argument that "readers in seventeenth-century England, because they read, began to develop a sense of the private self."[21] As scholars such as Adrian Johns have argued, characteristics often assumed to be inherent to the processes of producing and consuming printed materials arose instead from the specific activities of authors, stationers, and readers who advanced some characteristics of print rather than others.[22] If, as Jagodzinski claims, "the reading experience bred a new sense of personal autonomy" (1), this new sense of autonomy may be less an intrinsic result of reading than a result of reading books designed to foreground readers' capacity to choose. Books of epigrams therefore might be considered alongside the personal letters and conversion narratives that Jagodzinski examines, another seventeenth-century bibliographic form participating in the complex relation between reading and "the private self."

As Jagodzinski's emphasis on privacy suggests, such reflexive reading usually remains secret, and indeed, some epigrams advise readers to keep their readings close.[23] But Henry Harflete's reading of a single epigram by John Owen in *A Banquet of Essayes* records one highly individual reading in accordance with the promises extended in epigrams addressed to readers. Harflete fittingly selects as his text an epigram that emphasizes the multiple meanings of *legere*, a poem that repeats the commonplace that a book of epigrams contains "some good, some bad" and that a judicious reader must determine "good" and "bad": "*Qui legis ista, tuam reprehendo; si mea laudas. / Omnia, stultitiam: si nihil, invidiam.*"[24] Like many other epigrams, Owen's poem insists that only a fool would praise his entire book and only an envious reader would praise none of it, and like many other epigrams, Owen's poem leaves readers to select what in his book may be praiseworthy. At the end of his book, Harflete translates Owen's epigram thus:

> Reader, if thou do'st praise what e're I'ave writ,
> I must (perforce) rebuke thy flattering wit;
> If thou approv'st of nought in all my book,
> I must reprove thy heart, 'tis envies crooke. (86)

But before he translates it, Harflete devotes over eighty pages to unpacking the moral and religious applications of this distich, fragments of Owen's epigram serving as subject headings for Harflete's discussion:

—Si mea laudas.
Mea, not *me.*
Praise not my person. Personal proportion cannot be the true object of Praise: A small fall may soon dash that . . .

—Si me laudas.
Mea, not *quæ mei.*
Naturall endowments should neither be the objects of Praise. 'Tis for the fond lover to praise such things in his beloved. . . . *Quot homines, tot sententiæ*; As many men, so many mindes, saith our English proverb; for she may be faire in *oculo placiti*, who is not so in *oculo populi.* . . .

—Si mea laudas.
Mea, not *quæ mei.*
Riches do not make a man praise-worthy; they be *dona Dei data*, not *homini innata*; they be *quæ mihi*, not *mea propria*; things given to me, not properly mine own. . . . (34–36)

Although Harflete returns almost compulsively to the thirteen words of Owen's epigram, his reading here is remarkable for its consideration of words that do not appear on the page. In fact, Harflete reads the words Owen did not write at least as extensively as he reads the words of the epigram, and as a result, Harflete can derive a lesson about riches from an epigram that never mentions riches. As the epigraph from *A Banquet of Essayes* puts it, Harflete's reading unabashedly echoes his own words. "Of all Glasses Books be the best," Harflete writes (12), and just as his reading of Owen's epigram reflects Harflete's own predilections, other readers' readings reflect their spiritual states: "were not the Reader blear-ey'd he might quickly espy the lineament of his own soul in these Glasses by reflection; let him be but intentive in reading, and he may quickly collect the disposition of his own soule, and the disease being once known puts the patient in hope of a cure" (13). Harflete assumes that readers do not simply select material that suits their spiritual needs; their spiritual needs are discovered through the "intentive" activity of reading. Harflete intensifies epigrams' traditional curative function, their ability to expose readers' virtues and vices, and he shows how epigrams addressed to readers offered seventeenth-century readers a rich field for individuation. That Harflete draws spiritual instruction from an apparently secular epigram may seem surprising, but his reading complies with the configuration proposed by Owen's epigram and by many seventeenth-century epigrams addressed to readers: the process of reading/selecting inevitably reveals the defining attributes of a *lector*; or, in Harflete's more provocative words, "the reading of Books may anatomize the heart" (10). However appealing this prospect may have been for Harflete or for other seventeenth-century readers, it complicates the work of later scholars who position themselves as anatomizing rather than anatomized.

Lego Ego

Harflete's extraordinary response to Owen's epigram points to the complexity of the relation between implied and actual readers of seventeenth-century epigrams, a relation subtler than an outright struggle between "textual machinery" and subversive readers. Like the poems by Parrot, Herrick, and Owen, seventeenth-century epigrams addressed to readers regularly insist that readers recognize the shaping influence of their reading. This insistence is not a constraint that precedes and limits reading; instead, it is a theory of the relations within the "triangle" described by Chartier and others, "the relationship set up among the text, the book, and the reader."[25] The insistence on readers' shaping influence therefore cannot simply be resisted or overlooked by creative readers, for indeed, such resisting and overlooking would only confirm the theory. How, for instance, might a reader successfully resist the imperative that begins Herrick's address "To the generous reader," "See, and not see"? Even readers who skip the poem comply with its instructions and, by skipping the poem, shape *Hesperides* as Herrick requests.

If this model for the interactions of book, reader, and text complicates the familiar juxtaposition of restrictive authors and resistant readers, it even further complicates the rhetoric of impartiality characteristic of many scholarly accounts of past reading. In these accounts, scholars often eschew use of singular first-person pronouns and avoid assuming positions as readers. Descriptions of past reading tend to adopt the objective third person, or, in the rarer cases when the singular first person appears, the "I" does not so much read as meet or observe a prior reader (e.g., Robert Darnton: "I ran across a solidly middle-class reader in my own research on eighteenth-century France").[26] But of course past readers can only be read. The reunion of "reading" and "selecting" enacted in many epigrams recasts these encounters between current and past readers as further acts of reading in which fragments of text are assembled into coherence, even assembled into something as stable as "a solidly middle-class reader." Epigrammatic poems to readers draw attention to this process of assembling and suggest that there is no position outside of reading from which past reading may be studied. From this suggestion arise a number of challenging questions: are the influential, prescriptive methodologies for studying past reading attempts to regulate and standardize current reading? If scholars of reading champion the autonomy of past readers, why must those same scholars suppress the inevitable creativity of their own reading?

In my own case, reading seventeenth-century epigrams has made immediate the multiple meanings of *legere*. Confronting the massive corpus of epigrams published in seventeenth-century England, my reading has been unavoidably selective, and the representation of that reading in this essay has been more selective still. Yet if the essay had followed the initial plan and had compared "how authors and stationers wanted their books read to how contemporary readers actually read them," it would have been even more selective, despite following the guidelines for studying past reading proposed by Chartier: rather than picking samples only from the enormous corpus of seventeenth-century epigrams, I would have compared selected evidence of reading (gathered in a selection of three libraries, the Folger Shakespeare Library, the Huntington Library, and the British Library) to even fewer exemplary epigrams. Although I recognize that important differences between these approaches could have resulted in two significantly different essays, both approaches would have required highly selective reading. Either way, *lego ego*.

As Harflete and his contemporaries understood, by acknowledging my reading as reading, I risk isolating myself (this essay could stand out as the only essay in the volume to have been produced by a specific reader rather than to have emerged unmediated from objective evidence), and I risk exposing my prejudices, even to myself (I am surprised and dismayed to realize that, despite my enthusiasm for the multidisciplinary approaches to past reading, this essay depends heavily on literary texts as evidence and thus reaffirms the disciplinary boundaries in which I work). Because of these risks, I did not use first-person pronouns in the article on Herrick's *Hesperides*, nor have "I" appeared, outside the safety of endnotes and quotation marks, in other critical articles. Jagodzinski contends that "the flow of personal information is always opposite to the flow of authority" (5), but does the acknowledgment of reading necessarily diminish the authority of a scholarly essay, particularly an essay on texts that require readers to acknowledge their activity as *lectores*? Reversing the terms of Chartier's compelling questions in the epigraph, is it possible to consider the singular acts that comprise the shared regularities of scholarly reading? Who better than readers to write histories of reading?

Seventeenth-century collections of epigrams have much to contribute to such histories. No more complex than other early modern forms, seventeenth-century books of epigrams negotiate within a network of changing conditions, between patrons and shoppers, between satisfying and helping to realize readers' tastes, between classical topoi and contemporary concerns, between enduring texts and poignantly fragile books. It might be satisfying to stand above this turmoil, on the apparently stable foundation of current scholarly reading and writing practices, and to observe from a safe distance the fluctuating textual forms and practices of early modern Europe. But when have these forms and practices not been fluctuating? Certainly not now. Like other artifacts of their time, seventeenth-century books of epigrams can reveal our own involvement in a network of changing conditions, between excitement over newly relevant evidence and the realization that such evidence will not yield simple, unmediated truths, between discipline-specific training and multidisciplinary enterprises, between overstating continuities linking past to present and, maybe more acceptable, overstating discontinuities separating past from present. Satisfying as it might be to end an essay on epigrams with a resounding final *sententia*, negotiating within this network permits ad hoc compromises more than definitive conclusions, better suited to the social exchange of a collection of essays than to the monumental permanence of carving in stone.

Notes

1. Randall Ingram, "Robert Herrick and the Makings of *Hesperides*," *SEL: Studies in English Literature, 1500–1900* 38 (1998): 127–47.
2. Roger Chartier, "Texts, Printing, Readings," *The New Cultural History*, ed. Lynn Hunt (Berkeley: University of California Press, 1989), 156.
3. "Real Readers Reading," program presented at the 114th meeting of the Modern Language Association, San Francisco, December 1998.
4. In the discussion of "objects assembled in the image of their consumers' varied desires" that "materially shape those desires in the process," my reading of seventeenth-century books of epigrams resembles Nancy J. Vickers's reading of sixteenth-century French verse collections (183). Vickers's essay, "The Unauthored 1539 Volume in Which Is Printed the *Hecatomphile, The Flowers of French Poetry, and Other Soothing Things*," appears in *Subject and Object in Renaissance Culture*, ed. Margreta de Grazia, Maureen Quilligan, and Peter Stallybrass (Cambridge: Cambridge University Press, 1996), 166–88.
5. Dustin Griffin, *Literary Patronage in England, 1650–1800* (Cambridge: Cambridge University Press, 1996), 10.
6. Thomas Churchyard, *The Mirror of Man, and Manners of Men* (London, 1594), A2ᵛ. Since Churchyard's poem explicitly discusses the scene of selling early modern books, several scholars have cited it. See H. S. Bennett, *English Books and Readers, 1558 to 1603* (Cambridge: Cambridge University Press 1965), 259–60 and Paul Voss, "Books for Sale: Advertising and Patronage in Late Elizabethan England," *Sixteenth Century Journal* 29 (1998): 755.
7. The poem is attributed to "S.P." in William Slatyer's *History of Great Britanie* (London, 1632), ¶¶2ʳ.
8. John Heath, *The House of Correction; or, Certayne Satyricall Epigrams* (London, 1619), B5ʳ.
9. Christine Ferdinand, "Constructing the Frameworks of Desire: How Newspapers Sold Books in the Seventeenth and Eighteenth Centuries," *News, Newspapers, and Society in Early Modern Britain*, ed. Joad Raymond (London and Portland, Ore.: Frank Cass, 1999), 157–75. After noting that "employing the word 'advertisement' to promote products did not become standard practice until the nineteenth century" (734 n), Voss traces how a range of bibliographic features came to function as early forms of advertising in late sixteenth-century England.
10. *Wits A.B.C. Or A Centurie of Epigrams* (London, 1608), A4ʳ.
11. Robert Herrick, *Hesperides* (London, 1648), 3. Epigrammatists regularly give paper a voice to lament its mistreatment, as in John Davies's *Papers Complaint, compild*

in ruthfull Rimes Against the Paper-Spoylers of these Times in *The Scourge of Folly* (London, 1611).

12. John Davies, *Wits Bedlam* (London, 1617), A6ᵛ.

13. Francis Quarles, *Divine Fancies: Digested into Epigrammes, Meditations, and Observations* (London, 1632), A3ᵛ.

14. *Wits Recreations* (London, 1640), 463. Colin Gibson, the editor of the Scolar Press facsimile edition of *Wits Recreations* (Aldershot: Scolar Press, 1990) identifies "J. Tompson" as the author of this epigram (xxxiv).

15. Although some of these epithets for readers, such as "generous," can be found in many epigrams and epistles addressed to readers, here follow representative epigrams and epistles in the order of the epithets catalogued above: "To the soure Reader" and "To the generous Reader," Herrick, *Hesperides*; "An unfruitfull Reader" in Thomas Bancroft, *Two Bookes of Epigrammes, and Epitaphs* (London, 1639); "To a neate reader," *Wits Recreations*; "To the gentle Reader," Robert Heath, *Clarestella: together with Poems occaisionall, Elegies, Epigrams, Satires* (London, 1650); "To the equall Reader" and "To the captious Reader," Richard Brathwait, *A Strappado for the Diuell. Epigrams And Satyres alluding to the time, with diuers measures of no lesse Delight* (London, 1615); "To the Iudicious, Enuious, and foolish Reader," John Cooke, *Epigrams, Serued out in 52. seuerall Dishes* (London, 1604); "The Translator to the vertuous-minded English Scholler, and the indifferent Reader," John Penkethman, *Epigrams of P. Virgilivs, Maro, and others* (London, 1624); "To the plaine-dealing Reader," Henry Parrot, *The Movs-Trap* (London, 1606); "To the ungentilized Censurer," Henry Parrot, *Epigrams* (London, 1608); "To the vulgar Censurers," Henry Parrot, *Laquei ridiculosi: or Springes for Woodcocks* (London, 1613); "To the intelligent Reader," *Wits A.B.C.*; "To the kinde Reader, of the Censure of my Booke," William Gamage, *Linsi-Woolsie, or Two Centuries of Epigrammes* (London, 1613); "To my displeased Reader" and "On various Readers," Henry Killigrew, *A Book of New Epigrams* (London, 1695).

16. Pierre Bourdieu, *Distinction: A Social Critique of the Judgement of Taste*, trans. Richard Nice (New York: Routledge and Kegan Paul, 1984), 231.

17. Because Bourdieu does not focus simply on the demand of consumers or the influence of producers, his analysis helps make sense of seventeenth-century epigrams that seem more invested in disputing other producers than in appealing to consumers. To take an especially influential example, the first epigrams of Ben Jonson's collection scorn the "licentious" epigrams of other poets and the "vile arts" of advertising early modern books. See Jonson's *Workes*, (London, 1615), 769–70. According to Bourdieu, "[t]he producers can be totally involved and absorbed in their struggles with other producers, convinced that only specific artistic interests are at stake and that they are otherwise totally disinterested, while remaining unaware of the social functions they fulfill, in the long run, for a particular audience" (234). Jonson's opening epigrams extend the author's reach into the details of the book's circulation and thus imply a struggle among producers rather than concern for consumers, but Bourdieu's analysis shows that even grand assertions of authorial prerogative allow some consumers to realize their tastes—even Jonson's disdain for the "vile arts" of advertising can be, "for a particular audience," powerfully engaging.

18. Henry Parrot, *Cures for the Itch: Characters, Epigrams, Epitaphs* (London, 1626), C5ʳ.

19. Gordon Braden, *The Classics and English Renaissance Poetry: Three Case Studies* (New Haven: Yale University Press, 1978), 181.

20. Of course not all seventeenth-century collections of epigrams promise this individuation. Some translations of classical epigrams and self-help manuals portray epigrams as brief and easy access to an educated community. Other single-author collections demand to be read in their entirety, and all must please all or none please none. John Heath's epigram *"In librum suum"* from *Two Centvries of Epigrammes* (London, 1610) stakes a particularly rigid position: "My booke it must please all or some or none; / And one of these three must it needs embrace. / It cannot possibly please everyone, / And for to please none, that's a maine disgrace. / Yet for my will, what ere of it become, / I rather would, it should please none, then some" (A7^r). This extreme all-or-nothing stance is rare among epigrammatists; much more common is the hope that some poems within a collection will please some readers.

21. Cecile M. Jagodzinski, *Privacy and Print: Reading and Writing in Seventeenth-Century England* (Charlottesville: University Press of Virginia, 1999), 2.

22. Adrian Johns, *The Nature of the Book: Print and Knowledge in the Making* (Chicago: University of Chicago Press, 1998). For Johns's critique of "print logic," see especially the first chapter, "Introduction: The Book of Nature and the Nature of the Book."

23. Epigrammatists at least since Martial claim that the curative correction of epigrams should be applied in silence. For example, the address "To the Reader" from John Davies's *Scourge of Folly* states that the book secretly reveals a reader's faults and that those faults should be corrected secretly, behind a laughing façade: "And seeing closely it [the book] bewraies thy blame, / Mend it as close, and laugh to cloke the same" (A4^v).

24. Henry Harflete, *A Banquet of Essayes, Fetcht out of Famous Owens Confectionary* (London, 1653), 1. Hereafter cited parenthetically by page number.

25. Roger Chartier, *The Order of Books: Readers, Authors, Libraries in Europe between the Fourteenth and Eighteenth Centuries*, trans. Lydia G. Cochrane (Stanford: Stanford University Press, 1994), 10.

26. Robert Darnton, *The Kiss of Lamourette: Reflections in Cultural History* (New York: W. W. Norton, 1990), 156.

8

Devotion Bound

A Social History of The Temple

KATHLEEN LYNCH

Bookbinding is the final stage in a mechanical process of reproduction, but in early modern Europe it must also be understood as the first act of reception. For a customer had a say, at least potentially, about several important aspects of the binding, including the materials and methods of decoration and the limits and order of the contents within. In other words, any given binding could be custom work and therefore speak of a customer's tastes. With that idea in mind, this essay probes the role of binding as an act of reclamation, one that highlights the convergences of slippage and fixity—in texts and lives alike. As much as it promises stability, binding—like the process of publication as a whole—is also a means of extension that allows for destabilization, adaptation, and appropriation. The possibilities for reclamation have a particular resonance for a text as teasingly autobiographical as is *The Temple* by George Herbert. For the intimate portrayal of a spiritual life invites a reader to imagine the struggle described as one's own. The boundaries of identity are elided as the written representation of one's experience is reanimated in the reading of another.

This investigation assumes that customer is a category which includes but is not limited to readers: the author, the publisher, and a bookseller are among those who might function as the customer's proxy. The customer and reader may be identical or distinct; they may or may not be identifiable. Nevertheless, choices about a book's binding frame a reader's interests, strategies, and expectations. My own study is framed, too: by the resonant effect of bookbinding's marginalization, first in the Stationers' Company and now in contemporary academic disciplines, by the already well-mapped historical context in which this investigation fits, and by *The Temple*'s own liminal nature—determinedly devout and widely read.

In England, at least in the early modern period, bookbinding had a marginalized position in the book trade. The oldest of the crafts that were consolidated in the Stationers' Company, bookbinding rapidly lost both status and financial ground to printing and bookselling in the age of movable type. Bookbinders could compete for the retail trade, but their copies were liable to be more expensive: at the wholesale stage because they could not leverage a favorable exchange with their own stock, and at the retail stage because they could not match the prices of readily available unbound copies. Additionally, bookbinders were less protected by the company's statutes against competition from aliens and those in other guilds.[1]

Similarly, the study of bookbinding skirts the uncertain boundaries of academic disciplines today. The history of bookbinding remains an important part of connoisseurship. Books on bookbinding serve an audience of bibliophiles with lavish illustrations of fine craftsmanship well preserved. But the illustrations also provide the necessary evidence for the bibliographer's comparative study. Insofar as certain materials, methods, and tools may be localized, the study of bookbinding does the core work of identifying copies and schools. As David Pearson writes, that study remains a "distressingly inexact science when we are talking about such small tools of standard designs, which existed in multiple variant versions, all close copies of one another."[2]

An investigation of those details is by definition bibliographical. But bibliographers by and large have concentrated on textual questions, perhaps (as Graham Pollard speculated almost a half century ago) because bibliography owes so much to students of the drama of the period, "a class of book which has been more extensively disbound than any other."[3] Even Randall McLeod, who has done the painstaking work of "an exacting textual criticism of authoritative documents" in the publication history of *The Temple*, mentions the practice of binding Herbert's *Temple* together with another work, but does not integrate that into his assessment of the unacknowledged changes and appropriations that generally mark the history of editing.[4]

Scholars often depend on catalogers to analyze the salient material conditions of a rare book in copy-specific entries. The catalogues of rare-book archives are filled with detailed information about the nature and history of the bindings of their collections. Electronic databases have made it easier for scholars to search for this information with the introduction of notes fields. But scholars are less familiar with the critical mass of studies of bookbinding in this period. Many of these studies address texts and institutions with long histories supported by large archives and substantial paper trails. Collectively, they constitute an exciting conversation about the role of the history of bookbinding in a social history of readings.[5]

For instance, in the inaugural volume of *Transactions of the Cambridge Bibliographical Society*, J. C. T. Oates identified twenty extant presentation copies of gratulatory verse published by Cambridge to commemorate a series of royal occasions in the early seventeenth century. He also recovered relevant accounts in the university audit books as well as surviving bills from binders. By reading these records in light of each other, Oates sketched in important aspects of the relationships among the university, its printers, and its royal patrons. More recently, Mirjam Foot compiled and printed eight published lists of prices for binding as agreed upon by London stationers, an invaluable look at the practices of binderies. David McKitterick has presented a case study of one customer's purchase of a bible, supported by extensive correspondence over the matter. Finally, David Pearson has examined the bindings of Cosin's Library, the endowed public library founded by John Cosin, bishop of Durham. As Pearson describes it, the library is the collection of a single individual, formed within a lifetime, largely intact, not overrepaired, and thus a gold mine of physical evidence. With the exception of Foot's lists (to which I will return in the second half of this essay), each of these studies focuses closely on the Cambridge book trade, and provides an important model for the uses of the physical evidence of binding in the study of relations between the book trade and its customers.[6]

The Temple can play an important role in modeling those relations, for we know that Herbert's poetry was the touchstone of devotion for his seventeenth-century readers.[7] Herbert pronounced his intention to dedicate himself to a prayerful life in a pair of sonnets he presented to his mother as a New Year's gift when he was seventeen. None of his surviving writings indicate that Herbert ever retracted that vow. Nicholas Ferrar reinforced the impression of Herbert's as the distillation of devotion when Ferrar introduced the posthumous first publication to its readers as "a pattern or more for the age he lived in."[8] Herbert's eldest brother Edward, Lord Herbert of Cherbury, also commented on George's already well-established reputation for piety in his own autobiography, attesting that "about Salisbury, where he lived, . . . he was little less than sainted" (H xxxvi). From very early on, then, readers have acclaimed Herbert for achieving to a great degree the "Mark to aim at" that he set as a spiritual goal (H 224).

Even newer interpretive approaches that expose the political currency of Herbert's devotion are still dealing with a resolute and inescapable core of intentionality. And yet, shockingly like Donne's vision of the true church, *The Temple* is promiscuously available to multivalent readings and competing genealogical claims of church disciplines. I examine some of those seventeenth-century claims with this bifurcated study of two copies of the same edition of George Herbert's *Temple*, both housed at the Folger Library. The copies are bound in significantly different ways, affording opportunities to take up questions about the identification of tools and decorative styles with the first copy, about the choice of materials bound together in the second copy, and about the social, religious, and economic motivations that both bindings represent.

The sixth edition of *The Temple* was printed by Roger Daniel in 1641. It is the last edition published in Cambridge, the first without Thomas Buck's involvement. H1516 copy 1 is featured in the Folger Library catalogue of *Fine and Historic Bookbindings* (1992). There it is described as being sewn on four recessed alum-tawed thongs and bound with carefully mitred corners in citron goatskin over pasteboards. Prior to tooling, the covers and spine were marked with black ink dots to create a stencil-like pattern. Three concentric, rectangular panels on front and back are formed by rows of alternating small flower and toothlike tools. Fleurons jut out at angles from each of the corners and also embellish the central cartouche. The flat spine bears the same cartouche design with three lines of the small flower and tooth tools aligned with the panels on front and back. Ink dots and a six-pointed star decorate the edges of both boards. A fern-tip roll, also following the pattern of ink dots, runs around the turn-ins (Fig. 1).[9]

The elaborate cover is consistent with the careful embellishment of the pages inside. Double red margins frame each page and provide borders for running heads as well as the titles of individual poems. This kind of work was likely done by the binder. Such decoration is not restricted to a liturgical context, though the long history of rubrication in bibles and prayer books does support a strong association of the practice with reverence.[10]

H1516 copy 1 is also a book with a well-documented provenance, albeit one with tantalizing gaps. For it is the provenance that is not attested to by an overt mark of ownership—though perhaps it is articulated by the very craftsmanship—that has generated the most interest. At various times and with various levels of certainty, this has been identified as the work of the Ferrar family's Little Gidding community. The Ferrars' exemplarity as readers of Herbert is beyond question. That is not to say that the ways in and for which that exemplarity has been created and sustained is beyond investigation. Still, it is undoubtedly through Nicholas Ferrar's effort that there is a *Temple* to read in the first place. Additionally, book production was an acknowledged centerpiece of the family's own ritually organized life. So this copy would seem to speak with great immediacy about Herbert's first and closest circle of readers. It would seem to embody the deepest interests of both author and the text's implied reader, and it would seem to speak, too, of a withdrawal from, or even a transcendence of, the contemporary ecclesiastical fray. What follows, however, is a cautionary tale about the history of sentiment, the difficult process of establishing provenance, and by extension the arbitrary and uncertain nature of both bindings and boundaries.

In 1900, Cyril Davenport announced "Three Recently Discovered Bindings with Little Gidding Stamps" in the *Library*. Remarking that "there now exist only four known examples" of "absolutely certain Little Gidding workmanship," Davenport proposed to add three to the canon: a 1629 Cambridge bible, a 1649 *Eikon Basilike*, and a 1641 copy of *The Temple*.[11] Davenport pro-

Figure 1. Binding, *The Temple*, Folger shelfmark H151 6, copy 1. By permission of the Folger Shakespeare Library.

nounced the copy of *The Temple* (which is almost certainly Folger H1516 copy 1) and the *Eikon Basilike* to be "bound in an exactly similar way," though with different tools (D 210). Davenport buttressed his argument with the fact that Herbert was a "likely enough" candidate for a binding by Nicholas Ferrar's niece Mary Collet, D 210), and that the *Eikon Basilike* had a note on the flyleaf, dated 1678, also attributing the work to her.

Davenport's conclusion that bookbindings that do not share tools or patterns are "exactly similar" does not survive scrutiny. Still, his attribution is plausible. Noting that there was not as yet an example of Little Gidding binding in the British Museum, he offered his discoveries as the nuclei of "a new school of binding to admire and to look for" (D 212). His invitation has been astonishingly influential.

Edward Almack—identified by Davenport as the person who "brought to me" the 1641 copy of *The Temple*—was complicit in the attempt to reconstruct the Little Gidding canon at that time (D 210). Almack was himself a notable early twentieth-century bibliophile and editor of early works, including the *Eikon Basilike*. The binding on a copy of *The Temple* described by Davenport is not among the bindings in Almack's *Fine Old Bindings*, published in 1913. But Almack does feature Nicholas Ferrar's copy of John Valdesso's *One Hundred and Ten Considerations*, bound for him by Mary Collet.[12] This is a familiar circle of association, a ceremonial embrace of forefathers that both Davenport and Almack advocate. Theirs is one more instance of the high church Anglican tradition that has busily been claiming Herbert as one of its own since Nicholas Ferrar brought the little book to the printers at Cambridge and had it published as "a pattern or more for the age he lived in (H 3)."[13]

Folger 1516 copy 1 next appears at a Sotheby's auction of November 1918. There, lot 318 is a copy of the 1641 edition of Herbert's *Temple* from the estate of P. M. Pittar, esquire. The copy is described in the catalogue as a fine example of Little Gidding binding, with reference to a full account in the March 1909 issue of the *Library*. This book with bookplates of Lady Victoria Herbert and the Honorable P. Ashburnham is certainly the Folger volume, as the bookplates survive in the copy. Purchased by Quaritch for £60, it was sold again to (or perhaps had been purchased on behalf of) Sir R. Leicester Harmsworth, whose library was purchased whole by Joseph Adams for the Folger Library a year after it opened. It was a fortuitous purchase that neatly complemented and nearly doubled the holdings of the Folger's collection.

The volume in the Sotheby's catalogue is the Folger volume, but is it a near copy of the volume described in Davenport or the same copy? Though the Folger catalogue buttresses its identification as a Little Gidding binding with a recognition of others—the "school of binding" Davenport aimed to reconstruct—it is very likely the same copy as the one Davenport described. For the

Sotheby's reference to a March 1909 article by Davenport is a mistaken reference to the March 1900 article described above. A typographical error is responsible for the seeming confirmation (almost a century later in the Folger
catalogue) of Davenport's notion of a Little Gidding style of binding.

But G. D. Hobson had delivered a bracing reassessment of that bindery in
1929. With a fine disdain for the "dreadful monuments of a misdirected labour," he nevertheless catalogues fifteen known surviving products of Little
Gidding, including twelve "Harmonies." He does not accept any of Davenport's new discoveries into the canon, viewing them as reverential but un-
founded accretions. He is determined to reevaluate known Little Gidding
bindings in the context of contemporary binding practices. Little Gidding
bookbinding is wholly derivative of Cambridge bookbinding, as far as he is
concerned: "stamp-types, patterns, and materials are common to both cen-
tres."[14] That should not be surprising if indeed the Collet sisters were taught
binding by the daughter of a Cambridge bookbinder, as is legendarily alleged.[15]

In fact, derivative may be a particularly apt characterization of a community usually considered highly original. Their best-known works, the "Harmonies" mentioned above, are exquisite cut-and-paste jobs. Little Gidding's ethos
was one of radical reclamation. Theirs was a highly individual and assertive act
of appropriation. This is reading as remaking, and Folger H1516 copy 1 may or
may not be an example of that remaking. For attributions to Little Gidding
remain fluid. As a new generation of scholars investigates the work of the
family, the bases of past attributions are reexamined, sometimes with surprising results. For instance, a Little Gidding "Harmony" came up for auction (at
Sotheby's) seventy years after Hobson designated it numeral II on his short list
of accepted items. The large folio was trumpeted in the sales catalogue as "a
highly characteristics example of a Little Gidding 'Harmony,' and it is one of
the very few remaining in private hands or ever likely to appear for sale. Indeed,
it is probably the only one remaining outside institutional libraries which was
produced in Nicholas Ferrar's own lifetime."[16] In light of this promotionalism,
the caution about binding is even more striking. For following a description of
the bindery at Little Gidding is the conclusion that the book has a Cambridge
binding: "The tool used resembles Hobson's number 24 but is not the same."[17]

It is hard to judge resemblances from the sales catalogue. But the central
cartouche on the (otherwise chaste) front cover seems to be made up of four
repeats of two stamps. It is no more of a stretch to think that one resembles
Hobson's stamp number 28 than that the other resembles number 24. Which is
to say neither is a convincing match from a distance. But if this volume was
recognized by Hobson as belonging to the canon in 1629, why are its tools not
among those catalogued in his plate 48?[18] And if that attribution is not being
challenged, why not use this binding as a hallmark of a new set of tools for

Little Gidding work now? The establishment of provenance is indeed a tricky business.

Working with another set of books, David Pearson has suggested new candidates for inclusion in the Little Gidding canon. He argues that a group of eleven Cambridge bindings from Bishop John Cosin's library are the work of Little Gidding. These all employ a distinctive "chinese box" style of decoration, marked by a series of concentric rectangular frames that Hobson claimed as characteristically Cambridge. Pearson bases his attributions on the shared use of about thirty small tools, a group that includes the five tools that decorate a "harmony of King's Chronicles" (Hobson's numeral V) (Pearson 55).[19] Pearson also describes several shared methodological details as characteristic of the Little Gidding bindery. These include the sewing of sheets with an excessive number of narrowly spaced bands, the decoration of the top and bottom edges at the spine ends with the impression of tools, the gilt tooling of both the edges of the boards and the turn-ins, the gilding of the edges of the leaves, pastedowns of marbled paper, and the doubling of headbands (52–55).[20] Folger H1516 copy 1 displays these characteristics, with the exception of the number of sewing bands and doubling of headbands. In fact, the care taken to decorate the edges of the goatskin cover and the turn-ins sets the volume apart as a particularly fine example of workmanship. It is not an ostentatious piece, but it is nevertheless a little jewel of the bookbinder's art.

These characteristics may yet provide the basis for identifying further work of the Little Gidding bindery. For Pearson believes it was a larger operation than previously realized. He has found a letter Nicholas Ferrar's brother John sent to Isaac Basire after Nicholas's death in 1637. Ferrar asks Basire to spread the word around "worthy noble personages" that the community would accept bookbinding commissions. Additionally, Pearson has found a reference in an account book that indicates the Ferrars shipped more than two hundred copies of the *Eikon Basilike* to the American colonies in 1649 (55).[21] Helen Wilcox also refers to the ongoing contacts between the Ferrar family and Virginia colonists in her analysis of the ways several women read Herbert in the seventeenth century. Wilcox quotes from a 1650 letter from Edward Johnson to Ferrar's niece, aptly named Virginia. Johnson had received a consignment of books from the Ferrar family. "Herbert's poems I received," he writes, "and at the opening of [*The Temple*] I went into the Church and fell down on my knees to pray for you and your religious family."[22]

Such evidence of a bookbinding and bookselling relationship with colonists in America provides a tantalizing glimpse of a neglected aspect of the Ferrars' multiple relationships with the New World, extending well beyond the revocation of the Virginia Company's patent in 1624. Perhaps the family recognized in bookbinding the potential to address each of their various interests in profit, pedagogy, and piety. A craft practiced first for personal use and then for patronage purposes is expanded for trade.[23] Certainly, *The Temple* and *Eikon Basilike* constitute a dramatic inventory. By seeding Virginia soil with these volumes, the Ferrars were making pointed interventions in the politics of religion at a time of constitutional crisis. No doubt they did so with the conviction that Herbert's prophesy in "The Church Militant" was about to be fulfilled. "Religion stands on tip-toe in our land, / Readie to passe to the *American* strand," Herbert had written in lines that held up the initial publication of *The Temple* and that were widely referenced in contemporary commonplace books (H 196). Pearson reminds us that the westward movement of religion held as much promise for those like the Ferrars who wished to preserve the established church as for radical nonconformists who left England in search of freedom from such regulation. If the latter founded new communities in New England, the former were welcome in Virginia. In fact, following Charles's beheading, Governor William Berkeley's colonial government in Virginia provoked the English Parliament by refusing equally to abandon the Book of Common Prayer or to acknowledge Parliament's authority.[24] On both sides of the Atlantic, the Ferrars were turning *The Temple* into a powerful token for the royalist cause.

Given the current inventory of copies and tools, it may not be possible to determine if Folger H1516 copy 1 is the product of Cambridge or Little Gidding, the work of a professional or an amateur.[25] But it is safe to say that the binding is a product of the Cambridge sphere of influence. And that is to say that the binding is the work of those supportive of the widest possible definition of religious communion in the belief that separation posed a greater threat to the church than papistry. Whatever else Folger H1516 copy 1 is, it is a presentation book (and this, too, is part of the mentalité of the Cambridge book trade). It is an aesthetic treatment that complements, indeed highlights, a ritualistic and reverential approach to the word. It is an assertive appropriation, with the craftsmanship a redoing, an emphasis of, a laying claim to the acts of devotion within.

In 1641, such acts of devotion were increasingly hard to defend, let alone practice. Little Gidding suffered unwelcome public attention that year, with the London publication of the anonymous slander of *The Arminian Nunnery*. Though the sacking of the estate did not come until 1646, the published attack was an ominous sign of changed and more highly charged politics of devotion. A woman in nun's garb is depicted in the forefront of the woodcut that illustrates the title page (Fig. 2). She clutches rosary beads in her left hand and a little book in her right. There is no reason to identify the book as *The Temple*, but such a volume would be among the cherished possessions of the Little Gidding/Cambridge nexus of Herbert's first readers.[26] That it passed out of

THE
ARMINIAN
NVNNERY:
OR,
A BRIEFE DESCRIPTION
and Relation of the late erected *Mo-*
nasticall Place, called the ARMINIAN
NVNNERY at little GIDDING in
HVNTINGTON-SHIRE.

Humbly recommended to the wise consideration
of this present PARLIAMENT.

The Foundation is by a Company of FARRARS
at *GIDDDING*.

Printed for *Thomas Underhill.* MDCXLI.

Figure 2. Title page, *The Arminian Nunnery* (London: Printed for Thomas Underhill, 1641); 151306. By permission of the Folger Shakespeare Library.

those hands into the world of London publishing and wider dissemination is the doing of another man, one who also had close ties to Herbert, though on the face of things a different ideological agenda altogether from the Ferrars. Again, the binding is an important element of the transition. The binding is there in plain sight, in some sense an emblem of a proper Protestant reverence for the word, and yet still not quite "understood," to borrow Herbert's own characterization of an intuitive register of knowledge, or specifically in his case, of God's love ("Prayer 1," H 51).

Ann Ferry has described the ways in which the titles of the poems in *The Temple* prompt a commonplace-like or, more to the point, scriptural reading, an ordering that invites the reader's participation and work, the format of which fosters an intimacy between author and reader for the creation of meaning.[27] Building on Ferry's sense of the reading, I would like to argue that Philemon Stephens—a London bookseller with a forty-year career and a long association with Herbert—understood the invitation of the text and commercialized, even institutionalized, a response to it, in the form of a long-lasting, if little understood, binding practice that is exemplified in the other Folger copy of the 1641 edition.

Folger H1516 copy 2 is bound in black goatskin over pulpboard. It is sewn on three alum-tawed thongs. There are no pastedowns. The edges are gilt. On both front and back covers, a border is formed with two gilt decorative rolls run back-to-back. The outside roll is a small toothlike fillet. The inside roll is a larger swag design. Each corner is marked by a fleuron stamp facing the center cartouche which is built up of an oval shape surrounded by four symmetrical stamps of organic design. The top and bottom are further embellished with two stamps each—a round stamp and the fleuron that appears in the corners. The flat spine is divided into eight panels, tooled with back-to-back gilt fillet rolls, similar to the one forming the single border on the covers. A title label (probably a slightly later addition) overlaps one of the gilded panels, with the gilt words "Herberts Poems." The edges are gold tooled with a dotted roll. The headbands are front beaded (Fig. 3).[28]

The numeral 19 inked onto the fore edge could possibly indicate a place in a library. Could it also indicate a practice of shelving spine in? If it is a mark of ownership, it is matched by another: the initials E. C. and the date 1641 on the title page. The volume is also bound in goatskin rather than the more usual calf. Do these details collectively indicate that this binding a "fine" or custom job? Possibly not. Is the fact that so much else about the binding points to a commercial practice enough to indicate that this binding is a trade job? Again, possibly not. But the distinction between fine and trade may not be particularly useful, at least as it is currently understood. As Folger conservator Frank Mowery reminded me in conversations about the technical descriptions of these

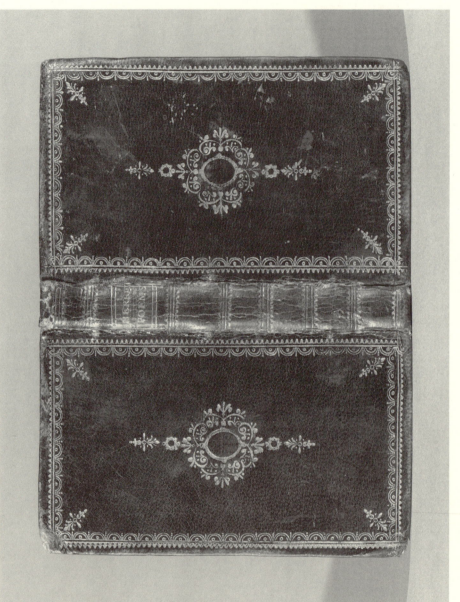

Figure 3. Binding, *The Temple*, Folger shelfmark H1516, copy 2. By permission of the Folger Shakespeare Library.

copies, binding was always a singular process. Binding was not a matter of mechanical reproduction, but one negotiated, often as not, between a customer and a craftsman. Nicholas Pickwoad also finds the distinction between fine and trade binding less than useful, writing that "the quality of the binding is not the main distinction, but how the order was placed."[29]

The markings in a volume, references in an account book, or correspondence that might indicate the manner of an order or the price of purchase (with or without binding) may or may not be available in any single case. On the basis of available information for this copy, we cannot determine if H1516 copy 2 is a trade or a fine binding. But for the sake of comparison, we might speculate that this copy is a trade copy, and consider several ramifications of that, beginning with the price. The seven extant price lists can provide useful evidence of bookbinders' attempts to establish a common price for trade bindings in the course of the seventeenth century—what we might call price fixing.

With the exception of the first list, where the organizing principle is the type of decoration, the organizing principle in the lists is more generally the type of book (i.e., Latin bible) and size (i.e., folio) with decorative styles as subcategories. The prices are for books bound in calf. *The Temple* falls into the category of "Books in 12 English" of the 1646 list. Bindings of that size, decorated with "rolles," would cost five pence.[30] A "small twelve" would still cost five pence, according to the 1669 list.[31] So, if H1516 copy 2 was bought in London in the 1640s, chances are that its binding would have added five pence to the cost of the book.

More intriguing is the question of what *The Temple* is bound *with*: Christopher Harvey's anonymous *Synagogue*, published in 1640 in a careful orchestration of typographical, poetic, and devotional imitation of *The Temple*. Philemon Stephens published *The Synagogue*. Stephens and (later) his successor-son would also publish the six remaining seventeenth-century editions of *The Temple*, possibly beginning with a "seventh" edition of *The Temple* without imprint or date in 1647, and then another "seventh" edition with Stephens's imprint in 1656.[32] The pairing of the two works was a durable one, surviving even a long eighteenth-century hiatus.[33]

Stephens has been credited with several innovations in the book trade. Edward Arber identified him as the first English publisher to put a list of his publications at the end of his books.[34] T. A. Birrell noted Stephens's marketing of *The Temple* in 1656.[35] In that edition, Stephens moved the table of alphabetized titles to the front of the book, away from the back where it has been all along. And he added a new alphabetical subject index to the back, "for ready finding out chief places." The index is equal parts guide to meditation, doctrinal controversy, and household minutiae (H lx).

Stephens was a shareholder in the English Stock, a collective of stationers enjoying the protected profits from the sale of English psalters and psalms.[36] He and Christopher Meredith operated a retail bookshop "at the Golden Lion" in a prime spot in St. Paul's churchyard.[37] Perhaps less obviously but no less effectively, he maneuvered around the tricky relations between Cambridge printers and the London stationers—each with letters patent protecting their conflicting rights—to secure the copy to the steadily selling *Temple.*

It is not clear precisely how he did this. And the most interesting bits of the story are situated in the civil war and interregnum years, the time of subsequent pairings of *The Temple* and successively expanding editions of *The Synagogue,* the same time the Ferrars were looking across the Atlantic for a new stronghold of episcopacy and monarchy. But even in 1641, we can see that Stephens is taking full advantage of the compromised position of Cambridge printers, operating as they did under a "covenant of forbearance." For the sum of £200 a year, the university had agreed in 1639 "not to exercise its right in respect of titles which the Company saw as the strong-selling lines of its chief members, or only to do so at the order of the company—and notably the partners in the English Stock."[38] Compounding the accommodations made by the Cambridge printers was the fact that some, like John Legate the elder, were themselves freemen of the Stationers' Company. Others, including Roger Daniel, operated retail shops in London as well as Cambridge. Like his father, John Legate the younger was a freeman of the Stationers' Company. He may have taken matters to their logical conclusion. He apparently printed the first two editions of *The Synagogue* for Stephens; once he succeeded Roger Daniel to the title of printer to the university in 1650, what was there to scruple about printing *The Temple* for Stephens as well?

This is far from a full explanation of the murky circumstances of the "seventh," undated edition of *The Temple,* the one that probably marks the transference of financial interest from Cambridge to Stephens or perhaps a sharing of it. But it does provide a rich background of trade and regulatory intrigue for the more personal interest Stephens had in Herbert's work. For Stephens had published *Memoriae Matris Sacrum,* Donne's funeral sermon and Herbert's Latin poems commemorative of the death of his mother, Magdalen Danvers, in 1627. The choice of publisher for this text had probably been Herbert's, since Donne published with the king's printer, Thomas Jones, in the 1620s. Further proof that the association was of Herbert's devising rather than Donne's is found in the fact that Stephens is mentioned in Herbert's will some six years later as having "diuers moneys" of Herbert's in hand, "wherof he is to giue as I know he will a Just account" (H 383).

Presumably, Stephens was successful with his matched and bound sets of texts. In 1636, he would again resort to the formula, publishing *The Conditions of Christianity* and *The Cure of Hurtful Cares and Feares* in a duodecimo edition. The authors are two respectable puritan divines, the sorts with which Stephens was associated throughout his career. But Stephens was not above virulent polemic. His first imprint (with Robert Milbourne in 1622) had been *The Anatomy of the English Nunnery at Lisbon*, Thomas Robinson's scurrilous narrative of convent life. In 1638, he published three editions of Nathaniel Bacon's *Relation of the Fearful Estate of Francis Spira*, the wildly popular anticonversion narrative, a cautionary tale of the dangers of reconversion. He also published twelve editions of John Owens's works after 1643.

Stephens's list of authors is solidly puritan, then, however fluid a category that may be. The authors of the works Stephens bound together in 1636 are well within that tradition. They also happen to be the father (Christopher Harvey the elder) and stepfather (Thomas Pierson) of Christopher Harvey the younger, he of *The Synagogue*. The younger Harvey had been named one of Pierson's literary executors, and he edited the pair of posthumous works of his fathers for Stephens.[39] In 1647, the year Stephens published the second, enlarged edition of *The Synagogue*, Harvey would edit another of Pierson's works for Stephens's press.

Stephens's record of publications makes perfect sense as business acumen informing godly fervor. It is an example, as well, of the establishment and maintenance of networks of an almost underground puritanism, which Jacqueline Eales has described in several recent studies.[40] As such, Stephens's sponsorship of Herbert assumes the role of an imprimatur in the process of claiming and repackaging him for a wider, more puritanically tinged audience of readers. True as this all may be, it does not yet account for the anomalous role in this puritan tradition of Christopher Harvey, especially in light of Harvey's increasingly tin-eared paeans to high church Anglicanism in the 1650s. Whatever his filial impulses or his understanding of the humanistic exercise of imitation may have been, Harvey's poetic corpus is insistently ceremonial and episcopal in a way that is clearly recognizable as a legitimate offspring of his poetic forefather Herbert but that no less clearly betrayed the stricter more presbyterian beliefs of his father, his stepfather, and his publisher.

Does commerce trump ideology? Or does devotion transcend sectarian divides? Whatever these lines of transmission and traditions of conformity and dissent, they are far too elastic to suit the ecclesiastical tradition we have constructed today: a solidly Calvinist consensus reached in the Elizabethan era and then sustained until threatened by a mid-century emergence of Laudian ceremonialism.

To further strain the fragile tissues of sectarian affiliations and doctrinal genealogies, Harvey and Stephens were facing a suddenly fierce application of regulatory oversight on the part of ecclesiastical authorities. Judith Maltby has found an letter from Stephens to Harvey bemoaning the lack of progress on the edition of Pierson and Harvey: "Sir, After all this expectation, often wailings, and many faire words importing[?] better dispatch; the copie is returned to me without an Imprimatur: it will not help you, nor me, to recite particulars. If you aske what is obiected; I answere no false doctrine; nor that there is any other then a very pious and good exhortation and fit for the pulpit; But for the press (say they) there is no need of it."[41] The letter is dated almost exactly one year after Herbert's death. So, three years prior to the official restatement and tightening of printing regulations in a Star Chamber decree of 1637, Stephens was already having trouble publishing moderate puritan sermons and meditations. But at the same time, Ferrar and Woodnoth were also having trouble publishing Herbert's translation of Luigi Cornaro's *Trattato de la Vita Sobria* (an edition to which Stephens seemed to have a competing claim), on the grounds that even dietary advice from an Italian Catholic was suspect.

The history of prepublication licensing in the period leads us to be particularly watchful for the nuanced interchanges between ideology and regulation in the book trade. The multifaceted and competing interests of monarchy, bishops, and trade guild are all at stake and equally subject to close scrutiny in 1637. And then they are just as quickly scrambled in 1640 when the Long Parliament abolished the Courts of Star Chamber and High Commission. The (again brief) period of freedom from regulation is a milestone in a long and indirect route to freedom of the press. As important, it was a serious challenge to the stationers' notion of copyright. Perhaps Stephens's binding together of Herbert and Harvey is as much a testing the limits of his newfound economic freedom as celebration of Laud's defeat.

However complexly textured Stephens's ideological, commercial, and sentimental motives may be, his binding practice frames a durable reading experience. The consequences of that framing can be somewhat bewildering and alienating for a modern reader. Most obviously, the act does not serve Stephens's ideological purposes. For Harvey is not the mainstream puritan whose work Stephens made a career of advancing. And if that was not especially evident in the first edition, it became inescapably clear with successive editions.

But the individual experience of each poet is also strangely elided in the pairing. The elision is in part a consequence of the pressure exerted by the binding to read the two within a range of expectations that extends from understanding their compatibility at the low end of the spectrum to finding them somehow mystically united at the high end. There are other material conditions adding to this pressure. For instance, Harvey was not identified by name on the title page of *The Synagogue*, facilitating the subsumption of the work of the acolyte into that of the master. A measure of Harvey's success may be found in the fact that Sarah Cowper mixed excerpts from both in her commonplace book, representing them equally as Herbert's work.[42]

Such a subsumption of identity, whether it be (even momentarily) achieved or remain always only potential, is a fair enough goal, given that the reach for greater powers is precisely the object of the traditional rhetorical exercise of imitation. And Herbert's single-minded purpose as poet-priest was to apply the techniques of those logocentric techniques to scriptural precedents. *The Temple*'s metatextual awareness of its own reading (and by implication writing) strategies is made explicit in the two sonnets on "The Holy Scriptures." The lines "[t]his verse marks that, and both do make a motion / Unto a third, that ten leaves off doth lie" invite a reading of *The Temple* even as they model a reading of the bible ("The H Scriptures II.," H 58). Such ways of reading transgress the boundaries of individual chapters and even books of the bible. For it is a reading founded on an understanding of the variously layered and interrelated narratives of the bible as a unified field in which one tests the strength of one's own belief.

It is not the singer who is ever supposed to matter in this exercise of Herbert's; it is the song. The experience of devotion is the common bond that "in another make me understood" (H 58). Herbert's way of reading taps into a deep exegetical tradition of reading in terms of precept, history, and prophecy, one that Sidney drew upon for his conflicted treatment of David in the *Apology*.[43] Herbert's way of reading also informs the humanist habit of keeping a commonplace book, of storing aphorisms for later motivated use and action. In one sense, the action for Herbert may be limited to an ephemeral apprehension of saving grace. But in another, the action is nothing less than the constitution and maintenance of the church in all its confounding communion, as an intimacy is forged in shared emotive beliefs. In the relationship between the individual and God, then, the position of the self becomes interchangeable. It is no accident that the deeply personal lyrics that describe "the many spiritual Conflicts that have past betwixt God and my Soul" are presented under the rubric of "The Church."[44]

The fluid boundaries of individual experience are physically embodied in the binding practices of the sixth edition of *The Temple*. In the differences of their bindings, the copies examined here complicate easy distinctions between authorial identities, ideological agendas, and the Cambridge and London book trades. The elision of those too easy distinctions marks the interchangeable positions of a reader. Such an elision of difference is the very means by which an inclusive church—George Herbert's church—was sustained as a normative model of devotion in seventeenth-century England. If we attend, then, to the strategic constructions of these copies, we are also attending to the social history of devotional literature.[45]

Notes

This essay has benefited from my many conversations with contributors to the NEH summer institute and to this volume. I am particularly indebted to Steve Zwicker, a masterful teacher and the father of so much of the work of this volume. Rachel Doggett, the Andrew W. Mellon Curator of Books at the Folger Library, spurred my casual interest in H1516 copy 1 with repeated cautions that there was probably more to the Little Gidding attribution than had yet been ascertained. Mirjam Foot, David Pearson, and Nicholas Pickwood generously responded to my inquiries and kindly reformulated some of my questions. Peter Stallybrass succinctly stated my thesis for me. And finally, Jennifer Andersen shared her own work in progress on the pedagogical uses of reading at Little Gidding; Judith Maltby puzzled over the pairing of Herbert and Harvey with me; and Suellen Towers guided me through the Folger's cataloguing archives with her own scholarly sympathy for this project.

1. Cyprian Blagden, *The Stationers' Company: A History, 1403–1959* (Cambridge, Mass.: Harvard University Press, 1960), 39.

2. Private correspondence (26 October 1998). Dr. Pearson, Librarian of the Wellcome Trust, responded generously to my inquiries.

3. Graham Pollard, "Changes in the Style of Bookbinding, 1550–1830," *The Library*, 5th ser., vol. 11 (1956): 71 n. 1.

4. McLeod also alludes to the cataloguing complications that ensue when different titles are bound together. For instance, the revised Short Title Catalogue includes an unnumbered cross-reference under Herbert for *The Synagogue* ("Fiat flux," *Crisis in Editing: Texts of the English Renaissance*, ed. Randall M Leod [McLeod] [New York: AMS Press, 1988], 154 n. 13).

5. In the profession's methodology, one researcher's process is not generally made available for replication by another. Instead, one researcher builds on another's work with a different set of materials, a different set of records to read them against, and each time a modified hypothesis. David McKitterick addresses this issue in contextualizing his own examination of a series of letters between the well-known Cambridge man Joseph Mede and Sir Martin Stuteville about the purchase of a 1629 Cambridge folio bible: "Customer, Reader, and Bookbinder: Buying a Bible in 1630," *Book Collector* 40 (1991): 382–406.

6. J. C. T. Oates, "Cambridge Books of Congratulatory Verses, 1603–1640, and their Binders," *Transactions of the Cambridge Bibliographical Society* 1 (1953): 395–421; Mirjam Foot, "Some Bookbinders' Price Lists of the Seventeenth and Eighteenth Centuries," reprinted in Foot, *Studies in the History of Bookbinding* (Aldershot, Hants.: Scolar Press, 1993), 15–67; David Pearson, "Cambridge Bindings in Cosin's Library, Durham," *Six Centuries of the Provincial Book Trade in Britain*, ed. P. Isaac (Winchester: St. Paul's Bibliographies, 1990), 41–60.

7. The quantitative case is presented in Robert H. Ray, ed., "The Herbert Allusion Book," *Studies in Philology* 83.4 (1986).

8. *The Works of George Herbert*, ed. F. E. Hutchinson (London: Oxford Univer-

sity Press, 1941), 3. Further references to this work are cited in the text as (H) followed by page numbers.

9. Frederick A. Bearman, Nati Krivatsy, and J. Franklin Mowery, *Fine and Historic Bookbindings from the Folger Shakespeare Library* (Washington, D.C.: Folger Shakespeare Library/Harry N. Abrams, 1992), 94–95.

10. Nicholas Pickwood, private correspondence (26 February 1999). The same treatment of margins is found in the Bodleian manuscript of *The Temple*, produced at Little Gidding.

11. Cyril Davenport, "Three Recently Discovered Bindings with Little Gidding Stamps," *Library*, new ser., 1 (1900): 205. Further references to Davenport are cited in the text as (D) followed by page numbers. Distinguished by a skull stamp not found elsewhere, the 1629 Cambridge bible is now in the British Library, shelfmark P850. Mirjam Foot ascribes it to the Cambridge bookbinder Daniel Boyes in *The Henry Davis Gift: A Collection of Bookbindings*, 2 vols. (London: British Library, 1978), 1: 59–69. The copy of *Eikon Basilike* is also distinguishable by its flyleaf annotation and is also in the British Library, shelfmark C.37.d.13.

12. Now in the British Library. In *Bindings in Cambridge Libraries* (Cambridge: University Press, 1929), G. D. Hobson accepted one of the stamps on this binding as number 13 in his list of Little Gidding stamps.

13. For a larger view of the historiography, see Diarmaid MacCulloch, "The Myth of the English Reformation," *Journal of British Studies* 30 (1991): 1–19.

14. Hobson, 124, refers to a copy of the fifth edition of *The Temple* with "the same stamps on its cover, though arranged in a different pattern" from those of H1516 copy 1. I cannot trace his reference to "Pickering's Catalogue of Bookbindings, n.d. No. 10718," but Sir Paul Getty has a copy of the fifth edition that may share two stamps with Folger H1516 copy 1. It is illustrated in Maggs Bros catalogue 966 (1975), item 28.

15. Oates speculates that Moody's daughter Katharine could be this "Dark Lady of English bookbinding," 421.

16. Lot 70, Sotheby's sale catalogue (11 December 1997), 54.

17. Sotheby's, 54.

18. Hobson, "Stamps used at Little Gidding," following p. 122.

19. The group includes the copy of John Valdesso's *One Hundred and Ten Considerations*, described above.

20. In H.IV.10, a penciled note by Cosin provides rare evidence of the cost of purchase: "in sheets 19s, binding 8s."

21. See also *Clare College, 1326–1926*, 2 vols. (Cambridge: Cambridge University Press, 1930), 2: 479–80.

22. Helen Wilcox, "Entering the Temple: Women, Reading, and Devotion in Seventeenth-Century England," *Religion, Literature, and Politics in Post-Reformation England, 1540–1688*, ed. Donna B. Hamilton and Richard Strier (Cambridge: Cambridge University Press, 1996), 196.

23. "I send you also three books of Mr. Herbert's," wrote Susanna Collet to her son Edward in the East Indies in 1634; *Nicholas Ferrar: Two Lives by His Brother John, and by Dr. Jebb*, ed. J. E. B. Mayor (Cambridge: Cambridge University Press, 1885), appendix.

24. See Thomas J. Wertenbaker, *Virginia Under the Stuarts* (New York: Russell & Russell, 1959), chpt. 4, "Governor Berkeley and the Commonwealth."

25. If Cambridge, perhaps John Holden. See Foot, *The Henry Davis Gift*, 59–75.

26. *The Arminian Nunnery* (London: Printed for Thomas Underhill, 1641); Ray, 1–17.

27. Anne Ferry, "Titles in George Herbert's 'Little Book,'" *English Literary Renaissance* 23 (1993): 314–44.

28. J. Franklin Mowery, Head of Conservation at the Folger, coached this description. The infelicities are my own.

29. Private correspondence (26 February 1999).

30. Foot, "Some Bookbinders' Price Lists," 40. Including the price of the book, a book this size would have cost 1 shilling in London, according to the 1620 list (the next earliest extant one).

31. The 1669 list, licensed by Roger L'Estrange, also carries the names of eighty-two bookbinders, eighteen of whom are known to be booksellers, and an additional five of whom are possibly booksellers.

32. Hutchinson, lix. He notes that the printing standards of the edition without an imprint are far below Cambridge's and that "there are printers' ornaments, notably the uncouth Gorgon's head on p. 16, which are not found in any Cambridge book of the period. The ornament below 'The Altar' on p. 18 is found on the title-page of the second edition of *The Synagogue . . .* (1647)."

33. Ilona Bell, "In the Shadow of The Temple," *Like Season'd Timber: New Essays on George Herbert*, ed. Edmund Miller and Robert DiYanni (New York: Peter Lang, 1987): 255–79.

34. Edward Arber, *Bibliographica*, III, part 9, 181–82. One such booklist survives in the folio edition of John Trapp's *Commentary on XII Minor Prophets* in 1654, one of only a handful of folio volumes in Stephens's career.

35. "The Influence of Seventeenth-Century Publishers on the Presentation of English Literature," *Historical and Editorial Studies in Medieval and Early Modern English for Johan Gerritsen*, ed. Mary-Jo Arn and Hanneke Wirtjes (Netherlands: Wolters-Noordhoff Groningen, 1985), 163–73.

36. Blagden, *Stationers' Company*, chapter 6, "The Stocks," esp. 92–101. Thanks to Peter W. M. Blayney for sharing with me his evidence of Stephens collecting his dividends in 1644, 1645, and 1667.

37. Right inside Paul's Gate. Peter W. M. Blayney, *The Bookshops in Paul's Cross Churchyard*, Occasional Papers of the Bibliographical Society, no. 5 (London, 1990), 39–41.

38. M. H. Black, *Cambridge University Press, 1584–1984* (Cambridge: University Press, 1984), 71.

39. See Judith Maltby, "From Temple to Synagogue? 'Old Conformity,' the Commonwealth, and the Case of Christopher Harvey," in *Conformity and Orthodoxy in Early Modern England*, ed. Peter Lake and Michael Questier (Rochester, N.Y.: Boydell and Brewer, 2000), 88–120.

40. Jacqueline Eales, "Thomas Pierson and the Transmission of the Moderate Puritan Tradition," *Midland History* 20 (1995): 75–102, and "A Road to Revolution: The Continuity of Puritanism, 1559–1642," *The Culture of English Puritanism, 1560–1700*, ed. Christopher Durston and Jacqueline Eales (New York: St. Martin's Press, 1996), 184–209.

41. B.L. Add. MS 70002, fol 82^r, dated March 7, 1633 [1634], and transcribed by Judith Maltby.

42. Wilcox, 196–98.

43. Anne Lake Prescott, "King David as a 'Right Poet': Sidney and the Psalmist," *English Literary Renaissance* 19 (1989): 131–51.

44. Izaak Walton, "Life of Mr. George Herbert," *The Lives*, intro. George Saintsbury (Oxford: Oxford University Press, 1956), 314.

III

Print, Publishing, and Public Opinion

9

Preserving the Ephemeral

Reading, Collecting, and the Pamphlet Culture of Seventeenth-Century England

MICHAEL MENDLE

In 1641, England experienced a culture shock—an explosion of small cheap books and broadsides reporting, commenting upon, and manipulating public events. That pamphlet culture waxed and waned until the Restoration, by turns more and less seductive. But it always remained a cultural presence, providing the greatest common denominator of public experience. Splitting the difference between high and low culture, pamphlets became the middlebrow point of contact of public life.[1] Peer and apprentice inhabited different material and mental worlds. So did conformist and sectarian, royalist and radical. Ostensibly defining their disagreements and differences, the pamphlet culture paradoxically brought the disparate voices together. In the Restoration, the press that royalists had learned to manipulate as well as the radicals ever had was put under greater control; but when the political thermometer soared in the later 1670s (and when the licensing act expired in 1679), the pamphlet reappeared as naturally as if it had never missed a step.

It may have been reflexive, but it was not un-self-conscious. From the earliest days of the pamphlet explosion, two vectors tugged on the pamphlet culture—"news" and "history." There is no mistaking that news drove the pamphlet explosion. Whatever their subgenre—"separates" of parliamentary speeches, copies of petitions, breathless reports of war news, the weekly newsbooks that began to appear in late 1641, or commentaries or satires upon public affairs—the little books of a sheet or less, usually costing 1d., were the core of the pamphlet culture. Weightier productions—the more learned tracts, treatises, and politically inspired sermons—consumed the little pamphlets as their daily bread, or better, their baguettes, fresh, cheap, and undemanding. By mid-1642 they often came day-dated as a sign of their newness. But like baguettes, news stales quickly. As one day's tracts were postdated by the next and the next, their marketability declined to the vanishing point. Those sold lost their value as news. The fate of nearly all of those penny texts—in runs characteristically of about 1,000 or 1,250 copies—was to be recycled. The commonest remark about the subsequent use of quarto pages is too obvious to bear further comment. Less crudely, one reader compared tracts to "pinns and needles," the archetypal throwaway objects of the age. But he also lamented that fate, wishing that someone would collect these books before they perished.[2]

He was not alone. As tracts ceased to be news, they became history; or, rather, some people perceived them immediately as incipient history and so to be *collected*. Thus the collection motto chosen by the greatest seventeenth-century pamphlet collector, George Thomason: "Actions y^t may be presidents to posteritie, ought to haue their records, & merit a carefull preseruation."[3] So too the London turner Nehemiah Wallington made a personal collection of godly petitions to Parliament because they testified to the Lord's hand in the stirring events of late 1641.[4] Such sentiments speak not only to the primacy of public affairs in contemporaries' sense of their era's significance; they also speak to the centrality of narrative. What turned one moment into history was the succeeding moment; one needed to collect the record of the story.

Publishers saw opportunity in the nexus of news and history. Ephemera could be gathered and reprinted, providing documentary histories of recent events. William Cooke's *Speeches and Passages* of parliamentary proceedings and Edward Husbands's two compilations of the declarations (*An Exact Collection*) exchanged between king and Parliament before were early examples of the genre. Cooke's compilation, Joad Raymond has shown, provided a spine for substantial stretches of John Rushworth's *Historical Collections*, and Husbands's first volume became almost scripture to the Leveller leader John Lilburne.[5] The New Model Army's declarations in 1647 were similarly gathered. An episcopal partisan in 1642 collected and published petitions designed to counter those so cherished by Nehemiah Wallington. Royalists later collected the scaffold speeches of their martyrs, and also published a collection of "moderate" declarations in favor of a Stuart restoration.[6]

These collections were one front of the contemporary war on ephemerality. The focus of this essay, however, is what can be gleaned of the efforts of individuals to gather and so preserve the record of their times as it first appeared in the press. Every tract existing today, it seems too obvious to state, has had a continuous existence since its publication. As Peter Blayney has sagely observed, while the odds of survival of any individual copy of a book are quite long, the chance that none at all will survive is small. What preserves individual copies of otherwise unremarkable items is that someone has seen fit to collect them.[7] Newsbooks are a most telling example. Late seventeenth-century auction catalogues, when they do list newsbooks, list them in sorted groups (usually by title), often consecutive runs. Leading surviving collections intact from the seventeenth century tell a similar tale. Thomason, with his omnivorous habits and date-focused organization collected titles systematically. Sir William Clarke, like most others, sorted his newsbooks by title, with complete or nearly complete runs within; Anthony Wood did the like, although he also relied on the collecting of others. The first earl of Bridgewater, who acquired newsbooks actively in 1647, operated more like Thomason in sorting his news-books, grouping them chronologically. But the point remains: it is all but impossible to see how the serial runs or date-related groupings could have been assembled, if not contemporaneously with publication. The converse is also apparently true. One short-run serial publication collected by Thomason, *The Grand Politique Informer*, was bound in a volume subsequently lost.[8] No other copies are known to have survived. The same point is attested by the vast holdings of the Folger Shakespeare Library. For all their richness, there are astonishingly few newsbooks of the civil war period. Apparently no newsbook runs were ever acquired, and as a consequence the few newsbooks that are in the collection seem to be strays, not unlike the odd copy of *Time* or *Life* to be found in a bargain box of books at rummage sale.

*   *   *

We can see how contemporaries collected the little books in several ways. The most direct is to examine the great surviving collections formed at the time of issue and preserved as their compilers arranged them, notably Thomason's in the British Library and Sir William Clarke's in Worcester College, Oxford. Other collections can also yield important insights. Anthony Wood's pam-phlets in the Bodley were formed partly after the fact, but are nonetheless interesting for his ways of categorizing and organizing. While the vast collec-tion of the earls of Bridgewater (now in the Huntington Library) has been rearranged, informative traces of the original organization persist.

Other evidence is provided by the book auction and other sale catalogues of the seventeenth century. First attempted in England in 1676 with the sale of the library of the divine and bibliophile Lazarus Seaman, by the 1680s auctions of private libraries had become accepted and fairly common.[9] While substan-tial learned works bulked largest in auction sale catalogues, from the Seaman sale onward, pamphlets, newsbooks, and contemporary tracts were also to be found, sometimes in considerable quantities. Then as now, auctioneers some-times obtruded lots from other sources into these catalogues, so that it is risky to conclude *tout court* that the lots of pamphlets actually belonged to the featured former owner. But, obviously, this was not universally the case, and in any event these lots had to have been gathered from somewhere, so that these catalogues do provide a glimpse of the place of the 1d.–6d. little books in the libraries of the learned, rich, and powerful.

Better to understand that place, we need to see how catalogues were compiled. English auction catalogues followed the pattern of general sales catalogues. Books were sorted by format, language, and subject, though the order of the sortings differed. For example, the primary sort might be by format—folio, quarto, or octavo. Within each format books would then be arranged by language or by subject. Topically, theology or divinity had pride of place, followed by others according to the collection's contents and the cataloguer's judgment. While there might be a miscellaneous heading, "history" and "philology" (frequently loosened by an "etc.") often served as nontheological catchalls. Alternatively, the primary sorting could be by subject or by language, with format becoming a subcategory. Within the categories individual titles were listed, sometimes with place and date of publication. Though a composite volume of several items might be listed, the usual pattern was one entry for one work.

The more substantial works having to do with public affairs found a home within this scheme. But the little pamphlets were not easily accommodated. There was, first, the sheer bulk of their numbers. Listing each title individually would have been as commercially pointless as it was tedious. Auction catalogues, of course, were not intended as memorials for the ages, but onetime listings with an eye to profit; few catalogues attempted complete descriptions of the pamphlets they offered for sale.[10] The overwhelming nature of the task can be glimpsed from the failure of the auctioneers of John Rushworth's very large pamphlet collection ever to make good on promises to describe it.[11] Another auction list stated that "besides the Books expressed in the Catalogue, there are to be sold at the said place, a Great Number of Stitcht Books or Pamphlets, together with about an Hundred Volumes of Curious Tracts bound together."[12] Usually, even when lots were identified, only sketchy information was provided about lot contents.

No less to the point, both because of their variety and their nature, the little books were difficult to accommodate into the scheme that had served to pigeonhole the books of the learned world. In instances where separate items had been bound together, a solution was offered by volumization, especially if the volume was thematic, generic (e.g., fast sermons), or chronological in constitution. But more often than not pamphlets were not bound together. They were offered for sale in "bundles" of "stitch't" or "stitched" pamphlets— groupings of separate pamphlets of one or a few sheets, with the cut pages of each title held together by nothing more than a knotted thread. These bundles, whether assembled by the owner or the auctioneer, are usually the most detailed breakdown of the tracts. Revealingly, they increasingly came to be category of their own—not another category's afterthought but a species in their own right. No less revealingly, they usually appear at the rear of the catalogues, an index of their lower standing.

The same uneasy attitude toward pamphlets can be seen in the ways in which pamphlets crept through the back door into the holdings of the Bodley. On the one hand, they were deemed inappropriate to a learned library, a factor that weighed heavily against the attempts later to acquire the Thomason collection. On the other hand, exuberance and engagement occasionally trumped learned prejudice. In 1646 John Milton, scanting the efforts of his left hand as he might, thought well enough of them to donate his prose works as well as his 1645 *Poems* to the Bodley. A bit earlier, in 1645, the Bodley made at least two purchases of pamphlets, even in its then extremely straitened circumstances. Eight "bundles of pamphlets . . . conteyninge the occurances of the times" were purchased in 1645–46 for £1 12s. The language suggests newsbooks or separates of news; at the going rate of 1d. per sheet the sum would have purchased 384 single sheets (or quarto pamphlets of eight pages), perhaps a little less because of carriage. Also, in June 1645, the Bodley purchased about two dozen significant tracts for £2 16s. 1d., with Prynne, John Goodwin, Henry Parker, Henry Burton, and John Milton among those represented.[13] But with the provision that the Company of Stationers send on to the universities one copy of each publication in almost total abeyance, the overwhelming bulk of the Bodley's vast holdings of civil war pamphlets and newsbooks came later, most notably through the bequest of Anthony Wood (which Wood originally made to the Ashmolean Museum, with the Bodley only receiving them in 1860), and, more recently, the Fairfax deposit, which was partly withdrawn in 1993.

Despite the prejudice against them and the bibliographical and descriptive complexities involved in selling them, pamphlets figured largely in the auction sales of private libraries. The evidence provided by the auction catalogues is at once frustratingly vague in particulars and overwhelming in the aggregate. It is never possible to give a precise count of the pamphlets available even as it is impossible to ignore the bulk of them. There was a fair sprinkling of 1640s pamphlets in the Lazarus Seaman sale, distributed amongst "Philologie, &c. in English." Another early sale, of the library of Thomas Manton, contained freestanding items of polemical divinity of the 1640s and 1650s within the category of "Divinity in English" as well as seventy bound volumes of pamphlets (primarily from the 1640s and 1650s), and some thirty-seven "Bundles," mostly from 1641–60 and 1660s and 1670s.[14] Benjamin Worsley's books yielded thirty-six volumes of fairly miscellaneous bound volumes, as well as 105 "Bundles," including those devoted to public papers, public sermons, William Prynne (seventeen of his own tracts and one devoted to replies to him).[15] Gabriel Sangar's and Lord Brooke's libraries offered thirty-eight bundles of "Tracts Sermons and Pamphlets" including a good number of newsbooks, as well as numerous similar items mixed in with the denominated categories.[16] An omnibus sale of the libraries of several divines in 1680 yielded large collections of civil war polemical divinity, a set of Engagement tracts, and runs of leading newsbooks.[17]

These examples are in the middle range of pamphlet collections by size. More remarkable was Dr. Richard Smith's library, which may have contained as many 1641–60 tracts as Sir William Clarke's library, including perhaps 1,800 newsbooks.[18] Bishop Brian Walton's library contained eighty-two thick-looking bound volumes (perhaps 2,000–3,000 items) heavily concentrated in 1641 to 1653, and sixteen "bundles" with a balancing thrust for the 1650s and 1660s.[19] The collection of Arthur, Lord Anglesey, sold in 1686, was composed in part of libraries he purchased whole, including a *"vast Collection of Pamphlets of all sorts, containing all the remarkable Ones relating to Government,* &c." "All" was too strong, of course, but the 118 bound volumes in octavo and folio show signs of careful arrangement, including a volume of 36 items for 1647, another for ship-money. Most items were from 1640 to 1660. The "bundles" held even more: 11 in folio, 162 in quarto; 16 in octavo, ranging across the century, and including hundreds of newsbooks.[20] An anonymous citizen of London's library, sold at auction on 12 March 1687/8, included amongst many other holdings of pamphlets a remarkable single lot, a ten-volume "Collection of Letters, Speeches, Remonstrances, Declarations, Orders, Ordinances, Diurnal Proceedings, Occurrences, Depositions and Articles, Votes, Messages, all relating to English, Scottish, and Irish Affairs in the time of the late Civil war, &c."[21]

No collection dispersal by auction was greater than the mountain of tracts heaped up by a London bookseller, William Miller. It was twice offered for sale after Miller's death in 1695,[22] first "by Retail, or otherwise" in *The Famous Collection Of Papers and Pamphlets of all Sorts, from the Year 1600. down to this Day, commonly known by the Name of William Miller's Collection.*[23] Since most items remained unsold, the catalogue was reworked as an auction catalogue, *A Curious Collection of Books and Pamphlets: Being the Stock of Mr. William Miller,* which announced that the sale would continue "until the Number of 1500 Bundles are Sold off."[24]

Miller, the son of a London printer active in the days of the first civil war, indicated his special field in an advertisement he placed in an auction catalogue of 1684: "All gentlemen, etc. may be furnished with most sorts of Acts of Parliament, as also the King's, and Chancellor's and Speaker's Speeches, with other Speeches, Declarations, Proclamations, Commissions, Orders, Ordinances, Remonstrances, Votes of Parliament, Letters, Articles of War and Peace, Of Religion, viz., Visitations Articles etc., with Books of Divinity, viz., of Church Government, Sermons on most Occasions, with Variety of School Books, History, Husbandry, Arts and Sciences, Poetry, Plays, Collections of

Gazettes, and all sorts of other News."[25] At some point Miller's business became an obsession; it was said that Miller "had the largest collection of stitched books of any man in the world."[26] The collection, first described in the *Famous Collection* through the efforts of Charles Tooker, consisted of both bound volumes and stitched bundles. The "Hundreds" of bound volumes were not listed, though they were on view at Mrs. Miller's.[27] The unbound bundles covered many fields, and were in Latin and the principal languages as well as English. Overwhelmingly, though, they were concerned with public affairs, even those in French. There were 240 folio entries, including seven bundles of state acts from 1648 to 1659, a bundle devoted solely to Titus Oates and another to last speeches of those sentenced to die for their parts in the popish and "presbyterian" plots, sixteen alphabetically sorted bundles of miscellaneous tracts of the time of Charles II, sets of gazettes and other newsbooks. The quartos comprised 1,123 entries. Only the first forty-one bundles were in Latin. Bundles 42–509, broadly categorized as "Divinity English," focused upon the public issues of the day. For example, bundles 60–71 were court sermons, while lots 62–97 held parliamentary sermons of 1640 to 1660 (again sorted alphabetically), with other sermon categories treated in lots 98–209. The remaining three hundred lots were tracts and pamphlets treating matters of public concern such as the liturgy, episcopacy (for and against), liberty of conscience, further treatments of church government, sectaries, popery, sabbatrianism, New England, and the Jews; only lots 403–57 treated "Practical Divinity." Much of the remainder of the quartos were news and political controversy. John Lilburne rated three bundles, William Prynne, seventeen and one devoted to replies to him. The 297 lots in octavo were similarly arranged, with a format-related category for almanacs. *A Curious Catalogue*, the list of the remainder put to auction, adds an important detail: some indication of lot sizes.[28] While many of the more numerous lots of single sheets were not indicated, most lots had ten or more items. One single page described twelve lots amounting to over one thousand items.

*   *   *

It remains to consider the great collections still intact. Four are particularly notable: the Bridgewater tracts at the Huntington Library, Wood's pamphlets in the Bodley, Sir William Clarke's at Worcester College, Oxford, and greatest of all, George Thomason's behemoth at the British Library.

The Bridgewater tracts cannot currently be counted. Apart from books retained by the family after acquisition of the main body by the Huntington, re-shelf-marking and disbinding early in the twentieth century of many original volumes, particularly the quartos, make even loose estimates impossible. Fortunately, the original Bridgewater shelfmarks have been preserved in the

Huntington's catalogues; the completion of the general Huntington catalogue in electronic form will allow a reliable count to be taken and may even permit reconstruction of the original library. However, most folio volumes were kept intact. By means of them, some intact quartos, and a few records of the original organization, the collection's richness and the care by the first and second earls (the two collectors of the seventeenth century) are readily apparent.

Huntington Library volumes of bound pamphlets (with the shelfmark prefix "P[art]V[olume].") have many Bridgewater items, easily spotted by the second earl's own part number written inside a box at the top right-hand number of the title page; many volumes are composed entirely of Bridgewater titles, though only the bulk of the folios and a few volumes in quarto remain untouched. A rough count of the folio items can be obtained, serving broadly to indicate the collection's substantiality. About 600 folio items date from 1640 or earlier, about 1,400 date from 1641–60, about 3,300 from 1661 to 1686 (the year of the death of the second earl), about 1,260 from 1687 to 1700.[29]

Numbers aside, something can be gleaned about the collection process from surviving intact volumes and from collection records. A set of contents pages from disbound and redistributed newsbooks reveals the care taken with newsbooks of 1647 and 1648 by the second earl, who gathered them in volume-sized chronological runs, and then divided them by title.[30] The second earl's intense concern for his pamphlets is best seen in the occasional quarto or smaller volume to escape disbinding,[31] and the vast number of accounts, trials, and tracts in folio purchased by the second earl, when in the late seventeenth century that larger format became de rigeur for items presumed eventually to be bound together in hefty volumes resembling the manuscript miscellanies of the sixteenth and early seventeenth centuries.[32] The folio volumes are tightly chronologized, and for most of them the earl supplied a contents list and the "box numbers" that are his hallmark.[33] His fastidiousness is seen in his treatment of large items (generally broadsides) folded into these volumes: the earl always placed the box number so as to orient it vertically on the first surface facing the reader. Items inserted and folded horizontally had their box numbers written diagonally, so as to be equally legible vertically and horizontally.[34]

Anthony Wood's tracts range across the century.[35] By one count there are 6,400 items in 1,000 volumes.[36] Duplicates, overlapping of volumes, and differing collection formats suggest that Wood expanded his collection through bulk purchase of other collections; Wood was an avid collector of book sale catalogues, including a very large set of auction catalogues.[37] Along with Wood's numerous comments, his categorization scheme, so far as it was actually achieved, bears attention. Volumes that Wood definitely supervised or established had an initial table of contents outlined in red ink, which also allowed for a volume heading. Wood occasionally cross-referenced to other volumes. For example Wood 209 contains three items having to do with either the regicides or royalist victims; Wood noted two others elsewhere, one in duodecimo (thus unsuitable for binding amidst the quartos) and another already bound "in my vol. of pamphlets entit [*sic*] *Tryalls, & Executions of Regicides*."[38] Wood 373, a volume of little news pamphlets of 1641–42, noted that pamphlets pertaining to Strafford were in another, distinct volume.[39] Such cross-referencing aside, Wood preferred topical or thematic categories wherever possible, except for the little news pamphlets, which tended to be placed in chronological series as tight as Wood could make them.

*   *   *

Two great contemporaneous, intact collections of civil war era pamphlets will always attract special notice, for they were formed in what might be described as the heroic age of pamphlet collecting. Sir William Clarke's books at Worcester College are certainly such a collection. A protégé of John Rushworth, Clarke later became an army secretary and secretary to the general of the army in Scotland, George Monck.[40] As such, he was peculiarly well placed to gather a great collection of news pamphlets. Along with his extraordinary set of army manuscripts, including the famed Putney debates, the books were bequeathed to Worcester College by his son, Sir George Clarke. While a few of Sir George's books mingle with the volumes assembled by Sir William, nearly one hundred volumes (some quite massive) preserve almost entirely their collector's original design. Apart from some utterly miscellaneous volumes, newsbooks were sorted by title and date, news separates were assembled chronologically, and political-constitutional, theological, and homiletic items were kept together. One exceptionally well-conceived volume gathered tracts from 1641 to 1660 about the successive oaths (the Protestation, Solemn League and Covenant, the Engagement) taken by or imposed upon the public.[41] Characteristically Clarke signed the first page of the first item in a volume, and often provided a table or contents list at the front or the back.

Clarke was cost-conscious. In some ways this has not served the collection well. Some volumes are thicker than the strength of binding will tolerate—one volume has 264 separate items.[42] Generally Clarke economized by folding large-format items into his quarto volumes, a practice that accelerates wear. But Clarke's close eye on his purse also produced one of the largely untapped resources of the collection: frequent, and, in a few volumes, systematic reporting of prices. Routinely the determinate of price was length; tables in some volumes simply count sheets, as if the sheet count equated to cost (at the usual 1d./sheet, although this was not invariable). However, Clarke acquired many items for free, noting on the copy or in an end-of-volume table "ob" (with a macron line of contraction drawn over the "o" and through the "b"), which stood, it seems likely, for "obtentus gratis."[43] In other cases he dickered, noting, usually on the last page of an item, the amount asked and the amount agreed upon, which was often less. In one instance he waxed triumphant: "preciu[m] 6d con: 3d valet 1s."[44] The hand of Clarke's early mentor John Rushworth is to be found at intervals, and one whole volume, in which Clarke as usual wrote his name on the first page of the first item, was in fact assembled and listed by Rushworth.[45]

The most intimate, largest, and most thoroughly organized of all collections is that of the London bookseller George Thomason. Given Thomason's and his partner Octavian Pulleyn's niche as vendors of learned books—they were prime suppliers to Oxford University[46]—Thomason's soul- and fortune-draining devotion to his pamphlets reveals again how the little books created a zone of commonality for otherwise separate, even fissiparous cultural strains. Thomason collected Hobbes's *Leviathan* along with a nonpareil assemblage of single sheets, puritan wranglings thick with distinctive idiom of the godly beside crude pornographic satires, writings with which he passionately agreed and those with which he as vehemently disagreed. The result was about 22,000 titles, arrayed originally in 1,955 volumes, almost all from 1641 through 1660.[47] Though Thomason's interests were obviously catholic, he never aspired (as is sometimes thought) to collect "one of everything" published. But within the realm of public affairs, save for a spell when he nearly gave his collection up, he assiduously bought nearly every newsbook to appear in London, a vast array of little pamphlets which have survived in no other collection, and a fair number of provincial printings as well. As he aged and as his views hardened, he "passed" on some items that by his own principles he ought to have collected—notably Quaker writings, not surprising for a man who judged George Fox a "Goose."[48] The lapses and lacunae, however, pale before the achievement.

No other major collector took greater pains in organizing his pamphlets, a fact that looms larger as the enormity of the collection dwarfs the others. Early on, he decided upon a chronological principle of organization (the "Method . . . is Tyme," as he put it), simply putting one item behind the other in its format category, without regard for contents.[49] Volumes were then formed as convenient.[50] Thomason did two other things that provided his collection with much greater utility than others. From mid-1642 onward, Thomason noted his date of acquisition on items where the publication date was not obvious, as it is, for example, with newsbooks.[51] He also constructed a twelve-volume manuscript catalogue (in two copies); every item was listed in order in its appropriate volume, with its date given. Of necessity, five different format categories had to be used: folio single sheets (broadsides), small quartos, large quartos, octavos and other small formats, and "Acts and Ordinances etc.," a category that essentially amounted to folios printed on both sides of the page.[52]

Like other collectors, Thomason scribbled attributions and comments on his books. Perhaps he did so less often than others—Anthony Wood and Narcissus Luttrell come readily to mind—but the sheer volume of the collection leaves much to captivate the modern reader. And it was principally through his collection that the pamphlet world of the seventeenth century was rediscovered in the nineteenth and early twentieth centuries. His manuscript catalogue guided early readers through the collection in the absence of a printed one. Despite the unwieldiness of twelve manuscript volumes in the five formats, readers could soon fathom the design. They learned the first lesson of the collection: browse. So successively William Godwin,[53] Thomas Carlyle, the Miltonist David Masson, and the great S. R. Gardiner came to rely on it. For Carlyle the "whole secret of the seventeenth century" was contained in that "hideous mass of rubbish."[54] Masson appreciated the immediacy of the collector as much as the value of the collection.[55] Gardiner's heavy use of the collection established it as a resource as fundamental to the period as the archives, a position that the microfilm and recent digital editions have enhanced.

* * *

The two great waves of pamphleteering (and pamphlet collecting) of 1641–60 and the later 1670s and 1680s are both continuous and discrete phenomena. Clearly, late seventeenth-century collectors did not discriminate between periods, except insofar as chronological principles of organization dictated separation. Recent tracts jostled those of a generation past in the auction catalogues; the availability of the earlier tracts and news accounts in the later age doubtless reinforced the dialectic of past and present. Nevertheless, there was a huge difference between the eras. In the 1640s and 1650s, worried collectors like Thomason, Clarke, and Rushworth thought that only their lonely heroics would preserve the ephemeral. But in the era of exclusion, the plots, and the Revolution of 1688, the exceptional had become normal. Catalogues were issued to keep them abreast. In 1680, one could find at the Green Dragon in St. Paul's Churchyard virtually every publication from every publisher having anything to do with the popish plot and its aftermath: a careful catalogue, issued serially in three parts, kept track of it all, even to the publication details of the serials, so collectors knew which titles had ceased publication and at which issue.[56] Similarly, in 1689, the recent victory of the Protestants was celebrated by a bibliography of their recent polemics: *The Catalogue of All the Recent Discourses Published against Popery, during the Reign King James II by the Members of the Church of England, and by the Non-Conformists.*[57] Publishers assumed that the "prints" of show trials were being collected; formats were uniform to assist in binding, and one trial's errata was corrected in another trial put out by the same publisher.[58]

One generation's Promethean labor had become another's routine expectation. At an auction in 1689, a scant thirteen years after the first one ever in England, amidst a collection rich in tracts and newsbooks, lot 80 was a collection of fifty auction catalogues.[59] Perhaps forty of them would have offered substantial numbers of the little pamphlets. The world of George Thomason and William Clarke was succeeded by the world of Anthony Wood and Narcissus Luttrell, when pamphlet collection had become a recognized hobby for some and a business for others. That indeed is one result of the English Revolution.

Notes

1. Arguably, the press supplanted the pulpit as the primary vehicle of a common national culture in the years in the ecclesiastically fissiparous 1640s and 1650s. For a current general survey of the news culture in early modern Europe, *The Politics of Information in Early Modern Europe*, ed. Brendan Dooley and Sabrina Alcorn Baron (London: Routledge, 2001).

2. *The Correspondence of Bishop Brian Duppa and Sir Justinian Isham, 1650–1660*, ed. Sir Gyles Isham, Northamptonshire Record Society 17 (Lamport, 1955), 117.

3. Thomason inscribed this in the margin of the first page of entries of the first volume of his manuscript catalogue (in two copies) of his collection [BL C. 38 h. 21 and BL C. 37. h. 13]. The source was Thomas Nabbes's continuation of Richard Knolles, *The Generall Historie of the Turkes*. Thomason apparently used the 5th ed. (London, 1638); see sig. SSSSSS1ʳ.

4. Nehemiah Wallington, *Historical Notices of Events Occurring Chiefly in the Reign of Charles I*, ed. R. Webb, 2 vols. (London, 1869), 2:1–22.

5. *Speeches and Passages of this Great and Happy Parliament* (London: for William Cooke, 1641). Cooke published a continuation: *The Diurnall Occurrences . . . of Both Houses* (London, 1641). Edward Husbands, comp., *An Exact Collection of All the Remonstrances* (London, 1642/3) and *A Collection of All the Publike Orders* (London, 1646). Joad Raymond, *The Invention of the Newspaper: English Newsbooks, 1641–1649* (Oxford: Clarendon Press, 1996), 302–10. Andrew Sharp, "John Lilburne and the Long Parliament's Book of Declarations: A Radical's Exploitation of the Words of Authorities," *History of Political Thought* 9 (1988): 19–44.

6. Army declarations were gathered in *A Declaration of the Engagements, Remonstrances, Representations* (1647). The conformist petitions are gathered in Sir Thomas Aston, *A Collection of Sundry Petitions* (1642). The royalist martyrology, including the late king's trial, was *England's Black Tribunall* (London, 1660). The irenic declarations were collected in *A Happy Handful* (London, 1660).

7. Peter Blayney, *The Texts of King Lear and Their Origins* (Cambridge: Cambridge University Press, 1979), 1:38.

8. No such title is to be found in Carolyn Nelson and Matthew Seccombe, *British Newspaper and Periodicals, 1641–1700: A Short-Title Catalogue* (New York, 1987), a point made to me by Carolyn Nelson in a personal communication. See BL C. 37. h. 13, vol. M, no. 12, marginal note of 1893 noting doubt that the volume containing the four issues of *The Grand Politique Informer* was ever received.

9. A still useful survey is provided by John Lawler, *Book Auctions in England in the Seventeenth Century (1676–1700)* (London, 1898; rpt. Detroit: Gale Research Co., 1968). Lawler, however, does not have a special interest in the pamphlet literature. Even as early as 1680, ordinary booksellers showed some concern that auctions were eating into their own trade: Robert Clavell's *General Catalogue of Books* (London, 1680), "To The Reader," claimed that "most Books bought in an Auction, may be had Cheaper in Booksellers Shops."

10. An interesting exception to the rule, since it contains Narcissus Luttrell's noting of the prices of the lots (though not the individual tracts within them), is the BL copy of *Catalogus Librorum ex Bibliotheca Nobilis cusjusdam Angli . . . Accesserunt Libri Eximii Theologi, D. Gabrielis Sangar* (London, 1678), 77–80. The anonymous nobleman was Lord Brooke.

11. *Bibliotheca Generalis ex Bibliothecis Duorum Doctissimorum Theologorum & Eximii cujusdam Medici, Nuper Defunctorum, . . . Tom's Coffee-House . . . Octavo Decemb. 1690* (London, 1690). To the reader on the verso of the title page: that inter alia the sale will include "*the Industrious* Rushworth's *Famous Collection* of Tracts *and* Pamphlets, *Bound as well as Stitch'd*." But none is to be found and there is a later notation that "*The Remaining Part of this Catalogue, from* Page 68 *near Printed* [this copy ends at p. 68], *will be suddenly distributed, viz. The* English, Libri Omissi, *and* Manuscripts." The additional part of the catalogue appeared as *The English Part of the Bibliotheca Generalis . . . As, also, a Collection of Stitch'd and Bound Tracts and Pamphlets, which Pamphlets were Chiefly Collected by Mr. Rushworth . . .* But at p. 114 of this addendum, the auctioneers reneged on the promise of the title page: "The entire famous Collection of pamphlets, and State Trials of the late ingenious and most industrious Mr. *Rushworth*, Author of the Collections in four Volumes, being above 300 Volumes bound, and as many others in bundles unbound. A particular account whereof will be exhibited a part [*sic*] to be perused 4 days before and at the time of Sale."

12. *Bibliotheca Selecta: sive Catalogus Variorum Librorum . . . 21 Die Mensis Maii,* A.D. *1688* (London, 1688). "Advertisement" on the verso of the title page.

13. Gwen Hampshire, "An Unusual Bodleian Purchase in 1645," *Bodleian Library Record* 10.6 (1978–82): 339–48; *The Bodleian Library Account Book*, ed. Gwen Hampshire, Oxford Bibliographical Society Publication, new ser., 21 (Oxford, 1983), 144, 150, 190–92. Other un- and ill-described purchases made of Thomas Robinson and Michael Sparke could conceivably be pamphlets as well. See also Ian Philip, *The Bodleian Library in the Seventeenth and Eighteenth Centuries* (Oxford: Clarendon Press, 1983), 42–43.

14. *Catalogus Variorum et Insignium librorum . . . Thomae Manton.* 25 Mar. 1678 (London, 1678).

15. *Catalogus Librorum . . . D. doctoris Benjaminis Worsley . . . Maii. 13. 1678* (London, 1678).

16. *Catalogus Librorum ex Bibliotheca Nobilis cusjusdam Angli . . . Accesserunt Libri Eximii Theologi, D. Gabrielis Sangar* (London, 1678).

17. *Catalogus Variorum Librorum in Selectissimis Bibliothecis Doctissimorum Virorum [H. Stubb, Dr. Dillingham of Oundle, Dr. Thos. Vincent, Dr. Cauthon of Westminster] . . . 29 Nov. 1680* (London, 1680).

18. *Bibliotheca Smithiana . . . Maii Die 15. 1682* (London, 1682). Smith, an obsessive bibliophile, amassed a great many learned and historical works; however impressive, the tracts were hardly the core of the collection.

19. *Bibliotheca Waltoniana . . . 30 Die Aprilis* (London, 1683).

20. *Bibliotheca Anglesiana* (London, 1686).

21. *A Catalogue of Books Viz, Divinity, History, Philology, Poetry and Plays, Romances, and Novels, Voyages, and Travels, &c. together with Volumes of Bound Tracts and Sermons, Contained in the Library of a Learned, and Eminent Citizen of London . . . the 12th Day of this Instant March, 1687/8* (London, 1687–8).

22. On Miller see H. R. Plomer, *A Dictionary of the Booksellers and Printers . . . from 1641 to 1647* (London: Bibliographical Society, 1907, rpt. 1968), 129, and *A Dictionary . . . from 1668 to 1725* (Oxford, 1922), 206–7. But the dates given of Miller's death (1698 in the first instance and 1696 in the second) both seem to be in error.

23. ([London, 1695?]). Wood dated his copy 10 May 1695.

24. (London, [1695?]). The total number actually listed was closer to 1,300.

25. Cited in Lawler, *Book Auctions*, 147–48.

26. Plomer, *A Dictionary . . . from 1668 to 1735*, 206.

27. *Famous Collection*, sig. N2^v, "Advertisement."

28. Though the lot categories are similar to those used in *The Famous Collection*, they appear in some spots to have been reworked, presumably in light of the earlier sale.

29. I am reluctant to be more specific because (1) exact counts depend on arbitrary decisions on how to treat works issued in parts or with multiple title pages but continuous signing; (2) I have simply distributed most undated items according to appearance, topic, and, where appropriate, volume contents, without checking standard bibliographical resources; (3) Huntington cataloguers were inconsistent in their own counting methods. I have made no effort to count post-1700 items. Non-PV Bridgewater items are not included. With these caveats, I suspect that my results would be within 5 percent of any other's.

30. A good many pseudo-mercuries (one-off pamphlets in the form of newsbooks) are also to be found. These pages are in a packet kept in the office of Alan Jutzi. This file is apparently the "catalogue" said to be compiled by the earl in *Guide to British Historical Manuscripts in the Huntington Library* (San Marino, Calif.: Huntington Library, 1982), 22.

31. Wholly or largely intact volumes include, for example, E-PV 8277-84, E-PV 8763-70, E-PV 11266-69, E-PV 60984-92, E-PV 62701-03, E-PV 77911-16, E-PV 95922-24-95926-30 [*sic*], E-PV 112702-707, E-PV 135336-53, E-PV 135703-24, E-PV 141042-49, E-PV 141299-310, E-PV 141327-43. Though a number of them are stamped "Miscellanies" on their spines, these volumes seem to have been undisturbed because they are fairly tight topical groupings or group together more loosely connected tracts in the smaller (and rarer) formats.

32. Manuscript items found their way into such volumes as well. Like the occasional intact volume in quarto or smaller, many of the folio volumes are labeled "Miscellanies" on the spine, a poor description of their often tightly chronologized contents, but an index perhaps of their connection to manuscript miscellanies common earlier.

33. The earl numbered his tracts within a box in the upper-right-hand corner of the title page or first page, or used the corner itself as two sides of the box. Occasionally a similar parallelogram was used.

34. Diagonal numbers are found, for example, in E-PV 133308-53, items 43–45., and E-PV 133826-82, items, 19 and 51.

35. We await the full presentation of Nicholas Kiessling's research into Wood

and his collection. For the present see "The Location of Two Lost Volumes of Ballads, Wood 399 and Wood 400," *Bodleian Library Record* 15 (1996): 260–91; "Anthony Wood, Thomas Gore and the Use of Manuscript Material," *Library* 21 (1999): 108–23; and, most importantly, "The Library of Anthony Wood from 1681 to 1999," *Bodleian Library Record* 16.6 (1999): 470–91, which I have only been able to use to correct my own much less thorough research into Wood's collection.

36. Kiessling, "Anthony Wood, Thomas Gore and the Use of Manuscript Material," 108. Cf. *The Life and Times of Anthony Wood, Antiquary, of Oxford, 1632–1695*, ed. Andrew Clark, 4 vols. (Oxford: Clarendon Press, 1891–1895), 1: 6–21, lists 959 volumes. Clark's methods and schemes of categorization are sometimes odd. Wood's books (not including those in the Wood A–E collections) are also cataloged in a manuscript volume, "Hand List of Wood Printed Books," made October–December 1922 by R. T. Milford. The list is kept on F Floor in the Bodley. Kiessling, "The Library of Anthony Wood," 470, estimates there were originally about 7,000 items.

37. While sale catalogues are found passim amidst the volumes, the auction catalogues constitute a tight chronological series in the volumes Wood E. 13–23. Wood's collection practices are briefly but entertainly described in Kiessling, "The Library of Anthony Wood," 471.

38. From the list at the beginning of the volume; an abbreviation silently expanded. But see Kiessling, "The Library of Anthony Wood," 482–84 and for a 1681 shelflist, 473–75.

39. Here Wood did bind in and fold large sheets amidst the tracts in quarto. The several numbering schemes also reveal prior ordering. Wood's comments on many of the tracts are a gold mine.

40. On Clarke, see Leslie Le Claire, "The Survival of the Manuscript," *The Putney Debates of 1647: The Army, the Levellers, and the English State*, ed. Michael Mendle (Cambridge: Cambridge University Press, 2001).

41. Worcester College AA. 8. 18.

42. Worcester College BB. 8. 11.

43. In Worcester College A. 1. 13, the items so marked are carried in the price list as 00.00.00. AA 1. 15, item 27, *A Second Remonstrance or, Declaration of the Lords and Commons Assembled in Parliament, concerning the Commission of Array* (London, 1642[43]), Clarke noted (sig. F4^v) the price as 3d. but added "ob [with the macron] gratis."

44. Worcester College BB. 1. 11, item 1.

45. Worcester College AA. 2 6.

46. *Bodleian Library Account Book*, 92, 100, 105, 109, 112, 117, 121, 125, 130 clearly show Thomason and Pulleyn as the Bodley's principal supplier of books in from 1632 to 1641 (when the library nearly stopped purchasing). A Thomason sale catalogue of 1647, *Catalogus Librorum Diversis Italiae Locis Emptorum*, makes clear that learned books remained a central part of Thomason's business. On this see also I. Abrahams, "The Purchase of Hebrew Books by the English Parliament in 1647," *Transactions of the Jewish Historical Society of England*, 8 (1915–17): 63–77.

47. I derive the volume count from Thomason's original manuscript catalogue; since some volumes were later split (and some in the catalogue never made it to the British Museum), the current volume total will differ. There are several items not listed in G. H. Fortescue, *Catalogue of Pamphlets, Books, Newspapers, and Manuscripts . . .*

Collected by George Thomason, 1640–1661, 2 vols. (London, 1908) from the 1630s, and some from 1640, but Thomason apparently did not *collect* until spring 1641. Some news serials continue beyond 1660.

48. In addition to BL E. 916 (4), *A Declaration of the Ground of Error & Errors* (London, 1657), which is cited in Fortescue, ed., *A Catalogue*, 1:xxiv, Thomason did the like in BL E. 812 (2), *A Message from the Lord, to the Parliament of England* (London, 1654).

49. Thomason described his method in a prefatory note bound into the first volume of small quarto entries of BL C. 38. h. 21. Initially Thomason segregated separates of parliamentary speeches and the first newsbooks but gave that practice up by 1642. The treatment of Acts and Ordinances also proved difficult; see n. 52 below. See Michael Mendle, "The Thomason Collection: A Reply to Stephen J. Greenberg," *Albion* 22.1 (spring 1990): 85–93; there are, however, a few errors of detail in that account.

50. Small-format volumes, for reasons of binding efficiency, were handled differently, but Thomason's chronological principle was rigorously maintained in the manuscript catalogue.

51. In this Thomason continued by hand a publisher's practice that was very common in the news-dense months of summer 1642. At that time day-dated imprints were common. Thomason seems to have begun his hand dating to fill out the record, and continued to do so for nineteen years. Some octavo items only bear month dates.

52. Thomason battled conceptual uncertainty with the Acts and Ordinances category. He used three different numbering schemes for the volumes, preserved his original segregation of Acts and Ordinances as a subject category in his catalogue, but let consistency prevail in the binding, transferring broadside acts to the single sheets, a fact he noted in the margin of each transferred entry.

53. William Godwin, *The History of the Commonwealth of England*, 4 vols. (London: H. Colburn, 1824–28), vol. 3, "Advertisement" comments upon the increasingly central role Thomason's pamphlets played in the writing of his history.

54. *Report of the Commissioners Appointed to Inquire into the Constitution of the British Museum; with Minutes of Evidence* (London, 1850), Minutes, 274, cited in *Catalogue of Pamphlets*, ed. G. K. Fortescue, 1: xx and n. Carlyle made similar remarks in his *Oliver Cromwell's Letters and Speeches*, 4 vols. (London, n.d.), 1: 8, 109.

55. David Masson, *The Life of John Milton*, 7 vols. (London: Macmillan, 1859–94), 2: 239, n. 1.

56. *A Compleat Catalogue of All the Stitch'd Books and Single Sheets* (London, 1680) and its *Continuation* (London, 1680) and *Second Continuation* (London, 1680).

57. (London, 1689).

58. At the conclusion of *The Tryal of Lawrence Braddon and Hugh Speke* (London, 1684), the publisher Benjamin Tooke advertised that his Hampden trial was shortly to be published, and also made a correction to the trial of Sir Samuel Bernardiston, which he had earlier published.

59. *Bibliotheca Selectissima seu Catalogus Variorum . . . Librorum . . . Sams Coffee-House, Octavo Die Mensis Maii, 1689* (London, 1689).

10

Licensing Readers, Licensing Authorities in Seventeenth-Century England

SABRINA A. BARON

Historians and literary scholars of seventeenth-century England have argued in recent years that if the political upheaval which occurred there midway through that century revolutionized nothing else, it revolutionized reading.[1] Most seventeenth-century contemporaries would have agreed that the revolution they experienced was in large part constituted in the highly politicized act of (and greatly increased opportunity for) reading. While it is the case that England was simultaneously experiencing a number of revolutionary events and the population was undoubtedly deeply affected by occurrences such as battlefield combat between the king and his Parliament, it is also the case that the vast majority of English people experienced these struggles vicariously and intellectually—in fact, primarily through reading about them.[2] Far more people purchased and read and heard about the contents of the cheap little pamphlets pouring out of the press than joined an army or a religious sect.

The early modern English state had long been concerned about the power reading printed matter exerted over the opinions and actions of the general population.[3] The huge increase in printed books and pamphlets following the demise of state mechanisms for regulating printing in 1641 and the concurrent rise of popular radicalism only served to deepen the conviction that the state must control the reading material available to its citizens in order to regulate their political activities. Likewise, the English church hierarchy was convinced that the freedom to print works about topics in religion led straight to heresy and schism (which, as John Milton in the 1640s would point out, had existed long before books).[4] The increasingly fractured plurality of religious sects emerging at midcentury was only cause for further alarm. It was the church that had been at the forefront of historic efforts to regulate printing in England, and it was clerics who carried on the crusade in the 1640s when civil officials were otherwise distracted.

Attempts on the part of both the state and the church to control, or limit, the reading material available for general consumption were fulfilled in the seventeenth century through prepublication licensing. Authors, printers, and publishers were obliged to present a manuscript of any work they planned to publish in print to an official licenser, whether secular or religious. These divisions among licensers were meant to employ expert knowledge in different subject areas. With the fragmentation of Charles I's government and the removal of Star Chamber, High Commission, and Archbishop of Canterbury William Laud in the summer of 1641, prepublication licensing came to an effective end. But when Parliament in its turn as the chief governing body sought ways to control the quantity and nature of reading material available to its constituents, prepublication licensing resumed.[5]

*　*　*

The reading revolution of the 1640s and attempts to control it through prepublication licensing passionately informed the thought, writing, and publishing of John Milton. It was especially pervasive in his AREOPAGITICA; A SPEECH . . . For the Liberty of VNLICENC'D PRINTING. Areopagitica is generally hailed as the benchmark argument for freedom of the press and free speech. But what Milton argued for in this work was free access to reading materials of all sorts—in short, the freedom to read.[6] Milton quite correctly viewed licensing for the press as fundamentally an attack on reading: with such a system in place "what is to be thought in generall of reading, what ever sort the Books be[?]," he asked—not once but twice—in Areopagitica (CPW 2:491, 507). English was the language of liberty, he wrote, and neither its writers nor its readers should be restricted (CPW 2:505, 551, 554). "Give me the liberty to know, to utter, and to argue freely according to conscience, above all liberties" (CPW 2:560). Milton's knowing came through reading, and he was "certain that a wise man will make better use of an idle pamphlet, then [sic] a fool will do of sacred Scripture" (CPW 2:521, 543, 554). Milton argued that "every acute reader" should have access to writing of all sorts in order better to formulate informed opinions of issues: "Read any books what ever come to thy hands, for thou art sufficient both to judge aright, and to examine each matter. . . . To the pure all things are pure, not only meats and drinks, but all kinde of knowledge whether of good or evill [sic]; the knowledge cannot defile, nor consequently the books, if the will and conscience be not defil'd" (CPW 2:511, 512).

Milton was objecting in Areopagitica specifically to the historical ecclesiastical monopoly controlling licensing ("a lordly Imprimatur, one from Lambethhouse, another from the West end of Pauls" [CPW 2:504]). He advocated the removal of the "illiterate and illiberal" clerics[7]—the "glutton Friers"—from any responsibility for print publication (CPW 2:503). By insisting on such a prominent role in this "cautelous enterprise" of licensing, the church was indicating a lack of faith in its own communicants, in its own teachings, in its own officials and structures, and in its own role as moral arbiter—all of which were under attack from a number of directions in the 1640s (*CPW* 2:520, 537, 541). Multifront attack caused the church to fight even harder to maintain the status quo.[8]

While Milton found the apparatus and operation of ecclesiastical pre-publication licensing repellent, he allowed that the state was justified in its concern about what its citizens were reading: "I deny not, but that it is of greatest concernment in the Church and Commonwealth, to have a vigilant eye how Bookes demeane themselves, as well as men. . . . For Books are not absolutely dead things, but doe contain a potencie of life in them to be as active as that soule was whose progeny they are; . . . they are as lively, and as vigorously productive, as those fabulous Dragons teeth; and being sown up and down, may chance to spring up armed men" (*CPW* 2:492).

Clearly Milton recognized the power of reading in the formulation of political ideas in this passage which he authored, as well as in others he recorded in his commonplace book. It was after all undeniably his own experience. But he was arguing that the state, like the church, should have faith, trust, in its citizens to judge reading material for themselves and to act in an acceptable manner (*CPW* 2:520–21, 536, 541). The state's response to print publication, like all other responses to print publication, should be temperate, free in fact—characteristics that the intercession of the church distinctly failed to exhibit. Indeed, Milton was arguing that the church should not instruct the state in matters touching its own security. Moreover, he argued that the state needed to exercise control over the institution of the church and its personnel rather than over the reading material of good and faithful English citizens (Cf. *CPW* 2:503 n). "The State shall be my governours, but not my criticks"—a mediation that should not limit learning, truth, or reading (*CPW* 2:534).

The call for unlicensed printing in *Areopagitica* has been a source of dissonance for scholars studying Milton and his writing.[9] How could he compose the original anthem of free speech, free press, and liberty of conscience only later to serve as a state licenser for the press himself? As shown above, Milton's objection to licensing was first and foremost an objection to the ecclesiastical role in the process and in particular, to the fact that ecclesiastics—"whom the change of their condition hath puft up, more than their late experience of harder times hath made wise"—continued to have responsibility for licensing the majority of printed works even under the parliamentary government (*CPW* 2:569). His quarrel with state oversight of the press, which he later nominally exercised, was negligible, and as will be discussed below, was mediated by his personal interpretation of the law under which he operated as licenser.

Much has been made over time of *Areopagitica*'s arguments and the intent of the author, but when it was published in November 1644, and for sometime thereafter, it seems to have had little impact. The first edition did not sell out and no reprint appeared until Milton's collected works were published at the end of the seventeenth century. It was not reprinted as an individual work until the mid-eighteenth century.[10] Moreover, *Areopagitica* on the surface looked very ordinary to seventeenth-century readers. It was indistinguishable from thousands of other unassuming print publications. The usual method of advertising early modern printed works to potential readers was displaying the title page, and *Areopagitica*'s title page was undistinguished, hardly worthy of notice (Fig. 1). The only element to perhaps set it apart from thousands of competing publications was a quotation from Euripides' *The Suppliant Women* in the original Greek, and an English translation, or at least Milton's idea of one, immediately beneath it. There is no printer's name, no bookseller's name, no indication of where the pamphlet might be available for sale, no mention of an official license—only the bold assertion that it was printed in London (home to most presses and most licensers) "in the Yeare, 1644."[11]

Up to this point in Milton's publishing career, seven of his nine polemical works, including the first edition of *The Doctrine and Discipline of Divorce*, appeared anonymously. The same number, although not the same works, appeared unlicensed. The license for one of his works, *The Judgment of Martin Bucer*, had been obtained from the "elderly" father of one of Milton's college mates. Milton's name as author was first printed on the title page of his fourth pamphlet publication, *The Reason of Church Government*. After *Areopagitica*, Milton published only two other polemical works before his pen became an instrument of the state. Both *Colasterion* and *Tetrachordon* appeared anonymously and unlicensed, with *Colasterion* blatantly attacking an ecclesiastical licenser (*CPW* 2:145; Parker, *Milton*, 1:196, 201, 208, 261, 276–82).

England had enjoyed for the first time from 1641 "de facto freedom" of the press, "the breaking forth of light," as Milton termed it (*CPW* 2:541). The print marketplace quickly became one where "the Printing of Pamphlets," as polemical-pen-for-hire Henry Parker noted, was "the utmost ambition of Stationers in *England*" (Mendle, "De Facto Freedom," 323, 330). Milton's writing and publishing reveal that he was keenly aware of the alluring "whiffe of every new pamphlet" (*CPW* 2:537). Everyone, whether Parliament or polemicist, king or balladeer, printer or publisher, wanted material in print as quickly and as economically as possible. In this freewheeling atmosphere, Milton published in print like everyone else—as he wished and generally without seeking a license. Neither was anonymous publication unusual in the early 1640s, although in the case of Milton, anonymity was a personal preference. "I was not eager to hasten the tardy steps of fame; nor willing to appear in public till a proper opportunity offered," he wrote in the *Second Defense*.[12] So when

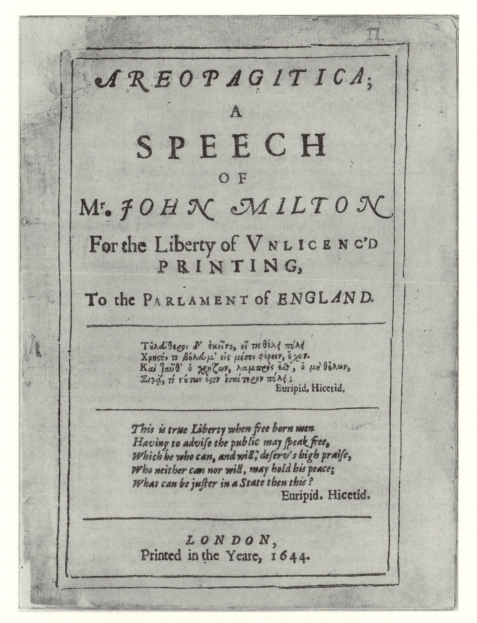

Figure 1. Title page, John Milton, *Areopagitica; A Speech of Mr. John Milton* (London, 1644); M2092. By permission of the Folger Shakespeare Library.

the publishing atmosphere was free-for-all, Milton was an enthusiastic, if largely anonymous, participant. And when the situation changed, when there was more attention to official attempts at regulation, Milton was willing to play by the rules.

While the descriptions in *Areopagitica* show that Milton was familiar with the licensing process as it had functioned under Charles I, there is no evidence that Milton sought to license a print publication under that regime. There is, however, evidence that he did seek a license to print as dictated by the Parliament's 1643 *Order... Regulating Printing*. Milton attempted to obtain a license for what proved to be his most controversial work of the 1640s, *The Doctrine and Discipline of Divorce* (*CPW* 2:534). He approached an ecclesiastical licenser, John Bachelor, likely at the suggestion of Milton's friend and fellow bishop basher, the radical author and publisher Richard Overton. Bachelor had been willing to license many of Overton's controversial works.[13] With *Doctrine and Discipline* Milton also tried to conform to the requirement that the author's name appear on any printed work. Although the first edition of *Doctrine and Discipline* did not have his name on the title page, he signed the preface with his initials, preserving his modesty while effecting compliance.

Bachelor, however, refused Milton a license and once again, in 1643—this time in direct contempt of an ecclesiastical licenser and an act of Parliament—Milton published an unlicensed work essentially anonymously. His motives in attempting to comply with the 1643 *Order* were likely mixed from the beginning. *Doctrine and Discipline* was a work he hoped would influence the Westminster Assembly of Divines which was convened to resolve religious differences of the early 1640s. If such a work carried official sanction, it might carry greater weight with those who read it. Maybe he was simply ready to shed anonymity and become a recognized author and public figure.[14] In any event, *Doctrine and Discipline* rather incensed the Westminster Assembly. The Assembly objected to the moral stance of the tract, but also took the opportunity to mention to Parliament Milton's violation of the licensing regulations.

On 6 August 1644, the collector George Thomason acquired Milton's follow-up work on divorce, *The Judgment of Martin Bucer*. It was a duly licensed and acknowledged work which Milton had translated and published to justify his own writings. But a week later, both of Milton's works on divorce were attacked in a sermon delivered before Parliament by Herbert Palmer, a member of the Westminster Assembly. A fortnight after that, a Stationers' Company petition naming Milton and Overton as violators of printing regulations was referred to the House of Commons' Committee on Printing. The Commons in response drafted new printing regulations that went up to the House of Lords for approval. Nothing further seems to have come of this draft, but the proceedings inspired Overton to launch his Martin Marpriest campaign against the Assembly and the Assembly kept Milton in its sights as well.[15]

Milton was infuriated by these proceedings, as well as with the more generalized negative response to *Doctrine and Discipline*. The specific attack in *Areopagitica* upon the 1643 *Order . . . Regulating Printing*, in addition to the larger diatribe about Parliament's motives and its slide back into the evil ways of the regime it had replaced, and beyond that into popery, were clearly provoked by the events surrounding *Doctrine and Discipline*. But if the responses offended his dignity and sullied his personal reputation, they were also great publicity for John Milton as an author. The first edition, probably 1,000 copies, of *Doctrine and Discipline* sold out in six months and was immediately reprinted. The second edition sold out in less than a year and *Doctrine and Discipline* was reprinted in third and fourth editions in 1645.[16] "Milton the divorcer" became the topic of international debate. This experience also inspired Milton to publish *Areopagitica* on or about 23 November 1644. It was unlicensed, but his name was splashed wall-to-wall in italic capitals near the top of the title page, thumbing his nose at both Parliament and the Westminster Assembly. This did not escape the Assembly's notice and in December 1644, Milton and Hezekiah Woodward, whose writings echoed Milton's, were summoned to appear before judges appointed by the House of Lords to investigate unlicensed printing. They were questioned and released after a few days, with no further action taken. Milton's *Tetrachordon*, published unlicensed and anonymously early in 1645, undoubtedly referred to these events when it thanked Parliament for sparing the author and his books.[17]

If anonymous and unlicensed publication was more the order of the day in the 1640s than it had ever been before, it was still the source of anxiety for everyone involved in the print publication process. A rump of church licensers had continued to function without their governing bodies while a group of clergy had continued to call for reinstitution of the Caroline licensing regime.[18] Quite quickly, in the 1643 *Order* their persistence was rewarded and as Milton said the "immediat [*sic*] image" of the licensing process established by a 1637 Star Chamber decree was restored by Parliament, down to reinstating a number of the same licensers who had exercised that power under Charles I and Archbishop Laud (*CPW* 2:569). In the wake of the 1643 *Order* there was clear tightening of enforcement and attitudes toward unlicensed and anonymous printing, despite Milton's personal disregard.[19]

Unlicensed printing was a straightforward criminal act. Anonymous publication was a somewhat more ambiguous offense, but it had long been a cause for uneasiness among regulatory authorities. If a print publication was not harmful and totally on the up-and-up, why was there a need to conceal the names of its producers? Numerous proclamations and decrees had specified that authors, printers, and publishers should be identified on the title pages of all print publications. But this was never enforceable historically, and in the political cauldron of the early 1640s, many authors had reasons to conceal their identity either through anonymity or noms de plume. Milton insisted he published anonymously out of modesty and a desire to serve the state, although it is clear that he also used the underinformed title page as a smoke screen behind which to conduct political and religious battles. It was always risky for a printer to print unlicensed and anonymous materials, even in the freer times of the early 1640s. Printing the work of someone like Milton, who was unquestionably a notorious figure after the *Doctrine and Discipline* scandal, was taking an even larger, calculated risk.

Whatever the official attitudes toward printing at a given moment, and whatever Milton's motivations for printing "meer unlicenc't," anonymous, publications at a given moment—be they modesty, avoiding ignorant licensers and official censure, or speedy production to compete in the marketplace—Milton needed to engage the services of a certain sort of printer and/or bookseller to achieve print (*CPW* 2:541). Milton's preference was to deal with a printer directly, without a middleman or "publisher," in almost all cases. Although recognizable "pure" publishers were beginning to emerge in this period, authors could and did continue to work directly with printers.[20] It was not difficult to discover which printers specialized in what sort of works, which printers were willing to print unlicensed materials, and which printers were willing to self-finance jobs based on word-of-mouth reputation or a browse through the book shops.[21] Milton was actively involved in the production not only of the much-studied 1645 edition of his collected poems, but of all his works printed in the 1640s.

Milton would have been looking for a printer willing to take a risk, and willing and able to print quickly and cheaply. This logically suggests he would have sought out more marginal printers of questionable integrity, a process no doubt facilitated by Milton's prior knowledge and experience of the book trade. He had acquired associations in the book trade through his father, also John, a professional scrivener at the sign of the Spread Eagle in Bread Street. The senior Milton was a well-known musical composer who collaborated with musicians from the royal household on the music for some of the most popular theater productions of the day, including Shakespeare's plays, as well as print publications. John Milton, Sr., wrote sonnets with John Lane, and has recently been identified as the "I. M." who contributed a sonnet to the prefatory material of the first folio publication of Shakespeare's collected works, printed in 1623. John Milton, Sr., was thus likely the conduit for his son's contribution to the second folio.[22] It was the father who introduced the son to one of his musical collaborators, Henry Lawes, who would also collaborate with and promote the younger Milton. Lawes wrote the music for and arranged for the 1637 publication of Milton's *Maske presented at Ludlow Castle, 1634,* better known as *Comus,* and at least in part made the connection with Humphrey Moseley to publish Milton's collected poems in 1645, as discussed below.[23] John Milton, Sr., also employed an assistant named Henry Rothwell, eldest son of a bookbinder and brother of a bookseller, both by the name of John Rothwell. Henry was himself a member of the Stationers' Company, but it was his brother, John Rothwell, Jr., who published a number of the works in the Smectymnuus controversy, including Milton's own contributions to that debate.[24]

Milton wrote in December 1634 from Hammersmith to his friend Alexander Gill, Jr., to "look for me (God willing) in London on Monday, among the booksellers."[25] Milton assembled a large personal library and would have certainly known the shop of Matthew Simmons "next door to the Gilded Lyon" in Aldersgate between 1636 and Simmons's death in 1654. Milton was living in Aldersgate from the fall of 1640 to 1645 (Parker, *Milton*, 1:192; STC, vol. 3). While Simmons was initially only a bookseller, his shop would have attracted the bibliophile Milton, and when Simmons started printing after 1641, occasionally printing material that got him into trouble with regulatory authorities, it would have been logical for Milton to approach Matthew Simmons to print his works. Early modern authors expressed a preference for working with printers close to home so they could more conveniently read and correct proofs of a work while it was in press. There are a number of recorded instances of authors even moving in with a printer to facilitate this process. Simmons printed for Milton the unlicensed *Doctrine and Discipline* and the equally controversial *Judgment of Martin Bucer.* He subsequently printed the first edition of *Eikonoklastes* and some of the early editions of the 1650s newsbook *Mercurius Politicus.*[26]

Milton was a devoted buyer of imported books at the Rose, and the Rose and Crown, George Thomason's shops in St. Paul's Churchyard. Thomason collected Milton's publications as they appeared in the 1640s through the author's donation, and may even have sold them in his shop. Milton wrote a sonnet in December 1646 on the death of Thomason's wife, who possessed a formidable library of her own, and possibly another sonnet on the death of their daughter. Milton clearly had relationships with Thomason on a number of levels, and it seems likely that Thomason had financed some of Milton's printing, such as the early anti-episcopal pamphlets. Thomason played a number of such financial roles in the book business as well as some hidden, "propagandist" roles in contemporary politics. His prosecution by the Commonwealth government for involvement in the Love Plot was likely mitigated by someone who had been a friend and business associate for years, namely John Milton, but who seems an unlikely ally at that stage, since they had developed differing views on Presbyterianism.[27]

Humphrey Moseley was a bookseller doing business at the Prince's Arms, a.k.a. the Three Feathers, in St. Paul's Churchyard, the location of the largest concentration of bookshops in London. Moseley became the foremost literary publisher of his day and his shop was among the most popular in the City. Milton would certainly have gone there to buy books. Moseley was later the publisher of the 1645 collection of Milton's poems, an association that has seemed an unlikely and even inexplicable one because Moseley was an overt royalist and Milton was not. But there were historic roots to their relationship. Moseley's original partner in the book business was Nicholas Fussell, who entered into the Stationers' Register in February 1631 *A Portraiture of master Hobson the Carryer of Cambridge and verses underwritten*. While an outpouring of verse by Cambridge students marked Hobson's death, the verses printed under the portrait must have been those written by Milton. The print publication of Milton's verses at this early date explains why his Hobson poems appear in so many manuscript verse miscellanies and commonplace books that pre-date Moseley's 1645 publication of Milton's collected *Poems* and the 1640 printing of Milton's Hobson verses in *A Banquet of Jests*.[28] Another printed work of Milton's early literary career, the masque *Comus*, was published by Humphrey Robinson in 1637. Robinson was also a partner of Moseley in the book business. Moseley probably knew Milton through one of these connections, or via another business associate, the Cambridge University printer, who had printed some of Milton's earliest poetry when he was a well known Cambridge scholar and poet. Or perhaps the publisher had been introduced to Milton by the musician Henry Lawes, the old Milton family friend who was John Jr.'s collaborator in *Comus*, who was named on the title page of the 1645 *Poems*, and who collaborated with Moseley in a number of poetry-publishing ventures.[29]

Whatever its origin, the relationship between Moseley and Milton was older, more enduring, and more comprehensible than is generally allowed by modern scholarship. If author and publisher held different political and religious outlooks, it made no difference. When the political climate changed in the 1640s, however sharply opinions diverged, individuals seldom disavowed business colleagues and acquaintances with whom they disagreed. Milton's brother served in the royalist army, and his in-laws, the Oxfordshire Powells, were royalists, one of them an informant for the king's secretary, Edward Nicholas (Campbell, *Chronology*, 76; Parker, *Milton*, 1:43–48, 53, 231, 234). It would have been nothing unusual for John Milton to do business with a royalist Stationer.

Besides being acquainted with book wholesalers, importers, collectors, and retailers, Milton also had associations with a number of printers, members of the book trade who produced reading material but did not sell it directly to the public and thus had no shops for browsers to encounter by chance. As noted earlier, word-of-mouth reputation and knowledge of product lines might have been an impetus for these associations. But these connections could also have been formed by Milton in other ways as well. Milton likely engaged his early printers, Richard Oulton and Gregory Dexter, through his friend Overton, although they were widely known for printing controversial material and had been in trouble with Charles I's government and Parliament a number of times. Edward Griffin, who did some printing early on for Milton, was also a lifelong business association of Gregory Dexter and the Eliot's Court Press where he printed, as well as Milton's friends Overton and John Rothwell. Rothwell had a personal connection to Milton and is known to have published Milton's contribution to the Smectymnuus debate. Rothwell was likely the publisher behind some of the unacknowledged tracts printed by Oulton and Dexter, as well as the connection to Thomas Underhill, who also had connections to George Thomason.[30] This was a network of friends, friends of friends, and printers known to be willing to take a risk. A number of these relationships were personal as well as professional, and a number of them endured over the course of Milton's career as a publishing author.

John Milton was equally long and well acquainted with the printing family of Raworth. The progenitor, Robert Raworth, had tried to buy his way into a master printer's slot early in the seventeenth century, but failed and eventually fell in with a group of marginal and even illegal printing operations which brought him frequent trouble with the regulatory authorities. Ultimately, Raworth was the protégé of Nicholas Okes, one of the most successful jobbing printers, who printed for Fussell and Moseley in the 1630s. Okes would have shared the work with Raworth. Robert's son John was by contrast accounted "an honest man." He was admitted to the Stationers' Company in the late 1630s, and to the position of a master printer in 1637. The Raworth press came into possession of type and ornaments used in *Comus* around the same time and, depending on the precise dating of its production, likely printed it.[31]

In the early years of parliamentary government, the Raworths printed a number of official publications and at least one of the pamphlets in the Smectymnuus controversy. Shortly after John Raworth's death in 1645, his widow Ruth Raworth was printing for the emerging publisher Moseley. She printed Milton's *Poems* for Moseley and part of Moseley and Humphrey Robinson's 1646 folio collection of Beaumont and Fletcher plays. Moseley purchased some lucrative copyrights from Ruth during her widowhood, including her share in some of the Beaumont and Fletcher plays and Richard Fanshawe's translation of *Il Pastor Fido*.[32] In fact, it is with Ruth Raworth and her second husband, the printer Thomas Newcomb, eventually the owner of a one-sixth share in the King's Printing House, that Milton had perhaps the most durable of his book trade associations.

Thomas Newcomb had served his apprenticeship with Gregory Dexter, an unruly printer who printed illegally for Milton in the early 1640s. Newcomb looked to be starting out his career as a disreputable printer too, when on 1 September 1649, Newcomb was arrested for printing his first work as a full-fledged member of the book trade, John Lilburne's *An Outcry of the young men and apprentices of London*. The printer was released three weeks later, possibly through the mediation of Milton, who the previous March had been appointed secretary for foreign tongues to the Council of State, and as such, served as the government licenser for the press and liaison with the book trade. His predecessor in that position had set a precedent of intervention with authorities on behalf of Stationers.[33]

If Newcomb came to know Milton through his master, his wife, and her associates Moseley and Robinson, as seems likely, it proved very beneficial for his career. In the 1650s Newcomb was printing the official state newsbook, *Mercurius Politicus* (sold by Thomason and licensed by Milton). Newcomb printed an enlarged edition of *Eikonoklastes* in 1650, *Pro Populo Anglicano Defensio Secunda* in 1654, and *The Ready and Easy Way* in 1660, among other Milton imprints. It was for good reason that he and Milton were closely linked in the minds of contemporaries as illustrated by an anonymous pamphlet of June 1660. *The London Printers Lamentacon, or, the Press opprest, and Ouerprest* attacked Newcomb as one of three printers who had done the most to destroy monarchy, describing him as "of Milton's strain, and so publiquely known." Newcomb like Milton survived the Restoration, and in the 1660s, as William Riley Parker discovered long ago, Newcomb continued to use the type and ornaments that had appeared in *Comus* thirty years earlier. By the end of his life, Newcomb had become one of the most successful and well respected Stationers in the Company and in London (*Stat. Reg. 1640–1708*, vol. 1; Plomer, *Dictionary*; Reed 141; Parker, "Contributions," 427 n). Like his friend Milton, he ended up far removed from his radical beginnings.

The Raworth-Newcombs and Milton were connected through an extended network of mutual book trade associations, personal cooperation in literary production, and a common early ethos about the freedom to print. They also had one other mutual association that must be considered in this analysis, that with Georg Rudolf Weckherlin. Weckherlin was Robert Raworth's brother-in-law, Ruth Raworth's uncle by marriage, and had been chief clerk to the senior secretary of state and ex officio secretary for the latin tongue in the government of Charles I. As such, Weckherlin had been the crown's licenser for the press since 1627, with a special responsibility for licensing news publications. He was also Charles I's primary contact with the Stationers' Company of London.[34] In addition to this official relationship with the Company and his family relationship with one of its members, Weckherlin himself had a personal business relationship with the Company. In 1631, for example, it voted to buy Weckherlin a piece of plate "Ouer & aboue the money agreed vpon for his extraordinary paines" (*Recs. Ct. Stat. Co.*, 228). The same year he obtained a royal patent for the printing of certain best-selling schoolbooks.[35] These relationships afforded Weckherlin a high level of influence with the administrators of the Company which he had exercised to the benefit of his Raworth in-laws in a number of instances over the years (*Recs. Ct. Stat. Co.*, 264).

Weckherlin, a native of Stuttgart, was also a member of the substantial émigré community around the royal court and intellectual circles in London. He was a well-known poet, writing primarily in German vernacular, but also authoring Italian sonnets. Among his friends were the medical doctors and royal physicians Theodore Mayerne and Matthew Lister, as well as diplomats and literary figures like Theodore Haak and Joachim Hübner. This circle intersected with that around the "visionary" Samuel Hartlib, who was involved in the pan-European Protestant movement. Weckherlin was part of this movement, as was their mutual friend, the English diplomat William Trumbull, whose son married Weckherlin's daughter. Hartlib and his circle were also, like Weckherlin, involved in Europe-wide news-gathering networks.[36]

Weckherlin successfully made the transition from crown bureaucrat to Parliament bureaucrat. In 1644 he was appointed secretary for foreign affairs to the Committee for Both Kingdoms. There he continued to execute many of the same duties he had performed for Charles I's administration. Weckherlin's authority to license for the press was never officially cancelled, although he last appears in the Stationers' Register as licenser in July 1641. As noted above, a number of the ecclesiastical licensers saw no reason why their authority to license should be invalid after 1641, and some of them made their own transitions to serve as parliamentary licensers under the 1643 *Order . . . Regulating Printing*.[37] Although Weckherlin was apparently not licensing for Parliament, his successor as secretary for foreign tongues in 1649, while directed by a new act regulating printing as well as a new form of government, was assumed to have Weckherlin's prior authority to license material for printing, especially newsbooks, and to be the state's liaison with the book trade. It was John Milton who succeeded Weckherlin as secretary for foreign tongues.[38]

Some years ago Leo Miller argued briefly that Milton had no personal acquaintance with Weckherlin, and while no correspondence between the two survives and there is no mention of Weckherlin in Milton's writings, when their social, intellectual, and book trade networks are analyzed, it is hard to imagine they had not met before 1649.[39] As the government licenser for the press, Weckherlin was a well-known figure, especially to authors and members of the book trade. Both Weckherlin and Milton were engaged in the unusual enterprise of writing Italian sonnets, and would certainly have been interested in each other's work. This likelihood is increased by the number of mutual acquaintances and social circles which they shared. Weckherlin's in-law Trumbull, for example, was an accomplished lutenist. He composed music and through that activity as well as his position as a clerk of the Privy Council would have known the royal household musician Henry Lawes, with whom both John Milton father and son collaborated.[40] Haak and Hartlib were friends and correspondents of Milton, and Lister rented for eleven years from the Milton family a property in Covent Garden which he purchased from them in 1638. Haak, who later translated Milton's *Paradise Lost* into German, acted as Weckherlin's agent with the Elsevier publishing house in Amsterdam.[41]

Hartlib especially was immersed in Milton's written works. He sent *Areopagitica* to German correspondents; encouraged Milton to write *Of Education*; and was party to the print feud between Milton and Adriaan Vlacq in later years. As Timothy Raylor has recently shown, Milton's association with Hartlib goes back further than previously known and extends to activities also previously unknown (Raylor 19–30). Hartlib and Weckherlin testified as witnesses for the prosecution in Archbishop Laud's 1644 trial, where much of the testimony centered on Laud's supervision of prepublication ecclesiastical licensing in the 1630s. This was a very high-profile trial, attracting the attention of many engaged in book production, and the issues addressed would certainly have been much on Milton's mind at the time since he was in the midst of the *Doctrine and Discipline* scandal. He was also possibly already contemplating *Areopagitica* (Forster, "Weckherlin in England," 114; *CPW* 2:87).

Weckherlin wrote verses to Hartlib, Haak, and his and Hartlib's associate in the international Protestant movement, John Dury. Dury was a royal and parliamentarian bureaucrat, who did some translations with Milton, and was the keeper of the royal library to which Milton donated some of his pamphlets. He was married to the sister of Edward King, Milton's *Lycidas*.[42] It is clear from papers of The States diplomat Hermann Mylius that he, Hartlib, Weckherlin, and other mutual friends sustained relationships over many years (Miller, *Oldenburg*, 12). In later correspondence with Mylius, Weckherlin wrote very complimentarily about Milton and his abilities. Weckherlin knew of Milton's talents in multiple languages, and the notice of Italian in particular, as Leo Miller has pointed out, indicates Weckherlin knew material in the 1645 *Poems* whether before or after it was printed (Miller, "Milton and Weckherlin," 1).

Weckherlin and Milton had a number of mutual friends and contacts in political circles. One example is mutual relationships with Sir Henry Vane the younger. Vane, Jr., conveyed the offer of employment with the Council of State to Milton in 1649 and Milton translated Latin treatises into English for Vane. In 1652 Milton wrote a sonnet to him (Campbell, *Chronology*, 59). Weckherlin had worked with Vane when he was treasurer of the navy under Charles I, and with Vane's father who had been Charles I's treasurer of the royal household and, briefly, a secretary of state by whom Weckherlin was directly employed in the early 1640s, and who had also chosen to follow Parliament. Both Vane Sr. and Jr. were members of the Committee for Both Kingdoms which Weckherlin served as secretary in the mid-1640s. The elder Vane would seem likely to have facilitated Weckherlin's transition from crown service to parliamentary service (*NDNB*, "Weckherlin").

Beyond this network of mutual associations and interests, Milton and Weckherlin may have worked together in Parliament's service prior to 1649. In July 1645 was published *The King's Cabinet Opened*, an edition of letters captured in the king's baggage after his defeat at the Battle of Naseby. It was entered into the Stationers' Register 9 July 1645 under license from Henry Parker and Thomas May, "Secretaries," and published by George Thomason's sometime partner, Robert Bostock (*Stat. Reg. 1640–1708*, vol. 1). Both Parker and May are believed to have edited the letters, as is John Milton since the form and focus of *The King's Cabinet Opened* strongly mirrors work that Milton later produced for the Commonwealth government. However, a number of deciphered letters from the king's correspondence, as well as the cipher keys used to decode them have turned up in Weckherlin's archive, part of the Trumbull Papers now in the British Library. Moreover, Weckherlin wrote to his fatally ill wife on 24 June 1645 that a "New Committee" had been set up to deal with the captured correspondence and in the previous two days, he had been called in five or six times to assist them with the work (*Trumbull Papers* 97–99). It may have been to this collaboration that Weckherlin referred when he wrote to Mylius in 1651 that Milton "'has already often edited state papers'" (Miller, *Oldenburg*, 54).

It is reasonable to believe that when Milton was chosen by the Council of State to be Secretary for Foreign Tongues and licenser for the press, Weckherlin, who had had twenty years of experience in the Secretariat of Charles I's government, and who had worked for Parliament since the early 1640s, would have been called on to train the new appointee. It was Weckherlin who had originally developed the role of the crown's licenser for the press and whose relatives printed for Milton; and it was he who was asked to turn over his papers to Milton to ensure familiarity with precedent and continuity in that office. Furthermore, it was Weckherlin who was called back to assist in the office when Milton's sight failed him in 1652 (Campbell, *Chronology*, 105; *Life*

Record 2:233, 295). All of this said, it is also the case that a letter written by Milton to the president of the Council of State at the death of Georg Weckherlin in 1653 shows Milton had chafed at having Weckherlin in the office with him.[43] It would of course be difficult to be the younger, less experienced incumbent in the same office with the older, long-serving predecessor. Beyond this, there was likely a divergence in many opinions between the lifelong bureaucrat who was an author on the side, and the literary figure who came to government service later in life. Such divergence becomes most obvious and most instructive in an examination of the views Weckherlin and Milton held about prepublication licensing and how they practiced it.

There is no statement from Weckherlin expressing his philosophy of licensing. In more than fifteen years of licensing, Weckherlin never mentioned it in his diary as he did his other bureaucratic duties.[44] His instructions from the secretary of state and his actions as licenser are the best illustrations of his views available. In February 1627, after several regulatory experiments, Weckherlin had been given authority to license printed news publications. He was ideally qualified to do this as a talented linguist, a newsletter writer, and a highly placed bureaucrat in the Caroline secretariat. Almost exactly two years later, Weckherlin's licensing authority was expanded to include "any matters of newes, relations, histories, or other things, in prose or in verse, that have reference to matters and affairs of State." Written works in these categories were to be submitted to his "view, approbation, and license," and he was to "acquaint [the senior secretary of state] of such things as he shall find cause." In January 1632, these regulations were reinforced by the king in a letter of reprimand to the Stationers' Company, upbraiding them for their "connivance" in illegal, unlicensed printing.[45] These sets of instructions, in their lack of specificity, suggest that Weckherlin, like the East German censors encountered by Robert Darnton late in the twentieth century, was expected to know at any given time what issues and topics would be most distasteful to Charles I's government, and what works written about them could and could not be printed at that given moment. Material that was perceived as dangerous and unacceptable at one juncture might well be viewed as harmless and allowable at another. It might also be altered by a licenser in the "more acceptable" direction to make it printable.[46] Milton expressed a sense of this in *Areopagitica*: "There is no book that is acceptable unlesse at certain seasons" (*CPW* 2:53, 534, 569).

Some judgments may be made about Weckherlin's licensing on the basis of entries in the Stationers' Register. When the Caroline government was under particular political stress, as in 1627 when the duke of Buckingham was making his ill-fated and unpopular expedition to the Ile de Rhé, Weckherlin paid close attention to the corantos and licensed them individually for publication. When current events and printed news shared lower levels of political resonance, Weckherlin paid less attention to the news publications, and licensed them only occasionally and en bloc. Beyond this evidence, there is one known item that Weckherlin refused a license to print: a manuscript of what seems to have been *Patriarcha* by Sir Robert Filmer. When the manuscript was presented to Weckherlin, on the basis of its content he brought it to the attention of the secretary of state, and ultimately King Charles I. Clearly, the licenser understood it to touch matters of state. Charles I personally annotated Weckherlin's memo on the manuscript with a curt "Non licet," which instruction Weckherlin followed (*Trumbull Papers* 97, 121–22). *Patriarcha* was refused a license and remained unprinted until the time of the Exclusion Crisis late in the seventeenth century.

There is also evidence of one item which Weckherlin did license for printing that subsequently caused some controversy. In 1637 the duke of Lorraine complained to Charles I that Weckherlin had allowed the print publication of an English-language account of the arrest and prosecution of the duke by the Parlement of Paris. Early in 1638, Secretary of State Sir John Coke, Weckherlin's direct supervisor, sent a letter of apology and reassurance to Lorraine, stating that this publication was undertaken without King Charles's knowledge, "no, nor with the knowledge of the State here, or any of his Majesty's Council." The printers were imprisoned and Coke asserted no books would be published hereafter without due examination. That Charles I and the Privy Council were unaware of the publication was a disingenuous defense since they were aware of very little that happened in the ordinary course of licensing. The letter of apology was signed by Coke, but written in the hand of Weckherlin, and in fact questioned the validity of Lorraine's complaint and the integrity of the person who had made it. The publication had occurred three or four years earlier, and "now on the sudden, when it was no more spoken of, presses it very much, by whose instigation I know not. . . . Weckherlin did herein mistake himself out of no ill affection, but by a little in these novelties complying with the time." The printer was arrested and the letter assured that in future all books would be examined before print publication was allowed.[47]

Weckherlin as the government licenser for the press worked for the most part within his brief. If his personal opinions differed from those of his superiors, as his diary and his defection to Parliament show they sometimes did, still he appears to have set his personal political opinions aside in fulfilling the duties of his post and to have enjoyed the full confidence and support of his superiors in that position. Weckherlin issued prepublication licenses to print on the basis of crown policy, and not his personal feelings or interpretations.

There are equally few sources of information about how Milton interpreted and exercised prepublication licensing. Among the evidence are the examples of his personal experiences with licensers as an author, discussed above, and the historical and contemporary descriptions of licensing systems and licensers in *Areopagitica*. Milton traced licensing back to ancient Greece and further to divine injunctions on what was permissible and what was forbidden, and then back up through the Caroline licensing regime and events in the summer of 1642 (*CPW* 2:493–505). He used this historical account to outline all the problems inherent in the very concept of licensing for the press and then went on to catalog the problems with the particular system and licensers then in place. Milton held the ecclesiastical licensers with "that jealous hautinesse of Prelates" in contempt, and believed their inadequacy made them of no consequence, especially compared to a thoughtful, learned, truthful author such as himself (*CPW* 2:489). "I know nothing of the licenser, but that I have his own hand here for his arrogance; who shall warrant me his judgement?" (*CPW* 2:533–34).

There is also evidence of Milton's licensing from the Stationers' Register and the State Papers Domestic. While there is some disagreement among scholars about Milton's role in the newsbook *Mercurius Politicus*, the entries in the Stationers' Register leave no doubt that Milton was licensing it for printing. He sometimes licensed it weekly, and sometimes only occasionally and en bloc as Weckherlin had done with the corantos of the 1620s. In addition, Milton licensed a French-language account of Charles I's trial in December 1649. He was possibly also the licenser behind entries in the register reading "by permission of authority," or "by the apoyntment [*sic*] of the Councell of State," or "by order of the Councell of State." If the Council of State wanted something printed, it was Milton they sent to make the arrangements and oversee the process. In 1651, in a role Weckherlin had also performed, Milton was mediating a complaint about the printing of pirated copies. He apparently also exercised this role in other instances like Weckherlin had done as illustrated by the examples of Milton's interventions on behalf of various Stationers in his network of personal associations presented above (Campbell, *Chronology*, 103–4, 115, 188; *Life Record* 2:276, 286).

But in contrast to the Weckherlin evidence, there is a personal statement from Milton on how he interpreted the duty of licensing when it became his in 1649. Sometime between May and October 1650, Milton discussed the latest regulations governing printing with Samuel Hartlib. Milton's interpretation was that since no licensers were named in the most recent act regulating printing, " 'everybody may enter his book without license. Provided the printer's or author's name be entered, that they may be forthcoming if required.' "[48] So, in Milton's view basic registration with the Stationers' Company for purposes of protecting copyrights should be followed (*CPW* 2:491, 569). This precluded any necessity for authors' manuscripts to be vetted for content by an official of the state or the church prior to printing. If there was a problem with any print publication, it could be called in and the producers dealt with ex post facto. This was the same interpretation he had given in *Areopagitica* of parliamentary proposals to regulate printing in 1642. It was also true to his concerns that readers—not "the presumptuous rashnesse of a perfunctory licencer"—should determine what was read, and whether or not it was dangerous (*CPW* 2:534). Milton's was a radical interpretation of the law and a radical involvement of personal opinions in state policy, as well as a radical extension of personal authority that a professional bureaucrat like Georg Weckherlin could never have made.

Nothing is known of material that Milton refused to license for the press. But something is known of at least one case of material Milton licensed to be printed, or at least did not prevent from being printed, that elicited parliamentary disapproval. On 27 January 1652, Parliament ordered the seizure and public burning of an English edition of the so-called Racovian Catechism, an antitrinitarian, Socinian work.[49] It was printed by William Dugard, a troublesome but official state printer with whom Milton worked closely and who had printed Milton's *First Defense* in 1651. Dugard revealed Milton's involvement to Parliament, leading to the secretary's own interrogation sometime between 10 February and 2 April 1652 on the subject. Milton defended to the committee his decision to allow it, or at least not stop it, and cited the principles he had laid out in *Areopagitica* in defense of his actions. As in his earlier confrontations with Parliament over unlicensed printing, there is no evidence Milton was punished in this instance. However, by January 1653, John Thurloe, also a secretary to the Council of State, was licensing *Mercurius Politicus*. Milton continued to perform his other duties as before, even though blind and often unable to attend the Council in person, and despite the rumor Mylius had heard in London in 1651 that Milton's duties were being given over to others. Milton's ceasing to license *Mercurius Politicus* does seem to be connected to his degenerating eyesight and inability to do all the reading required in his job.[50] Whether Thurloe replaced Milton because the Council was displeased with Milton, or because he was unable to read for himself any longer, or because Thurloe was expanding his own influence, remains unclear (Cf. Dobranski, "Licensing Milton's Heresy," 141–43).

Milton's views on licensing appear consistent, if personal and radical. But if his basic operating principle was that everything should be printed and the press should be free, why did he license *Mercurius Politicus*? One answer is that this was likely a pro forma action, necessary for the Stationers' Company to allow the printing process to begin, rather than any approval or prohibition of content.[51] Milton believed in registration for the protection of copyrights (*CPW* 2:491, 569). Milton viewed his role as licenser—the only acceptable role of a licenser—as facilitating print publication rather than prohibiting it. His attitude was laissez faire. Allow everything to clear the press and the market of readers will decide for themselves what is worthy to be read (*CPW* 2:530, 569). Milton was unable to keep his personal beliefs and opinions out of what should have been a purely bureaucratic process. When this inability conflicted seriously with government policy, either the Council decided it could no longer employ Milton as licenser or Milton decided he could no longer operate within the context of government service as his beliefs about reading and licensing required him to act.

* * *

John Milton's connections to the book trade were quite ordinary for the time. Milton as a publishing author was not an isolated ideologue nor a reactionary radical; he was, in fact, a somewhat conventional participant in 1640s English print production. He was only one among the large numbers of authors who published in print anonymously, unlicensed, and unregistered. He was simply one of hundreds of authors who sought out marginal printing operations of questionable integrity to print his works expeditiously in standard formats with humble appearances. Like other authors, he exploited his personal, business, family, and intellectual contacts to achieve print publication of his writings. He would engage royalist or radical, respectable or disreputable, male or female, rich or poor Stationers in his need to provide reading material for mid–seventeenth century readers.

Milton was an extraordinary prepublication licenser as comparison with Weckherlin shows. With all they had in common, it should come as no surprise that Weckherlin and Milton as licensers actually performed for the most part in similar ways. But there was one very crucial difference in their performances. When Weckherlin encountered a manuscript with a clear political message such as *Patriarcha*, he recognized it as something he could not, or should not, deal with under the authority delegated to him as licenser. When Milton encountered a similar situation with the religiously controversial Racovian Catechism, he acted in the completely opposite manner. He relied only on his own authority and his own interpretation of licensing to allow the publication to go forward. When Milton was taken to task by Parliament, he did not acquiesce to their authority nor would he admit any wrongdoing. Milton instead continued to defend his position with indignation based on his personal beliefs: "that which purifies us is triall, and triall is by what is contrary" (*CPW* 2:515).

This is where Milton was a radical: in the ideas about reading and licensing which he had developed through his own experience, practiced in his own print publication, articulated in *Areopagitica*, and disseminated in his service as government licenser for the press. He had developed his ideas about reading from a lifetime of reading and study. His ideas about licensing came from recent life experience as well as from acquaintance with the history of its practice—that "all Presses might be open . . . was the peoples [*sic*] birthright and priviledge" (*CPW* 2:541). Milton was not the radical proponent of a free press who recanted on his position later in life; his beliefs about reading simply transcended both politics and authorship. Milton is better understood not as the enemy of licensing, but rather as the proponent of the freedom to read, the advocate of the reader with a book "to know, to utter, and to argue freely according to conscience"; "A fool will be a fool with the best book, yea or without book" (*CPW* 2:521). What Milton believed should be utterly unregulated was not necessarily the printing industry as such, but the relationship between the reader and reading material. This was especially relevant in times of turmoil like the 1640s and 1650s in England when "the people . . . should be disputing, reasoning, reading, inventing, discoursing . . . [about] things not before discoursed or written of" (*CPW* 2:557).

Notes

This essay grew out of a 1997 NEH Summer Institute at the Folger Shakespeare Library in Washington, D.C. I would like to thank the director, Steven N. Zwicker, and all the participants, as well as Frederic Baron, Philip Hamburger, Kathleen Lynch, Steve Mentz, and two anonymous readers for the University of Pennsylvania Press for their comments on earlier drafts. All dates are given old style, with the assumption that the new year began 1 January rather than 25 March.

1. For example, Sharon Achinstein writes "The English Revolution was a revolution in reading" in *Milton and the Revolutionary Reader* (Princeton, N.J.: Princeton University Press, 1994), 3. See also Derek Hirst, "'The Politics of Literature in the English Republic," *The Seventeenth Century* 6 (1991): 133–55; Steven N. Zwicker, *Lines of Authority: Politics and English Literary Culture, 1649–1689* (Ithaca, N.Y.: Cornell University Press, 1993); Michael Mendle, *Henry Parker and the English Civil War: The Political Thought of the Public's "Privado"* (Cambridge: Cambridge University Press, 1995); Nigel Smith, *Literature and Revolution in England, 1640–1660* (New Haven: Yale University Press, 1997); and David Norbrook, *Writing the English Republic: Poetry, Rhetoric and Politics, 1627–1660* (Cambridge: Cambridge University Press, 1999). Kevin Sharpe's *Reading Revolutions: The Politics of Reading in Early Modern England* (New Haven: Yale University Press, 2000) appeared after this essay was completed.

2. Ann Baynes Coiro, "Milton and Class Identity: The Publication of *Areopagitica* and the 1645 *Poems*," *Journal of Medieval and Renaissance Studies* 22 (1992): 269; Achinstein, 3–14.

3. Frederick S. Siebert, *Freedom of the Press in England, 1476–1776* (Urbana: University of Illinois Press, 1952; rpt. 1962); Philip Hamburger, "The Development of the Law of Seditious Libel and the Control of the Press," *Stanford Law Review* 37 (1985): 661–765. I am grateful to Philip for a copy of this essay and much discussion of this topic.

4. *Areopagitica, Complete Prose Works of John Milton*, vol. 2 (1643–1648), ed. Ernest Sirluck (New Haven: Yale University Press, 1959), 501–2, 529. Hereafter cited as *CPW*.

5. *An Order of the Lords and Commons Assembled in Parliament. For the Regulating of Printing . . . 14 June. 1643* [hereafter *Order . . . Regulating Printing*] (London, Printed for I. Wright in the Old-bailey, Iune 16.1643). Wing E1711.

6. William Riley Parker, *Milton: A Biography*, 2 vols. (Oxford: Clarendon Press, 1968), 1:268.

7. *Second Defense, The Student's Milton*, ed. Frank Allen Patterson, rev. ed. (New York: Appleton-Century-Crofts, 1957), 1147.

8. Michael Mendle, "De Facto Freedom, De Facto Authority: Press and Parliament, 1640–1643," *Historical Journal* 30 (1995): 307–32.

9. Stephen B. Dobranski, "Licensing Milton's Heresy," *Milton and Heresy*, ed. Dobranski and John P. Rumrich (Cambridge: Cambridge University Press, 1998), 139–58. This essay became known to me only when I was revising my own, and Dobranski's recent monograph, *Milton, Authorship, and the Book Trade* (Cambridge: Cambridge University Press, 1999), became available to me after this essay was completed and is not considered here.

10. *CPW* 2:480; Parker, *Milton*, 1:273; Charles S. Osgood, "*Areopagitica*—1644," *Proceedings of the American Philosophical Society* 89 (1945): 495, 497. Cf. David Norbook, "*Areopagitica*, Censorship, and the Early Modern Public Sphere," *The Administration of Aesthetics: Censorship, Political Criticism, and the Public Sphere*, ed. Richard Burt (Minneapolis: University of Minnesota Press, 1994), 30 n. 39.

11. Graham Pollard and Albert Ehrman, *The Distribution of Books by Catalogue from the Invention of Printing to A.D. 1800* (Cambridge: Cambridge University Press, 1965), 148–49; Paul J. Voss, "Books for Sale: Advertising and Patronage in Late Elizabethan England," *Sixteenth Century Journal* 29 (1998): 733–56; David Davies and Paul Dowling, "'Shrewd books with dangerous Frontispieces': *Areopagitica*'s Motto," *Milton Quarterly* 20 (1986): 33; John K. Hale, "*Areopagitica*'s Euripidean Motto," *Milton Quarterly* 25 (1991): 25–27; John Milton, *Areopagitica; A Speech of Mr. John Milton for the Liberty of Vlincenc'd Printing, To the Parlament of England* (London, 1644). See Fig. 1. Observations on physical properties of the book here are based on the Folger Shakespeare Library copy, Wing M2092, and the copy in the Thomason Tracts, E.18(9). Cf. Norbrook, "Early Modern Public Sphere," 17–18.

12. *Second Defense*, 1140–41, 1144; Barbara K. Lewalski, "How Radical Was the Young Milton?" *Milton and Heresy*, 59–60. Cf. David Lindenbaum, "Milton's Contract," *The Construction of Authorship: Textual Appropriation in Law and Literature*, ed. Martha Woodmansee and Peter Jaszi (Durham, N.C.: Duke University Press, 1994), 175–91.

13. Bachelor's note that he had refused *Doctrine and Discipline* a license was published in John Goodwin's *Twelve Considerable Cautions*, 17 February 1646, as cited in Gordon Campbell, *A Milton Chronology* (New York: St. Martin's Press, 1997), 87. See also *A Transcript of the Registers of the Worshipful Company of Stationers from 1640–1708* [hereafter *Stat. Reg. 1640–1708*], 3 vols. (London: Privately printed, vol. 1: 1640–1655); *DNB*, s.v. Overton, Richard; *The Life Records of John Milton*, ed. J. Milton French, 5 vols. (New Brunswick, N.J.: Rutgers University Press, 1948–53), 2:54, 146; Parker, *Milton*, 262–68, 290. Cf. William R. Parker, "Milton, Rothwell, and Simmons," *The Library*, 4th ser., 18 (1937): 96, on Milton's intent for *Doctrine and Discipline*.

14. Thomas Corns, "Milton's Antiprelatical Tracts and the Marginality of Doctrine," *Milton and Heresy*, 39–40.

15. Campbell, *Chronology*, 81–82; *CPW*, 2:142–43; Parker, *Milton*, 1:263–65; *Life*

Records, 2:106; *DNB*, s.v. Overton, Richard; [18 September 1644], draft ordinance against printing seditious and libelous books and pamphlets, House of Lords Record Office, Main Papers, unfoliated; Herbert Palmer, *The Glasse or God's Providence Towards his Faithfull Ones . . .* (London, Printed by G. M. for Thomas Underhill at the Bible in Woodstreet, 1644), 55–57.

16. *CPW* 2:493–505; Campbell, *Chronology*, 87; Parker, *Milton*, 1:244–45, 259. Cf. Parker, "Milton, Rothwell, and Simmons," *The Library*, 4th ser., 18 (1937): 96, on licensing of *Doctrine and Discipline* and *CPW*, 2:138–39, on its reception.

17. *Journals of the House of Commons* (Printed by order of the House of Commons), 3:201, 606; *CPW* 2:143–45; Campbell, *Chronology*, 82–83; *Life Records*, 2:116, 122; Parker, *Milton*, 1:281–82.

18. Mendle, "De Facto Freedom," 320–21; Sheila Lambert, "The Beginning of Printing for the House of Commons, 1640–42," *The Library*, 6th ser., 3 (1981): 47. Lambert's assertions about the overarching importance of the Stationers' Company's commercial motivations must be treated with caution.

19. *CPW*, 2:162, 569; *20. Junii, 1643. A Particular of the Names of the* LICENSERS, *who are appointed by the House of Commons for Printing; According to an Order of the Lords and Commons, Dated the 14. of June, 1643* (London, Printed by John Field for Edward Husbands, 1643); W. W. Greg, *Licensers for the Press, & c to 1640* (Oxford: Oxford Bibliographical Society), 1962, s.v. individual names; Mendle, "De Facto Freedom," 330–31. William Riley Parker's example of numbers of entries in the Stationers' Register is graphic: 1641–240 items entered, 1642—76, 1 January–16 June 1643—17, 16 June–31 December 1643–350 items entered of which approximately one-half were newsbooks. Parker, "Milton, Rothwell and Simmons," 95.

20. Phoebe Sheavyn, "Writers and the Publishing Trade, Circa 1600," *The Library*, 2nd ser., 7 (1906): 337, 339, 350.

21. E.g., Richard Mountagu to John Cosin, 21 January 1625, 7 February [1625], 21 February 1625, *The Correspondence of John Cosin, D. D. Lord Bishop of Durham . . .*, 2 vols. Surtees Society, vol. 52, 1868, 1: 51, 53, 57–58; 19 March 1628, list of printers in London; 1 May 1629, 5 September 1629, John Davies to Owen Wynn, *Calendar of the Wynn of Gwydir Papers in the National Library of Wales* (Aberystwyth: National Library of Wales, 1926), 509–10, 509 n.

22. *Life Records*, 1:37; Campbell, *Chronology*, 45; Ernest Brennecke, Jr., *John Milton the Elder and His Music* (New York: Columbia University Press, 1938), 46, 49, 57, 59, 63–66, 82, 90–91, 117; Gordon Campbell, "Shakespeare and the Youth of Milton," *Milton Quarterly* (1999): 95–105; Parker, *Milton*, 1:10–11, 15–17.

23. *A maske presented at Ludlow Castle, 1634* (London, for Humphrey Robinson, 1637). STC 17937; Parker, *Milton*, 1:80.

24. *Second Defense*, 1145; Brennecke, 122, 127, and passim; Campbell, *Chronology*, 44; Rose Clavering and John T. Shawcross, "Anne Milton and the Milton Residences," *Journal of English and Germanic Philology* 59 (1960): 680; Parker, "Milton, Rothwell and Simmons," 90–91. Milton also would have heard the admonition to read from the rector of All Hallows, Bread Street, Richard Stock. Parker, *Milton*, 1:9, 14.

25. *Milton's Familiar Letters*, trans. John Hall (Philadelphia: E. Littel, 1892), 12–13, 23.

26. Sheavyn, 359, 364; Plomer, *Dictionary*, s.v. Simmons; *Stat. Reg. 1640–1708*, vol. 1; *Life Records*, 2:9; Mendle, "De Facto Freedom," 326–27; Campbell, *Chronology*, 89–90; Raylor, "New Light on Milton and Hartlib," *Milton Quarterly* 27 (1993): 21, 33;

Cyprian Bladgen, "The Stationers' Company in the Civil War Period," *The Library*, 5th ser., 13 (1958): 8–11.

27. Richard M. Johnson, "The Politics of Publication: Misrepresentation in Milton's 1645 *Poems*," *Criticism* 36 (1994): 58 (I am grateful to Steve Zwicker for this reference); *Catalogue of the Pamphlets, Books, Newspapers, and Manuscripts Relating to the Civil War, The commonwealth, and Restoration, collected by George Thomason, 1640–1661* (London: British Library, 1908), 1: introduction; Lois Spencer, "The Professional and Literary Connexions of George Thomason," *The Library*, 5th ser., 13 (1958): 105–6, 108–10, 111; Lois Spencer, "The Politics of George Thomason," *The Library*, 5th ser., 14 (1959): 12–13, 14, 18–19, 22–23, 24; *Dictionary of Literary Biography* (Sumter, S.C.: Bruccoli, Clark, Layman, 1998), vol. 213, s.v. Thomason.

28. *A Transcript of The Registers of the Company of Stationers of London: 1554–1640 A.D.*, ed. Edward Arber (London: Privately printed, 1876), 4:248; John Curtis Reed, "Humphrey Moseley, publisher," *Proceedings and Papers of the Oxford Bibliographical Society* 2 (1927–30): 62, 128; John T. Shawcross, "A Note on Milton's Hobson Poems," *Review of English Studies*, n.s., 18 (1967): 433–37; Shawcross, *Milton: A Bibliography for the Years 1624–1700* (Binghampton: Medieval and Renaissance Texts and Studies, 1984), entries 2–26. See also Coiro, 279, on Moseley's clientele as decidedly not royalist.

29. Reed, 62, 61, 141; Shawcross, *Bibliography*, entry 41; Johnson, 59; A. S. P. Woodhouse, "Notes on Milton's Early Development," *University of Toronto Quarterly* 13 (1943): 66–101. The Cambridge connection would go some way toward explaining why Moseley had Marshall portray Milton in the frontispiece portrait as a younger man in academic robes. See also Moseley's comments on the frontispiece to Cartwright's 1651 poems cited by Johnson, 68 n. 28.

30. Bradford F. Swan, *Gregory Dexter of London and New England 1610–1700* (Rochester: Printing House of L. Hart, 1949), 9–24, 30–46; Parker, "Milton, Rothwell, and Simmons," 92–94; H. R. Plomer, "The Eliot's Court Printing House, 1584–1674," *The Library*, 4th ser., 2 (1921–22): 179–81.

31. [July 1637], Sir John Lambe's notes on printers, P[ublic] R[ecord] O[ffice], S[state] P[apers] D[omestic] 16/364/11; [?1637], "The 20 Printers," SP16/376/16; Peter W. M. Blayney, *The Texts of King Lear and their Origins: Volume I. Nicholas Okes and the First Quarto* (Cambridge: Cambridge University Press, 1982), 64–65; William R. Parker, "Contributions Toward a Milton Bibliography," *The Library*, 4th ser., 16 (1936): 426–27, 431–32. The key factor here is when Mathewes was forced out as a master printer, lost his shop, and his materials and place were obtained by John Raworth in 1637.

32. Reed, 62; Spencer, "Professional and Literary," 107; *Stat. Reg. 1640–1708*, 1: passim; Johnson, 70 n. 53; Johan Gerritsen, "The Printing of the Beaumont and Fletcher Folio of 1647," *The Library*, 5th ser., 3 (1949): 234; Standish Henning, "The Printers and the Beaumont and Fletcher Folio of 1647, Sections 4 and 8D-F," *Studies in Bibliography* 22 (1969): 166; R. C. Bald, *Bibliographical Studies in the Beaumont and Fletcher Folio of 1647* (Oxford: Oxford Bibliographical Society, 1938), 1–49. Cf. Johnson, 70 n. 53.

33. Swan, 10–12, 18–19; *Stat[ioners'] Co[mpany] Appr[entices] 1641–1700*, ed. D. F. McKenzie (Oxford: Oxford Bibliographical Society, 1974), 996; Campbell, *Chronology*, 102; David Masson, *The Life of John Milton . . .* , 7 vols. (rpt. New York: P. Smith, 1946), 4:120, 146–47.

34. 17 April 1628, Robert Raworth from Westminster to Francis Raworth at

Dover, BL, Downshire Manuscripts, Trumbull Papers, Misc. Corr., vol. 18, unf.;
Leonard Forster, "G. R. Weckherlin in England," *German Life and Letters* 3 (1938–39):
107–8; S. A. Baron, "Georg Rudolph Weckherlin, 1584–1653," *New Dictionary of National Biography*, gen. ed. Colin Mathew (Oxford: Oxford University Press, forthcoming) [hereafter *NDNB*]. I consulted Weckherlin's diary when the Trumbull Papers were on deposit at the Berkshire Record Office, prior to their acquisition by the British Library.

35. *Recs. Ct. Stat. Co.*, 228; 20 February 1631, Weckherlin's petition to the King, *C[alendar of] S[tate] P[apers] D[omestic]* 1629–31, 514; 28 March 1631, grant to Weckherlin to print Latin school books, *CSPD* 1629–31, 557.

36. Forster, 114; Baron, "Weckherlin"; Raylor, 21. The father of Milton's closest friend, Charles Diodati, was also a physician attached to the royal household. Parker, *Milton*, 1:15, 2:715.

37. Forster, 112; *20, Junii, 1643. A Particular of the Names of the* LICENSERS, *Who are appointed by the House of Commons for Printing* . . . (London, Printed by John Field for Edward Husbands, 1643). Michael Mendle was the first to notice this, but there was more than one old licenser reappointed under the *Order*. Mendle, "De Facto Freedom," 330–31.

38. Forster, 114; Masson, 4:116–18. It should be noted that Milton did not decide to serve in the position of licenser. He accepted the position of secretary for foreign tongues to the Council of State. The position of licenser was appended to that position and not a separate office. Cf. Dobranski, "Licensing Milton's Heresy," 141.

39. Leo Miller, "Milton and Weckherlin," *Milton Quarterly* 16 (1982): 1–3.

40. *Life Records*, 1:272, 2:81; Brennecke, 144; Leonard Forster, "The Weckherlin Papers," *British Library Journal* 19 (1993): 133, 136–37; Sabrina A. Baron, "William Trumbull," *The House of Commons 1604–1629*, ed. J. P. Ferris and A. P. Thrush (London: Secker and Warburg, forthcoming); Sonia Anderson, "The Elder William Trumbull: A Biographical Sketch," *British Library Journal* 19 (1993): 125–27, 129. Trumbull was also something of a bibliophile and was well known among the Stationers. At his death, there was a library of forty volumes in his London lodging alone.

41. Brennecke, 114; Clavering and Shawcross, 685, 688; *The Trumbull Papers* (London: Sotheby's, 1989), 111; Barbara K. Lewalski, "Milton and the Hartlib Circle: Educational Projects and Epic *Paidea*," *Literary Milton: Text, Pretext, Context*, ed. Diane Trevino Benet and Michael Lieb (Pittsburgh, Pa.: Duquesne University Press, 1994), 202–20. Lewalski asserts that Haak and Dury were far closer to Milton than Hartlib, and while Milton had lots of acquaintances in the circle, he was not part of the circle.

42. Leo Miller, *John Milton and the Oldenburg Safeguard* (New York: Loewenthal Press, 1984), 2, 27; Campbell, *Chronology*, 80, 84, 118; *Life Records*, 3:103, 143; Lewalski, "Milton and the Hartlib Circle," 203. Weckherlin had known Dury from the mid-1630s at least. 10 April 1634, John Dury to Sir Thomas Roe, *CSPD* 1633–4, 547; *Life Records*, 1:90, 3:227; *Trumbull Papers*, 111, 112.

43. 21 February 1652/3, Milton to Lord President Bradshaw, *CSPD* 1652–53, 176–77.

44. British Library, Downshire Manuscripts, Trumbull Papers, Misc. Corr. 61.

45. *Trumbull Papers*, 125. The editor has read the dates wrong for these instructions, seemingly oblivious of the new year beginning on 25 March, old style. It seems that "Advisoes" has also been incorrectly transcribed. February 1628/9, [Dorchester] to

the Company of Stationers, draft, BL, Downshire Manuscripts, Trumbull Papers, Misc. Corr. 18, unf.; January 1631/2, Charles I to the Company of Stationers, draft, Trumbull Papers, Misc. Corr. 19, unf.

46. Robert Darnton, *Berlin Journal, 1989–1990* (New York: W. W. Norton, 1991), 199 and passim (I am grateful to Michael Mendle for this reference and this point); Anthony Milton, "Licensing, Censorship, and Religious Orthodoxy in Early Stuart England," *Historical Journal* 41 (1998): 628–30. Anthony Milton, however, considers only ecclesiastical licensers.

47. [?1637], petition of Anthony Fortescue, agent of the duke of Lorraine, to the king, *CSPD* 1637–38, 117; 1 February 1637/8, Coke to [?Sir William Boswell], ibid, 223–24.

48. Hartlib's *Ephemerides*, Sheffield Library, Hartlib Papers, Hartlib 28/1/61b cited in Campbell, *Chronology*, 107–8; *CPW* 2:569.

49. A Latin edition of this printed in London was dedicated to James I. STC 20083.45. The only English edition shown by Wing, R121, was allegedly printed in Holland by Broer Jansz in 1652. See also Leona Rostenberg, "William Dugard, Pedagogue and Printer to the Commonwealth," *Papers of the Bibliographical Society of America* 52 (1958): 197.

50. Parker, *Milton*, 1:395; Rostenberg, 198; *Life Records*, 3:206, 212, 231, 279, 288; 3 November 1653, proceedings of the Council of State, *CSPD* 1652–53, 227; Campbell, *Chronology*, 127, 135.

51. If Milton was writing *Mercurius Politicus*, or at least editorials for it, he would have known what the content was from its inception. Or perhaps Masson was right that licensing was not primarily Milton's job. It was certainly the lesser part of the duties when Weckherlin held the post (Masson, 4:154).

Licensing Metaphor

Parker, Marvell, and the Debate over Conscience

LANA CABLE

As English citizens weary of sectarian battles welcomed their restored monarch in a groundswell of public concord, some might reasonably have hoped that the impulse toward national unity would help to settle long-standing disputes over liberty of conscience. King Charles II in the Breda Declaration had expressed willingness to "declare a liberty to tender consciences."[1] Meanwhile, less magnanimous Restoration leaders felt they could afford to think of nonconformist sectarians, the most vociferous free conscience advocates, as a defeated, hence nonthreatening, minority. After 1660 it became increasingly acceptable to portray nonconformist language and habits of thinking as the remnants of a fashion now discarded by up-to-date rationalist political and cultural arbiters. "The better sort of Hearers are now out of love with these things," affirms Simon Patrick in 1669, with an urbanity that conveys what Derek Hirst calls "a sociology of hearing."[2] Conduct that in prior decades might have been viewed as a testament of absolute faith, truth, and conviction was coming to be treated as the ephemera of changeable style.

It would be wrong to take the victors' words at face value, however, and simply equate silencing of nonconformist political opposition with defeat of nonconformist oppositional culture. As N. H. Keeble has shown, loss of political power in fact worked subtly to consolidate nonconformist influence on English thought: "political defeat was the condition of cultural achievement."[3] This was so not only for writers like Bunyan and Milton, whose art was transformed by the need to construct spiritual triumph out of the ruins of millennial expectation. Political defeat became the condition as well of a more diffuse achievement, expansion of individual social and political rights. By driving inward the Puritan demand for spiritual autonomy, political defeat confirmed already developing popular notions about the sanctity of individual conscience, notions strengthened by literature that valorized the solitary wayfarer: "The idealism remained: the challenge was not compromised: but it was issued now not to systems or organizations but to the individual conscience. . . . Nonconformist literature bore an invaluably sympathetic witness to the apprehensions and aspirations of individuals in an age of increasingly complacent dismissal of any manifestation of individuality as a reprehensible aberration" (Keeble 24). The cry for liberty of conscience that had formerly been amplified by the collective energies of republican parties in dispute was now left for articulation to the resources of the relatively isolated individual explicator.

Certainly, in a society struggling to maintain a new and still fragile civil order, public institutions promoted behavioral conformity for the sake of peace and also for the sake of their own survival. This was particularly true for the ecclesiastical establishment when it came to questions of conscience. But the line that separated the domain of religious behavior from that of social or political behavior remained ambiguous at best. Indeed to some pragmatic Anglican divines, the interests of the church lay in keeping the distinctions blurred: church authority over private consciences justified ecclesiastical power in the state. Meanwhile, for dissenting individuals who had little left to lose by resisting pressure to conform, the experience of defeat was molding a new kind of autonomy, a personal sovereignty available only to those who undertook the arduous task of building the unassailable domain that Milton called the "Paradise within."[4] Thus the old republican cause may have been lost, but the claims of free conscience remained a force to be reckoned with.

One indication that the outwardly defeated remained inwardly undaunted was the frequency and ruthlessness with which Archbishop Sheldon thought it advisable to enforce the Clarendon Code, a set of statutes forbidding religious gatherings that departed from Anglican liturgy.[5] By compelling at least an outward show of religious unity, Sheldon's expectation was that nonconforming "tender consciences" would be isolated where they might wither silently into oblivion. But a burgeoning and largely uncontrollable print trade circumvented true isolation, leaving formal gatherings as only one of many venues for continuing the debate over conscience.

Since unlicensed printing thrived even under censorship in the discursive marketplace, a more ingenious way to breach the sanctity of nonconformist conscience was needed.

That cause was taken up by the ambitious Samuel Parker, Sheldon's personal chaplain and official licenser, later bishop of Oxford. Parker thought he had isolated the very germ that spread the pestilence of social and political deviation: "Had we but an Act of Parliament to abridge Preachers the use of fulsom and luscious Metaphors," he argued, "it might perhaps be an effectual Cure of all our present Distempers." It was metaphor that authorized the workings of private conscience, in Parker's view, metaphor and not doctrine that makes a religious fanatic. Simply by banning the "gawdy Metaphors" and "lascivious Allegories" whereby nonconformists have "turn'd all Religion into unaccountable Fansies and Enthusiasms," Parliament could arrest dissenting consciences in the very act of conceptualizing unauthorized ideas, that is, ideas that are *unaccountable*.[6] As Parker saw it, unaccountability constituted a threat even more dangerous than alien religions: "We condemn neither Turks nor Papists for their forms and Postures of Adoration. . . . Let them but address the same worship to its proper object, and we will never stand stiffly with them about the outward Rites and Ceremonies of its expression, but will freely allow them to conform to the significant Customs of their own Countrey, as we do to those of ours."[7] In other words, the doctrinal differences that separate Muslims from Roman Catholics from Protestants amount to nothing more than variations in style or taste attributable to the "significant customs" of sovereign states. But sovereignty itself requires that such customs be regularized within each state. If somehow the ungovernable activity of English metaphor could be brought under rule, then Parker saw hope for official dominion over private conscience.

Parker's digressional attack on metaphor in a treatise concerned primarily with freedom of conscience bears close examination. For this intervention provides insight into the cultural significance of the era's discursive shift from focus on questions of truth to focus on matters of style. Parker's indictment of metaphor documents an intuitive and only partially theorized grasp of the crucial linguistic link provided by figuration between that which can be accounted for in individual thought and that which cannot. Whereas Turks and Papists can easily be accounted for, what pushes "our modern Sectaries" beyond the pale of "The sober Christians of the Church of *England*" is the fact that "*we* express the Precepts and Duties of the Gospel in plain and *intelligible* Terms, whilst *they* trifle them away by childish *Metaphors* and *Allegories*, and will not talk of Religion but in barbarous and uncouth *Similitudes*" (*EP* 74–75; pronoun italics added). By driving a linguistic wedge between ways of thinking and being in the world that are tolerable (religious discourse "in plain and *intelligible* Terms") or intolerable ("talk of Religion . . . in barbarous and uncouth *Similitudes*"), Parker hoped to establish a rational standard whereby sectarian religious conduct would be perceived as in bad taste. For, if banning metaphor cannot work, subjecting it to the subtle censorship of social convention might. So to bring unruly eloquence into public disgrace, Parker loads upon metaphor and its practitioners every unmannerly, unattractive, contaminating, or disreputable characteristic he can glean from the social landscape: "*Effeminate* Follies," "*illiterate* Enthusiasms," "*gawdy* Metaphors," "Fansies and Enthusiasms dressed up with *pompous and empty* Schemes of Speech," "*clownish and slovenly* Similitudes," "*wanton and lascivious* Allegories." Ironically, the more contempt Parker heaps on the linguistic frippery and supposed vacuousness of dissenting style, the more substantial seems its cultural presence.

Parker's indictment of metaphor reveals that what was actually at stake in the seemingly ancillary quarrels over expressive style during the toleration debate was in fact not style but freedom of conscience itself.[8] Parker was clever enough to frame his impracticable metaphor-banning proposition with a wink and a nudge as a piece of idiosyncratic pleasantry: "Let not the Reader smile at the odness of the Proposal," he confides. But as he presses on, his meaning becomes clear: "For were Men obliged to speak Sense as well as Truth, all the swelling *Mysteries of Fanaticism* would immediately sink into flat and empty Nonsense" (*EP* 76). Despite the moderate, even genial tone of his banter, Parker knew from the growing currency of rationalist discourse that making objective "Sense" a criterion of "Truth" would prevent unorthodox opinions from gaining public exposure. More to the point, he knew that rationalist criteria, when applied by a rising clergyman not to scientific discourse but to the free conscience debate, would deflect concerns having to do with individual hope, expectation, desire, fear—the entire spectrum of subjective experience that was essential to the articulation of personal conviction. In other words, Parker knew that he did not need literally to outlaw metaphor in order to accomplish his aim of curbing the authority of individual conscience. By publicly redefining the language of inspired (hence divinely authorized) belief, by construing such language as no more than the rhetoric of a self-aggrandizing style, he could achieve virtually the same end without resorting to impractical legislative schemes.

Marvell's Parker and Parker's Hobbists

Interestingly, the language of inspired belief was a medium in which Samuel Parker had himself at one time acquired a certain facility. Having been sent to Oxford for ministry studies by his Cromwellian father, young Parker fell in with a group of earnest-minded students who gathered around one Elizabeth Hampton, a nonconformist recognized for the scriptural authenticity of her teaching. Described by Anthony Wood as "an old and crooked Maid that drove the trade of Laundrey"[9] but by Andrew Marvell as "a plain devout Woman," Hampton provided the nurturing conventicle wherein Parker "train'd himself up in hearing their Sermons and Prayers, receiving also the Sacrament in the House, till he had gain'd such proficience that he too began to exercise in that Meeting, and was esteem'd one of the *preciousest* young men in the University."[10] From the influence of this apprenticeship, according to Marvell, Parker did not break away even after the Restoration. Instead, he applied his training to a vociferous defense of nonconformity, protesting the return of episcopacy until political developments finally forced him to earn his keep. As Marvell tells the story, Parker "at last satisfyed himself that the Episcopal

Government would indure as long as this King lived, and from thence forward cast about how to be admitted into the Church of *England*" (*RT* 182). In his capacity as an Anglican clergyman, then, Parker pursued an opportunistic polemical career that brought credit neither to the established church he had entered nor to the nonconformist upbringing he had left behind. If Elizabeth Hampton were to witness her old pupil in action today, Marvell observes, "she would go near, although she were bed-rid, to kick you: did she but see that so *precious* a young man, of her own Education, should in this manner stir up persecution[,] . . . run down and baffle that serious business of Regeneration, Justification, Sanctification, Election, Vocation, . . . only *as a Horse* to gain *Provender*, or *like a Hog*, to procure yourself *Beans*" (*RT* 287). Although hardly an objective biographical sketch, Marvell's caricature of the future bishop as a man unhampered by religious conviction tallies with the politic shifts and contradictions that emerge from Parker's argument.

Parker's diatribe against metaphor might at first glance seem quixotic, a relatively brief (7-page) digression on linguistic style that he has inserted into his 372-page antitoleration treatise, the *Discourse of Ecclesiastical Politie*. Marvell himself gives the metaphor-banning proposal merely passing notice in his refutation, *The Rehearsal Transpros'd*, when he jabs at Parker for culling out only "fulsom" and "luscious" metaphors: "What of the dull and lazy one[s] too?" Marvell wants to know (*RT* 197). Indeed, if bad style had really been what prompted Parker's antimetaphor campaign, Marvell's riposte might have ended the dispute. But Parker's momentary fixation on linguistic style indicates that he had a more long-range, and also more self-serving, agenda in mind.

Within Parker's frame of reference the attack on metaphor identifies him immediately as one of that company of prominent writers, philosophers, scientists, and men of affairs who belonged to the Royal Society: men like Robert Boyle, John Wilkins, Joseph Glanvill, John Evelyn, John Dryden, Edmund Waller, and Marvell's own patron the Duke of Buckingham.[11] All subscribed to Francis Bacon's view that rhetorical devices can lead to "distemper of learning, when men study words and not matter"; all were on record for their recommendations or schemes for "reforming" and "improving" the English language, and ultimately English society, by paring away the irrational excesses of metaphorical "enthusiasms."[12] Yet like the society historian Bishop Thomas Sprat, all would have conceded that if metaphor were outlawed, only outlaws would have metaphor, leaving "the *naked Innocence* of vertue . . . upon all occasions expos'd to the *armed Malice* of the wicked."[13] Thus they were more tempered than Parker in their arguments for linguistic reform. But the Royal Society included the influential sorts of men among whom the ambitious Parker, himself a relatively new member, relished being publicly counted.[14]

Parker's roll of notables also included Thomas Hobbes, who was neither a member of the Royal Society nor capable of being ignored by those who were. Parker denounces Hobbes in *Ecclesiastical Politie* for reducing divine Nature to a kind of warfare, and worse, for reducing the religious establishment itself by subordinating it to the absolute monarch. Indeed, it is this latter reduction that provokes some of the most sustained and substantive arguments in *Ecclesiastical Politie*, arguments calculated not only to reinforce the political authority of the church, but interestingly, also to enhance among a powerful group of agnostic thinkers the intellectual prestige of Samuel Parker. For Parker's seemingly indignant censure of atheism in fact provides a smoke screen for arguments meant to invest the institutional authority of the church with a sinecure quite independent of religious belief.

Parker's conception of an ecclesiastical establishment answered perfectly to his understanding of a secular government's needs. It is no doubt true that, as Jon Parkin has recently argued, "Parker was not as Hobbesian as his opponents would have liked to imply."[15] Parker takes great care to convey the theological concepts that underpin his absolute monarchy. He bases his argument not on the desperately isolated individualism of Hobbes's state of nature, but rather, on a foundation of divinely ordained communitarian principles. As Parker's argument unfolds, however, those principles appear not as an article of faith, nor even as a practical framework for communal relations. Parker's divine communitarianism acts rather as a pragmatic hypothesis, an originary myth required to legitimize arbitrarily imposed human political order. *"For, take away the Divine Institution of Government, and the Obligations of Conscience to Obedience, and then all Government is Usurpation, and all sense of Obedience Folly: and Princes have no other Right to their Crowns, but what is founded upon Force and Violence; . . . And therefore I leave it to Authority to consider, how much it concerns them . . . to punish those, who . . . propagate Irreligious Principles, as the worst and most dangerous Enemies to the State"* (*EP* xxxv). What Parker leaves "to Authority to consider" is how difficult governance would be if threats of eternal punishment were not readily available to prop it up. Religion functions simply to validate monarchical government: "Irreligious Principles" must be prosecuted not because they endanger souls but because they endanger absolute rule. For Parker, divinely authorized individual conscience exists for one reason only—to secure obedience to the sovereign state: "If all humane Laws have their main force and efficacy from the apprehensions of Religion, if Oaths, Promises, and Covenants, and whatsoever else whereby Civil Societies are upheld, are made firm by nothing but the bonds of Religion; then let Authority judge, how much it is beholden to those men, who labour to bring it into Publick Disreputation" (*EP* 143). Like the "Obligations of Conscience to Obedience," the "apprehensions" and "bonds of Religion" are tools of political power. Moreover, apart from its obligation to obedience, any activity of conscience is by definition politically and socially subversive: "*Princes may with less hazard give Liberty to mens Vices and Debaucheries, than to their Consciences*" (*EP* lxv). Thus while Parker vehemently denies Hobbes's atheistical vision and pays lip service to "the Divine Institution of Government," his vision for state authority depends substantially on the rationalist and materialist terms used by Hobbes himself (*EP* 114).

For example, in order to deride the "Mushroom Wits" who parrot Hobbes, Parker adopts an attitude of particular condescension. "How huffingly will they assert," he jibes, "*that men have no Faculties but of Sense and Imagination . . . that Religion is the belief of Tales publickly allowed; that Power is Right, and justifies all Actions whatsoever . . . How boldly do they take up with these and other resembling Principles of Baseness and Irreligion, upon the bare Authority and proofless Assertions of one proud and haughty Philosopher?*" (*EP* xxv–xxvi) Having chastised the "Hobbists" (and thus the "proud and haughty" Hobbes himself) as befits an Anglican priest, Parker demonstrates, in materialist terms that might have impressed a Hobbesian monarch, "*the inconsistency of* Liberty of Conscience, *with the first and Fundamental Laws of Government*" (*EP* xxxvi). Parker defines these fundamental laws by incorporating into the magisterial domain whatever men may do that is capable of being apprehended by the senses. He debars private conscience from effecting any sort of concrete action, thereby completely severing human affairs from the exercise of individual prerogative. "Let all matters of *meer Conscience*, whether purely Moral or Religious, be subject to Conscience meerly," Parker urges: "This is the Prerogative of the Mind of Man within its own Dominion; its Kingdom is intellectual, and seated in the thoughts, not Actions of Men" (*EP* 89). Thus for Parker, the workings of individual conscience rightly end where they begin: enclosed within the isolated mind, unvoiced, unwitnessed, unacted upon. Thus every discernible act of human imagination would be proscribed.

To implement that proscription, Parker justifies in the name of civil order the magistrate's right to decree what words may mean, what "Tales" may be "publickly allowed," and what manners are to be tolerated. Significantly, he delivers his argument for totalitarian control of the imagination in terms of progressivist linguistic theory: "For as Words do not naturally denote those things which they are used to represent, but have their Import Stampt upon them by consent and Institution, and may, if Men would agree to it among themselves, be made Marks of Things quite contrary to what they now signifie: So the same Gestures and Actions are indifferently capable of signifying either Honour or Contumely; and therefore that they may have a certain and setled meaning, 'tis necessary their Signification should be Determined" (*EP* 108). Parker's conventionalist approach to words aligns him with the anti-occultists whom Brian Vickers has identified as subscribing to a scientific perspective on language: words gain their meanings not from intrinsic identification with things, as Renaissance "natural language" proponents would have it; rather, words are arbitrary signs.[16] But Parker carries these theoretical terms beyond scientific description to prescribe social discipline. If words are arbitrary signs, he reasons, then the arbitrary signifiers should be made to achieve the "certain and setled" meanings whose "necessary . . . Signification" has *already been* "Determined" by the authorities. Such determinations would enforce those "Duties of Morality" which, in Parker's view, constitute "the most weighty and material concerns of Religion" (*EP* 77). Parker's casual rescission of spiritual concerns from religious worship prompted Marvell's famous jibe: "I am resolved instead of *his Grace* to call him alwayes *his Morality*" (*RT* 62).

Indeed, it is the "material concerns" of religion that command Parker's most sustained polemical attention. Within the realm of the material he sums up the overriding purpose of religion, portraying it as an instrument of state, albeit a secretive and potentially fraudulent one: "So that though Religion were a Cheat, they are apparently the greatest Enemies to Government, that tell the World it is so. . . . Nothing more concerns the Interest of the Civil Magistrate, than to take care, what particular Doctrines of Religion are taught within his Dominions; because some are peculiarly advantageous to the ends of Government, and others as naturally tending to its disturbance" (*EP* 144). Having apparently fashioned his own religious faith into a vehicle for career ambition, Parker now promotes religion as a skillfully engineered political utensil. The terms he employs to characterize visible religious practices betray this utilitarian perspective: "And as for all that concerns External Worship, 'tis no part of Religion itself, but only an *Instrument* to express the Inward Veneration of the Mind by some Outward Action or Posture of the Body" (*EP* 99). Since the isolated and circumscribed conscience is prohibited from expressing the "Inward Veneration of the Mind," it is "Religion itself" that finally lies beyond the pale of Parker's institutional church.

Even as Parker disburdens religion of its individual and spiritual significance, his arguments about the relation between Christian liberty and Mosaic law or ceremonial ordinance relieve law itself from the necessity of "matter" or legal significance. Laws are enacted for the sake of our obedience, not our understanding: "The Duty of our Acting according to the Laws arises not from any Opinion of the Necessity of the thing it self, but either from some Emergent and Changeable Circumstances of Order and Decency, or from a sense of the Absolute Indispensableness of the Duty of Obedience" (*EP* 95). Since the true objective of laws is to enforce obedience, the content of any given law is irrelevant. Indeed, the power of the magistrate to impose law depends precisely on the arbitrariness, the "indifferency," of its content and on our acknowledg-

ment that the law is indeed "indifferent": "And therefore whatsoever our Superiours impose upon us, whether in Matters of Religious Worship, or any other
Duties of Morality, it neither is, nor can be any entrenchment upon our Christian Liberty, provided it be not imposed with an Opinion of the Antecedent
Necessity of the thing it self" (*EP* 97). So long as the magistrate avoids claiming
divine ordinance for the sake of imposing a *particular* law (these words, this
statute, a specific code of conduct), then the imposition cannot infringe on
"Christian Liberty": it affirms no "Antecedent Necessity." Since Christian liberty is identical with individual conscience in Parker's argument, it shares with
conscience the same "freedom": provided they remain mute and motionless,
individuals are free to think whatever they wish. To explicate such empower-
ment, Parker neatly distinguishes between "the Power of things" and "that of
Government," so as to empty "things" (like "matter") of all possible substance:
"Though the Gospel has freed our Consciences from the Power of things, yet it
has not from that of Government; we are free from the matter, but not from the
Authority of Humane Laws; and as long as we obey the Determinations of our
Superiours with an Opinion of the Indifferency of the things themselves, we
retain the Power of our Christian Liberty, and are still free as to the matter of
the Law, though not as to the Duty of Obedience" (*EP* 95). It is our "Opinion of
the Indifferency of the things themselves" on which our "Power" over "things"
in fact depends: Parker's Christian liberty requires unqualified passivity. Meanwhile, as for words and tales, or manners and gestures, the true meaning of laws
concerning them derives not from their "matter" or content but from their
enforceability. The reason laws exist is so that they may be obeyed.

Given the arbitrary logic of Parker's authoritarian vision, the consequen-
tiality of his views on deity may seem diminished. But his rhetorical stances at
least hint at how he wished to be perceived. Although he castigates aspiring
freethinkers as "Mushroom Wits," Parker speaks of *true* atheists in a manner
that approaches reverence. " *'Tis not for you to pretend to Atheism,*" he repri-
mands upstart Hobbists; " *'tis too great a Priviledge for Boys and Novices. 'Tis
sawsiness for you to be Prophane, and to censure Religion Impudence and ill Manners: and whatsoever Rational Pleas Atheism may admit of, 'tis not for such as you to
pretend to Wit and Learning enough to understand them*" (*EP* xxiii–xxiv). That a
future bishop should publicly censure budding atheists not for spiritual error
but for unmannerly intellectual trespass dramatically illustrates the extent to
which the discourse of truth had by 1669 lost ground to discourse of style.
Implicit in the discursive shift as negotiated by Parker is a class statement as
well: "*They have nothing to make them fancy themselves more witty and refined
people, than illiterate Peasants and Mechanicks, but a readiness and pregnancy to
rally upon Religion*" (*EP* xxxiii). Exclusive right to freethinking is thus reserved
by Parker to an elite circle that resembles, not surprisingly, the Royal Society.

Once he has secured into the province of the cultivated few not only "Wit and Learning" but also the "Privilege" of censuring religion, profaning it, or ignoring it altogether, Parker dubs "the most Learned and Inquisitive" of such "Philosophers" devotees of "a Grand Perhaps": those who, while explaining natural phenomena, instead of openly denying God happen to stumble upon the idea *that possibly there might be none*" (*EP* xxiv). An ecclesiastical establishment structured entirely on the premise of a "Grand Perhaps" coincides perfectly with Parker's argument for retaining even corrupt clergy as instruments requisite to a smoothly running state. In Marvell's arch phrase, "No Atheist could have said better" (*RT* 139).

Parker's Politics of Style *vs.* Nonconformist Poetics

Marvell stops short of directly accusing Parker of atheism, but his demonstration of the slippage between sacred and profane in Parker's critique of nonconformist language makes the charge superfluous. If Parker's utilitarian perspective on religion had not already convicted him, that judgment would have been assured by his reduction of varied spiritual expression to mere rhetorical style. When Marvell deconstructs Parker's view of nonconformist metaphor, Marvell's readers cannot help detecting the churchman's solecism. Marvell begins by quoting Parker's jeering representation of nonconformist terms for the spirit: "*The Non-conformist Preachers*, you say, *make a grievous noise of the Lord* Christ, *talk loud of getting an interest in the Lord* Christ, *tell fine Romances of the secret Amours between the Believing Soul and the Lord* Christ, *and prodigious Stories of the miraculous feats of Faith in the Lord* Christ. Did ever Divine rattle out such profane Balderdash!" (*RT* 264). Since on first reading, Marvell's "profane Balderdash" could easily refer to the nonconformist language that Parker describes, Parker might initially agree. But then, Marvell launches his counterattack with a metaphoric backhand calculated to scandalize: "I cannot refrain, Sir, to tell you that you are not fit to have Christ in your mouth." Marvell's iconoclastic image provokes the complex response often associated with nonconformist metaphor. Here, initial shock gives way to ambivalence as the startling picture of Christ in the cleric's mouth is momentarily registered, then revised, as the reader recognizes that *this* mouth has after all been declared "not fit" for such a morsel. But the inference that *other* mouths *are* fit to have Christ in them can hardly be more visually welcome. So literal image yields to figuration in a more decorous reading: Parker's mouth must be unfit to contain *the name* of Christ. But still, as is characteristic of such evocative and malleable imagery, the metaphoric activity declines to rest. Marvell's iconoclastic image lends itself to a final reading, one available from the start yet elusive to immediate sensory grasp: Parker's mouth is unfit for the eucharist. Marvell's seemingly scandalous metaphor is in the end perfectly orthodox. Regardless of whether one regards the eucharist as literally Christ's body or as only symbolic of it, if there remains a scandal here, Marvell's words make it lie in Parker's unfitness for ecclesiastical office rather than in the Protean quality of nonconformist metaphor.

With that indictment, then, Marvell launches his exposure of the atheistical inferences to be drawn when "so great an Artist" of profane manners as Parker presumes to set stylistic standards for religious expression:

> You talk like a Mountebanke. . . . Is this our great champion against Atheisme? . . . What Distinction do you make betwixt the Amours of the French Court, and the secret Amours betwixt the believing Soul and the Lord *Christ*? What between the Feats of Faith in the 11*th.* to the *Hebrews*, and the Chivalry of *Don Belianis* or *Don Quixote*? What betwixt the Romances of the Lord Christ, and those of the *Grand Cyrus* or *Cleopatra*? . . . was it not here that, as you told Doctor *Bathurst, the Recreation you took to frame your Thoughts and Conceptions into Words, did almost equal the Ravishing delight you derive from their first Births and Discoveries? (RT* 264)

As Parker sees it, no distinction is called for between the sacred and the profane, because all sensory language, whether words or the Word, strives to serve a single purpose: not faith or conviction, not inspired truth, not even the ingenuous desire to lead a holy life, but always and only sensory pleasure, "Ravishing delight." In Marvell's view, it is exactly such leveling of linguistic value that leads Parker to reduce divine faith to mere civilized behavior: " 'Tis the fifth to the *Galatians* where you had before expounded the Fruits of the Spirit to be meer Moral virtues, and the *Joy, Peace*, and *Faith* there spoken of to be only *Peaceableness, Chearfulness* and *Faithfulness*, as if they had been no more than the three Homileticall conversable Virtues, *Veritas, Comitas,* and *Urbanitas" (RT* 265). In the battle over conscience, just as Parker translates inner faith into outward manners, he evacuates conviction by transmuting its spontaneous verbal expression to manipulable style. By operating as if style rather than conviction is at the heart of the free conscience debate, Parker gives language the same treatment that he gives religion: he makes language an instrument for the uses of the world and worldly institutions rather than a medium for articulating the search for truth. For purposes of carrying on the latter enterprise, Parker's curtailment of metaphor would have circumscribed even Learned and Inquisitive subscribers to a Grand Perhaps.

Parker's politicization of language brings him into conflict with the radical poetics of the age's most profoundly literary nonconformist, John Milton. Paradoxically, the clash is inevitable because, on at least one point regarding metaphor, Milton and Parker would have agreed. This is the point at which, through metaphor, the transforming power of imagination intersects with the liberty of conscience. For Parker and Milton alike, it is metaphor that enables us to articulate that which, though felt, can neither be empirically verified nor objectively replicated. Analogous to the pattern of Saint Paul's "faith," metaphor was understood by Milton as the *expressive* "substance of things hoped for," the *verbal* "evidence of things not seen." This intersection between transforming imagination and individual autonomy I have elsewhere called Milton's poetics of desire—an approach to affective rhetoric that, while working as an aesthetic principle, operates also as a visionary pattern of spiritual self-transformation.[17] For Milton, the poetic process must always be twofold. Rhetorically, his poetics of desire facilitates iconoclastic liberation from—and power over—the seductive illusions of sensory language. Spiritually, Milton's poetics of desire enables iconoclastic redefinition of the individual, and of the world within which individual action acquires significance, in a radical and transgressive act of carnal, yet visionary, self-authorship.

While the fruits of Samuel Parker's thinking about metaphor are rather less sublime than Milton's, he makes the same essential connections that Milton does in linking the transforming powers of metaphor to religious belief, individual conscience, and disparate patterns of dwelling in the world. We have no evidence that either Parker or Milton was aware of the mutuality of their insight into metaphor as an instrument of imaginative transformation, or of the disparity between the kinds of concrete inferences each would draw from that insight. What we do know is that the two men had met. In the early days of the Restoration, before Parker's commitment to monarchical Anglicanism had solidified, he had, according to Marvell, "frequented *J.M.* incessantly and haunted his house day by day." In fact, Marvell himself happened to have met Parker in Milton's home. At a time when Parker was still sympathetic with the republican cause, he enjoyed Milton's hospitality and sufficiently familiarized himself with the poet's career to enable him—once he became a monarchist— to take a personalized potshot at Milton for the Salmasius exchange in Milton's 1651 *Defence of the People of England*. It is not difficult to imagine that Parker would have made use of any other insights he might have gained during these visits, especially insights into the vital connections drawn among affective language, thought, and religious belief by the nation's most renowned literary advocate of free conscience.

Clearly both Parker and Milton *equate* religion with conscience. Here is Milton in *A Treatise of Civil Power*: "I here mean by conscience or religion that full persuasion . . . that our belief and practice . . . is according to the will of God."[18] Similarly, in *Ecclesiastical Politie*, Parker asserts that there is "nothing so necessary to the reverence of Government . . . as a sense of Conscience and

Religion" (*EP* 140–41). But in contrast to Parker's "reverence of Government," Milton makes *his* equation of religion with conscience serve the interests of spiritual progressivism, what he calls "the advancement of religion," a concept answering only to "the will of God & his Holy Spirit within us, which we ought to follow much rather then any law of man" (*CPW* 7: 241–42).

The claims for conscience that Milton makes in *Civil Power* are identical to the ones he had made a decade earlier in his "tailed sonnet," "On the New Forcers of Conscience," where he skewers the *"New Presbyter"* for turning out to be "but *Old Priest* writ Large" (*Complete Poems*, ed. Hughes, p. 145, l.20). Similar claims continued to be made by dissenters throughout the Restoration period. Parker, meanwhile, speaks not of "advancing" religion but of "settling" it, as he points to the *"utter inconsistency"* of free conscience *"with Publick Peace & Settlement"* (*EP* xii). The *"peremptory Conceptions"* of *"a rout of unlucky Boys and Girls,"* he says, are *"enough to overturn the present Settlement,"* which the public cannot hope to solidify except by *"reducing the minds of men to . . . Unity in Religious Worship"* (*EP* xl–xli). By contrast, Milton had long recognized "settlement" as a political buzzword. In *Civil Power*, he explicates with mounting irony the metaphor by which "reducing . . . minds" is transformed into securing "Publick Peace." Those, he says, who cannot think the gospel safe "unless it be enacted and *settled*, as they call it, by the state, a statute or a state-religion . . . understand not that *the church itself* cannot . . . *settle* or impose one tittle of religion upon our obedience . . . unless they mean to . . . give to the state in their *settling* petition that command of our implicit beleef, which they deny in thir *setled* confession both to the state and to the church" (*CPW* 7: 257–58). Milton's restless exploration of the word "settlement" exposes by contrast the complacency with which Parker's official terminology would harden *"the present Settlement"* into civilized fossil.

As Milton and Parker both knew, what made free use of metaphor a threat to institutional rigidity was metaphor's subversive capacity for *world-making*: "Whoever among them can invent any new Language, presently sets up for a man of new Discoveries," frets Parker (*EP* 74–75). For "the present *Settlement*," the prospect of "new Discoveries" could only be a threat. Primacy of conscience had led Milton to argue for separation of church from state in *A Treatise of Civil Power in Ecclesiastical Causes*. Primacy of conscience signals to Parker, however, that civil power unquestionably *is* an ecclesiastical cause. Barely gesturing toward the "antecedent necessity" of such primacy ("notwithstanding that Conscience is the best, if not the only security of Government") Parker delineates the power of that Inner Discipline with mounting wonderment. "Government [has] never been controul'd or disturbed so much by any thing as [by] Conscience," he laments:

Are Governours Gods Vicegerents? so is this. Have they a power of deciding all Controversies? so has this. Can they prescribe Rules of Virtue and Goodness to their Subjects? *so may this*. Can they punish all their Criminal Actions? *so can this*. And are they subject and accountable to God alone? *so is this*, that owns no superiour but the Lord of Consciences. And of the two Conscience seems to be the greater Sovereign, and to govern the larger Empire. For whereas the Power of Princes is restrain'd to the outward actions of men, this extends its Dominion to their inward thoughts: Its throne is seated in their minds, and it exercises all that Authority over their secret and hidden sentiments, that Princes claim over their publick and visible practices. (*EP* 4–5)

The passage is remarkable for its unabashed envy of the *material* power wielded by *immaterial* conscience. For Parker, the throne of the mind, the dominion of "secret and hidden sentiments," is a prize to be coveted. His uneasy acknowledgement of the true source of peace and civil order ("Conscience is the best, if not the only security of Government") shows his essential agreement with Milton about the primacy of the discipline within. But the inference he draws from that recognition is diametrically opposed to Milton's. At a time when King Charles's tolerationist policies threatened the authority of the church, Parker's strategy for extending the Prince's "public and visible" dominion over men's "secret and hidden sentiments" provided new hope for the ecclesiastical establishment. By reining in metaphor, by harnessing the builder of kingdoms of the mind, the Anglican authorities might once again—this time more securely—command the civil power they had enjoyed before the revolution.[19] As Marvell points out, Parker's magisterial appropriations of spiritual life are in the end designed to benefit not Hobbes's absolute monarch, but rather the ecclesiastical establishment: "he first makes all that he will to be Law, and then: whatsoever is Law to be Divinity" (*RT* 185).

The Royal Society and Language Reform

Parker's metaphor-licensing proposal of course failed to be taken up in parliamentary debating chambers. And Andrew Marvell's satires famously laughed the cleric off the polemical stage. But Parker announced his scheme for stigmatizing nonconformist thought and feeling through expressive style in a culture that enabled it to acquire a life of its own. Richard Foster Jones's once influential argument, which credited Royal Society linguistic reforms with shifting English prose style "from humanist subjectivity to scientific objectivity," is now recognized as narrowly positivistic and historically inaccurate. But signs of the Restoration backlash against "enthusiasm" nevertheless abound. Paul Arakelian locates the important change not in rationalist simplification of diction and syntax, but in newly analytical habits of thought.[20]

Parkin's reference to Parker's "unequivocal championing of the magis-
to order the church" seems to me to underestimate Parker's true political
nd his vision of the actual role in government to be played by the ecclesiasti-
ment. See Parkin, "Liberty Transpros'd," 276.
he Myth of a Restoration Style Shift," *Eighteenth Century* 20 (1979):

anguage and Loyalty: Plain Style at the Restoration," *Literature and His-*
o): 2–18.
Two-Edg'd Weapons: Style and Ideology in the Comedies of Etherege, Wycherley
reve (Oxford: Clarendon Press, 1988), 26. Subsequent page references will
the text. For further development of the history of style as a dynamic rather
ar process, see Robert Markley, *Fallen Languages: Crises of Representation in*
an England, 1660–1740 (Ithaca: Cornell University Press, 1993).

Roger Pooley demonstrates a new movement pressing forward on multiple
fronts from the sixteenth-century "plain style" tradition, as widely differentiated seventeenth-century writers invoked the time-honored term to articulate
their own political, social, artistic, and philosophical values.[21] Robert Markley
has shown how complex and subtle could be the thinking about language of
people like Robert Boyle. Boyle's writing displays the "dialogical tension"
among multiple authorial voices in an era acutely conscious of style as "the
writer's struggle against convention and towards an elusive individuality that is
itself bounded culturally and ideologically."[22] The idea of language reform was
being discussed throughout the post–civil war decades by leaders across the
political spectrum. Reformers who belonged to or actively supported the Royal
Society shared the common view that civil conflict had left the linguistic landscape as well as the political and economic one in disarray, and all agreed that
matters required putting into order. The Restoration's dual "strategies of con-
tainment," Markley points out, included both censorship and reformist propaganda such as the Royal Society produced:

The former is a blatant exercise of political power, the latter an attempt ultimately to
obviate the need for censorship by a complex deployment of power to encourage self-
censorship and self-policing. As Foucault has demonstrated, the techniques for deploying political power—for making the individual an *effect* of power—become more
sophisticated in the eighteenth and nineteenth centuries. What is fascinating about
late seventeenth-century writings on language is that we can observe these techniques
taking shape and analyze the mechanisms by which Sprat, Glanvill, and Boyle promote
their views of language and culture as rational, "natural," and irrevocable. (*Two-Edg'd
Weapons* 39)

"Self-censorship and self-policing" aptly describe the behavioral objectives
that Parker's strictures on metaphor were ultimately designed to achieve. Like
the attacks on linguistic enthusiasm mounted by Sprat and Glanvill, and like
the more indirect and idealized language schemes such as John Wilkins offered, Parker's language reform effort must be recognized as seeking, alongside
overt censorship and printing press closures by Roger L'Estrange, to impose a
new social order. Thus if the Royal Society campaign against figurative language in scientific discourse is more symptomatic than causal in the larger
movement, it nevertheless supplied a vital forum for exchange of related ideas
for social reform. Floridity of verbal expression came increasingly to be regarded as old-fashioned or provincial, while religious nonconformity fell into
the silence of virtual internal exile. At the same time, the civil religion of
Anglican decency became central to the public myth of national identity. By
1680, the censor Roger L'Estrange could talk about the highly metaphoric style
of the dissenters as if it were a foreign language, and the dissenters themselves

as undesirable aliens: "These are *Words*, and *Expressions*, that signify quite another thing to *Them*, than they do to *Us*. . . . This is not to be taken now, as the *Language Currant* of the *Nation*, . . . they make it a point of *Honour* to maintain the Freedome of their *Owne Tongue*; in token, that they are not as yet a *Conquer'd Nation*" (Keeble 245). L'Estrange's tacit recognition of the linguistic foundation for liberty of conscience ("the Freedome of their *Owne Tongue*") is worth noting. If the dissenters remained, in his words, "not as yet a conquered nation," the rhetoric of estrangement used by this aptly named censor nevertheless invests dissenters with the dignity of nationhood. In other words, L'Estrange acknowledges the specifically *political* force in the linguistic dimension of free conscience, even as he anticipates its ultimate defeat.

Notwithstanding that acknowledgment, however, L'Estrange's championship of stylistic conformity to "the *Language Currant* of the *Nation*" makes it clear that for him, and for his readers, language itself is now assumed to be determined by national consensus and changeable style rather than by personal conviction or individual thought. When Parker first published *Discourse of Ecclesiastical Politie* in 1669, he expected his public statement against the unfettered use of metaphor to situate him among Simon Patrick's "better sort of Hearers," the social and intellectual elite. By 1680, to make such a statement was to take what amounted to a patriotic stand. In just over a decade, Parker's campaign to appropriate private conscience to the public domain through an attack on metaphor could be said to have met with a measure of success.

Notes

1. Andrew Browning, ed., *English Historical Documents, 1660–1714* (London: Eyre & Spottiswoode, 1966), 57–58.

2. I am greatly indebted to Professor Hirst for allowing me to read in manuscript his essay "Samuel Parker, Andrew Marvell and Political Culture, 1667–73," *Writing and Political Engagement in Seventeenth Century England*, ed. Derek Hirst and Richard Strier (Cambridge: Cambridge University Press, 1999). The quotation appears on page 148.

3. N. H. Keeble, *The Literary Culture of Nonconformity in Later Seventeenth-Century England* (Athens: University of Georgia Press, 1987), 22. Subsequent page references will appear in the text.

4. *Paradise Lost*, 12.575–87. Citations from Milton's poems are from *John Milton: Complete Poems and Major Prose*, ed. Merritt Hughes (New York: Odyssey Press, 1957).

5. See Keeble, chpt. 1, especially 45–55 for discussion of the complex evolution and execution of the Clarendon Code, rigorous implementation of which is more properly associated with Archbishop Sheldon than with the code's framer, Edward Hyde, Earl of Clarendon.

6. Samuel Parker, *A Discourse of Ecclesiastical Politie: Wherein The Authority of the Civil Magistrate over the Consciences of Subjects in Matters of External Religion is*

Asserted. The Mischiefs and Inconveniences of T[...] Pleaded in Behalf of Liberty of Conscience are ful[...] 1671), 74–75. Subsequent page references to [...] appear in the text with the initials *EP*.

7. Samuel Parker, *A Defence and Continu[...]* don, 1671), 285–86.

8. Hirst documents the complexities of inte[...] why "The traffic between style and conscience [...] polemical issue of the middle years of Charles II's r[...]

9. Anthony Wood, *Athenae Oxonienses, Volu[...]* (Printed in London for R. Kraplock, D. Midwinter, [...]

10. Andrew Marvell, *The Rehearsal Transpros'd a[...] Second Part*, ed. D. I. B. Smith (Oxford: Clarendon P[...] references will appear in the text with the initials *RT.*

11. Hirst interestingly explores the reason why M[...] menting his patron, chooses to parody and weave allusi[...] *hearsal* throughout the multiple levels of aesthetic, satiric a[...] *Rehearsal Transpros'd*. See Derek Hirst, "Samuel Parker."

12. See Richard Foster Jones, "Science and English [...] printed in *Seventeenth-Century Prose: Modern Essays in [...]* (New York: Oxford University Press, 1971), 53–89.

13. Sprat's statements on metaphors are quoted at leng[...] ence and English Prose Style," Fish, ed., *Seventeenth-Cen[...]* quotation is on p. 62.

14. Lotte Mulligan lists Parker as one of eight nonlatitudi[...] who joined between 1665 and 1667. Parker had been recommen[...] losopher John Wilkins. Mulligan's article "Civil War Politics, R[...] Society," *Past and Present* 59 (May 1973) is reprinted in *The Intelle[...] Seventeenth Century*, ed. Charles Webster (Boston: Routledge & [...] 317–46.

15. "Liberty Transpros'd: Andrew Marvell and Samuel Parker, [...] *erty*, ed. Warren Chernaik and Martin Dzelzainis (London: Macmill[...] New York: St. Martin's Press, 1999), 269–89. The present quotation [...]

16. "Analogy Versus Identity: The Rejection of Occult Symbol[...] *Occult and Scientific Mentalities in the Renaissance*, ed. Brian Vicke[...] Cambridge University Press, 1984), 95–163.

17. See *Carnal Rhetoric: Milton's Iconoclasm and the Poetics of De[...]* N.C.: Duke University Press, 1995). Although Brian Vickers helpfully [...] "occult tradition" in natural language theory that influenced nonconformi[...] even his rich account of that tradition seems to me unable to explain what n[...] ists strove to accomplish through language. Regardless of whether word m[...] derived from convention in scientific language theory, or from intrinsic valu[...] ral language theory, Vickers's focus on word meaning alone leaves out the im[...] power of linguistic affect and its capacity for transforming individual and [...] human ways of being in the world. See Vickers, "Analogy Versus Identity."

18. *A Treatise of Civil Power, Complete Prose Works of John Milton*, ed. Don[...] et al., 8 vols. (New Haven: Yale University Press, 1953–82), 7:241. Subsequen[...] references to this edition of Milton will appear in the text as *CPW*.

19. Jon[...] trate's right[...] objectives a[...] cal establis[...]
20. "[...] 227–45. [...]
21. "[...] *tory* 6 (198[...]
22. [...] *and Con[...]* appear i[...] than lin[...] *Newton[...]*

John Dryden's Angry Readers

ANNA BATTIGELLI

When we consider John Dryden's achievement today, it is rightly as the Restoration writer who most completely defines his age. A narrative of his ascent to national prominence would point first to his appointments as poet laureate in 1668 and as historiographer royal in 1670. It would note that in 1671 the success of *The Conquest of Granada* and of *Marriage a-la-Mode* confirmed his standing as one of London's leading playwrights. By 1672, William Ramesey, physician in ordinary to Charles II, was recommending Dryden together with Chaucer, Ben Jonson, Shakespeare, Beaumont, and Fletcher to would-be gentlemen readers in *The Gentlemans Companion*.[1] After acknowledging Dryden's leading role as a Tory satirist in the early 1680s, such a narrative would note that, despite losing his public posts as a consequence of the Revolution of 1688, he continued to engage his public through his successful career as a translator. Finally, it would note Dryden's ongoing, though increasingly subtle, political commentary in *Fables* (1700).[2]

Though these details are in themselves accurate, such a narrative is, however, incomplete. Missing is the fact that during every phase of Dryden's career, readers contested his work—and often sharply. He was attacked publicly in satires, plays, prefaces, dedications, and in commentaries on his works. Privately, readers registered their resistance in manuscript annotations in the margins of his texts still visible today in a surprisingly high percentage of extant copies. That verbal objections could become physical became evident when on the evening of 18 December 1679, three men with cudgels attacked Dryden in Rose Alley. As James Winn notes, the beating was severe: "an account published in the *Gazette* two days later suggested that his life was in danger, and the painful crippling of his limbs to which Dryden refers in his later writings may have been the result of fractures suffered in this brutal beating."[3] The beating was probably the result of the wrongful attribution to Dryden of the earl of Mulgrave's *Essay upon Satire*.[4] That a wrongful attribution could result in physical violence suggests an existing readiness to attack Dryden's work. His readers acted on that readiness, leaving their marks on his body as well as on his texts.

Criticizing poets was, to be sure, a legitimate recreational sport in Restoration England, as is evident in Thomas Shadwell's *The Virtuoso* (1676), in which the play's main characters are invited to discuss a dissection and "to sport an author over a glass of wine," activities that Dryden's experience suggests may be more closely linked than they first appear.[5] But Dryden seems to have had greater success than most at driving readers into vituperative frenzies, and by 1693, he rightly lamented, "more Libels have been written against me, than almost any Man now living."[6] His character, his morals, his sexuality, his playwrighting, his prosody, his politics, his religion, his wife—all were attacked viciously in responses to his work.

Dryden's personal demeanor would not seem to account for the anger he provoked in his readers; his own testimony and that of friends like William Congreve and foes like Thomas Shadwell agree in describing his temperament as being naturally reserved. Congreve described Dryden as being "something slow, and as it were diffident in his Advances to others. He had something in his Nature that abhorr'd Intrusion into any Society whatsoever. Indeed it is to be regretted, that he was rather blameable in the other Extream: For by that means, he was Personally less known, and consequently his Character might become liable both to Misapprehensions and Misrepresentations."[7] Dryden's public reserve is also suggested, though less generously, by Thomas Shadwell, who lampooned Dryden by having him say "Nor Love nor Wine cou'd ever see me Gay, / To writing bred I knew not what to Say."[8] Shadwell was only caricaturing Dryden's own self-description. As early as 1668, in *A Defense of an Essay of Dramatique Poesie*, Dryden had acknowledged that he lacked the disposition to write comedy: "My Conversation is slow and dull, my humour Saturnine and reserv'd: In short, I am none of those who endeavour to break Jests in Company, or make reparties" (*Works* 9:8). Much later, Colley Cibber corroborated these claims when he reported that Dryden's reading of *Amphytrion* to actors was delivered "in so cold, so flat, and unaffecting a manner" that a true account of the reading would not be believed.[9] Slow, saturnine, reserved, cold, flat, unaffecting—these attributes, however unattractive, seem unlikely in themselves to have motivated Dryden's enemies to annotate their copies of his texts, lampoon him in their own works, or arrange to have him beaten.

When we turn to Dryden's texts, however, many factors can be identified as potentially irritating. His haughty confidence in his own taste and judgment, his false modesty, his mercenary flattery, his frequent self-promotion, and his razor-edged satire surely annoyed readers. If, however, we look at the printed responses to Dryden's work, it becomes evident that the single most disruptive characteristic troubling readers was Dryden's irrepressibly ironic disposition.[10] Irony pervades Dryden's works and is the key ingredient of his wit, but it also posed interpretive difficulties for partisan readers who wished for fixed or determinate readings of his plays and poems. If we look at two very different controversies—the heated literary debate over heroic drama in the early 1670s and the vituperative political responses to *Absalom and Achitophel* following its publication in 1681—we find that in both instances, Dryden's tonal instability troubled readers. As Roland Barthes would put it, Dryden's texts are "plural," "indeterminate," and "multivalent."[11] *The Conquest of Granada*, for example, is both parodic *and* straightforward, making a determinate interpretation impossible. Similarly, *Absalom and Achitophel* is both a defense and an indictment of Charles II. Dryden's willingness to elicit his readers' interpretive difficulties signals his interest in creating a reading experience in which readers are forced to sense alternative opinions without the guidance of authorial judgment. As William Bowman Piper has noted, reading Dryden's works forces one to "breathe the atmosphere" of late seventeenth-century literary and political conflict, and this was Dryden's goal.[12] For him, the act of reading was more closely tied to ephemeral controversy than to more conservative efforts at assimilating fixed, durable meaning.[13] Although the two debates—one literary, the other political—differ from one another, both reflect Dryden's interest in expanding and complicating the experiential nature of reading. In both instances, Dryden's predominantly partisan readers resented and resisted his efforts—and they publicized their resistance.

The Controversy over *The Conquest of Granada*

The highly artificial nature of heroic drama lent itself to parody, but what is particularly interesting about Dryden's heroic plays is his willingness to exemplify and parody the genre simultaneously. The two-part, ten-act *The Conquest of Granada* exhibits this indeterminacy. By exemplifying and parodying heroic drama, he both reached and irritated two opposing audiences: one audience was prepared to relish heroic drama's hyperbolic idealism; the other, to laugh at it. Unsure whether Dryden's huffing hero, Almanzor, was meant to represent or to parody heroism, readers discussed the play in print at length, alternately attacking the absurdity of Almanzor's speeches or charging Dryden with moral laxity in creating a Hobbesian hero. Thus, the play serves as an emblem for Dryden's paradoxical status within Restoration literary culture: if Dryden had attained a highly visible position as poet laureate and playwright, it was a highly contested position as well.

The play's contests of love and honor can be and were read unironically by contemporaries. Mary Evelyn, for example, felt that Almanzor represented the heroic ideal. She reported that the play was "so full of ideas that the most refined romance I ever read is not to compare with it; love is made so pure, and valor so nice, that one would imagine it designed for an Utopia rather than our stage. I do not quarrel with the poet, but admire one borne in the decline of morality should be able to feigne such exact virtue; and as poetic fiction has been instructive in former ages, I wish this the same event in ours."[14]

A more recent straightforward interpretation of the play is offered by Anne Barbeau Gardiner, who rightly notes that Almanzor learns to correct himself throughout the course of the play:

Almanzor . . . learns to bridle his lofty passions for the sake of the common good. His original vision of himself as an irresistible natural force, and earthly god, is belied by the trials he must face: he is reduced to bondage, sent into exile, and finally defeated in battle. In adversity he begins to control his impulses to revenge and love; he curbs his will and puts the safety of Granada above private considerations. Out of Almanzor's humiliation—his military and political defeat—comes his redemption: he is discovered by his father, the Duke of Arcos, given a noble title by Ferdinand, and because of Boabdelin's death, promised the hand of Almahide.[15]

Similarly, for Michael Alssid, Almanzor is educated through the course of the play, moving "from savagery to civilization."[16]

That Dryden fully intended to satisfy readers like Evelyn, Gardiner, and Alssid seems entirely likely. Heroic plays like *The Conquest of Granada* clearly quenched the thirst of a generation of theatergoers like Evelyn, who had been denied theatrical activity during the interregnum and had turned for entertainment to the reading of platonically driven romances. Appropriating the language of platonic love doctrine helped to elevate the tone of a play, and the use of rhymed couplets also signaled a level of discourse that was removed from the ordinary. When the king asked Roger Boyle, earl of Orrery, to write a play, Boyle produced a play in rhymed couplets because, as he put it, "I thought it was not fit, a Command soe Extraordinary, should have bin obeyed in a way that was Common."[17] Boyle's recognition that rhymed couplets would not be "common" and would thus be suitable for royal entertainment points to their main appeal: their ability, if used skillfully, to transport the audience to an elevated world.

Dryden became the chief defender of rhymed heroic drama, and in his printed defenses, he makes clear that mere realism was not its chief goal. In fact, imitation alone was, he explained, antithetical to what he strove to achieve: "It is very clear to all, who understand Poetry, that serious Playes ought not to imitate Conversation too nearly. If nothing were to be rais'd above that level, the foundation of Poetry would be destroy'd" (*Works* II:8). When, in *The Essay of Dramatic Poesy*, Crites argues that blank verse is "nearest Nature," and thus is most appropriate for dramatic dialogue, Neander responds by correcting Crites's definition of "nature": "I answer you . . . by distinguishing betwixt what is nearest to the nature of Comedy, which is the imitation of common persons and ordinary speaking, and what is nearest the nature of a serious Play: this last is indeed the representation of Nature, but 'tis Nature wrought up to an higher pitch. The Plot, the Characters, the Wit, the Passions, the Descriptions, are all exalted above the level of common converse, as high as the imagination of the Poet can carry them, with proportion to verisimility" (*Works* 17:74). The interest in "Nature wrought up to an higher pitch" helps to explain one of the effects that heroic drama intended to achieve. Part of the pleasure of Dryden's heroic plays is the intensified, hyperbolic atmosphere created by their language. We listen to the characters speak and watch in wonder as their language creates a compelling, though highly artificial, world around them.

Yet however much Restoration dramatists enjoyed playing to the audience by creating elevated scenes and deploying refined language, they were decidedly more cynical than their Caroline predecessors, and the language of platonic love had to be adapted to the current climate. Dryden, who was by temperament no platonist, and who demonstrates throughout his work a keen sensitivity to the demands made by the flesh on the spirit, furthermore understood that having professional actresses whose reputations were in question assume the roles of spotlessly virtuous platonic lovers demanded a more complex handling of such scenes than had before been necessary. And though he appreciated the marketing value of using platonic love doctrine to elevate the setting of his plays, he also understood that the libertine court wits—highly visible members of the audience whose reactions could determine a play's reception—were likely to laugh outright at the unironic handling of platonic love doctrine. He thus purposefully evoked libertine smiles by deliberately exaggerating the language of platonic love to the point at which he appears to be using it satirically. As D. W. Jefferson has noted, Dryden's seriousness is often "modified by a lurking comic intention."[18]

There can be little question that Dryden's satirical bent is deployed in *The Conquest of Granada*. The platonic love rhetoric is pointedly and comically exaggerated so as to reveal the overblown nature of the characters' ideals. Almanzor's hyperbolic "huffing" speeches are blatantly humorous. His ease in switching sides, his casuistry in building a case for his right to Almahide, and his Hobbesian individualism make him at best a flighty candidate for heroism. To the extent that the play parodies heroic drama, it was designed to amuse a sophisticated libertine sensibility. Ultrasophisticated court wits, who were tired of war and cynical about the abstract ideals that fueled it, were likely to view heroism less as an attractive or attainable ideal than as a subject of derision. For them, the hero's bombastic language proved humorous and the play's handling of platonic love doctrine was decidedly parodic. In fact, when the duke of Buckingham caricatured Almanzor in *The Rehearsal* (1672), he had his hero, Drawcansir, echo Almanzor's most ridiculous lines nearly word for word: "He who dares love; and for that love must dy, / And, knowing this, dares yet love on, am I" becomes "He that dares drink, and for that drink dares dye, / And, knowing this, dares yet drink on, am I."[19] The ease with which Almanzor could be parodied points to Dryden's own proximity to parody throughout *The Conquest of Granada*. In fact, Dryden's heroic plays have even been read as satires "of the social, political, and intellectual ideas current in his time."[20]

But satire alone was an unlikely goal unless Dryden was prepared to lose a large portion of his audience. As Evelyn's and Buckingham's divergent readings suggest, Dryden aimed for the balancing point between satirical and straightforward treatments of platonic love. Thus, the hyperbolic language and activity of a character like Almanzor can be read as a parody of heroic drama, a reading intensified by the fact that Nell Gwyn, one of the king's mistresses, played Almanzor's virtuous love interest, Almahide. Alternatively, however, as Derek Hughes has taken pains to demonstrate, Almanzor's exaggerated rhetoric can also be read as an exploration of the absurdity of human experience, in which hopelessly idealistic aspiration repeatedly collides with the force of physical desire.[21] Thus, the comic element that can be detected in Almanzor's absurd rants allows cynics to smile, but that same exaggerated elevation of the characters' language lends a sort of transporting awe to those in the audience predisposed to be pleased by it.

Readers, however, were not uniformly amused by Dryden's sophisticated ironic sensibility. The two parts of his play were performed in late December of 1670 and early January of 1671, probably within weeks of one another. A few attacks emerged before the text of the play was printed: Thomas Shadwell quickly lampooned Dryden in his comedy, *The Humourists*, and in December, Buckingham produced *The Rehearsal*, which had been written earlier but was updated to target Dryden and *The Conquest of Granada*. The text of *The Conquest of Granada* was published in February of 1672, and after its publication, attacking Dryden and *The Conquest of Granada* became something of a blood sport: in 1673, at least nine pamphlets discussed the play.[22] Long quotations and detailed analyses of passages characterize these attacks, suggesting that some of the authors worked from texts of Dryden's play and of his other works. In addition to these printed attacks, the heroic drama craze was ridiculed in the prologue to Edward Ravenscroft's *The Careless Lovers* (1673) and in Joseph Arrowsmith's full-scale parody of Dryden as the conceited and self-promoting tutor in *The Reformation* (1673), a play that rivals Buckingham's in its researched caricature of Dryden.

Particularly problematic for many of these readers was Almanzor's Hobbesian tendencies. Throughout most of the two parts of the play, he is in a Hobbesian state of nature. He has no loyalties other than to himself, and he engages in the competitive blood sport of war only so as to prove his superior strength. When Almahide prepares an evening of dancing, he insists that the men first "sally out, and meet the foe" (I.i 366). When he captures the duke of Arcos, he claims to be so pleased by the prospect of fighting that he promises to free him so "that I again may fight and conquer thee" (II.i 66). His disregard for the fact that freeing Arcos might harm Granada furthermore reflects his single-minded interest in the sport of combat rather than in loyalty. Hostile contemporaries like Richard Leigh sneered at this representation of "Men in a Hobbian [sic] State of War."[23] Without attachments or loyalties to a nation or culture, Almanzor's self-interested behavior indeed resembles that of Hobbes's natural man, a resemblance that Dryden surely knew to be problematic for a hero.

That Dryden nevertheless insisted on highlighting Almanzor's Hobbesian individualism is evident in a famous scene in the second part of the play. King Boabdelin becomes angry that Almahide has given Almanzor a yellow scarf. Irritated by the ease with which Boabdelin's anger is roused, Almanzor refuses to help when the Spaniards attack. He draws an imaginary circle around him into which he invites Almahide. The small empire of that circle is all he professes to care about or defend:

> I care not; perish; for I will not fight.
> I wonnot lift an arm in his defence:
> Yet will I not remove one foot from hence:
> I to your Kings defence his town resign;
> This onely spot whereon I stand, is mine.
> Madam, be safe; and lay aside your fear,
> You are, as in a Magique Circle, here. (Part II: III.i.158–64)

Contained with the "Magique Circle" of the self, Almanzor exemplifies Hobbesian individualism.

In fact, Almanzor is only saved from the doom of Hobbesian individualism when toward the conclusion of Part II he confronts the duke of Arcos in battle. Arcos recognizes a diamond bracelet with a ruby cross on Almanzor's wrist and a heart-shaped tattoo on his right arm that identify Almanzor as his long-lost son. With this recognition scene, Almanzor gains a father, a family, and a nation to which to be loyal. When he learns that a Zegry has killed Boabdelin, the opportunity to marry Almahide lawfully presents itself. With Queen Isabella's urging, Almahide agrees to marry him within a year. Both convert to Catholicism, embrace Spain as their home country, and find in one another a stabilizing force. Rescued from a Hobbesian state of nature, Almanzor's heroism has, finally, been confirmed. But confirmation cannot erase the play's forcible presentation of Hobbesian ideas nor can it diminish Dryden's active efforts at problematizing Almanzor's heroism through his hyperbolic huffing speeches. It is clear from the attacks that members of the audience and readers of the text alike were troubled by the ease with which competing interpretations of the play and its hero could be produced.

Not surprisingly, one group of readers found Dryden and his play to be politically and socially dangerous. This group of readers did not pick up on the parodic elements of Dryden's play; like Mary Evelyn, though without her enthusiasm, they read the play straightforwardly and found Almanzor deficient as a hero because of his Hobbesian leanings. Almanzor's extreme individualism was read as a license for unregulated behavior of all kinds and even as an indication of Dryden's tolerance for or promotion of Hobbesian behavior. The same William Ramesey who had earlier recommended Dryden to would-be gentlemen readers complained in 1673 that the portrayal of the unsuccessful struggle with desire for a married woman—exemplified by Almanzor's struggle with his passion for Almahide—was "not to be termed Rational, it being, indeed, nothing but filthy lust, and so, the truth is, deserves not the name Heroick."[24] The author of *Remarques on the Humours and Conversations of the Town* must have had Almanzor's Hobbesian individualism in mind when he warned against the fashionable cynicism promoted by those, like Dryden, who were close to the court. Such people were, he continued, "blundering Hectors, who think, that the modish non-sense which they bring from London, should be more valued, than the civility and agreeableness of rural conversation."[25] Almanzor's struggle with his physical desire is reduced to "the hot passion of an hour; tried by Chymaerical and odd experiments; unpracticable to the World, and rather an Idaea fit to misguide the leisure and the sentiments of Youth, than capable of giving any just assistance to the occasions of life" (52–53). "Never in any Age," this writer continues, "was there such a violent and universal thirst after the Fame of being wits, and yet no Age has possibl[y] discharg'd it self, with less real applause in those pretenses" (93). The idea that Dryden was a Hobbesian lingered, and when John Aubrey later noted rightly that Dryden "oftentimes makes use of [Hobbes's] Doctrine in his Playes," he concluded wrongly—as have many others since Aubrey—that Dryden was "a great admirer of Hobbes."[26]

Those who tried to defend Dryden's play thus found themselves having to defend Dryden's morality. When, for example, Charles Blount responded to the unfriendly *Friendly Vindication of Mr. Dreyden*, he had to argue that not only was *The Conquest of Granada* not profane but that attacking Dryden's morality was simply a measure "to advance the sale of your Book among the pretended Zealots."[27] Similarly, the anonymous author of *Remarks upon Remarques: Or, a Vindication of the Conversations of the Town* countered that "there was more practical Divinity in [Dryden's play] then in several Country Sermons I have heard."[28] Claims for the "practical Divinity" of Dryden's play, like Mary Evelyn's claim that she admired Dryden's willingness, despite the "decline of morality" surrounding him, to "feigne such exact virtue" ran alongside condemnations of the play as a vehicle for "filthy lust." The range of readings generated by the play suggests its indeterminacy.

Another portion of the attacks followed Buckingham's lead in parodying *The Conquest of Granada*'s bombast. These readers seem troubled by the fact that the play's hyperbolic language and action had succeeded in moving theatergoers and readers. By focusing exclusively on the play's bombast, parodists denuded the play of its generic complexity and stabilized its tonal instability. Buckingham, for example, took aim at the length and scale of Dryden's two-part play when he caricatured Dryden as Mr. Bayes, who prides himself on the extravagant scale of his play: "Why, I have design'd a Conquest, that Cannot possibly, I gad, be acted in less than a whole week: and I'l speak a bold word, it shall Drum, Trumpet, Shout, and Battle, I gad with any the most warlike Tragedy we have, either ancient or modern" (IV.i 18–22). Similarly, Joseph Arrowsmith caricatured Dryden's aesthetic sensibility by having him provide a formula for tragedy. In the process, he narrowed Dryden's interest exclusively to spectacle:

I take a subject, as suppose the Siege of *Candy*, or the conquest of *Flanders*, and by the way Sir let it alwayes be some war-like action; you can't imagine what a grace a Drum and Trumpet give a Play. Then Sir I take you some three or four or half a dozen Kings, but most commonly two or three serve my turn, not a farthing matter whether they lived within a hundred years of one another, not a farthing Gentlemen. . . . You must alwayes have two Ladies in Love with one man, or two men in love with one woman; if you make them the Father and the Son, or two Brothers, or two Friends, 'twill do the better. There you know is opportunity for love and honour and Fighting, and all that. . . . Then Sir you must have a Hero that shall fight with all the world; yes i'gad, and beat them too, and half the gods into the bargain if occasion serves. . . . in all you write reflect upon religion and the Clergy; you can't imagine how it tickles, you shall have the Gallants get those verses all by heart, and fill their letters with them to their Country friends; believe me this one piece of art has set off many an indifferent Play.[29]

The debate recorded in Richard Leigh's *The Censure of the Rota* opens with an ironic defense of the play's bombast:

An Heroick Poem never sounded so nobly, as when it was heightned with Shouts, and Clashing of Swords; and that Drums and Trumpets gain'd an absolute Dominion over the minds of the Audience . . . Here an Aquaintance of the Authors interpos'd, and assur'd the Company, he was very confident, that Mr. Dryden would never have had the Courage to have ventur'd on a Conquest had he not writ with the sound of Drum and Trumpet; and that if there was any thing unintelligible in his rants, t'was the effect of that horrour those Instruments of War with their astonishing noise had precipitated him into, which had so transported him, that he writ beyond himselfe. (3–4)

Targeting the play's indulgence in spectacle—signaled in each of these accounts by the focus on "drums and trumpets"—obscures Dryden's own awareness of the natural proximity between the heroic and the parodic; it also overlooks entirely his success at creating a moving and successful performance of the kind that Evelyn and others admired. That Dryden's success with a hero who "could Kill and Damne you with a Look" unsettled these readers is made clear in the prologue to Edward Ravenscroft's *The Careless Lovers*: "They that observe the Humours of the Stage, / Find Fools and Heroes best do please this Age, / But both grown so extravagant, I scarce / Can tell, if Fool or Hero makes the better Farce."[30] For these readers, Dryden's willingness to respond to the culture's craze for heroic drama signaled a mercenary willingness to please a paying audience, a willingness that furthermore suggested that he was aesthetically deficient, fad prone, and rather silly.

The bipolar nature of the responses to Dryden's play makes clear that he had, through his ironic indeterminacy, created a hero who presented himself differently to different audiences. If Dryden succeeded in reaching multiple audiences through his ironic handling of Almanzor, so, too, did he succeed at offending multiple audiences. Cynics were disturbed that the play was taken seriously, while moralists failed altogether to see that the very source of their anxiety—Almanzor's Hobbesian leaning—could parody the same fashionable cynicism to which they objected in the first place. The interpretive anarchy that resulted says a great deal about Dryden's familiarity with his audience. Some writers argued that public disputes like those over *The Conquest of Granada* were unlikely to benefit a reading public. Wary of a "Frantick Age so tollerably pester'd with whimsical Pasquils, Ralleries, and Rota's," one bemused pamphleteer concluded, "The principal end of Reading is I am sure to enrich the Mind; . . . But where every Man thinks what he lists, speaks what he thinks, writes what he speaks, and prints what he writes, from such kind of scribling, carried on by a frantick [vagary], I do not well apprehend what Advantage can in the least accrue one way or other to the Readers, either to the enriching their Discourse, or advancing their Knowledg."[31] But while this reader blamed the "Frantick Age" for the heated controversy over heroic drama, it seems evident that the real cause of the controversy was Dryden himself. It was Dryden who manipulated the conventions of heroic drama to draw an admiring and paying audience; it was Dryden who created a hero whose Hobbesian leanings were sure to antagonize theatergoers spooked by Hobbes; it was Dryden who parodied his hero even as he used him to represent heroic ideals. Dryden's ironic indeterminacy prevented any single fixed interpretation from becoming dominant. Readers in search of fixed meaning could find it only at the expense of simplifying the play, and their irritation with the play's indeterminacy informs their attacks.

The Controversy over *Absalom and Achitophel*

The results of Dryden's provocative indeterminacy are also evident in the responses to *Absalom and Achitophel* (1681). By 1681, Dryden found himself fully engaged in partisan politics, and the volatility of the current crisis to which he responded is indicated by the fact that the number of publications dated 1680 is matched only by those years of national crisis, 1649 and 1660.[32] If his indeterminate treatment of genre had elicited hostile commentary in the literary debate over heroic drama, his indeterminate treatment of Charles II drove readers into frantic rages.[33] *Absalom and Achitophel* was published anonymously, but it was quickly identified as Dryden's. That it captured national attention is evident in the many printed responses that appeared quickly, in the keys, both printed and marginal, that also appeared, and in the marginal comments that readers registered in their copies of the text.[34] The poem was published on 17 November 1681, the anniversary of Queen Elizabeth's accession, and one week before the earl of Shaftesbury was to go to trial. Phillip Harth has ably demonstrated that the satire had a clear political purpose: it was designed to strengthen the Tory use of the trial. Knowing that Shaftesbury would be acquitted, the Tories meant to use the trial as an opportunity to showcase the existence of a Protestant plot organized by Shaftesbury. The trial itself would be "a public performance staged for the benefit of the public and designed to show once again that the king's recent actions, far from being arbitrary, were necessary to the continued existence of the lawful government."[35]

But the trial was over before the first printed response to *Absalom and Achitophel* appeared, and responses continued for six months before attention turned to Dryden's subsequent satire, *The Medal*. Though *Absalom and Achitophel* surely helped to frame Shaftesbury's trial, it also acted in other contradictory ways that suggest Dryden's interest in forcing readers to take in the alternative opinions of partisan politics, seeing beyond partisanship. For example, even as the poem clearly defends the king, it can be and was read as a critique of Charles's kingship. Howard Weinbrot has noted that contemporaries were quick to recognize that the extended parallel between Charles and David was meant in part to chastise Charles: "The poem's deservedly famous opening lines . . . are not an 'apology' or 'insinuated condonement of . . . promiscuity' in the king's private life. . . . Rather, they lay out a theory of causation: unacceptable conduct breeds unacceptable conduct."[36] The poem's satiric norms—James Butler, duke of Ormond, and his son, Thomas, earl of Ossory—serve as "instructive paradigm[s]" for the king, whose lawless sexuality had threatened his family and his nation (Weinbrot, "'Nature's Holy Bands,'" 144). The fact that the poem was published on the anniversary of Elizabeth's accession might further indicate an interest in criticizing Charles, since celebrations of Elizabeth's accession had long been associated with criticism of Stuart monarchs.[37]

Contemporary responses reflect readers' anxiety over Dryden's equivocal portrait of Charles. Readers had only to read the first ten lines to discover the startling strategy of justifying Charles's sexual behavior through the precedent set by the Old Testament patriarchs:

> In pious times, e'r Priest-craft did begin,
> Before Polygamy was made a sin;
> When man, on many, multiply'd his kind,
> E'r one to one was, cursedly, confind:
> When Nature prompted, and no law deny'd
> Promiscuous use of Concubine and Bride;
> Then, Israel's Monarch, after Heaven's own heart,
> His vigorous warmth did, variously, impart
> To Wives and Slaves: And, wide as his Command,
> Scatter'd his Maker's Image through the Land. (lines 1–10)

The wit of these ten lines serves to debase both the patriarchs and Charles; that same wit, however, also works to deflect the severity of the charges against the king. William Bowman Piper has noted Dryden's syntactic equivocation throughout the poem: read in isolation, lines 7–9 "add a grotesque extension to a statement of sexual license: David not only made love with all the females in his court; he also loosed his lechery to the very boundaries of his political control" (Piper, "Invulnerability," 19). Yet if these lines are read within the context of the complete couplet and passage that contains it, they suggest that "David had piously augmented the population of his country" (Piper, 19). This kind of equivocation, which Piper traces throughout the poem, was calculated to unnerve partisan readers who wanted fixed and determinate readings of their flamboyant and transgressive king. Just as Dryden had portrayed Almanzor as both a parody and an exemplification of heroism, so, too, does he portray Charles as both a parody and an embodiment of good kingship.

Readers must also have been annoyed by a paradox within the poem: although the poem refuses to yield a fixed or determinate interpretation of Charles, it nevertheless places great pressure on the act of reading. Within the poem, poor reading leads to politically dangerous action. Thus, Absalom is tempted and falls, for example, when he fails to read the self-interest behind Achitophel's deployment of typology. And the poem's villain, Achitophel, is a villain in part because he uses a sacred reading practice for his own political purposes. His abuse of typology is evident when, in an attempt to boost Absalom's ego, he calls him the peoples'

> ... cloudy Pillar, and their guardian Fire:
> Their second *Moses*, whose extended Wand
> Divides the Seas, and shews the promis'd Land:
> Whose dawning Day, in every distant age,
> Has exercis'd the Sacred Prophets rage:
> The Peoples Prayer, the glad Deviners Theam,
> The Young-mens Vision, and the Old mens Dream! (lines 233–39)

As Paul Korshin has noted, Absalom is presented as "a false messiah . . . , a mistaken antitype, and a false prophet."[38] The ease with which typology could be used to support a false prophet suggests its dangers, which Dryden highlights when he has Achitophel use typology to attribute satanic qualities to Charles in the course of persuading Absalom to rebel against him: Charles is "like the Prince of Angels" who "Comes tumbling downward with diminish'd light" (lines 273–74).

The Whigs are thus portrayed as archetypal poor readers, and the poem serves as a cautionary warning of the dangers of typology. As Gerard Reedy notes, "by putting typological imagery into the mouths of the advocates of 'innovation' in the poem, Dryden asks the reader to muse at the distortions that can be made of such language."[39] In fact, when Dryden introduces the catalog of malcontents as being "not Wicked, but Seduc'd by Impious Arts," he may well have had in mind as one of those "Impious Arts" the rhetorically powerful and "impious" abuse of typology (line 498). Reedy concludes that "the use of typology in political contexts seems to be not only the medium of *Absalom and Achitophel* but also part of the message" (88). By questioning the political application of typology, Dryden was, in fact, questioning a standard mode of political engagement. Portraying the Whigs as poor readers—self-interested typologists who were willing to distort Holy Scriptures in order to make their case—was a way of calling into question any sort of opposition to the crown, since typology would naturally be used in constructing political arguments.

Not surprisingly, the attacks on *Absalom and Achitophel* work to reverse the charge, portraying Dryden as the fanatically misled exegete. In a direct response to Dryden's portrayal of Shaftesbury, Henry Care reverses the terms of the poem by portraying Dryden as a mad dog in *Towser the Second, A Bull Dog* (London, 1681). Referring to Dryden as "Towser the Second" was a way of accusing him of partisanship by linking him with Roger L'Estrange, who had been dubbed "Towser" by Whigs irritated by his seizure of pamphlets as surveyor of the press and by his work as a propagandist (Winn, *Dryden*, 343). Caricaturing Dryden as a mad dog was also a way of suggesting that it was Dryden and not Shaftesbury who had abused exegetical modes:

> Like a mad Dog he runs about the Streets
> Snarling and Biting every one he meets.
> The other day he met our Royal Charles,
> And his two Mistresses, and at them Snarles.
> Then falls upon the Ministers of State
> Treats them all A-la-mode de Billingsgate:
> But most of all, the glory of our gown,
> He must be bark't at, Drivil'd, pist upon.[40]

Dangerous to the king and overcome by his own exegetical frenzy, Dryden is revealed here as alternately dangerous or mad.

Poetical Reflections, published on 14 December 1681, similarly attacks Dryden's "National Libel" in characterizing the king "as a broad figure of scandalous inclinations" (sig. B1r) and in "darken[ing]" the "sanctity" of King David (sig. B1r–B1v). Christopher Nesse's *A Key (With the Whip)*, which first appeared on 13 January 1682, also took issue with Dryden's debasement of typology: "The Type of Christ he makes our Charles's Type, / Yet draws foul Figures of the Antitype; / As if embracing Queans o're all his Land, / Instead of's Royal Queen with's Royal Hand" (page 18). No prosodist himself, Nesse contends, "Had Plutarch made such parallels as This / Fond Poet doth, he had deserv'd an Hiss" (Nesse, 18). Point by point, Nesse attacks Dryden's "Jewish Allegories" (p. 17). He objects, for example, to Dryden's admittedly blunt reference to Queen Catherine's barrenness: "Next is our English Queen the Poets Scorn, / Because she's Barren, She must be forlorn: / . . . / How dare this black-mouth'd wretch blaspheme a Queen, / To' Afflict th' Afflicted base hath ever been" (p. 19). Nesse also finds the comparison between Monmouth and Absalom to be objectionable, and he complains, "Oh thou Incongruous Fool, what parallel / That's Congruous 'twixt these two canst thou tell?" (p. 19). Privately, one writer articulated his objection to Dryden's extended parallel by handwriting in the margins of his copy of the text, next to the opening ten lines: "The Poet an Atheist Exceeding Lucretius."[41] Although this writer expresses shock at Dryden's irreverent use of typology, others saw Dryden's assault on typology as a way of limiting who could engage in political debate.

Other responses to *Absalom and Achitophel* try not only to reverse Dryden's damage but also to label him as mercenary. Samuel Pordage borrowed much of Dryden's language and imagery to reverse the terms of Dryden's poem in *Azaria and Hushai*.[42] In Pordage's poem, Monmouth is the hero who, aided by Shaftesbury, counsels the people to stay loyal to their king. Exclusion is arrived at obliquely, allowing Monmouth to succeed lawfully. In fact, Pordage's Shaftesbury (Hushai) cautions Monmouth to wait for a lawful way to become king:

> You should without a Crown for ever live,
> Rather than get it by the Peoples Lust,
> Or purchase it by ways that are unjust.
> David your Ancestor, from whom you spring,
> Would never by Rebellion be made King;
> But long in Gath a Warring Exile stay'd,
> Till for him God a *lawful* way had made. (emphasis mine; p. 17)

Pordage's Shaftesbury maintains a reverent attitude toward the Old Testament patriarchs that leads him to do the right thing. The villain of Pordage's poem, then, is not Shaftesbury but the poet laureate, Shimei:

> *Shimei* the Poet Laureate of that Age,
> The falling Glory of the *Jewish* Stage,
> Who scourg'd the Priest, and ridicul'd the Plot,
> Like common men must not be quite forgot.
> Sweet was the Muse that did his wit inspire,
> Had he not let his hackney Muse to hire:
> But variously his knowing Muse could sing,
> Could *Doeg* praise, and could blaspheme the King:
> The bad make good, good bad, and bad make worse,
> Bless in Heroicks, and in Satyrs curse.
> Shimei to *Zabed's* praise could tune his Muse,
> And Princely *Azaria* could abuse.
> *Zimri* we know he had no cause to praise,
> Because he dub'd him with the name of *Bays*.
> Revenge on him did bitter Venome shed,
> Because he tore the Lawrel from his head;
> Because he durst with his proud Wit engage,
> And brought his Follies on the publick Stage.
> Tell me, *Apollo*, for I can't divine,
> Why Wives he curs'd, and prais'd the Concubine;
> Unless it were that he had led his life
> With a teeming Matron ere she was a Wife:

Or that it best with his dear Muse did sute,
Who was for hire a very Prostitute. (p. 29)

In Pordage's poem, Dryden's considerable talents—his "sweet" muse—are
wasted by his mercenary ways. His skill is suggested by the claim that he can
"the bad make good, good bad, and bad make worse," but Pordage makes clear
that Dryden's motives are merely mercenary: he lets "his hackney Muse to
hire." By the end of the verse paragraph, Pordage draws a connection—made
frequently in the attacks on Dryden—between his prostituted muse and his
wife, who according to Pordage was a "teeming Matron" before she married
Dryden.

The charge that Dryden was mercenary, which was repeated throughout
these attacks, was a way of attacking Dryden's indeterminacy. Dryden's detrac-
tors argued that his wit—his ironic sensibility and verbal dexterity—could be
used to argue for or against any position, regardless of its intrinsic merit.
Ironically, these attacks complain that Dryden was not sufficiently partisan.
The anonymous *Panegyric on the Author of Absalom and Achitophel*, published
on 19 December, considers the dangers of wit, which could be used to argue for
or against any position with equal ease:

How vast an Orb has a Poetick Soul?
Grasps all from East to West, and Pole to Pole.
Its warbling Voice, Right, Wrong, Truth, Falshood Sings,
Tuned to all States, Religions, Gods or Kings.
Oh Wit how wide is thy Circumference?
Where thy Attractive Center's Bread and Pence. (lines 78–82)

Worried that Dryden's irony signaled a sort of invulnerability to the pull of
party politics, and that Dryden might be perfectly willing to use his powers to
support any argument given a sufficient financial motive, writers like this one
and Samuel Pordage engaged in antirhetorical arguments that had long been in
fashion. Thomas Hobbes had considered rhetoric "that faculty, by which we
understand what will serve our turn concerning any subject to win belief in the
reader"; similarly, these writers argued that Dryden's ease in constructing arguments for any occasion signaled a willingness to sell his wit for profit.[43]

Finally, readers were alarmed by the success of Dryden's satire. Thus, the
preface to *Poetical Reflections* objects to Dryden's use of his wit as a form of
"Hangman's Ax" which "his Muse does in effect take upon her to hasten" (sig.
B1v). The desire for commercial gain has, according to the author of *A Panegyric*, led Dryden to "despise" "All Laws and Bounds" "And raign the Prince o'
th' Air, in which it flyes" (lines 97–98). Just as Dryden had suggested the

dangers of typological reading, respondents to *Absalom and Achitophel* countered that wit, too, had both political and sociological dangers. Dryden's wit was, in fact, perceived as defying sociological laws. The irritated comparison of Dryden's satirical force to a political hangman's axe acutely reflects the threat Dryden posed to noblemen who deeply resented his unequivocal intrusion into their traditional sphere of literary and political activity. That a gentleman poet could succeed at disparaging an earl and a duke signaled a new age in which the professional writer's rhetorical skill supplanted the nobility's traditional hold over the world of letters.[44]

Dryden's rhetorical power threatened his contemporaries because he was transforming the literary landscape and insisting on new modes of reading. Whether he wrote a heroic play that could be read straightforwardly even as it parodied its genre, or a satire that both defended and criticized the king, Dryden forced readers to experience the tug of alternative opinions, first in literary affairs, and later in political affairs. Although *The Conquest of Granada* and *Absalom and Achitophel* are the most clear embodiments of Dryden's practice, they represent an interest in the experiential nature of reading that can be found throughout his work. Dryden had recognized the emergence of a growing reading public for whom the public sphere was shaped increasingly through print controversy, and he designed his work so as to immerse his readers in that controversy and familiarize them with alternative points of view. His willingness to court his readers' resistance—to elicit the angry responses we have examined—signals his awareness of a readership for whom reading itself was more closely tied to a public sphere of ephemeral controversy than to more conservative efforts at assimilating fixed, durable meaning. That he understood his readers perhaps better than they understood themselves did not, clearly, heighten their appreciation of him. If, then, Dryden defines his age—and he surely does—it is not because he represents it in any simple or direct way. Rather, he deployed his irony to unsettle his readers' comfortable habits of reading: in doing so, he not only recognized the existence of a new emerging readership; he helped to shape it, ironically, by eliciting his readers' resistance.

Notes

1. William Ramesey, *The Gentlemans Companion* (London, 1672), 129.
2. See Cedric Reverand, *Dryden's Final Poetic Mode: The Fables* (Philadelphia: University of Pennsylvania Press, 1988), and David Bywaters, *Dryden in Revolutionary England* (Berkeley: University of California Press, 1991).
3. James Anderson Winn, *John Dryden and His World* (New Haven: Yale University Press, 1987), 325.
4. Winn, *John Dryden and His World*, 326; Paul Hammond, *John Dryden: A*

Literary Life (New York: St. Martin's, 1991), 85; Charles E. Ward, *The Life of John Dryden* (Chapel Hill: University of North Carolina Press, 1961), 143–44.

5. Thomas Shadwell, *The Virtuoso*, ed. Marjorie Hope Nicolson (Lincoln: University of Nebraska Press, 1966), I.i 258.

6. *The Works of John Dryden*, ed. H. T. Swedenberg et al. (Berkeley: University of California Press, 1978), 4:59. All subsequent citations are to this edition and will be placed within the text.

7. William Congreve, ed., *The Dramatick Works of John Dryden*, 6 vols. (London, 1717), 1: sig. A8r.

8. Thomas Shadwell, *Satyr to His Muse* (London, 1682), 4.

9. Cited in Emmett Avery and Arthur Scouten, *The London Stage, 1660–1700: A Critical Introduction.* (Carbondale: Southern Illinois University Press, 1968), cli.

10. Overviews of attacks on Dryden begin with Edmond Malone's biographical study of Dryden in the first volume of *The Critical and Miscellaneous Prose Works of John Dryden* (London, 1800). Sir Walter Scott's *The Life of Dryden* in *The Works of John Dryden* (Edinburgh, 1882) and George Saintsbury's *John Dryden* (New York: Harper & Brothers, 1901) also trace these attacks. The only study that focuses exclusively on these attacks, however, is Hugh Macdonald's excellent "The Attacks on Dryden," *Essays and Studies by Members of the English Association*, vol. 21 (Oxford: Clarendon Press, 1936), 41–74. More recently, Harold Love has commented in passing on the antipathy directed at Dryden in an interesting article, "Shadwell, Rochester, and the Crisis of Amateurism," *Restoration* 20.2 (fall 1996): 199–234.

11. Roland Barthes, *S/Z: An Essay*, trans. Richard Miller (New York: Farrar, Straus and Giroux, 1974): 41, 44. Barthes distinguishes between "irony" and "multivalence" by suggesting that "multivalence" is less determinate than irony. For Barthes, irony presents two meanings, one of which cancels the other out. For the purposes of this essay, it is helpful to consider a broader definition of the word "irony" in which multiple meanings are presented with no clear "signposts" attributing authority to one meaning over others.

12. William Bowman Piper, "The Invulnerability of Poetic Experience," *South Central Review* 4.1 (1987): 11–23.

13. This claim is meant to complicate Roger Chartier's claim that "reading, by definition, is rebellious and vagabond." See *The Order of Books* (Stanford, Calif.: Stanford University Press, 1992), viii. In Dryden's case, writing, too, can be seen as "rebellious and vagabond" in its consciousness of the experiential nature of reading and in its indeterminacy.

14. Mary Evelyn, 29 May 1660, *Diary and Correspondence of John Evelyn, F.R.S.*, ed. William Bray (London: Routledge, 1906): 739–40.

15. Anne T. Barbeau, *The Intellectual Design of John Dryden's Plays* (New Haven: Yale University Press, 1970), 114.

16. Michael Alssid, *Dryden's Rhymed Heroic Tragedies: A Critical Study of the Plays and of their Place in Dryden's Poetry*, 2 vols. (Austria: Institute für Englische Sprache und Literatur, 1974), 1:192. Derek Hughes offers a compromise position worth investigating. For him, *The Conquest of Granada* reveals "love and heroism [to be] chimerical and destructive of ideals, bewitching their adherents with infinite dreams but betraying them into impotence and self-destruction." See Derek Hughes, *Dryden's Heroic Plays* (Lincoln: University of Nebraska Press, 1981), 114.

17. *The Dramatic Works of Roger Boyle*, ed. William Smith Clark, 2 vols. (Cambridge: Harvard University Press, 1937), 1:25.

18. D. W. Jefferson, "Aspects of Dryden's Imagery," *Dryden's Mind and Art*, ed. Bruce King (Edinburgh: Oliver and Boyd, 1969), 27.

19. John Dryden, *The Conquest of Granada* (*Works* 11: 157–58); George Villiers, Duke of Buckingham, *The Rehearsal*, ed. D. E. L. Crane (Durham: University of Durham, 1976), 48. All subsequent citations are to this edition and will be placed within the text.

20. Bruce King, *Dryden's Major Plays* (New York: Barnes & Noble, 1966), 2. King argues that Dryden's heroic plays "are a form of satire: that is, the values and sentiments of the characters are often humorous or ironic" (2). Much of my article develops King's ideas, qualifying them by adding that Dryden was parodying genre as much as he was satirizing current ideas and that his interest in addressing an audience broader than the court circle led him to allow for "straight" as well as parodic readings of the heroic plays. See *Dryden's Major Plays*, 59–81. Alan Fisher addresses the play's interest in paradox. See "Daring to be Absurd: The Paradoxes of *The Conquest of Granada*," *Studies in Philology* 73 (1976): 414–39. Another treatment of the play's generic complexity, different from the one I present here, can be found in James Winn's "Heroic Song: A Proposal for a Revised History of English Theatre and Opera, 1656–1711," *Eighteenth-Century Studies* 30 (1997): 113–37.

21. Derek Hughes, *Dryden's Heroic Plays*, 1–21 and 79–117.

22. Four discuss *The Conquest of Granada* directly. These are Richard Leigh's *The Censure of the Rota* (Oxford, 1673), *The Friendly Vindication of Mr. Dryden from the Censure of the Rota* (Cambridge, 1673), Charles Blount's *Mr. Dreyden Vindicated, In a Reply to the Friendly Vindication of Mr. Dreyden* (London, 1673), and *A Description of the Academy of the Athenian Virtuosi* (London, 1673). Five others target Dryden and his success at heroic drama generally. They are *Remarques on the Humours and Conversations of the Town* (London, 1673), *Remarks upon Remarques: Or, A Vindication of the Conversations of the Town* (London, 1673), *Reflexions on Marriage* (London, 1673), *Raillerie a la Mode Consider'd; Or the Supercilious Detractor* (London, 1673), and William Ramesey's *Conjugium Conjurgium* (London, 1673).

23. Richard Leigh, *The Censure of the Rota* (Oxford, 1673), 3.

24. William Ramesey, *Conjugium Conjurgium, Or, some Serious Considerations on Marriage* (London, 1673), 61.

25. *Remarques on the Humours and Conversations of the Town* (London, 1673), 36.

26. *Aubrey's Brief Lives*, ed. Oliver Lawson Dick (Ann Arbor: University of Michigan Press, 1957), 157.

27. Blount, *Mr. Dreyden Vindicated*, 6. See also *The Friendly Vindication* (London, 1673).

28. *Remarks upon Remarques: Or, a Vindication of the Conversations of the Town* (London, 1673), 56.

29. Joseph Arrowsmith, *The Reformation* (London, 1673), 47–48.

30. Edward Ravenscroft, *The Careless Lovers: A Comedy* (London, 1673), sig. A1ʳ, lines 1–4.

31. *Raillerie a-la-Mode Consider'd: or the Supercilious Detractor* (London, 1673), 43–44.

32. Wilmer G. Mason, "The Annual Output of Wing-Listed Titles, 1649–1684," *Library* 29 (1974): 219–20. See also Paul Hammond, *John Dryden*, 93.

33. George Saintsbury noted that the "frantic rage which Dryden's satire produced in his opponents" resulted from a certain coolness at the center of his scorn. This essay argues that the "coolness" Saintsbury mentions results from Dryden's ironic detachment. See George Saintsbury, *Dryden* (New York: Harper & Brothers, 1901), 76.

34. Printed responses include the following: Henry Care, *Towser the Second, A Bull-Dog* (London, 1681); *Poetical Reflections on a Late Poem Entituled, Absalom and Achitphel* (London, 1681); *A Panegyrick On the Author of Absalom and Achitophel* (London, 1681); Christopher Nesse, *A Whip for the Fools Back* (1681); Christopher Nesse, *A Key (With the Whip) To Open the Mystery & Iniquity of the poem called Absalom and Achitophel* (London, 1682); *Absalom's IX Worthies; Or, a Key to a late Book or Poem, Entituled A.B. & A.C.*; Samuel Pordage, *Azaria and Hushai* (London, 1682); and Elkanah Settle, *Absalom Senior: Or, Achitophel Transpros'd* (London, 1682).

Printed keys (some of which served as responses) included *Absalom and Achitophel. A Poem. The Key* (London?, n.d.); *The Second Part of A & A*, which provided keys to both parts; Christopher Nesse's *A Key (With the Whip) To Open the Mystery & Iniquity of the Poem Called Absalom and Achitophel* (London, 1682); and *Absalom's IX Worthies: Or, A Key to a late Book or Poem* [no imprint].

Additionally, a surprisingly high number of extant copies of the poem have keys written in by hand. For example, manuscript annotations can be found in the following Folger Library copies of *Absalom and Achitophel* D2212; 2216; D2216. The following annotated copies of *Absalom and Achitophel* exist at the Bodleian Library: Vet. A3 c. 76; Malone G.1. 19; AA 73(12) Art; Ashm. G 16(2); Mason H 185. Manuscript annotations also appear on copies of the printed responses to the poem. See, for example, *Absalom Senior* (Folger Library S2652) or the following copies of Buckingham's *The Rehearsal*: Bodleian Library: Mal. 123(1); Vet. A4f. 1904. Some of these manuscript annotations may have been added after the controversy, but many resemble late seventeenth-century manuscript. I plan on discussing these marginal annotations more comprehensively elsewhere.

35. Phillip Harth, *Pen for a Party: Dryden's Tory Propaganda in Its Contexts* (Princeton, N.J.: Princeton University Press, 1993), 102. Harth's careful scholarship has contributed richly to our understanding of Dryden's rhetorical strategies. This article is meant not to contradict Harth's learned argument but to augment it by suggesting that in addition to being an expert polemicist Dryden was also always interested in expanding and complicating the experiential act of reading.

36. Howard Weinbrot, "'Nature's Holy Bands,' *Absalom and Achitophel*: Fathers and Sons, Satire and Change," *Critical Essays on John Dryden*, ed. James A. Winn (New York: G. K. Hall, 1997), 141. Weinbrot quotes Alan Roper, *Dryden's Poetic Kingdoms* (New York: Barnes & Noble, 1965), 185–86.

37. Larry Carver has argued that the poem's publication on the anniversary of Elizabeth's accession day "provided Dryden the occasion not only to uphold but to praise the patriarchal ordering of society," which he did by defending Charles in *Absalom and Achitophel* (37). I would like to augment Carver's interpretation by suggesting, as I do within this essay, that Dryden's purposes are always multiple rather than single. See "Absalom and Achitophel and the Father Hero," *The English Hero, 1660–1800*, ed. Robert Folkenflik (Newark: University of Delaware Press, 1982), 35–45.

38. Paul Korshin, *Typologies in England, 1650–1820* (Princeton: Princeton University Press, 1982), 70.

39. Gerard Reedy, S.J., *The Bible and Reason: Anglicans and Scripture in Late Seventeenth-Century England* (Philadelphia: University of Pennsylvania Press, 1985), 88.

40. Henry Care, *Towser the Second, A Bull-Dog* [no imprint], lines 33–40. Narcissus Luttrell dated his copy of this poem 10 December 1681.

41. This heavily annotated copy of *Absalom and Achitophel* can be found in the Folger Shakespeare Library, Washington, D.C. See D2212.

42. Samuel Pordage, *Azaria and Hushai* (London, 1682); rpt. *Anti-Achitophel* (1682), *Three Verse Replies to Absalom and Achitophel by John Dryden*, ed. Harold Whitmore Jones (Gainesville, Fla.: Scholar's Facsimiles & Reprints, 1961).

43. Thomas Hobbes, *The Art of Rhetoric* (1637), *The English Works of Thomas Hobbes*, ed. Molesworth, 6:424.

44. Although Harold Love only discusses Dryden as a contrast to Shadwell, he makes interesting points about the threat Dryden posed to members of the nobility like Buckingham. See Harold Love, "Shadwell, Rochester, and the Crisis of Amateurism," *Restoration* 20.2 (fall 1996): 199–234.

Afterword

Records of Culture

STEPHEN ORGEL

The revolution in modern bibliographical studies has in large measure been effected through a willingness to notice what had been unnoticeable, to find evidence in the hitherto irrelevant; so that, for example, habits of reading, marginalia, and traces of ownership become as central to the nature of the book as format and typography, watermarks, and chain lines. The history of the book, we are coming to realize, is not simply a history of print technology; more important, the history of any particular book does not conclude with its publication. The fact that this collection focuses on readers, booksellers, and collectors rather than on printers and publishers, on bindings and inscriptions rather than on foul papers, copy texts, scribes, and compositors, is indicative of how far we have come from the bibliographical world of Greg and Bowers. The print revolution as it is presented here was, in fact, a reading revolution, a revolution not of technology but of dissemination and reception. I am flattered to be asked to write a concluding word, and rather than attempting to summarize a rich and various collection, would like instead to follow out a few lines of thought that these essays have prompted.

The early modern printed book could be a monument, like the Gutenberg Bible, the Nuremberg Chronicle, or the *Hypnerotomachia*; but it could also be, and much more often was, mercurially transient. Ephemera, indeed, were what kept printers in business. While the typesetting slowly proceeded on the monuments of early printing, the same presses were turning out innumerable broadsheets, pamphlets, decrees, edicts, proclamations, prayers, calendars; and a few decades later, ballads, accounts of battles, festivals, funerals, lurid stories—these paid the bills. During times of crisis and debate polemical pamphlets filled the bookstalls in huge numbers, and were swiftly replaced by the replies they generated. Those leading up to the English Civil War, discussed by Ann Hughes and Michael Mendle, were characteristically unstable, full of changes of mind, often sent to the press incomplete, often attacked or refuted before they were even published. They were also almost instantly outdated; for the publisher, indeed, this was their greatest virtue, their creation of a continuing market for instantaneous refutation. The book in such cases was less a product than a process, part of an ongoing dialectic—as Hughes says, not a record of events, but events in themselves.

The radically unstable polemical press was not, however, a mid-seventeenth-century innovation; I do not believe that Hughes and Mendle mean to suggest that it was, but their concentration on the 1640s might give that impression. The Lutheran revolution a century earlier had been similarly fought through printing. The innovation, as both writers observe, was the decision to treat the myriad of ephemera as history, the fact that, for the first time, somebody considered instantly obsolete pamphlets worth collecting and preserving, and thus created a market, and thereby a value, for them, and an archive for us. Survival in this case depends on the collector—it is not printing that effects continuity and promises permanence, but connoisseurship and bibliophily. These are, however, largely antithetical to the printers' interests, which are precisely in the ephemeral character of their production, the rapidity of its transformation from irresistible to worthless, its almost instant obsolescence. What is new is the connoisseurship of the ephemeral. The innovation is in readers, not publishers: the agent of change is not the press but its audience. It is worth reminding ourselves that scarcely a century earlier even the monuments of incunabula were considered by the great collectors to be vulgar products. In the age of Aldus Manutius and Anton Koberger, the Duke of Urbino's factor notoriously praised his master for refusing shelf space in his magnificent library to printed books.

If connoisseurship is not a constant, neither is reading itself. Peter Stallybrass's fascinating essay charts a history of modes of attention. The transition from roll to codex, in his reading, is a transition from continuous to discontinuous reading—the history of the book, as he puts it, is the history of the bookmark—and the bible is his central example. The material reality of the Torah, a double scroll, would seem to preclude a discontinuous reading; it is all but impossible to read the book any other way than consecutively. And yet the rabbis, over many centuries, produced a commentary that demanded the most discontinuous of readings, a code of ethics that depended on the constant comparison of widely separated passages; they assumed that the scripture was amenable to any amount of reordering and recontextualization. The Christian bible, through its narrative structure, at least, seems no less to demand consecutive reading: it runs from Genesis to Apocalypse, beginning at the beginning and ending with, or even a little after, the end. But the material history of the sacred texts positively inhibits such a reading. "Scripture," as Locke memorably puts it, "crumbles into verses, which quickly turn into independent aphorisms." And Stallybrass moves on to show how, increasingly, the bible looks less and less like a whole continuous work, more and more like a compilation of exerptible fragments; and shows particular readers reading it as such. Anne Askew, in an age before bibles had numbered verses or concordances, was nevertheless able to cite chapter and verse to her ecclesiastical interrogators; clearly she read not only for the edification of her soul, but to gain precisely this sort of authority over the sacred text, the authority to shape it to her arguments. A less inflammatory but equally telling example is Lady Grace Mildmay, "who began her autobiography . . . by extolling a reading of the bible as continuous narrative," but in actual practice, as Mildmay herself says, "did read a chapter in the books of Moses, . . . another in the Epistles to the end of Revelation," and so forth.

The history Stallybrass elegantly describes has, as he indicates, some curious consequences for modern notions of the norms of reading, a transition not only to the Enlightenment, but to modernity; but if we press on Locke's assumption that continuity ought to be the norm—that, in effect, the thousand-year tradition of discontinuous reading, the very tradition presumed by the invention of the codex, is nothing but a childish error—we find ourselves confronting a quite unrecognizable form of literacy. For example, is Lady Grace Mildmay's practice really an example of discontinuous reading? Perhaps, confronted with her duplicity, she would invoke a temporal defense: certainly she has read through her bible from beginning to end, but that is not the only way to read the bible. Now she is returning to her favorite parts, or to those sections that will provide the wisdom to enable her to negotiate her present trials. Analogously, even those of us who would insist that a Dickens novel cannot be read in any way except consecutively (who would disagree?), will surely also agree that readers are entitled to go back and reread their favorite chapters—or even to read chapters of novels they have never read—without concerning themselves with what comes before or after: who wants to plough through *The Old Curiosity Shop* just to understand what Oscar Wilde found so irresistibly funny about the death of Little Nell?

Moreover, we might press the point and demand that Locke explain what is so self-evidently good about consecutive reading. It is certainly an essential mode of attention if we are undertaking to follow a narrative, or a logical argument. But historically, reading has always had many other ends. Suppose we are reading for wisdom? Then the extraction of dicta might very well be our primary purpose, and separable nuggets of philosophy would take precedence over narrative or logical coherence. Consider the history of the "ut pictura poesis" crux in Horace's *Ars Poetica*. Sir Philip Sidney, following a tradition of many centuries, took it to mean that poetry and painting had essential qualities in common, that poetry was "a speaking picture"; this assumption, with Horace's authority behind it, informs a great deal of Renaissance aesthetic theory. If we read Horace's dictum in context, however, we will find that it means nothing of the sort. All it says is that just as some paintings are designed to be viewed from afar, and need not be scrupulous about detail, and some are miniatures designed to be closely scrutinized, and must be composed with the most meticulous attention to detail, so it is with poetry. The only similarity claimed for the two arts has to do with the necessity for both poet and artist to keep the purpose of the work of art in mind.

Does this mean that Sidney was ignorant of the context? Had he not read the rest of the sentence? No doubt he had; but in his defense, we might observe that the phrase as a dictum actually makes much better sense than the phrase in context. Horace seems to argue that some poems need not be as carefully written as other poems. Can this be right? What poems? Big poems versus small poems, epics on the one hand and lyrics on the other? Did Virgil not need to worry about details? (It is difficult to come up with untendentious examples—the Roman equivalents of rap lyrics and sonnets perhaps?) Whatever Horace meant, however, surely the only way to claim that Sidney's reading of this passage is incorrect is to argue that Horace did not mean it to be read that way. This is doubtless true, but I also doubt that anyone involved in this collection intends to limit the possibilities of reading to those defined by the author's intentions—an especially problematic move when the example is the bible.

And of course there are many books, even now, that we do not read consecutively: dictionaries, encyclopedias, almanacs, handbooks of all sorts. In fact, most modern books of information depend for their usefulness not on their narrative coherence or even on the persuasiveness of their argument, but on the capaciousness of their indexes; we go to them to find primarily what we are looking for, and the coherence in this case is that of the reader's narrative, not the author's. The model here is unchanged from the one described by Randall Ingram in his discussion of seventeenth-century books of epigrams, in which the reader is urged, and expected, to construct the book.

If readers construct books, books also construct readers. Questions of presentation and format recur throughout these essays: what is on the title page, what guides are there to the material, what sort of information is the potential buyer conceived to require to turn him—or her: the presence of women throughout these essays is notable—into a reader? To begin with, not necessarily the author's name, which for a modern reader would be a primary selling point. Despite the fact that by 1609 Shakespeare's name was sufficiently famous to sell a number of books with which in fact he had no connection, most of the early quartos of his own plays were issued anonymously. The appeal of published drama was more likely to be that of the theatrical company, or a particularly impressive performing venue—for example, a play will be presented to readers as performed by the King's Men before the King's Majesty at Whitehall. As David Kastan observes, there is no reason to assume that the publishers of Shakespeare's early quartos even knew that he was the author—the author's name was largely irrelevant. In contrast, Milton's incendiary pamphlets appeared anonymously for just the opposite reason: because the author's name was all too relevant; and as Sabrina Baron notes, Milton's authorship is acknowledged (by initials, to be sure) only in the pirated editions.

If a spurious anonymity sold the pamphlets, however, Milton's poems, published within a year of the divorce tracts, positively traded on his name and authority: *Poems of Mr John Milton, Both English and Latin, Compos'd at several times. Printed by his true Copies.* Let us pursue the point a little further: the interplay of genre, format, and ascription is complex. Shakespeare's play quartos are anonymous, but his name, like Milton's, is an indispensable part of his poetry: *Venus and Adonis, Lucrece, The Passionate Pilgrim,* the *Sonnets,* are all explicitly (though not always correctly) ascribed to him; and as Kastan points out, for early readers, *Venus and Adonis* was by far his best-known work. The fact that the poetry is not included in the great folio of 1623 is simply a matter of intellectual property: the folio collected what the King's Men owned or could acquire the rights to do. But it is also to the point that the company apparently had no interest in acquiring the rights to Shakespeare's best-sellers, the nondramatic poetry. What would Shakespeare's career look like if the model for the 1623 folio had really been what we are always told it was, the Jonson folio of 1616? For the two books, in fact, are crucially different: Jonson's is *Workes,* and includes his lyric poems, epigrams ("the ripest of my studies"), and masques—the startling thing, for Jonson's contemporaries, was that the plays were included at all, plays could be considered "works." For Jonson, the poems were essential—it was the poems that enabled the inclusion of the plays. But *Shakespeare's Comedies, Histories & Tragedies* are not works; they are, unashamedly, nothing but plays, and their appearance as such in a folio format is probably the most audacious part of the enterprise.

The genres in the Renaissance have their separate rules and conventions, and those that deal with information look quite different from imaginative or polemical works. Christopher Grose is surely correct to refer to Burton's *Anatomy of Melancholy* as encyclopedic, but consulting it for information is a daunting task at best. What is the appropriate format for an encyclopedia? Burton supplied the book with an elaborate synoptic outline, but this gives little help, not least because it includes no page references. This is a case where an encyclopedic index would seem called for. The 1621 first edition has none. The 1624 second edition was "corrected and augmented"—the improvements involved a promotion from quarto to folio and a good deal of new material, but also the removal of one critical piece of information from the encyclopedic volume: Burton's name, which now appears nowhere in the book. An index is now provided, but it is singularly erratic and vague: characteristic entries under *A* include "All are melancholy" and "All beautiful parts attractive in love"; under *B*, "Best site of an house" and "Black eyes best." Though bugloss wine is said in the text to be effective in curing leprosy, neither bugloss nor leprosy is indexed. Examples could be multiplied ad infinitum: what are readers expected to use this index for? Nor, as the work went through its many revisions, was the index revised: the seventh edition of 1660 has the same index as the second. The *Anatomy* is in fact fairly unusual in this respect: Renaissance encyclopedias often have splendid indexes. G. P. Valeriano's *Hieroglyphica*, first published in 1556, was in its subsequent editions provided with an increasingly detailed analytic index, which was placed before the text, not at the end, and was clearly felt to constitute a significant part of the book's value. Similarly, Philemon Holland's translation of Pliny's encyclopedic natural history, published in 1601 under the title *The Historie of the World*, justifies its claim to compendiousness in part through the inclusion of a very elaborate and genuinely usable index. This was, however, by no means an invariable practice, and the English seem to have had more resistance to it than Continental publishers: for example, both that classic repository of early modern knowledge *Batman upon Bartholome* and Plutarch's great biographical compendium, the *Lives*, in Sir Thomas North's translation, were issued without indexes. It is probably the halfhearted quality of Burton's effort that is most striking.

Moreover, as the example of Burton reveals, even when books acknowledge the value of an index, there is often considerable uncertainty about the proper form for the reference—that is, about how readers will construe what they are looking for. Halle's *Chronicle*, for example, indexes Anne Bullen under *Anne* and Stephen Gardiner under *Stephen*, and groups all its various abbots and bishops under *Abbot* and *Bishop* respectively. A stranger case is found in Thomas Wilson's *Arte of Rhetorick*, which in its 1567 edition includes an index keyed to the book's folio numbers. The same index is reprinted in the 1584 edition, which, however, is foliated with *page* numbers, not folios, rendering the index basically useless. Why then is it included? Presumably simply because the format seems to require it. No wonder William Sherman found so many books with marginal subject headings supplied by their owners.

How much, and how many kinds of things, readers add to their books appears especially clearly in these essays, and bibliography must come to terms with the reader as an essential element in the history of the book—and that means coming to terms with the marginal as in a real sense central. The fact that people commonly wrote in their books is something that tends to infuriate modern collectors and librarians. But inscriptions constitute a significant dimension of the book's history; and one of the strangest phenomena of modern bibliophilic and curatorial psychology is the desire for pristine copies of books,

books that reveal no history of ownership. This passion is always claimed to be a nineteenth-century phenomenon, but it is no such thing: modern first editions especially lose a large percentage of their value if they have an owner's name on the flyleaf. It is, indeed, not uncommon for collectors to attempt to obliterate early marginalia, as if to restore the book's virginity, to stop its history at the door of the printing house. A 1997 Quaritch catalogue lists a first edition of *Areopagitica* with two manuscript corrections, which are "very faint . . . all but washed out during some restoration in the past" (item 50 in Catalogue 1243). But the same corrections are also found in a presentation copy of the essay, and are almost certainly in Milton's hand—the price of virginity was here, ironically, the obliteration of the author.

What is a book without is history? Books are the records of culture, and not only—and sometimes not even principally—through the agency of the printing press. Books are, most basically, as Sherman correctly insists, not texts but paper; and for the owners of books the uses of paper were not exhausted, or even inhibited, by what was printed on it. Marginalia and inscriptions were the norm; it is a rare book that remained unmarked. But the marks were not invariably related to the subject—or the value—of the book. In the margins of my copy of Richard Tottel's 1553 edition of *The Fall of Princes* (even in its own time a dauntingly precious object to be using as scratch paper) a sixteenth-century child with an eerily proleptic name practiced her penmanship: "Elizabeth Taylor the beutie of Shanell Row," she carefully inscribed on the first page of text in the italic hand appropriate to ladies; and she and several other young women subsequently adorned Tottel's margins with bits of verse copied from the poem, as well as with the alphabet and the opening of the Lord's Prayer. (And what, I wonder, happened next? Did an outraged bibliophile father banish these children from his library for defacing his book? Or did he perhaps acknowledge instead that books have many uses, and literacy, after all, is writing as well as reading?) In a striking number of cases, seemingly important documents, things one would have thought their owners would want to file away and would need easy access to, have been inscribed on the blank pages of a book to which they have no relevance whatever. Sherman suggests that a principle of simple economy lies behind this—paper was very expensive, and using the paper in a book was cheaper than buying paper for record keeping—but I doubt that this is the whole story. For example, the Stanford library's copy of the splendid folio of Thomas Lodge's translation of Seneca's essays, 1614, contains, on the verso of its engraved title page, a handwritten deposition concerning a dispute between a landowner and the writer of the document. Clearly this is a quasi-legal testimony; it might be a dry run for the actual document, with somebody using the blank page as a piece of scratch paper, but it does not have the look of a rough draft. There are no false starts or changes of

Contributors

Jennifer Andersen teaches English at California State University, San Bernardino. She is interested in hot spots of polemic and propaganda in early modern England. Forthcoming articles examine links between Elizabethan conformity and grub street through Thomas Nashe's *Unfortunate Traveller*; Andrew Marvell's "Upon Appleton House" and the impact of civil war newsbooks; and the politics of publishing William Dugdale's *Monasticon Anglicanum* (1655).

Sabrina A. Baron, Visiting Assistant Professor of History, University of Maryland, Baltimore County, was awarded a Fulbright Scholarship in 1998. Her research interests are publishing history, news in early modern England, and the relationship between politics and literature. Recent publications include a coedited book (with Brendan Dooley) *The Politics of Information in Early Modern Europe* (2001) and *The Reader Revealed: Creating, Consuming, and Conserving Manuscript and Print*, the catalogue for an exhibition at the Folger Shakespeare Library (2001).

Anna Battigelli, Professor of English at Plattsburgh State University, is the author of *Margaret Cavendish and the Exiles of the Mind*, which was chosen as a *Choice* Outstanding Title for 1998. She is currently working on a book on John Dryden.

Lana Cable is Associate Professor of English at the University of Albany, State University of New York. Her book *Carnal Rhetoric: Milton's Iconoclasm and the Poetics of Desire* (1995) won the James Holly Hanford Award for the most distinguished book on John Milton of 1995. She is currently researching a book on metaphor and the early modern freedom of conscience debate.

Christopher Grose, Professor of English at the University of California, Los Angeles, is the author of *Milton's Epic Process* (1973) and *Milton and the Sense of Tradition* (1988). He has also coedited *Riven Unities: Authority and Experience, Self and Other in Milton's Poetry* (1993).

Heidi Brayman Hackel teaches English at Oregon State University. She has published an essay on early modern libraries in *A New History of Early English Drama* (1997) and on varieties of early modern readers in *A Companion to Shakespeare* (1999). She is completing a book entitled *Impressions from a "Scribbling Age": Readers and Reading Practices in Early Modern England.*

Ann Hughes, Professor of Early Modern History at the University of Keele, is the author of numerous studies on politics and religion under the Stuarts. Her publications include *Politics, Society, and Civil War in Warwickshire, 1620–1660* (1987), *The Causes of the English Civil War* (1991, 2nd ed., 1998), and the coedited volumes *Conflict in Early Stuart England* (1989) and *The English Civil War* (1997). She is completing a book-length study of Edwards's *Gangraena*.

Randall Ingram is Associate Professor of English at Davidson College. He specializes in English Renaissance literature, and has recently published articles in *Studies in English Literature, 1500–1900*, *Milton Studies*, and the *Journal of Medieval and Early Modern Studies*.

David Scott Kastan is Professor of English and Comparative Literature at Columbia University. He is the author of *Shakespeare and the Shapes of Time* (1982) and *Shakespeare After Theory* (1999); he has edited *A Companion to Shakespeare* (1999), as well as (with Peter Stallybrass) *Staging the Renaissance* (1991), and (with John Cox) *A New History of Early English Drama* (1997). He also serves as a general editor of the Arden Shakespeare.

Kathleen Lynch, Executive Director of the Folger Institute, has published essays on the ecclesiastical politics of *The Temple* and the dramatic festivity of *Bartholomew Fair*. Her article on "The Narrative Ventures of Agnes Beaumont" appeared in *English Literary History* in 1999.

Michael Mendle is Professor of History at the University of Alabama. He is the author of two books in the history of political thought, *Dangerous Positions* (1985) and *Henry Parker and the English Civil War* (1995); he also edited *The Putney Debates of 1647: The Army, the Levellers, and the English State* (2001). His current project, "Bottling the Air: Keeping and Finding the Seventeenth Century," is a study of the creation and recovery of historical memory.

Stephen Orgel, Jackson Eli Reynolds Professor of Humanities at Stanford University, has published widely on the political and historical aspects of Renaissance literature, theater, and art history. His most recent book is *Impersonations: The Performance of Gender in Shakespeare's England* (1996). He is the general editor of Cambridge Studies in Renaissance Literature and Culture, and of the new Pelican Shakespeare. Professor Orgel is a Fellow of the American Academy of Arts and Sciences.

Elizabeth Sauer, Professor of English at Brock University, Canada, is the author of *Barbarous Dissonance and Images of Voice in Milton's Epics* (1996). She has edited (with Janet Lungstrum) *Agonistics: Arenas of Creative Contest* (1997), as well as (with Balachandra Rajan) *Milton and the Imperial*

Vision (1999), winner of the Milton Society of America Irene Samuel Memorial Award. A SSHRCC-funded book, *Print, Performance, and the Public Sphere in Early Modern England*, is in progress, as is an edition on early women writers.

William H. Sherman, Associate Professor of English at the University of Maryland, is the author of *John Dee: The Politics of Reading and Writing in the English Renaissance* (1995) and the editor (with Peter Hulme) of *The Tempest and Its Travels* (2000). He is currently working on Renaissance marginalia, Elizabethan travel writing, and the cultures of intelligence in early modern England.

Peter Stallybrass, Professor of English at the University of Pennsylvania, has published widely on Renaissance literature and culture. He coauthored *The Politics and Poetics of Transgression* with Allon White and *Renaissance Clothing and the Materials of Memory* with Ann Rosalind Jones. He also coedited several volumes, including *Language Machines: Technologies of Literary and Cultural Production* (1997), and is an editor of the New Cultural Studies series for the University of Pennsylvania Press.

Index

Achinstein, Sharon, 20n19, 114n16, 237n1
advertisement, 12, 33, 139, 164, 174n9, 189
Allde, Edward, 36
Almack, Edward: *Fine Old Bindings*, 182
almanacs, 130, 146, 207, 285. *See also* calendars
Alssid, Michael, 264
Anabaptist, 97, 109, 112
Andersen, Jennifer, 1–20
Anderson, William, 130
Anglicanism, 12, 15, 182, 191, 244, 247, 249, 254, 256, 257
Anjou Match, 13
Annales School, 9
annotation, 2, 10, 119–21, 124, 139, 146
anonymity, 10; anonymous, 34, 220, 222–24, 285, 286
Antinomians, 106
Anti-Theatrical Campaign, 13
appropriation, 9, 177, 185
Arakelian, Paul, 256
Arber, Edward, 189
Archer, John: *Comfort for Believers*, 106–7
Ariosto, Lodovico: *Orlando Furioso*, 38
Arminian Nunnery (anon.), 185, 188
Arrowsmith, Joseph, 266, 269; *The Reformation*, 266
Arthur, Lord Anglesey, 206
Askew, Anne, 16, 69–73, 284, 286
Aston, Margaret, 63
atheism, 246–58 passim, 274
Aubrey, John, 268
authenticity, 1
authorial intention, 3, 82; authorial control, 15; authorial judgment, 16; authorial manuscript, 29, 31
authorized publication, 30; unauthorized publication, 29
authorship, 1, 169; coauthor, 25; conditions for Shakespeare, 24; as a marketing strategy, 34, 38–39; self-authorship, 254. *See also individual authors*

Bachelor, John, 16, 104, 110, 222
Bacon, Francis, 16, 82, 94n7, 131, 132, 143, 247; *Advancement of Learning*, 131–32, 137n46
Bacon, Nathaniel: *Relation of the Fearful Estate of Francis Spira*, 191
Bacon, Nicholas, 138
Baillie, Robert, 104, 106, 109
Baldwin, William: *Mirror for Magistrates*, 146
Banquet of Jests (anon.), 226
Baptist, 100–101, 104
Barker, Nicolas, 133
Barlow, William, 80
Baron, Sabrina, 14–15, 20n19, 217–42, 286
Barthes, Roland, 263
Basire, Isaac, 184
Bastwick, John, 109
Bate, John: *Mysteryes of nature, and art*, 130
Battigelli, Anna, 15–16, 261–81
Battle of Naseby, 231
Beaumont and Fletcher, 26, 227, 261
Bellany, Alastair, 3
Berridge, John, 61
Best, Paul, 107
best-seller, 99, 286
Bevington, David, 37
bible, 5, 7, 10, 44, 47–53, 60–61, 67, 127, 141–43, 148–53 passim, 179, 180, 189, 193, 283, 284; Authorized Bible, 49, 51, 63; Bishops' Bible, 51, 63, 66–68, 126; Geneva Bible, 51–53, 60–61, 63, 71–72; Septuagint, 43; "Wicked" Bible: definition of, 60
bibliophiles, 178, 182, 283, 287, 288
Birrell, T.A., 189
Blair, Ann, 7
Bland, Mark, 39n2
Blayney, Peter, 6, 27, 28, 40n7, 202

Blount, Charles, 268

Blount, Edward, 34

Blundeville, Thomas: *Exercises*, 123

Boccaccio, Giovanni: *Amorous Fiammetta*, 130–31; *Decameron*, 10, 145

Bodley, Thomas, 27

Bodley, 203, 205, 207

Boethius: *Books of Philosophical Comfort*, 145, 147

Bonner, Edmund (bishop of London), 70

book auctions, 203–12 passim

bookbinding, 12, 122, 145, 177, 178, 182–84, 189, 193, 204, 207; disbinding, 208; rebinding, 52, 122, 130; unbound, 207

book buyer, 165, 170

book closets, 142, 157n26

book history: movements in, 1–20

bookmark, 42–46 passim, 283; book-marking, 46–47

Book of Common Prayer (Church of England), 48, 52, 72, 185

Book of Homilyes, 145, 146, 147

book of hours, 46. *See also* prayer book; psalters

book owners, 138–47 passim; marks of ownership, 124, 126, 142, 145–46, 154n1, 187, 282, 288

books and licensing, 217–42

bookseller, 104, 107, 122, 163, 164, 177, 187, 220, 224, 225

bookshop, 224

bookstall, 32, 163, 166, 169

book trade, 52, 177, 189, 192; in Cambridge, 185; in London, 224, 227; Milton's connections to, 226–28

Bostock, Robert, 231

Bourdieu, Pierre, 167–68, 169, 175n17

Bowers, Fredson, 30, 282

box number, 208

Boyle, Robert, 247, 257

Boyle, Roger (Earl of Orrery), 264

Braden, Gordon, 169

Brahe, Tycho, 145, 153; *Astronomicall Conjectur*, 145

Brayman Hackel, Heidi, 11, 138–59

Breda Declaration, 243

Brinsley, John, 16, 107, 121–22; *Ludus Literarius: Or, the Grammar Schoole*, 121

British Library, 173, 203, 207, 231

broadsides, 157n17, 201, 208, 210, 282

Brome, Richard, 6; *Antipodes*, 25, 33

Buck, Thomas, 179

bugloss wine, 287

Bunyan, John, 243

Burby, Cuthbert, 32, 35–38

Burn, Edmund, 60

Burroughs, Jeremiah, 103, 107–10

Burton, Henry, 16, 97, 205

Burton, Robert, 5, 16, 80–97, 286–87; *Anatomy of Melancholy*, 80–97

Butler, James (Duke of Ormond), 272

Butter, Nathaniel, 33–34

Byrd, William: *Gradualia*, 46

Cable, Lana, 15, 243–60

calendar, 48, 282

Calvert, Giles, 16, 104

Calvinism, 52, 191

Cambridge, 177–97 passim

Campion, Edmund, Affair, 13

Care, Henry: *Towser the Second, A Bull Dog*, 273

Carlyle, Thomas, 211

Carroll, D. Allen, 36

Casas, Bartolomé de Las, 91

Casaubon, Isaac, 131–32

catalogue, 11, 14, 44, 124, 141–46, 178, 202, 205, 208, 210–12, 215n37; auction catalogues, 203–4

Catalogue of All the Recent Discourses Published Against Popery, 211

Catholicism, 47–48, 50, 60, 63, 67, 70, 192, 245, 267; anti-Catholicism, 53, 127, 143

Caxton, William: *Royal Book*, 127

censorship. *See* licensing

Cervantes, Miguel de: *Don Quixote*, 145

Chambers, E. K., 36

Chapman, Alison, 48

Charles I (king of England), 218, 222, 223, 227–29, 231–34; *Eikon Basilike*, 181–82, 184, 185

Charles II (king of England), 15, 243, 256, 261, 263, 271

Chartier, Roger, 4–5, 9, 12, 17n2, 160, 166, 172, 173, 278n13

Chaucer, Geoffrey, 261; *Canterbury Tales*, 42

Chettle, Henry, 36
Christina of Sweden, 140, 156n13
Churchyard, Thomas, 163
Cibber, Colley, 262
City (of London), 52, 106, 110, 112
civil war, 103, 190, 203, 205, 206, 209, 282
Clanchy, Michael, 7
Clarendon Code, 244, 258n3, 258n5
Clarke, Sampson, 34
Clarke, Samuel: *Golden Apples*, 112
Clarke, Sir William, 14, 16, 202–12
Clarkson, Laurence, 16, 109, 111; *Lost Sheep Found*, 111; *Pilgrimage of Saints*, 111
Clifford, Lady Anne, 11, 139, 146, 155n8
Clifford, James, 82
Cobbler's Prophecy, 38
Cobham, Robert, Lord Brooke, 205
codex, 7, 42–43, 73, 74nn3–5, 283–84
Coke, Sir John, 233
Cole, Peter, 106
Coleman, Thomas, 103
collector, 135n16, 202–26 passim, 283, 287
Collet, Mary, 182, 183
Collier, Thomas, 107
Collinson, Patrick, 48, 51, 52, 67, 102
Committee for Both Kingdoms, 231
Common Council (of London), 105, 106
commonplace, 12, 119, 139, 187, 193, 219, 226, 137n46
Commonwealth government, 225, 231
computers, 42
concordance, 52–53, 60, 72
Conditions of Christianity, 191
conformity, 191
Congregationalists, 97
Congreve, William, 3, 262, 283
connoisseurship, 122, 178
conscience, 15, 207, 243–60
conventicle, 246
Cooke, William, 202; *Speeches and Passages*, 202
Cooper, Anthony Ashley (earl of Shaftesbury), 271, 273, 275–76
copyright, 6, 28, 192, 234
copy-text, 3
corantos, 232, 234. *See also* newsbooks
Cornaro, Luigi: *Trattato de la Vita Sobria*, 192

Cornhill, 106–7
Cosens, Robert, 106–7, 110
Cosin, John, 179, 184
Cotton, Robert, 120
Council of State, 228, 231–32, 235
courts: High Commission, 192, 218
Coverdale, Miles: *Crummes of Comfort*, 150
Cowper, Sarah, 193
Creede, Thomas, 37, 40n12
Cressy, David, 9–10, 116n35
Culpeper, Cheney, 100
Culpeper, Nicholas: *Culpeper's Directory for Midwives*, 138
Cure of Hurtful Cares and Feares, 191
Curious Collection of Books and Pamphlets, 206–7
Cust, Richard, 18n10

Dagenais, John, 123
Daniel, Roger, 179, 190
Daniel, Samuel, 29, 37, 140; *Vision of the Twelve Goddesses*, 29
Danter, John, 16, 27, 35–38
Danvers, Magdalen, 190
Dare, Christopher, 69–70
Darnton, Robert, 4, 10, 17n1, 172, 232
Davenport, Cyril, 180–81, 183
Davies, John, 140, 164–65; *Wits Bedlam*, 164–65
Davis, J. Colin, 100–102, 108
Davis, Natalie Zemon, 126
Dawlman, Robert, 97
dedications, 15, 23, 29, 261
Dee, John, 11, 119, 120, 145
defenses, 109, 264
De Grazia, Margreta, 3
Dekker, Thomas: *Honest Whore*, 36
DeMaria, Robert, 127
Dent, Arthur: *Exposition on the Revelacion*, 150
Dering, Edward: *Brief Catechisme for Housholders*, 150
Dewe, Thomas, 34, 52
Dexter, Gregory, 227
diary: as evidence, 119; of Thomas Edwards, 108
dissenters, 61, 73, 255
Dobranski, Stephen B., 235, 238n9

Dolan, Frances, 144

Donne, John, 51–52, 148, 149, 153, 179, 190; *Pseudomartyr*, 148

Drake, William, 120

Drapes, Edward, 100

Drayton, Michael, 148; *Baron's Wars*, 31

Dryden, John, 15–16, 247, 261–81; *Absalom and Achitophel*, 263, 271–81; *Conquest of Granada*, 261–71; *Defense of an Essay of Dramatique Poesie*, 262; *Essay of Dramatic Poesy*, 264; *Fables*, 261; *Marriage a-la-Mode*, 261; *The Medal*, 271

Dugard, William, 235

duodecimo, 192, 209

Dury, John, 230

Eales, Jacqueline, 191

Earle, John, 67, 72

Eaton, Samuel, 110

Edwards, Thomas, 5, 8–9; *Antapologia*, 104, 107; *Gangraena*, 97–112

Egerton, Frances (Countess of Bridgewater), 11, 16, 138–59

Egerton, John (Earl of Bridgewater), 14, 203, 207, 208

Egerton, Stephen, 29, 37

Eisenstein, Elizabeth, 3, 108; *Printing Press as an Agent of Change*, 3

Elizabeth I (Queen of England), 271–72

Ellis, John, 110

encyclopedism, 7, 71, 81–85, 130, 286

Enemy to Atheisme, 146, 151

Engagement, 206

English Stock, 189–90

enthusiasm, 256, 257

epigrams, 11, 160–76, 285, 286

episcopal/episcopacy, 191, 202, 207, 246; anti-episcopal

Erasmus, Desiderius: *De Copia*, 130, 131

Erastian, 103

Euripides, 220; *Suppliant Women*, 220

Eusebius: *Ecclesiastical History*, 148

Evelyn, John, 247

Evelyn, Mary, 16, 263–64, 266, 268, 269, 270

Exchange, 106

Exclusion Crisis, 233, 275

Ezell, Margaret, 3, 11

Fanshawe, Richard, 227; *Il Pastor Fido*, 227–28

Feather, John P., 17n1

Febvre, Lucien and Martin, Henri-Jean: *Coming of the Book*, 1, 17n1

Ferdinand, Christine, 164

Ferrar, Nicholas, 12, 179–84, 192

Ferry, Ann, 187

Field, Richard, 23

Filmer, Sir Robert, 233; *Patriacha*, 233, 236

Fish, Stanley, 127

Fisher, John (Bishop of Rochester), 71

Flower, Francis, 36

flyleaf, 10, 182, 288, 289

Folger Library, 42–79 passim, 173, 177–97 passim, 203

folio, 44, 142–3; Countess of Bridgewater's folios, 147–48; 183, 204, 208; first folio, 26, 34, 35, 224, 286; second folio, 224

Foot, Mirjam, 179

Foucault, Michel, 90, 257

Fox, George, 210

Foxe, John, 8, 63, 67, 69–71, 100, 102; *Acts and Monuments*, 8, 67, 71, 100, 102

freemen, 36, 190

freethinkers, 251

freewheeling, 220

Freist, Dagmar, 20n19, 114n18

Frye, Northrop, 80, 81, 83

Fussell, Nicholas, 226, 227

Gardiner, Anne Barbeau, 264

Gardiner, S.R., 211

Garland, John of, 47

Gataker, Thomas: *Gods Eye on his Israel*, 106

gazette, 206. *See also* newsbooks

Ghent Altarpiece, 7, 46, 76n10

gilding, 184

Gill, Alexander, 225

Ginzburg, Carlo, 4, 9–10, 17n2

Glanville, Joseph, 247, 257

Globe Theater, 87

goatskin, 180, 184, 187

Godwin, William, 211

Goltzius, Hendrik, 46

Goodwin, John, 100, 104, 108–9, 205

Goodwin, Thomas, 16, 97: *Apologeticall Narration*, 104

gossip: London networks, 106

Grafton, Anthony, 7, 127, 17n1, 18n8
Greene, Robert: *Quip for an Upstart Courtier*, 149
Greenes Ghost Haunting Conie-Catchers (anon.), 144, 152
Greenhill, William, 107
Greetham, D. C., 17n1
Greg, W. W., 36, 282
Gregory, Edmund: *Historical Anatomy of Christian Melancholy*, 93
Greville, Fulke: *Tragedy of Mustapha*, 144, 149
Griffin, Dustin, 163, 166
Griffin, Edward, 227
Grose, Christopher, 7, 80–96, 286
Guildhall, 106
Gwyn, Nell, 266

Haak, Theodore, 229–30
Habermas, Jürgen, 13
Hall, Joseph: *Contemplacions*, 150
Hamburger, Philip, 237n3
Hampton, Elizabeth, 246, 247
Harflete, Henry, 162, 170–73
Harmonies, 183
Harsnett, Samuel: *Declaration of Egregious Popish Impostures*, 31
Harth, Philip, 271
Hartlib, Samuel, 16, 229–30, 234
Harvey, Christopher, 12, 16, 189, 191–93; *Synagogue*, 12
Harvey, Gabriel, 119, 120, 127
Hastings, Elizabeth (Countess of Huntingdon), 141
Hawkins, Richard: *Philaster*, 33
Hawkins, William, 105
Hayes, Thomas, 31
Heath, John, 163–64; *House of Correction*, 163
Heinlein, Michael, 121, 123–24
Helgerson, Richard, 81
Helme, Anne, 52
Helme, John, 34
Heminge, John, and Henry Condell, 24, 26
herbals, 127, 144, 146
Herbert, Edward (Lord of Cherbury), 179
Herbert, George: "The British Church," 49–50; "The Church Militant," 185; "The H. Scriptures. II," 51, 193; *Memoriae Matris*

Sacrum, 190; "Prayer I," 187; *The Temple*, 143, 177–97
Herrey, Robert, 52–53, 58; *Two Right Profitable and Fruitfull Concordances*, 52–53, 60
Herrick, Robert, 160–76; *Hesperides*, 160–61, 168, 172, 173
Heywood, Thomas, 6, 25, 33, 147, 148; *Greene's Tu quoque*, 33; *History of Women*, 147; *Rape of Lucrece*, 25
High Mass, 47
Hill, Christopher, 100–101
Hirst, Derek, 237n1, 243
Hobbes, Thomas, 210, 248–49, 251, 256, 263, 266–68, 270, 276; *Leviathan*, 210
Hobson, G. D., 183, 184
Hooker, Richard, 16, 81–83, 92, 147; *Laws of Ecclesiastical Polity*, 81–82, 147
Horace, 284–85
House of Commons' Committee on Printing, 222
Hübner, Joachim, 229
Hughes, Ann, 3, 8–9, 97–116, 282
Hughes, Derek, 266
Hull, Suzanne, 144, 154n1
Hulvey, Monique, 122
Humanism, 7, 10, 191, 193, 256
Hunt, Elizabeth, 142
Huntington Library, 10, 120, 122–33 passim, 154–59, 173, 203, 207–8
Husband, Edward, 202
Hyde, Edward (Earl of Clarendon). *See* Clarendon Code
hypertext, 42

Ile de Rhé expedition, 232
Imitacion of Christ, 150
Independents, 97, 99, 101–12
indexes, 44, 46–47, 80, 189, 285, 286, 287
Ingram, Elizabeth, 63
Ingram, Randall, 11–12, 160–76, 285
Innocents' Day, 49
inventories, 119, 138–39, 145, 154n3

Jaggard, Isaac, 34
Jaggard, John, 52
Jaggard, William, 52
Jagodzinski, Cecile M., 170, 173

James I (king of England), 80, 83, 91, 131; *Daemonologie*, 83
Jardine, Lisa, 127, 19n15
Jayne, Sears, 154
Jefferson, D. W., 265
Jesus Psalter, 36, 143, 151
Johns, Adrian, 1, 3, 8, 124, 170; *Nature of the Book*, 1, 17n2, 114n19, 176n22
Johnson, Edward, 184
Johnson, Gerald, 31
Johnson, Samuel, 80, 89, 90
Jones, Inigo, 120
Jones, John, 109
Jones, Richard Foster, 256
Jones, Thomas, 190
Jonson, Ben, 1, 6, 25, 120, 143, 175n17, 261; *Every Man Out of His Humor*, 25; *Gypsies Metamorphosed*, 144, 147, 153; *Masque of Beautie*, 140; *Masque of Queenes*, 140; *Sejanus*, 25; *Workes, The New Inne*, 143, 148, 286
Judaism: adoption of scroll, 43

Kastan, David Scott, 6, 23–41, 286
Keeble, N. H., 114n16, 243, 244
keys, 43, 280n34, 231
Kiffin, William, 109
King, Edward, 230
King's Cabinet Opened (anon.), 231
King's Men, 34, 38, 285, 286
Knox, John: *History of the Reformation*, 102
Koberger, Anton, 283
Koran, 10
Korshin, Paul, 273
Kyd, Thomas: *Spanish Tragedy*, 26

Lake, Peter, 3, 13–14
Lane, John, 224
Lanseter, John, 107, 109
Laud, William (archbishop of Canterbury), 52, 192, 218, 223, 230; Laudian, 12, 104, 191
Lawes, Henry, 225, 226, 230
lectures (London), 106
Legate, John, 190
Leigh, Richard, 267, 269; *The Censure of the Rota*, 269
leprosy, 287
L'Estrange, Roger, 16, 257, 258, 274

Leveller, 8, 97, 105, 110, 202. *See also* Lilburne
library, 11, 139–45, 179, 182, 184, 205, 206, 225
licenser, 14, 15, 104, 218, 220, 223, 224, 228–37; license, 37; licensing: 15, 104, 201; ecclesiastical and state, 217–42; unlicensed printing, 223–34, 244; prepublication, 218–37
Lilburne, John, 93, 103, 202, 207, 228; *Outcry of the young men and apprentices of London*, 228
Ling, Nicholas, 30–31, 35, 38–39, 40n12
literacy, 4, 6, 9–10, 103, 141, 166, 217, 19n2, 284, 288, 289; illiteracy, 218; in Latin, 145
Little Gidding, 12, 177–97 passim
Locke, John, 50–51, 73, 283; *Paraphrase and Notes on the Epistles of St. Paul*, 50–51
Lodge, Thomas, 288–89
London Printers Lamentacon, or, the Press opprest, and Ouerprest, 228
London Prodigall (anon.), 34
Long Parliament, 192
Love, Harold, 3, 281n44
Love Plot, 225
Lownes, Matthew, 52
Lumley, Lady Jane, 138
Luttrell, Narcissus, 14, 16, 211, 212
Lynch, Kathleen, 12, 177–97

Maguire, Laurie, 28, 40n7
Maltby, Judith, 192, 76n14
Mandeville, Sir John: *Travels of Sir John Mandeville*, 10
Manton, Thomas, 205
manuscript, 105, 107, 218, 234; army ms, 209; medieval, 123; miscellanies, 226
Manutius, Aldus, 283
Marcus, Leah S., 40n11
marginalia, 42–79 passim, 119–33 passim, 146, 161, 282, 288; margins, 120, 122, 180, 261, 274, 287
Markley, Robert, 257
Marlowe, Christopher: *Dr. Faustus*, 26
Marmion, Shakerley: *Fine Companion*, 126
Marotti, Arthur, 3, 18n4
Marprelate Controversy, 13
Marriot, John and Richard, 52
Martial, 168, 169
Martin Marpriest, 222
Martin, Henri-Jean, 1

Martson, John: *Malcontent*, 37

Marvell, Andrew, 15, 246, 247, 252–60; *Rehearsal Transprosed*, 15, 247–60 passim

Marxism, 9

Mascall, John, 107

masque, 140, 143, 286

Masson, David, 211, 242n51

Master of the Revels, 26

May, Steven, 140

May, Thomas, 231

Mayerne, Theodore, 229

McGann, Jerome, 3, 17n2

McKenzie, D. F., 2–3, 50, 17n2

McKerrow, R. B., 36

McKitterick, David, 179

McLeod, Randall, 178

Mede, Joseph, 43, 45; *Key of the Revelation*, 43–46

Mendle, Michael, 14, 201–16, 282

Menocchio, 10

Mercurius Politicus, 225, 228, 234, 235. *See also* newsbooks

Meredith, Christopher, 190

Merricke, Lady Anne, 144

Middle Ages, 6, 124

Middleton, Thomas: *The Family of Love*, 33

Milbourne, Robert, 191

Mildmay, Lady Grace, 16, 50, 73, 284

Miller, Leo, 229

Miller, William, 14, 16, 206, 207

Milton, John, 1, 14, 81, 83, 100, 140, 141, 205, 217–43, 244, 253, 254–56, 286, 288; *Areopagitica*, 15, 218–37, 288; *Colasterion*, 220; *Comus*, 225, 227, 228; *Doctrine and Discipline of Divorce*, 220, 222, 223, 224, 225, 230; *Eikonoklastes*, 225, 228; *First Defense (Defensio pro populo Anglicano)*, 235; *Judgment of Martin Bucer*, 220, 222, 225; *Of Education*, 230; "On the New Forcers of Conscience," 255; *Paradise Lost*, 83, 230; *Poems*, 226, 227, 230, 286; *Second Defense (Pro Populo Anglicano Defensio Secunda)*, 220, 228; *Ready and Easy Way*, 228; *Reason of Church Government*, 220; *Tetrachordon*, 220, 223; *Treatise of Civil Power*, 254–55

Milton Sr., John, 224, 230

missal, 7, 47

Monck, George, 209

Montaigne, Michel de, 83, 91

Montefeltro, Guidobaldo (Duke of Urbino), 283

More, Richard, 52

Morton, Thomas: *Grand Imposture of the (Now) Church of Rome*, 143, 149

Moseley, Humphrey, 16, 93, 225–28

Mowery, J. Franklin, 187: *Fine and Historic Bookbindings*, 180

Mucedorus (anon.), 26

Muslims, 245

Mylius, Hermann, 230, 231, 235

Nesse, Christopher: *A Key (With the Whip)*, 274

New Criticism, 3

New Model Army, 99, 112, 202; soldiers in, 111

New World, 184, 185

Newby Bible, 7, 51–57, 59, 60–62, 65, 73

Newcomb, Thomas, 16, 228

newsbooks, 2, 103, 201–12, 214n30, 234, 235; separates, 14, 201, 205, 209; *Grand Politique Informer*, 203; *Mercurius Politicus*, 225, 228, 234, 235

newspaper, 164

Nicholas, Edward, 226

nonconformists, 15, 185, 243, 246, 252–58

Norbrook, David, 20n19, 237n1

notepad, 10; notebook, 43

Oates, J. C. T., 178

Oates, Samuel, 111

Oates, Titus, 207

octavo: Countess of Bridgewater's books in, 150–52; 204, 210

Okes, Nicholas, 34, 227

Order . . . Regulating Printing, 222, 223, 229

Orgel, Stephen, 282–89

Oulton, Richard, 227

Overbury, Thomas, 144; *Characters*, 144, 151

Overton, Henry, 16

Overton, Richard, 105, 222

Owen, John: *Banquet of Essayes*, 162, 170, 171

Owens, John, 162, 170–72, 191

Oxford University, 210

pagination, 44, 286, 287

Palmer, Herbert, 222

pamphlets: collectors of, 14; explosion of cheap pamphlets, 13, 201–16; Milton's anti-episcopal pamphlets, 225; plays published as, 29; polemical, 101–11 passim, 282; published by John Danter, 36; radical, 103

Panegyric on the Author of Absalom and Achitophel (anon.), 276

paper: made of cloth, 1; *Gangraena* used as lavatory paper, 100; price of, 131, 288

papists/popery, 100, 207

Parker, Henry, 205, 220, 231

Parker, Samuel, 15, 244–60; *A Discourse of Ecclesiastical Politie*, 248–58 passim

Parker, William Riley, 228

Parkes, Malcolm, 43

Parkin, Jon, 248

Parlement of Paris, 233

Parliament, 2, 8, 99, 106, 185, 192, 202, 206, 217, 218, 220, 223, 227, 236, 244

parliamentarian/parliamentary, 103, 201, 207, 256

Parrot, Henry: *Cures for the Itch*, 168, 172

Parsons, Robert: *Christian Directory*, 127–29

pasteboard, 180

pastedowns, 187

Patrick, Simon, 243, 258

patronage, 140, 163, 179

Pauls, 106, 218

Paul's churchyard, 190, 211, 225

Peacham, Henry: *Gentleman's Exercise*, 130

Pearson, David, 178, 179, 184

Pearson, Jacqueline, 144, 154n1

Peter, Hugh, 16, 99, 103, 105–7

petitions, 109, 201

Pickwood, Nicholas, 189

Pinnell, Henry, 107

Piper, William Bowman, 272

piracy, 6, 28, 30, 32, 37, 234, 286

Platt, John and Susan, 97, 99

Pliny, *The Historie of the World*, 287

Plomer, Henry R., 36

Plutarch: *Lives*, 145, 148, 287

Poitiers, Dianne de, 140, 156n13

Pollard, Graham, 178

Pooley, Roger, 257

Pordage, Samuel, 274–76; *Azaria and Hushai*, 275

Portrature of master Hobson the Carryer of Cambridge and verses underwritten, 226

powers-that-be, 14

prayer book, 127, 143, 146, 180. *See also* psalters

preface, 2, 7, 11, 15, 48, 144, 164, 261; of Hooker's *Laws*, 82–84; 88, 163

preprint, 7

Presbyterian, 99, 100, 103–4, 109–11, 191, 207, 226

print culture, 2, 8, 13, 99, 102, 103; print: and performance, 23–41; printing revolution: concept of, 7, 44, 282

Prior, Mary, 138

Privy Council, 230, 233

Promethean, 212

proprietary right, 6, 26

Protean, 88

Protestantism, 5, 7, 8, 47–50, 61, 67, 69, 87, 100, 127, 143, 187, 211, 245; pan-European movement, 229–30

Protestation, 209

provenance, 2, 3, 6, 28, 180

Prynne, William, 104, 106, 109, 205, 207; *Fresh Discovery of Some Prodigious New Wandering Blasing-Stars & Firebrands*, 106

psalters, 7, 47, 123, 143, 150; profits protected by English Stock, 190

public opinion, 5, 13

public sphere, 13, 16, 19n19, 277

Pulleyn, Octavian, 210

pulpboard, 187

Puritan, 5, 7, 8, 12, 88, 111, 191, 192, 210

Putney debates, 209

Quakerism, 210. *See also* Fox, George

Quarles, Francis: *Divine Fancies*, 165

quartos, 32, 52, 141; Countess of Bridgewater's books in, 140, 148–49; 202, 204, 207, 208, 210; bad quarto, 5, 6, 29, 30–32; play quartos, 25, 286

radical, 61, 97–111 passim, 185, 201, 236

Ralegh, Sir Walter, 88, 89

Ramesey, William, 261, 268

Ramism, 64, 80, 84

Ranter, 101

Raven, James, 4; *Practice and Representation of Reading*, 4

Ravenscroft, Edward, 266; *The Careless Lovers*, 266, 270

Rawlinson, John: *Romish Judas*, 143

Raworth, Robert, 227

Raworth, Ruth, 227

Raylor, Timothy, 230

Raymond, Joad, 4, 114n18, 202

reader-response, 9, 136n32

readers: actual, 127, 160–62; anonymous, 165–66, 170; appropriative, 11, 127, 130; autonomy of, 13, 170; case studies, 42–79, 138–59; implied, 120, 160–62, 167, 172; epithets for, 175n15; ordinary, 9; partisan, 262, 263; puritan, 191; real, 10, 11, 12; taxonomies of, 166; women, 138–59; would-be gentlemen, 261, 268

readership: active, 8, 145; broad, 165; female, 144; national, 8; partisan, 16; print, 109

reading: biblical, 5; consecutive, 284; continuous, 42–74 passim, 283; discontinuous, 7, 42–74 passim, 283, 284; extensive, 127; intensive, 127; liturgical, 7, 73; nonconformist, 15; passive, 124

reception, 9, 12, 24, 177, 265, 282

recipes, 126, 130, 146

recusant, 36, 143. *See also* Catholicism

Reedy, Gerard, 273

regulation of printing, 217–18

Remarks upon Remarques: Or, a Vindication of the Conversations of the Town (anon.), 268

Remarques on the Humours and Conversations of the Town (anon.), 268

republican, 244, 254; turncoats—Samuel Parker and John Streater, 15

Restoration, 15, 201, 228, 246, 254, 255, 256, 257, 261, 263

Revolution of 1688, 211, 261

Ricraft, Josiah, 109

Right Godly Rule, 143, 151

Roberts, Colin H., and Skeat, T. C.: *Birth of the Codex*, 42

Roberts, James, 30–31

Robinson, Humphrey, 226, 228

Robinson, Thomas: *Anatomy of the English Nunnery at Lisbon*, 191

Rothwell, Henry, 225

Rothwell, John, 225

Rouse, Mary and Richard Rouse, 43–44

Royal Society, 15, 247, 251, 265

royalist, 185; use of pamphlet press, 201, 202, 209; Moseley as royalist printer, 226

rubrication, 44, 124, 180

Rushworth, John, 202, 204, 209, 210, 211; *Historical Collections*, 202

Saenger, Paul, 43, 121, 123–24

St. Paul's churchyard, 190, 211, 225, 226. *See also* Pauls

Salisbury, John, 87

Saltmarsh, John, 16

Sangar, Gabriel, 205

Scoggin, John: *Jests*, 144, 152

scriptures, 50, 63, 70, 72–73, 82, 141, 187. *See also* bible

scrivener, 224

scroll, 42–43, 74

Seaman, Lazarus, 203, 205

Second Part of the Return from Parnassus, 27

sectarianism, 9, 97, 99–111 passim, 191, 201, 207, 217, 243–60 passim

Shadwell, Thomas: *The Humourists*, 266; *The Virtuoso*, 262

Shakespeare, William, 5, 23–41, 87, 91, 143, 144, 285; *Hamlet*, 30–32; *1 Henry IV*, 26, 32, 33; *Henry V*, 25; *2* and *3 Henry VI*, 32; *King John*, 34; *King Lear*, 33, 34; *Love's Labors Lost*, 32; *Lucrece*, 23, 286; *Merchant of Venice*, 31; *Othello*, 30, 34; *Passionate Pilgrim*, 286; *Richard II*, 26, 32, 33; *Richard III*, 26, 32, 33; *Romeo and Juliet*, 32, 35–38; *Sonnets*, 286; *Taming of a Shrew* (Shakespeare?), 26, 32; *Taming of the Shrew*, 32; *Titus Andronicus*, 32, 35–38; *Venus and Adonis*, 23, 27, 286

Sharpe, Kevin, 19n13, 137n46, 237n11

Sheffield, Edmund (earl of Mulgrave), 261

Sheldon, Gilbert (archbishop of Canterbury), 244

shelfmark, 187, 207

Sherman, William, 10, 119–37, 161, 287–88

shorthand, 29

Short Title Catalogue (STC), 3, 11, 120, 122, 124, 131

Sidney, Mary: *Antonius*, 144

Sidney, Philip, 284–85; *Apology*, 193

signatures, 9, 11, 120, 139, 145, 156n12, 209

Simmons, Matthew, 16, 225

Sion College, 106

Slatyer, William: *History of Great Britanie*, 163

Slights, William, 77n24

Smectymnuus controversy, 225, 227

Smethwick, John 31, 35, 38–39, 52

Smith, Nigel, 20n20, 114n18

Smith, Ralph, 107

Smith, Dr. Richard, 206

Solemn League and Covenant, 209

Southwell, Lady Anne, 11, 139,

Spenser, Edmund, 126, 148; *Colin Clout Comes Home Again*, 140; *Faerie Queene*, 148; *View of the Present State of Ireland*, 126

Sprat, Thomas (Bishop of Rochester), 247, 257

Spufford, Margaret, 9

Stallybrass, Peter, 6–7, 42–79, 283–84

Stanbridge, John, *Accidence*, 36

Stanley, Alice, 140

Star Chamber, 192, 218, 223

State Papers Domestic, 2

stationers, 160–76 passim

Stationers' Company, 28, 37, 104, 177, 190, 205, 222–41 passim

Stationers' Court, 36

Stationers' Register, 2, 6, 38, 226, 234; entries of James Roberts, 30–31, 232

Stephens, Philemon, 16, 187, 189–92

Stoddard, Roger, 119, 122

Streater, John, 15, 39n4

Tableau historique des ruses et subtilitez des femmes, 147

Tasso, Torquato, *Godfrey of Bulloigne*, 145, 148

Temple Bar, 52,

theater, 23–41, 261–81; theatergoers, 32, 264, 269; theatrical player, 8, 9, 88; play text, 25, 27, 38; playbook 6, 25–38 passim, 34, 144; playgoers, 33; playwright, 6, 25, 27, 28, 34, 263

theatricalism: antitheatricalism, 88, 89

Thomas, Keith, 10, 19n14

Thomason, George, 14, 202, 205, 210–16 passim, 222, 225, 227, 231

Thurloe, John, 235

title pages, 25, 63, 67, 164, 187, 208, 220, 223, 285, 288; as evidence, 2; of Milton's tracts,

14; of Shakespeare's play quartos, 32–33; of 1608 *King Lear*, 33; 35, 38

Tooker, Charles, 207

Torah, 283

Tory, 261, 271

Tottel, Richard, 288

translation, 145; bible translations, 51; by Dryden, 261

Treasurie of Amadis of Fraunce, 124, 125

Tribble, Evelyn, 77n24

Troublesome Raigne of King John (anon.), 34

True Chronicle History of King Leir (anon.), 34

Trumbull, William, 229–30; Trumbull Papers, 241n45

Trundle, John, 30–31

turn-ins, 184

typology, 273, 274, 277

Underhill, Thomas, 227

Valdesso, John: *One Hundred and Ten Considerations*, 182

Valeriano, G. P.: *Hieroglyphica*, 287

Van Eyck, Jan, 46, 76n10

Vane Jr., Sir Henry, 230–32

Vane Sr., Sir Henry, 231–32

Vicari, E. Patricia, 88

Vicars, John, 109

Vickers, Brian, 32, 250, 259

Villiers, George (Second Duke of Buckingham), 247, 265, 266, 269, 232; *The Rehearsal*, 265, 266

Virginia Company, 184

Vischa, Johan, 90

Vlacq, Adriaan, 230

Voss, Paul, 164

Walkley, Thomas, 34–35

Waller, Edmund, 247

Wallington, Nehemiah, 202

Walsham, Alexandra, 20n20

Walton, Bishop Brian, 206

Walwyn, William, 109

Watt, Tessa, 20n20

web, website, 46

Webb, Thomas, 107, 109, 110,

Weckherlin, Georg Rudolf, 16, 228–42

Weinbrot, Howard, 271–72

Wentworth, Thomas (earl of Strafford), 209
West, R.: *Wits A.B.C., or, a Centurie of Epigrams*, 164–65, 169
Westminster Assembly, 8, 106, 107
Westminster Assembly of Divines, 222, 223
Whigs, 273
Whitaker, Elaine E., 127
White, Edward, 35
Whitehall, 286
wholesaler, 226
Wilcox, Helen, 184
Wilkins, John, 247, 257
wills, 154–55n3, 155n4. *See also* inventories
Wilson, Thomas: *Arte of Rhetorick*, 287
Winder, George, 52

Winn, James, 261, 274
Wither, George, 28
Wits Recreations, 165
Wolfreston, Frances, 126, 139–40
women: and books, 138–59
Wood, Anthony, 14, 16, 203, 205, 207–9, 212, 246
woodcut illustration, 127
Woodnoth, Arthur, 192
Woodward, Hezekiah, 223
Worsley, Benjamin, 205
Writer, Clement, 106, 109

Zaret, David, 19–20n19
Zwicker, Steven, 17, 19n13, 77n24, 237n1